EMOTION:
Theory, Research, and Experience

Volume 4

The Measurement of Emotions

EMOTION
Theory, Research, and Experience

EDITED BY

Robert Plutchik
Albert Einstein College of Medicine
Bronx, New York

Henry Kellerman
Postgraduate Center for Mental Health
New York, New York

EMOTION
Theory, Research, and Experience

Volume 4

The Measurement of Emotions

Edited by

Robert Plutchik

Albert Einstein College of Medicine
Bronx, New York

Henry Kellerman

Postgraduate Center for Mental Health
New York, New York

ACADEMIC PRESS, INC.
Harcourt Brace Jovanovich, Publishers
San Diego   New York   Berkeley   Boston
London   Sydney   Tokyo   Toronto

Academic Press, Inc.
San Diego, California 92101

United Kingdom Edition published by
Academic Press Limited
24–28 Oval Road, London NW1 7DX

Library of Congress Cataloging-in-Publication Data

The Measurement of emotions / edited by Robert Plutchik and Henry
    Kellerman.
        p.   cm. -- (Emotion, theory, research, and experience ; v. 4)
    Includes bibliographies and indexes.
    ISBN   0-12-558704-X   (alk. paper)
    1. Emotions--Research. 2. Psychometrics.   I. Plutchik, Robert.
    II. Kellerman, Henry.   III. Series
        [DNLM: 1. Emotions--physiology. 2. Psychophysiology. W1 EM668
    v. 4 / EL 102 M484]
    BF561.E48   vol. 4
    [BF531]
    152.4 s--dc19
    [152.4'028'7]
    DNLM/DLC
    for Library of Congress   89-174
                                                                  CIP

Printed in the United States of America
89 90 91 92   9 8 7 6 5 4 3 2 1

CONTENTS

Chapter 1
Measuring Emotions and Their Derivatives 1
Robert Plutchik

Chapter 2
Models and Methods for Measurement of Mood 37
Maurice Lorr

Chapter 3
Assessing Emotion by Questionnaire   55

Harald G. Wallbott and Klaus R. Scherer

Chapter 4
Measures of Emotion   83

James A. Russell

Chapter 5
The Dictionary of Affect in Language   113

Cynthia M. Whissell

Chapter 6
Information Integration Approach to Emotions and Their Measurement

133

Norman H. Anderson

Chapter 7
Projective Measures of Emotion

187

Henry Kellerman

Chapter 8
Methodology in the Anthropological Study of Emotion

205

Robert I. Levy and Jane C. Wellenkamp

269079

Chapter 9
Vocal Measurement of Emotion   233
Klaus R. Scherer

Chapter 10
Measuring Animal Aggression   261
David Benton

CONTRIBUTORS

Numbers in parentheses indicate the pages on which the authors' contributions begin.

NORMAN H. ANDERSON (133), Department of Psychology, University of California, San Diego, La Jolla, California 92093

DAVID BENTON (261), Department of Psychology, University College of Swansea, Swansea, Wales SA2 8PP, United Kingdom

HENRY KELLERMAN (187), Postgraduate Center for Mental Health, New York, New York 10016

ROBERT I. LEVY (205), Department of Anthropology, University of California, San Diego, La Jolla, California 92093

MAURICE LORR (37), Life Cycle Institute, Catholic University of America, Washington, D. C. 20064

ROBERT PLUTCHIK (1), Albert Einstein College of Medicine, Bronx, New York 10461

JAMES A. RUSSELL (83), Department of Psychology, University of British Columbia, Vancouver, British Columbia, Canada V6T 1Y7

KLAUS R. SCHERER (233, 55), Department of Psychology, University of Geneva, Geneva, Switzerland

HARALD G. WALLBOTT (55), Department of Psychology, University of Giessen, D-6300, Giessen, Federal Republic of Germany

JANE C. WELLENKAMP (205), Department of Anthropology, University of California, Los Angeles, California 90024

CYNTHIA M. WHISSELL (113), Department of Psychology, Laurentian University, Sudbury, Ontario, Canada P3E 2C6

PREFACE

This is the fourth volume in the series entitled *Emotion: Theory, Research, and Experience*. In the first volume, *Theories of Emotion*, the contributors presented a variety of models and conceptualizations concerning the nature of emotions. Contemporary theories reflecting the various historical traditions were represented. These included the Darwinian evolutionary tradition, the Jamesian psychophysiological tradition, and the dynamic or Freudian tradition. As a consequence of examining these various viewpoints, the beginning of a synthesis of the field of emotions could be recognized.

In the second volume, *Emotions in Early Development*, the issue of emotion in relation to neonatal and infant development was considered. The contributors examined the question of how inferences are made about emotions in infants in both humans and lower animals. They examined the connections between cognitive and emotional development and considered the relations between personality and emotions. The role of parent–child interactions in the appearance and development of emotions was also of special interest.

It became apparent that there was considerable agreement that emotions in young organisms serve subtle communication, behavioral, and biological regulatory functions. In addition, it was pointed out that cognitive development is generally inferred on the basis of such emotional indicators as smiling, crying, and attachment behaviors. Emotions emerge as complex, genetically-based dispositions that play a major role in the formation of an individual's character structure.

In the third volume, *Biological Foundations of Emotion*, the relations among brain structures, brain functions, and emotions were examined. Some of the contributors presented general models of brain functioning, while others considered emotions from an evolutionary and comparative–neurological viewpoint. Contributors also focused their attention on particular emotions, such as aggression, or particular brain structures, such as the amygdala. The role of genetics and brain biochemistry was also considered in some detail. The reports are rich in content, and a wealth of information about brain functioning and emotions is given.

The present volume, *The Measurement of Emotions*, examines a key issue involved in constructing a theory of emotion; namely, how the concept is to be measured. Some of the contributors examine the issue of mood measurement and the complexities that are involved. Some are concerned with the cross-cultural examination of triggers of emotion and subjective reactions to them, and some are concerned with the possible dimensions that underlie the language of affect. Measurement issues in the assessment of affect from vocal indices are considered as well as how emotions are measured in lower animals. Important chapters are included that deal with broad theoretical issues in the measurement of emotions and their derivatives. The chapters present a rich set of both broad and deep ideas.

INTRODUCTION

The problem of measurement is a central issue in the psychology of emotions. Inherent in any theory are implications for the measurement of the concepts involved. If emotions are conceptualized solely as subjective feelings, then mood checklists are reasonable ways to attempt to measure these states. If emotions are special classes of behavior, then behavioral indices are required. If, however, emotions are conceptualized as more complex multidimensional processes, then still other approaches to measurement are necessary.

This volume examines these various issues. It looks at the many psychometric problems associated with mood checklists. It considers problems in the measurement of emotional behavior in lower animals as well as the vocalizations that serve as indirect markers of emotional states. It also looks at the issue of measuring some of the concepts which are conceptually connected to the study of emotions.

In the first chapter Plutchik begins by considering general issues involved in all measurement and concludes that the measurement of emotional states is fundamentally similar to the measurement of any other inferred state. He then presents the basic postulates of his psychoevolutionary theory of emotion emphasizing the concept of emotion derivatives. The concept of derivatives refers to the idea that certain conceptual domains are systematically related to emotions. These domains include personality, psychiatric diagnoses, ego defenses, and coping styles. For example, the affective state of anger is seen as related to the personality trait of irritability. In extreme form, the diagnostic term "aggressive" might be applied, while the ego defense of displacement could be used to deal with inhibited aggression. These ideas are systematically elaborated and their implications for test construction are described. Several new tests of the concepts involved in these derivative domains are described and their use in a variety of contexts is elaborated. The emphasis of the chapter is on relating measures of emotions to theories about emotions.

The second chapter by Lorr examines many of the complex issues associated with the measurement of mood, one of the domains described by Plutchik. He begins by distinguishing between states and traits and emphasizes the essential ambiguity of the distinction. The concept of overlapping fuzzy categories appears to be a better description of emotions than does the idea of sharply discrete categories. Various investigators who have looked at the problem of defining moods have used factor analytic techniques for the most part and have arrived at widely divergent conclusions concerning the issue of how many basic mood states there are. Estimates have varied from 2 to as many as 16. In contrast to such a dimensional approach to mood, Lorr describes the circular or circumplex model which assumes that emotions show a graded similarity structure as well as bipolarities. Some of the differences among researchers are related to the analytic tools which they use, particularly to the differences between factor analysis and multidimensional scaling. Another set of variables that influence the outcome of research are the response sets such as acquiescence, extreme response style, and social desirability. Lorr concludes that the concept of bipolar moods is likely to have the richest pay-off for research.

The third chapter by Wallbott and Scherer continues the discussion of the measurement of subjective mood states. The authors compare questionnaire techniques for assessing subjective emotional experience to laboratory induction procedures. They emphasize that however theoretical and inferential one becomes in conceptualizing emotion, most people consider subjective experience as a key, if not major, aspect of emotions. For them, emotions can be studied primarily by introspective reports.

Given this perspective, the authors describe a questionnaire study of emotions that they have carried out involving thousands of subjects in a dozen different countries. The questionnaire they developed focused on the emotion-arousing situation, the characteristics of the subjective experience, the expressive and physiologic reactions, and the attempts made to regulate or control those reactions. Considerable information was obtained on the four basic emotions of joy, sadness, fear, and anger. Open-ended questions were used as well as precoded categories of response. Of considerable interest is the high degree of generality found for many of the variables despite different cultures, languages, and modes of upbringing.

A further attempt to identify generalities in the language of emotions is presented in the chapter by Russell in which he deals with the implicit relations among emotion words. Rather than think of the language of emotions as reflecting discrete entities, Russell points out that emotion terms are systematically related and that the best description of the relations is by means of a circumplex. He describes the emotion circumplex that he has obtained through his research and presents the implications of integrating diverse reports by recognizing that emotion categories are systematically and highly interrelated.

A number of lines of evidence are consistent with a circumplex organization of emotions. These are based on direct judgments of the similarity between emotion terms, verbal self-report data, and judgments of facial expressions of emotion. Russell also points out sources of bias in previous research as a result of overlooking context effects in judging emotions. Judgments of emotion are strongly influenced by the linguistic terms available to the judge. This effect can be demonstrated in several classic experiments such as the Schachter–Singer studies. Mood induction typically arouses multiple affects, all of which need to be assessed. The major point of the chapter is that emotion terms are embedded in a cognitive similarity network of beliefs and concepts and that all verbal measures of emotion need to be interpreted within that network.

One way to explicate the network of ideas associated with the language of emotions is considered in the fifth chapter by Whissell which deals with the development of a special kind of dictionary of the language of emotion. She points out that the research literature in this field describes a large variety of stimulus materials used to produce emotional states and an equally large range of responses used to measure how subjects feel. In an effort to standardize this kind of language, Whissell has identified approximately 4000 English words culled from various sources to define the basic language of affect. Each word in the list is described in terms of a score along two dimensions: a dimension of activation or arousal and a dimension of evaluation or pleasantness.

Evidence for test–retest reliability has been obtained, as well as concurrent validity. It is possible to use the dictionary of affect to score an individual's self-descriptions as well as to score written or video-taped interactions. Another value of the dictionary is its capacity to assess emotions in terms of the connotative rather than the denotative meanings of words. The dictionary promises to be a new tool for affective research.

Considering the various issues that have been raised thus far, Anderson in the sixth chapter attempts to apply his theory of information integration, first developed in the area of psychophysics and social attitudes, to the domain of emotion. The focus is on information flow within an individual and on the multiple sources of input that influence affective states. In terms of the model that Anderson presents, nonaffective, cognitive variables, such as proximity and expectancy, interact with more purely emotional stimuli to produce the complex reactions and states called emotions.

The theory presents the basic integration rules that determine how multiple sources of information are combined. Such rules can also be used in reverse to fractionate out the determinants of observed emotional responses. One of the implications of the model is that there are both conscious and unconscious contributors to emotional states. Another is that emotions are forms of goal-oriented adaptive behavior. The theory is applied to such diverse issues as the validity of conscious reports, rating methodology and scale types, the state–trait distinction, single subject designs, phobias, mood, pain, cerebral organization, and the problem of recognizing emotion. The chapter is thus a deep and thoughtful attempt to deal with a multitude of complex problems in the psychology of emotions.

One of the methodologies used to deal with specific issues in relation to the measurement of emotions is considered in Chapter 7 by Kellerman who focuses on projective measures of emotion with a particular emphasis on the Rorschach. He demonstrates that a widely recognized distinction between extratensive and introversive profiles, obtained on the basis of Rorschach responses, can be interpreted within a broader framework. This framework assumes that personality traits are connected with particular diagnoses in a systematic way and that Rorschach responses are an additional way in which the connectedness of these domains and concepts can be expressed. The value of the approach is that it reveals a unity among emotions, personality traits, and diagnoses that become visible when expressed through projective responses.

Another area in which deep inferential techniques are necessary is presented in the chapter by Levy and Wellenkamp who examine important issues in the measurement of emotions in different cultures, particularly non-Western communities. They review the expanding literature in this field which reflects a renewed interest in emotion in both the social and behavioral sciences. However, as is true in all sciences, anthropology has its own special methods that are used in investigations, and the rest of the chapter is devoted to an explication of these methods. Anthropologists need to determine the local schemata used by members of a community for understanding and communicating about emotions. They need to recognize how cultural forms serve to express, discharge, and disguise emotions in everyday life. And they need to explore various approaches to explanation, for example, developmental, adaptational, or psychodynamic.

These issues are dealt with by various techniques of observation. Most are naturalistic and some rely upon open or structured interviews, but all depend heavily on an understanding of the context of the culture as well as on empathic understanding. The success of such observations and interviews depends on long periods of acquaintance with the people involved and the development of trust, an issue that rarely arises in other types of research. Levy and Wellenkamp conclude that emotions mediate the integration of individuals into social groups and that emotion has co-evolved with the capacity for culture.

Another special area of concern in the measurement of emotions is the assessment of emotions in lower animals. Ever since Darwin, it has been taken for granted that the concept of emotion applies in some sense to lower animals as well as humans. The chapter by Scherer is an important synthesis of the literature on vocal expression of affective states in both animals and humans.

He begins by examining the phylogenetic history of vocal emotion expression and then considers the different ways in which vocal encoding and decoding have been studied. Scherer notes that a major problem in this field has been the essentially atheoretic approach that has been adopted by most researchers. In contrast, he outlines his component process model of emotions and develops a number of predictions from it. In the final section of his chapter, Scherer summarizes a number of studies that have provided support for his hypotheses. The interplay of theory and new technology is of considerable importance in determining what and how to measure.

A further effort to describe the problems of measuring emotions in lower animals is considered at length by Benton. Using the methods of the ethologist, Benton describes in detail the nature of offensive and defensive behavior in rodents. He then analyzes the concept of aggression as an ethological, adaptive pattern of interaction and reviews the various category systems that have been used to describe its subtypes. He concludes that the most meaningful way to measure aggression is to use settings that are ecologically appropriate for the animal. Testing situations should reflect as much as possible the natural social organization and life experiences of the species in question. Based on this criterion, he evaluates the various induction and measurement approaches to aggression and rejects some as inadequate. Benton concludes by pointing out that aggression is not a unitary phenomenon and that different measures may reflect different underlying biological mechanisms. This again implies the need to relate measurement methods to theoretical models.

Seen as a whole, the chapters of this volume demonstrate by theory and example the connectedness of general models and measurement techniques. They illuminate the complex nature of emotions and raise new questions for future theory and research.

Chapter 1

MEASURING EMOTIONS AND THEIR DERIVATIVES

ROBERT PLUTCHIK

ABSTRACT

The general nature of measurement is described and illustrated in a physical science context. The chapter then presents a psychoevolutionary theory of emotion and shows how general principles of measurement can be applied to the measurement of emotions. A key element in the theory is the concept of emotional derivatives. This concept implies that other conceptual domains such as personality, diagnoses, ego defenses, and coping styles are related to the basic emotions in a systematic way. New self-report tests of these derivative domains have been developed and they are described in some detail. The fundamental point made is that the study of emotions comprises a vast array of phenomena, and that the ideal measures of emotions and their derivatives are those that are diverse, based on theory, and systematically related to these complex phenomena.

INTRODUCTION

Emotions are often described as subjective, personal, and idiosyncratic, and are therefore difficult to define and measure. One result of this belief is an emphasis on qualitative rather than quantitative descriptions of emotion. Another is a proliferation of arbitrary rating scales that have limited generality. In contrast

1

EMOTION
Theory, Research, and Experience
Volume 4

to these practices, the present chapter is concerned with describing some key issues in measurement theory and in showing how a general theory of emotion helps to define what aspects of emotion to measure and how to measure them.

WHY MEASURE?

Most of the events or objects that scientists are concerned with vary in magnitude in a continuous fashion. Although people may be described as introverted or extroverted, neurotic or well-adjusted, or happy or sad, we generally recognize that such dichotomies are simply convenient names representing the extremes of continuous variables.

In our effort to describe events that vary in magnitude, we use numbers because numbers are a well-understood system of concepts involving magnitude. Numbers function as a general analog or model of the relations that exist among many events. Generality exists because the very same kinds of numbers are used to represent the magnitudes of very different kinds of events. Numbers thus provide a kind of universal language useful for describing continuously changing events. Another reason for using numbers is that they enable us to make fine distinctions in situations where our everyday language allows only broad distinctions. Thus numbers allow distinctions not only between normal and depressed patients, but between patients who experience degrees of depression.

If we define measurement as *the assignment of numbers to objects or events according to certain rules,* it is evident that there are at least two good reasons for doing so. One is that numbers represent a universal language for describing many different kinds of things; the other is that numbers enable us to make fine distinctions in the magnitude of events (Plutchik, 1983).

EMOTIONS AND SCALES OF MEASUREMENT

Ever since the work of Stevens (1946, 1959) on scales of measurement, there has been a widespread belief that most (if not all) psychological quantities such as intelligence, personality, emotions, and defenses can only be measured on ordinal or rank-order scales. It is believed that since we can never be certain that the psychological distance between 1 and 2 on a 7-point scale of anxiety is equal to the distance between 5 and 6, (or any other pair of numbers), we can only use statistics that apply to rank-order data. If we accepted this restriction literally we would be forever prohibited from adding and subtracting such numbers and from applying routine statistical tests such as the *t*-test or analysis of variance.

Despite these recommended restrictions, most psychologists apply routine statistics to their data and ignore the prohibitions. In so doing, they are, in fact, following the lead of physicists who have likewise ignored the same issue. Physicists have long recognized that there is no need to prove the equality of intervals of their fundamental units of measurements. For example, any recurrent process in nature can be used as a clock. The rising and setting of the sun, the movement of a pendulum, the vibrations of a tuning fork, and the speed of radioactive decay have all been used to measure the passage of time. But one fundamental assumption is made, and that is that the unit of time tomorrow is the same length as the unit of time today. In short, equality of units is assumed and not proved. The physicist is not generally concerned with the question of whether his scale has equal units. However, he is very concerned about the *consistency* and *reliability* of his data. He is also concerned with their *relations to other kinds of data.*

AN ILLUSTRATION: THE MEASUREMENT
OF EARTHQUAKES

There are over 6000 earthquakes throughout the world each year, although only about 500 are strong enough to be felt or to cause damage. In their efforts to describe and categorize earthquakes, geologists tried to create ways to measure their magnitudes. One of the earliest methods was developed in 1902 by an Italian seismologist named Mercalli. His scale required a direct estimate on a 12-point scale of the ground movement associated with the earthquake, as well as its effects on humans and buildings. The system was useful in providing a rough measure of the intensity of the earthquake in populated regions, but was not useful in unpopulated areas. Its consistency was also limited.

In the mid-1930s, Richter developed an alternative scale of earthquake magnitude that was based on a good deal of empirical data as well as physical theory about energy propogation in liquids and solids. As is well known, earthquakes are generally caused by the sudden movement of tectonic plates past one another. When stresses exceed the breaking strength of rocks, slippage and shock waves occur. These shock waves are of three types: compressional waves traveling at a speed of about 5 miles per second, shear waves traveling at a speed of about 2 miles per second, and surface waves traveling at speeds that are slightly less than shear waves. The result of this complex pattern of energy transfer is that a given point on the surface of the earth is subjected to a highly variable and complex energy flow that varies over time. Any attempt to measure the magnitude of the earthquake is therefore at best an average energy over brief periods of time.

The Richter Scale is based on a mathematical equation that relates the theoretical magnitude of the earthquake to a series of variables. These include the amplitude of ground motion due to surface waves, the wave period in seconds, several empirical terms that relate to the depth of the earthquake focus, and various factors that attenuate the energy. The scale is logarithmic so that each unit on it indicates a 10-fold increase in wave amplitude and a 30-fold increase in energy. Thus a magnitude-8 earthquake releases about 30 times more energy than a magnitude 7, about 900 times more energy than a magnitude 6, and 27,000 times more energy than a magnitude 5. Unequal size units are thus deliberately created in order to be able to cover the large range of energies involved in earthquakes.

There is only a rough correspondence between scores on the Richter Scale and subjective estimates of earthquake strength on the Mercalli Scale. Reliability of estimates are within one-half scale unit on the Richter Scale, and partial calibration of the scale is based on the use of explosives of known strength to create seismic waves. The scale is also based on the obviously incorrect assumption that the focus or origin of the earthquake is a point, when, in fact, the slippage of two plates may sometimes extend for hundreds of miles (Stacey, 1977).

It is also of interest to note that there are many phenomena associated with the development of an earthquake. These include the sudden lowering of groundwater levels, tilts and bulges in the earth's surface, changes in the velocity of propogation of compressional surface and shear waves, increased concentrations of rare gases in well water, and electrical changes in certain rocks. These associated phenomena have been used to try to predict the onset of earthquakes.

What is true for the measurement of earthquakes is also true for the measurement of other scientific concepts. A theoretical model defines the concept by identifying the major elements of the concept and by specifying their probable relations to each other. Measurement then involves attaching numbers to each of the key elements of the model, including the indirect, implied, or derivative correlates. Simplifying assumptions are made along the way to enable reasonable approximations to be made. What is learned is then fed back to influence the nature of the theoretical model. Standardization of key points along the measurement scales are made to enable the reliable assignment of numbers to the scale. Issues of validity are not dealt with by arbitrary definitions of scale types, but by determining the relations of the scale numbers to real world events.

IMPLICATIONS FOR THE MEASUREMENT OF EMOTIONS

Emotions, too, are complex events which have a variety of associated properties. They usually involve subjective experiences, but not all emotional states are clearly perceived by the individual. Some are distorted, modified, defended against, or repressed. Many emotional states are inferred in individuals such as schizophrenics or the mentally retarded, who cannot adequately report on their emotions. And emotions are obviously inferred in both infants and lower animals, from whom subjective reports of inner states are not available.

It is thus evident that emotions are complex, hypothetical states that are inferred on the basis of various kinds of evidence, which may include subjective reports, display behavior, goal-directed behavior, physiological changes, and peer reactions, among other things. In order to be able to use these indicators as measures of emotion we require a fairly explicit theoretical model that describes the relations between the theoretical state called an emotion and the various indicators. Thus, a theory of emotion is a fundamental prerequisite for a rational theory of measurement of emotions.

THE PSYCHOEVOLUTIONARY THEORY OF EMOTION

The general theory of emotion developed by Plutchik (1958, 1962, 1970, 1980a, 1980b, 1984) has many implications for the measurement of emotions. Before examining these implications, a brief description of the theory will be presented.

There are a number of basic ideas associated with the psychoevolutionary theory of emotions. The first is that emotions can best be understood in an evolutionary context. This idea simply reflects the Darwinian and ethological view that there are continuities of emotional expression from lower animals to humans. Examples include the snarl, the smile, and expressions of terror, disgust, and surprise, and various display behaviors, such as the apparent increase in body size during rage due to the erection of body hair or feathers, changes in postures, or expansion of air pouches or lungs. According to Darwin (1965), emotions in all animals, including humans, act as communication signals of intentions, and tend usually to be reactions appropriate to emergency events in the environment. Their fundamental function is to increase the chances of individual survival.

Both Scott (1980) and Wilson (1975) have pointed out the similarity of behavioral adaptations in humans and lower animals. For example, almost all animals show agonistic (fight or flight) behavior, care-soliciting and care-giving behavior, imitative behavior, and investigative behavior. They generally form cooperative groups that occupy more or less defined territories, and communicate such states as alarm, threat, dominance, and reproductive status by means of identifiable signals or displays.

The psychoevolutionary theory assumes that a small number of types of adaptive behaviors are the prototypes that form the bases for emotions in lower animals and humans. The theory assumes that the environments of all organisms create certain common problems—for example, identifying prey and predator, food and mate, and care giver and care solicitor. Emotions are attempts of the organism to achieve control over those events that relate to survival (of oneself or one's genes). Emotions are the ultraconservative evolutionary behavioral adaptations, based on genetic codings, that have been successful (such as amino acids, DNA, and genes) in increasing the chances of survival of organisms. Therefore, they have persisted, in functionally equivalent forms, throughout all phylogenetic levels.

A second key idea of the psychoevolutionary theory is that an emotion is more than a feeling state, a facial expression, or a display behavior. In contrast, emotions are considered to be complex chains of events having a number of important elements or components. These chains can be triggered by ideas or images, but are most often triggered by environmental events associated with other individuals. Environmental events, however, need to be interpreted (as threats, losses, gifts, rewards, punishments, etc.) so that cognitive evaluations of the triggers are part of the complex chain. Depending on the nature of the interpretation, certain feelings, autonomic changes, preparations for action, and display behaviors will follow, resulting in a final overt action. The final action can be considered to be a kind of vectorial sum of various emotional impulses (e.g., urges to fight and run away, or to mate and attack).

It is important to emphasize that emotional behavior is not random, meaningless, overflow behavior, but is directly related to the stimulus event that triggered the complex chain in the first place. For example, distress signals by a puppy or the crying of an infant will increase the probability that the mother, or a mother substitute, will arrive. Therefore, the overall effect of the complex feedback system is to reduce the threat or emergency and to establish a kind of behavioral homeostasis.

A third important implication of the theory derives from the complexity of the emotional state. This complexity prevents an observer from knowing all about an emotion from any one of its components. Another way of saying this is that subjective feelings of an emotion are never a complete description of that emotion, nor is any overt behavior a complete description of an emotion. Verbal reports of feelings can be attempts to deceive or a distortion of the feeling, or an incomplete description of it, and will in any case depend on an individual's experience with language. Similarly, overt behavior may reflect attempts to deceive, or may be an ambiguous expression of conflicting impulses. What we say about emotions is always an inference based on multiple sources of information.

A fourth element in the psychoevolutionary theory of emotion concerns the structure of emotions. This idea refers to a geometric analog designed to describe the relations among emotions, in the same sense that a circle may describe some important relations among colors.

It is evident that emotions vary in *intensity* (e.g., fear vs panic), in *similarity* (shame and guilt are more similar than love and disgust), and in *polarity* (joy is the opposite of sadness). These characteristics of intensity, similarity, and polarity may be represented geometrically by means of a three-dimensional structure shaped like a cone, somewhat like the three-dimensional color solid. In addition, the cone can be considered to be made up of eight sectors or slices, each of which represents a basic or primary emotion.

The names for the primary emotions are based on factor-analytic evidence, similarity scaling studies, and certain evolutionary considerations. The complexity of the states we call emotions make any labels somewhat arbitrary. However, the emotions designated as primary should reflect the properties of intensity, similarity, and polarity. If one uses the ordinary subjective language of affects, the primary emotions may be labeled as joy and sadness, anger and fear, acceptance and disgust, and surprise and anticipation. This issue is discussed more fully in Plutchik (1980a).

Finally, the fifth central idea in the psychoevolutionary theory of emotion is the concept of *derivatives*. This idea has several aspects. One is that there are many different words that may be used to describe emotions. Words such as joy and ecstasy, annoyance and rage, or disgust and loathing reflect different intensities of the same emotion. Other words, such as gloomy and sad, cooperative and friendly, or surprised and astonished, tend to be synonyms of the same emotion.

However, one may also focus on different aspects of the complex chain of emotions. One may focus on feeling states (as illustrated above), or on associated behaviors instead. Thus, instead of talking about "fear," one may describe flight. Instead of talking about anger, one may describe threat or attack. And instead of talking about sadness, one may describe crying or distress signals. Feeling states represent one type of derivative of the chain of emotion, and associated behaviors represent another.

A further derivative language concerns the functions of emotions. From an adaptive point of view, the function of flight associated with fear is to *protect* the individual. The function of attack associated with anger is to produce *destruction* of a barrier to the satisfaction of one's needs. And the function of crying when sad is to try to provoke nurturance or support from a lost person or surrogate, a process that is here called *reintegration*.

The three derivatives of emotion thus far described (Table 1.1) may be thought of as different languages used to describe the same fundamental process. Table 1.1 places this idea in a broader perspective. It implies that there are many possible "languages" that may be used to describe various aspects of emotions, e.g., their subjective feelings, the associated behaviors, their functions, and others. The information in Table 1.1. implies that emotions also express funda-

TABLE 1.1

A MODEL OF EMOTIONS AND THEIR DERIVATIVES OR ASSOCIATED DOMAINS

Biological regulatory process	Behavioral expression	Adaptive function	Subjective state	Personality trait expression	Diagnostic extreme	Ego defense regulatory process	Coping style	Social control institution
Avoid	Withdraw	Protection	Fear	Timid	Anxious	Repression	Avoidance	Religion
Approach	Attack	Destruction	Anger	Quarrelsome	Aggressive	Displacement	Substitution	Police, war, sports
Fuse	Mate	Reproduction	Joy	Affectionate	Manic	Reaction formation	Reversal	Marriage and family
Separate	Distress signal	Reintegration	Sadness	Gloomy	Depressed	Compensation	Replacement	Religion
Ingest	Eat	Incorporation	Acceptance	Trusting	Hysterical	Denial	Minimization	Psychiatry, shamanism
Eject	Vomit	Rejection	Disgust	Hostile	Paranoid	Projection	Blame	Medicine
Start	Examine	Exploration	Expectation	Demanding	Obsessive–compulsive	Intellectualization	Mapping	Science
Stop	Freeze	Orientation	Surprise	Indecisive	Borderline	Regression	Help-seeking	Games, entertainment

mental biological regulatory processes that apply even at the level of single-celled organisms. At this level processes such as approach and avoidance, fusion and separation, or starting and stopping are interpreted as "emotional" patterns.

If one moves up the phylogenetic scale to increasingly complex derivatives of emotions, there are a number of other languages that may be used. Although anyone may experience a transient emotion of any type, the repeated expression of a given emotion in a variety of situations leads to a new conceptual domain. For example, someone who frequently expresses fear in social situations is usually called timid. Someone who frequently expresses anger is quarrelsome, while someone who is frequently sad is likely to be described as gloomy. These terms are part of the language of personality traits, and it is reasonable to assume that personality traits reflect frequent expressions of particular emotions or combinations of emotions. Plutchik has shown that the language of personality can be conceptualized as mixtures of the basic emotions (1962, 1980a), and that this view has a number of empirical consequences. For example, it has been shown that personality traits exhibit the same circular (or circumplex) structure of relations as do emotions (Conte & Plutchik, 1981; Fisher, Heise, Bohrnstedt, & Lucke, 1985, Wiggins, 1979).

When certain traits are expressed in extreme form, a new language is created to describe this situation, the language of diagnostic labels. For example, an extremely affectionate and sociable person may be diagnosed as manic, an extremely gloomy one as depressed, and a very suspicious one as paranoid (Kellerman, 1979, 1980). Empirical research has shown that these diagnostic concepts also form a circumplex similarity structure, just as do personality traits and emotions (Plutchik & Platman, 1977; Schaefer & Plutchik, 1966).

Another derivative domain of emotions is the regulatory processes called ego defenses. One may conceptualize ego defenses as mechanisms that have developed phylogenetically, and also ontogenetically, as ways by which the conceptual apparatus handles difficult situations involving emotions. For example, a little boy may become angry at his mother because she has disciplined him. Because of his training and ambivalent feelings of affection for her, he may be reluctant to express his anger directly toward his mother. Instead, he may kick the dog or start a fight with a sibling. This process of *displacement* of his anger is actually one way of (unconsciously) dealing with his ambivalent feelings of anger toward his mother.

Similarly, a person who has difficulty completing a job or assignment may feel increasingly anxious. However, instead of blaming himself for the poor performance he may criticize his boss or teacher for being out to get him or for putting unfair pressure on him. This process of *projection* is one way of handling feelings of rejection of oneself by attributing one's own feelings of hostility to another person. The theoretical connections between emotions and defenses have been described by Kellerman (1979, 1980, 1987) and Kellerman and Plutchik

(1977). Empirical support for these ideas have also been published (Plutchik & Conte, 1985; Plutchik, Kellerman, & Conte, 1979).

Two other derivative domains may be related to emotions; one concerns coping styles and the other concerns social institutions. The assumption made by most clinicians is that ego defenses are unconscious, that the individual who uses repression or displacement is unaware of the process itself. Although this may often be true, it is not a necessary aspect of the theory. For example, psychotherapy may help an individual recognize his (or her) reaction formations or denials and yet the individual may consciously decide to continue to engage in these patterns of behavior. In such a case, the person may be said to be using a defense as a conscious coping style simply because it works for him. Thus, instead of using denial as a defense, the individual may choose to minimize conflicts or their seriousness. This coping style has been labeled *minimization*. Similarly, instead of engaging in regressive, childlike behavior in the face of stress and frustration, one may consciously choose to *seek help* from others as a way of coping with a problem. Other examples of coping styles include conscious decisions to avoid unpleasant situations, or to engage in substitute behaviors, or to map out a problem by getting as much information as possible before taking action. Examples of the use of these ideas in stress management training and in psychotherapy research may be found in work by Wilder and Plutchik (1982) and by Buckley, Plutchik, Conte, and Karasu (1984).

The most speculative idea about the derivatives of emotion concern the role of social institutions in controlling the expression of emotions. Since emotions appear to be universal and are found in similar forms in all cultures (see Levy and Wellenkamp, this volume), it is at least plausible to assume that various social institutions have evolved to deal with them. For example, some form of religion exists in every culture. Although the details of expression and rituals may vary widely, some functional aspects are relatively invariant. Every society needs to be able to help its members deal with inevitable losses and with inevitable deaths. The sadness of loss and the fear of death are handled in a variety of ways by different religions—heaven, reincarnation, or deification—but religion as an antidote to fear appears to be a universal phenomenon. Similarly, anger and aggression are channeled into socially acceptable pathways through the social institution of sports as well as the social institution of war. Science may be conceptualized at least in part, as a way of controlling the emotion of curiosity. And certain games and entertainments are ways of systematically creating and thus controlling the emotion of surprise.

These suggestions are obviously oversimplifications, and with things as complex as social institutions, it is evident that they may serve multiple functions. But among their functions, it seems very likely that the creation, organization, and control of emotions are paramount. An elaboration of this idea may be found in the work of the sociologist Elias (1977).

IMPLICATIONS FOR MEASUREMENT

The theoretical model that has been outlined above has some important implications for the measurement of emotions and their derivatives. First of all, it is evident that the concept of emotion as a complex chain of events implies that one may attempt to measure each of the components separately. To fully grasp an emotional state it would be important to be able to measure subjective states, associated behaviors, personality traits, diagnostic implications, ego defenses, and coping styles. In addition, it should be possible to use the structural model of the emotions and its implied circular (or circumplex) form as a guide to test construction and scoring. Of course, the usual psychometric criteria for adequate measurement—reliability, generality, and validity—must also be observed. From this point of view, in the following sections we will examine various tests and scales that have been developed in connection with the psychoevolutionary model. The focus is on four domains: subjective feelings, personality traits, ego defenses, and coping styles.

THE MEASUREMENT OF SUBJECTIVE FEELINGS

The decision concerning what to measure when studying emotions may appear to be arbitrary. However, to be able to interpret meaningfully one's results, a theory is necessary of what an emotion is. For example, if one considers emotion to be a subjective experience that is described in words, then it becomes impossible to study emotions in either animals or infants. Similarly, if one considers fatigue, arousal, and energy level as emotions, then factor analyses of subjective reports produce different factor structures than if these states are not considered to be emotions. For a fuller discussion of this issue, see Lorr (this volume).

From the point of view of the psychoevolutionary theory, an emotion is a complex chain of events that includes the eight basic emotions, their different intensity levels, their mixtures, and their derivatives. The further assumptions of bipolarity and relative similarity of emotions implies certain relations among these various states. It is expected, for example, that circular or circumplex structures should be found in all these domains. It also implies that the state–trait distinction is largely arbitrary. Thus, the study of personality traits is implicitly a study of emotions, just as is the study of diagnoses, ego defenses, and coping styles.

MOOD CHECKLISTS

One of the most common and deceptively simple ways to measure emotional states in human adults is by means of adjective checklists. Such lists consist of a series of adjectives—such as *calm, nervous, fearful,* or *bored*—that the subject identifies as reflections of his or her feelings. Sometimes the instructions ask for descriptions of immediate feelings, sometimes for feelings experienced during a recent period (e.g., 2 weeks), and sometimes for feelings that are frequently experienced over long periods. In the first case, we describe the responses as transient states of emotion; in the second case, we usually refer to the responses as moods; and in the third case, we talk of dispositions or traits. There are no sharp lines of distinction between these terms, and they are, in fact, often used interchangeably. For a critique of several earlier adjective checklists, such as the Gough Adjective Check List (GACL) and the Multiple Affect Adjective Check List (MAACL), see Plutchik (1980a). Recent checklists are reviewed by Lorr (this volume).

The various checklists differ in a number of ways. They vary in length, from as few as 8 adjectives (Plutchik, 1966) to as many as 235 (Scherer, 1984). Some require a simple "yes/no" response, while most ask for a graded intensity judgment or a graded frequency of occurrence judgment. Forced-choice formats have also been used (Plutchik & Kellerman, 1974).

A Comparison of Adjective Checklists

In an effort to discover the role of test format and context in checklist sensitivity and stability, the following experiment was conducted. Six different adjective checklists were prepared and administered to a class of college students on three different occasions. There were 6 males and 19 females with an average age of approximately 24 years. On the first test administration the students were simply told that the tests would illustrate for them different ways of measuring current moods or emotions. The same battery was administered 2 weeks later during class and the students were told that the tests were being given to determine how stable moods are. Another 2 weeks later, the same battery was administered just prior to a midterm examination. On all administrations the tests were randomized for each student.

Each test in the battery was differently constructed and differently scored:

Test 1 consists of the following eight adjectives: *happy, fearful, agreeable, angry, interested, disgusted, sad,* and *surprised.* The students were asked to describe their feelings "right now" using a 5-point intensity scale ranging from *not at all* to *very strongly.* This scale has been used in several previous studies (Plutchik, 1966; Plutchik, McCarthy, & Hall, 1975).

Test 2 consists of eight groups of three or four adjectives each. Each group of adjectives was selected as near synonyms from the emotion circumplex empirically determined by Plutchik (1980a). Thus, for example, the loss sector of the circumplex is represented by the terms *sad, worried, unhappy,* and *disappointed,* and the protection sector of the circumplex is represented by *afraid, anxious,* and *ashamed.* The students were asked to rate the strength of their immediate feelings on a 100-point scale. The average score for each group of terms was used to represent each sector.

Test 3 consists of eight groups of five words each. Each group represents a basic emotion dimension, with the words in each group varying in intensity. The words were selected from Plutchik's (1980a) list of emotion terms scaled for intensity on an 11-point scale. Thus, for example, the destruction dimension is represented by the following words (with the number in parentheses describing the intensity level of each word): *annoyed* (6.3), *irritated* (6.8), *hostile* (7.1), *angry* (8.4), and *furious* (10.1). The students simply circled the word in each list that best described their feeling ''right now''; the score they received was pre-coded on the basis of independent intensity estimates by a separate group of judges.

Test 4 consists of nine lists of eight words each. The first eight lists are synonyms for the eight basic emotions, and the ninth list expresses general level of arousal (*weak* to *energetic*). The students simply checked as many of the terms as they wished in each list that described their current feelings. For each dimension, the scores ranged from 0 to 8 representing the number of adjectives checked within each list.

Test 5 (the *Mood Profile Index*) consists of 36 pairs of emotion words, with each pair being matched for intensity on the basis of independent assessments (Plutchik, Platman, & Fieve, 1968). Examples of the pairs are *timid–gloomy, fearful–irritated, surprised–aggressive,* and *revolted–furious.* All of the eight basic emotions are represented in the pairs. The students were asked to select one word from each pair to express how they felt ''now.'' For each basic emotion dimension a percentage-of-maximum score was obtained.

Test 6 (the Profile of Mood States, or POMS) consists of 65 words representing six dimensions which have been labeled by McNair, Lorr, and Droppleman (1971) in the following way: Anger–Hostility, Depression–Dejection, Vigor–Activity, Fatigue–Inertia, and Tension–Confusion. Examples of the words used on the scales are *friendly, tense, angry,* and *worthless.* Students make intensity of feeling judgments on a 5-point scale ranging from *not at all* to *extremely.* Scoring is based on published percentile norms (McNair, Lorr, & Droppleman, 1981).

Results of the Adjective Checklist Study

The results of this study were evaluated in two general ways. First, which tests and which emotions are most sensitive to the classroom situation in revealing emotional reactions to a major examination stress? Second, to what extent do

TABLE 1.2
SENSITIVITY OF THE VARIOUS ADJECTIVE CHECKLIST TESTS TO THE
CLASSROOM EXAMINATION STRESS[a]

Test	Number of significant changes	Emotions that changed significantly
No. 1 8 adjectives; intensity scale	2	Disgusted ↑ **; fearful ↑ *
No. 2 28 adjectives on 0–100 scales	3	Agreeable ↓ ***; afraid ↑ ***; disgusted ↑ *
No. 3 40 adjectives; scaled for intensity	5	Disgusted ↑ ***; surprised ↑ **; fearful ↑ **; agreeable ↓ **; happy ↓ *
No. 4 72 adjectives; synonym groupings	4	Trusting ↓ **; afriad ↑ ***; sociable ↓ **; slowed down ↑ *
No. 5 36 pairs of intensity-matched adjectives (forced choice)	2	Protection (fearful) ↑ *; reproduction (sociable) ↓ *
No. 6 65 adjectives on 5-point intensity scales (POMS)	3	Tension ↑ **; vigor ↓ *; confusion ↑ **

[a]Based on analysis of variance.
*Significant at the .05 level.
**Significant at the .01 level.
***Significant at the .001 level or better.

scales that are designed to measure the same dimensions correlate with one another?

Table 1.2 is based on an analysis of variance computed for each emotion scale in each test across the three repetitions. In almost all cases there is very little difference between mean scale scores for each emotion on the first and second administration of the battery. When a significant change occurs it is typically on the third administration, just before the midterm examination.

The table reveals that some of the emotion scales show significant changes over the three administrations for different tests. Test number 3, which consists of 40 adjectives scaled for intensity, shows significant changes on five emotions; test 5 (the 36 pairs of intensity-matched adjectives) shows significant changes on only two emotions.

On three of the tests, feelings of *disgust* increased significantly. In addition, feelings of *agreeableness, trust,* and *sociability* decreased significantly on several of the tests. On the POMS, whose six scales have only limited overlap with those of the other tests, feelings of *tension* and *confusion* increased, while feelings of *vigor* decreased. It appears that test number 3, consisting of 40 adjectives scaled for intensity, is most sensitive in revealing the effects of the classroom stress.

Table 1.3 examines the question of the correlations between scales of different

TABLE 1.3

PERCENTAGE OF SIGNIFICANT CORRELATIONS BETWEEN EACH SCALE AND ALL OTHER SCALES FOR EACH EMOTION OVER THREE ADMINISTRATIONS[a]

Test	Percentage of significant correlations with other scales designed to measure the same emotions								
	Fear	Joy	Anger	Sadness	Trust	Disgust	Surprise	Curiosity	Mean (%)
No. 1. 8 adjectives; intensity scale	75	83	67	80	25	58	13	50	56.4
No. 2. 28 adjectives on 0–100 scale	67	75	80	73	58	67	13	42	59.4
No. 3. 40 adjectives; scaled for intensity	58	67	40	47	17	42	0	25	37.0
No. 4. 72 adjectives; synonym groupings	75	75	80	60	25	75	13	58	57.6
No. 5. 36 pairs of intensity-matched adjectives (forced choice)	8	33	40	60	8	42	27	8	28.3
No. 6. 65 adjectives on 5-point intensity scales (POMS)	—	—	80	93	—	—	27	—	66.7
Mean (%)	56.6	66.6	64.5	68.8	26.6	56.8	15.5	36.6	—

[a]Each figure represents the percentage of the total number of correlations for each emotion.

tests designed to measure the same emotions. For example, the emotion of *anger* is measured by all six tests in different ways. The correlation between the anger scales varies from a low of +.21 (not significant) to a high of +.79 (significant at better than the .001 level). In fact, all but one of the 15 correlations between anger scales are significant on the first administration of the test battery. This is also largely true for the emotions of *fear, joy, sadness,* and *disgust.* There are relatively fewer (and lower) significant correlations between similarly named scales for the emotions of *trust, surprise,* and *curiosity.*

Table 1.3 also reveals that there is considerable consistency among most of the different tests in measuring the same emotions. Overall, about 60% of the correlations are significant between different tests measuring the same emotions. There are two exceptions: Test 5 (the forced-choice test) is relatively inconsistent with the others, and test 3 (the 40 adjectives scaled for intensity) is also somewhat inconsistent with the others.

IMPLICATIONS

A midterm examination produces appreciable stress in most college students. The emotion checklists used here are fairly consistent in revealing significant increases in feelings of fear (or anxiety), feelings of disgust (or rejection), and feelings of surprise. They also are consistent in demonstrating significant decreases in agreeableness, sociability, and trust. These changes were demonstrated despite large differences in the format of the tests used. However, the tests were based upon the same eight underlying emotion dimensions. It thus appears that there are many different adjective checklist formats possible for measuring the same emotions. Correlations among similar emotion scales on different tests are also fairly high. This implies a reasonable level of interconvertability of different emotion scales. This is similar to the physicist's ability to measure temperature using different kinds of measuring instruments.

Interconvertability is possible only so long as the different tests measure the same dimensions. That this is often not the case may be illustrated by Table 1.4, where 10 different adjective checklists for measuring emotions are described in terms of the dimensions being measured. It is interesting to note that certain states which are not clearly emotions are included in the tests. Examples are *tired, thoughtful, fatigued, clear-thinking,* and *sleepy.* These observations emphasize the point made earlier; that is, that the consistent measurement of a domain presupposes a theory that defines the categories of measurement.

THE MEASUREMENT OF PERSONALITY TRAITS

The psychoevolutionary theory of emotion assumes that personality traits are derivatives of emotions. Evidence has been presented to demonstrate that the

TABLE 1.4

DIMENSIONS MEASURED BY VARIOUS ADJECTIVE CHECKLISTS

Checklist	Adjectives	Checklist	Adjectives
Borgatta (1961) 40 adjectives	Lonely, (depressed); warm hearted; tired; thoughtful; defiant (aggressive); startled (anxious)	Izard (1972) 30 adjectives	Interest; joy; suprise; distress; disgust; anger; shame; fear; contempt; guilt
Clyde (1963) 132 adjectives	Friendly; aggressive; clear thinking; sleepy; unhappy; dizzy	Plutchik and Kellerman (1974) 66 adjectives	Sociable; trusting; dyscontrolled; timid; depressed; distrustful; controlled; aggressive
Zuckerman and Lubin (1965) 89 adjectives	Depression; hostility; anxiety	Curran and Cattell (1975) 96 adjectives	Anxiety; stress; depression; regression; fatigue; guilt; extraversion; arousal
Plutchik (1966) 8 adjectives	Happy; agreeable; fearful; angry; interested; disgusted; sad; surprised	Howarth (1977) 60 adjectives	Concentration; anxiety; anger; depression; potency; sleep; control; cooperation; optimism; scepticism
McNair, Lorr, and Droppleman (1971) 57 adjectives	Anger–hostility; depression–dejection; vigor–activity; fatigue–inertia; friendliness; confusion	Lorr and McNair (1984) 72 adjectives	Composed; anxious; agreeable; hostile; elated; depressed; confident; unsure; energetic; tired; clearheaded; confused

language of interpersonal personality traits is also the language of emotions (Plutchik, 1980). Words such as *aggressive, friendly,* and *stubborn* can be used to describe both transient feelings and persistent traits. The theory assumes that traits are fundamentally mixed emotions.

For any given trait it is possible to identify its emotion components. For example, the trait of *docility* is described by judges in terms of the emotions of *fear* and *acceptance.* Similarly, *aggressiveness* is judged to be composed of *anger* plus *expectancy.* In general, personality traits tend to fall into families, or clusters, for example, *spiteful, sarcastic, scornful, revengeful, resentful, quarrelsome, vicious,* and *cruel.* All these traits contain anger and disgust as major emotion components. They differ in the relative intensity of these components and in the presence of "traces" of additional emotions. In addition, since personality traits reflect the presence of mixed emotional states, conflict is implied. Someone who is *sullen* has an impulse to *cry* as well as to *attack* (Plutchik, 1962, 1980a).

The theory implies that the inherent characteristics of emotions are reflected in the characteristics of one of its derivatives, i.e., personality. This means that personality traits should show a circumplex ordering, as do emotions. They should also reveal bipolarities as well as conflicts.

That these characteristics exist is well known. There is an increasing literature that reveals the circumplex structure of personality traits (Conte & Plutchik, 1981; Fisher et al., 1985; Wiggins, 1980; Wiggins & Broughton, 1985). Psychoanalytic theory and practice describe character traits (personality) as "precipitates of instinctual conflicts" (Fenichel, 1945). And several personality tests have been published that are based upon the concept of a circular ordering of traits (Benjamin, 1974; Freedman, Leary, Ossorio, & Coffey, 1951; Lorr & Youniss, 1986; Stern, 1958). Wiggins (1980) demonstrated that many well-known personality tests demonstrate circumplex structures, even though they were not so designed. These tests, however, are based only on the idea of a circular ordering of traits and do not fully utilize the ideas inherent in the structural model of emotions that has earlier been described. The following section describes a test, the *Emotions Profile Index,* that utilizes many of the features of the theory.

THE *EMOTIONS PROFILE INDEX*

The *Emotions Profile Index* (EPI) provides measures of the eight basic emotions first postulated by Plutchik in 1958 and described more fully in subsequent publications (1962, 1970, 1980a, 1984). It is based on the idea that all interpersonal personality traits can be conceptualized as resulting from the mixture of two or more primary emotions. This means, for example, that those who describe themselves as shy or gloomy are implicitly telling something about the primary emotions that go to make up these traits. Shyness, for example, implies frequent feelings of fear, whereas gloominess implies frequent feelings of sadness.

The EPI was developed initially by having 10 clinical psychologists rate the primary emotion components of a large number of traits. Twelve trait terms were finally selected on the grounds of high interjudge consistency on the components and a wide sampling of the trait universe described by Schaefer's (1959, 1961) factor-analytic studies. These 12 terms were then paired in all possible combinations, yielding 66 pairs. Four of the pairs were found to have identical scoring categories and so were dropped, thus leaving 62 pairs of trait terms for the final form of the test (Kellerman & Plutchik, 1968).

The EPI is a forced-choice test. The person taking it is simply asked to indicate which of two paired words is more personally descriptive; for example, is he or she more quarrelsome or shy? The choices are scored in terms of the primary emotions implied by the trait word. Each time the respondent makes a choice between two trait words, he or she adds to the score on one or more of the eight basic emotion dimensions. Thus, the test simultaneously measures anger, sadness, joy, and so on. Because the implications of the choices are not always clear to the respondent, the test has something of a projective quality, since the subject does not usually recognize the implicit scoring system. Finally, because of the forced-choice format of the EPI, it tends to reduce response bias associated with a set to choose socially desirable traits. This is true because many of the choices must be made between two equally undesirable or two equally desirable traits. In addition, a bias score is built into the test as a measure of the respondent's tendency to choose socially desirable (or undesirable) traits in those cases where the items are not matched.

The 12 terms used in the EPI are as follows: *adventurous, affectionate, brooding, cautious, gloomy, impulsive, obedient, quarrelsome, resentful, self-conscious, shy,* and *sociable.* A brief definition is provided in the test for each term. The total score for each of the eight primary dimensions is converted into a percentile score based on normative data obtained from 500 men and 500 women. These people represent a broad range of individuals characterized by a lack of overt pathology or psychiatric hospitalization. The percentile scores are then plotted on a circular diagram, as illustrated in Figure 1.1 for a group of severely depressed patients (Plutchik et al., 1968). The center of the circle represents zero and the outer circumference of the circle is the 100th percentile. The larger the dark wedge-shaped area, the stronger the emotional disposition that is revealed. Each of the eight scales of the EPI has been shown to have high internal reliability. Short-term test–retest reliability is also high (Plutchik & Kellerman, 1974).

The EPI has been used in a variety of clinical and research settings and has been used to describe clinical populations or subgroups (Albrecht & Brabender,

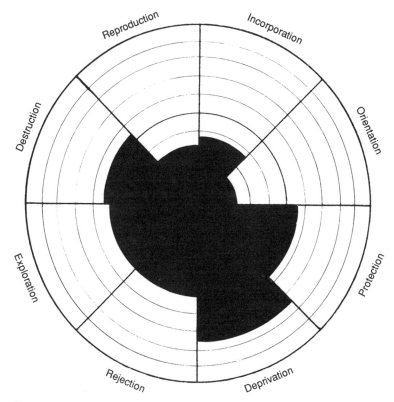

FIGURE 1.1. Depression profile obtained from a group of manic-depressive patients.

1983; Conte & Plutchik, 1974; Fahs, Hogan, & Fullerton, 1969; Fiorentino, Sheppard, & Merlis, 1970; Fracchia, Sheppard, & Merlis, 1974; Hama, Matsuyama, Hashimoto, & Plutchik, 1982; Kellerman & Plutchik, 1978; Platman, Plutchik, Fieve, & Lawlor, 1969; Plutchik, 1971; Plutchik & DiScipio, 1974; Sheppard, Fracchia, Collins, & Merlis, 1969; Sheppard, O'Neill, & Fracchia, 1970). The EPI has also been used in several studies concerned with psychosomatic issues (Edwards, 1980; Fieve, Platman, & Plutchik, 1968; Grunert, Lynch, Erdmann, & Vasudevan, 1979; Unden, Orth, Edwards, & Hedling, 1985), ethological problems (Buirski, Plutchik, & Kellerman, 1978; Plutchik & Landau, 1973) and a variety of other problems (Elizur & Klein, 1974; Fracchia, Sheppard, & Merlis, 1972, 1973; Kellerman, 1977). The test has been translated into Japanese (Hama and Plutchik, 1975), Italian (Perini & Plutchik, 1981, 1983), Czeckoslovak (Koukola, 1977), and several other languages.

A major value of the EPI is that it represents one of the few tests that is based directly on a general theory of emotions. The theory has determined the choice of

basic dimensions, decided on the circular order of elements, provided the basis
for identifying emotional components of personality traits, and provided a systematic and numerical basis for measuring degree of conflict implied by the
existence of mixed emotions or traits. In addition, the theory has created hypotheses that have been tested through the use of the EPI as well as other instruments.

THE *LIFE STYLE INDEX* FOR THE
MEASUREMENT OF EGO DEFENSES

One of the most important contributions of psychoanalysis to personality
theory is the concept of ego defenses. As stated earlier, according to psychoanalytic theory, defenses are mental processes that attempt to resolve conflicts
between emotions or between action tendencies. A child who has been punished
by his mother for misbehaving may wish to retaliate, to express his anger toward
her, to achieve revenge. The fear of further punishment or loss of her love may
lead to an indirect expression of the anger toward a younger sibling, a pet, or
some other vulnerable individual. Such indirect expressions of anger are an
unconscious way of handling the conflict between anger and fear and are defined
as *displacement*. The view will be presented here that all defenses are unconscious ways that individuals use to handle a conflict of emotions, and it is in this
sense that ego defenses are considered to be derivatives of emotions.

At present, clinicians do not agree on the total number of defenses, nor on their
degree of overlap, nor on their explicit definitions in all cases. Although the
Psychiatric Glossary of the American Psychiatric Association (Frazier, 1975) lists
23 ego defenses, various psychiatric sources have pointed out the extensive
overlap of meanings that exist, so that it is impossible to say exactly how many
defenses exist. For example, Vaillant (1971) has stated that the term
intellectualization includes the concepts of *isolation, rationalization, ritual, undoing,* and *magical thinking.*

The literature implies at least three concepts in terms of defenses. One is that
defenses overlap and vary in their degree of similarity to one another. The second
is that some defenses, at least, are polar opposites. The third point frequently
made is that some defenses are more primitive than others. From an analog point
of view, these ideas can be represented by a three-dimensional circumplex model
in precisely the same way that the subjective language of emotions can be so
represented. This structural view of the relation between ego defenses and emotions has been elaborated by Plutchik et al., (1979) and will be briefly summarized here.

The model assumes, as implied in Table 1.1, that each major ego defense has
developed ontogenetically to deal with a basic emotion. For example, the theory

assumes that displacement has evolved primarily to deal with issues of anger, repression has evolved to deal with issues of anxiety, denial has evolved to deal with issues of trust, and projection has evolved to deal with issues of distrust (or rejection). In every case, fear is assumed to be a common element involved in the conflict between emotions.

This model has some implications for measurement. It suggests that there should be eight basic defenses that are intimately related to the eight basic emotions of the psychoevolutionary theory. These defenses should have certain specific similarity and polarity relations to one another. Furthermore, the existence of defenses should provide an indirect measure of levels of conflict in the personality so that severely maladjusted individuals (determined by independent methods) should utilize defenses much more than do "normal" individuals. All of these implications have been confirmed. Before summarizing the data, however, a description will be given of how an ego defense scale was constructed.

RATIONALE FOR A SELF-REPORT
EGO DEFENSE SCALE

In order to identify the conceptual domain of defense mechanisms, a large number of psychoanalytic, psychiatric, and psychological sources were examined. Based on this review, 16 defense mechanisms were identified as constituting the domain of ego defenses. These defenses were *acting out, compensation, denial, displacement, fantasy, identification, intellectualization, introjection, isolation, projection, rationalization, reaction formation, regression, repression, sublimation,* and *undoing.* Based on the definitions of these terms, test items were developed to sample each of the 16 defenses. The statements were of a type that a person might use if he was expressing a particular defense. For example, the statement "I always see the bright side of things" reflects denial. Repression is expressed by a sentence such as "I never remember my dreams." The initial test, with a total of 224 items, was administered to a large group of college students. Item analyses reduced the number of items to 184. A series of studies was then instituted to determine the properties of the test. For example, 36 experienced clinicians completed the test (the *Life Style Index*) for patients they had or had known who met various DSM-III personality diagnoses such as hysteric, psychopathic, paranoid, etc. Using intraclass correlations, it was found that there was high interjudge agreement on the scales that characterized a given diagnosis in most cases.

Based on the data from the college students an intercorrelation matrix was computed for the 16 ego defenses and then was factor analyzed. The results showed some bipolarity plus strong loadings of many items on the first factor. This was interpreted as reflecting the core anxiety underlying all defenses. The overlap of scales suggested that 16 defenses were too many. The items were regrouped based both on empirical data as well as psychoanalytic theory, producing a new version of the *Life Style Index* that contained 138 items distributed into eight scales. The defenses being measured now consisted of compensation (including identification and fantasy), denial, displacement, intellectualization (including sublimation, undoing, and rationalization), projection, reaction formation, regression (including acting-out), and repression (including isolation and introjection).

The new scales were then given to 17 clinicians, who were asked to rate the appropriateness of the items for the various defenses. Although there was good agreement on some items, others were judged inappropriate. The results of this procedure further reduced the number of items to 97 and this version was used in most of the further research described.

Another study examined the issue of degree of primitiveness of the various defenses. Six psychiatrists were asked to rank a list of the eight defenses in an order that represented the level of development of each defense. There was good agreement among the psychiatrists (Kendall's Coefficient of Concordance was .71) in producing the following list from most to least primitive: denial, regression, projection, displacement, repression, reaction formation, intellectualization, and compensation. These results are largely consistent with those of Vaillant (1971, 1976) and others.

The *Life Style Index* was then administered to a group of 29 schizophrenic patients in a state hospital and their scores were compared with those of the normal college students. The results revealed that the schizophrenics had significantly higher scores on seven of the eight defenses. It thus appears that schizophrenics use defenses much more than do normal college students, a finding consistent with reports by Vaillant (1971), and a confirmation of one of the original hypotheses. This result indicates that the test has some degree of discriminant validity.

A further study was conducted in which the *Life Style Index* was given to 58 normal adults along with a test of self-esteem based on the Tennessee Self Concept Scale (Fitts, 1965), and a brief version of the Taylor Manifest Anxiety Scale (Bendig, 1956). The results of this study revealed that scores on all but one of the defense scales correlated positively and significantly with anxiety level, thus again supporting the hypothesis that fear is a common element in all defenses. The one exception, denial, is interesting. The negative correlation with denial suggests that high deniers do not recognize or acknowledge their own anxiety, a finding consistent with psychoanalytic theory. The self-esteem scale correlated negatively to a significant degree with five of the eight defenses,but particularly with regression and intellectualization. Thus, not only do psychiatric patients use defenses much more than do normal individuals, it is also the case that, among the normals, those who use defenses a great deal tend to have lower self-esteem. These findings provide evidence for the construct validity of the scale.

More recently the *Life Style Index* has been used in a study of variables that might predict the outcome of psychotherapy (Buckley, Conte, Plutchik, Wild, & Karasu, 1984). In this study, 21 medical students were seen in psychotherapy over a period averaging 42 sessions. Each student completed a self-report battery of tests at the time psychotherapy was begun that included measures of symptoms, general adjustment, coping styles, and ego defenses (as measured by the *Life Style Index*). Outcome was measured by psychiatrists' ratings of change. Of the many measures used in the study, reaction formation, undoing, rationalization, and projection, taken from the *Life Style Index,* correlated significantly with outcome. This implies that the nature of the defenses individuals use influences their openness to change as well as their ability to form a therapeutic alliance.

Finally, there have been several studies of the similarity structure of the different ego defenses. In one study the 16 ego defenses first identified were compared using a modified method of paired comparisons. Details of the method are given in Conte and Plutchik (1981). A separate analysis was carried out using a semantic differential approach designed to measure similarity on the basis of degree of overlap of connotations. The results of the two analyses are summarized in Figure 1.2.

Examination of Figure 1.2 reveals that a circle is a reasonable approximation to the similarity and polarity relations among ego defenses. It demonstrates that the defenses grouped under the heading of intellectualization are, in fact, quite similar to one another (sublimation, rationalization, and intellectualization), and that acting-out, displacement, and projection are also similar (that is, are negative, outwardly directed, hostile actions). Denial and repression are similar, as are reaction formation and regression.

Also, if one considers the polarities inherent in the circle, it appears that the displacement–projection cluster is opposite the fantasy–introjection cluster, and that the relatively primitive defense of regression is opposite the more evolved defenses of sublimation and rationalization. Another way to describe these polarities is to point out that the displacement–projection defenses are outwardly directed and action-oriented while fantasy–introjection and identification are inwardly directed and inherently passive. Similarly, regression suggests a loss of control, while its opposite (sublimation and rationalization) suggests cognitive control.

The *Life Style Index* has been further refined by changing some items and eliminating others. It has been used in both individual counseling and industrial consulting. An illustration follows. In a recent investigation, 110 middle managers from a large multinational corporation agreed to participate in a study of factors related to stress (Bunker, 1982). They provided information on a battery of tests, including the Eysenck Personality Questionnaire, the SCL-90, the

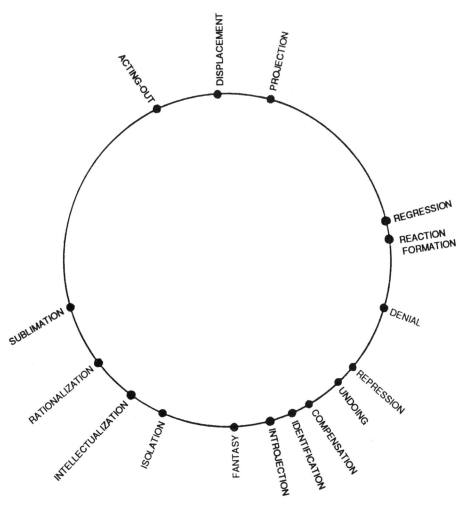

FIGURE 1.2.   Similarity scaling of 16 ego defenses.

Holmes–Rahe Life Events Scale, the Rorschach, the *Life Style Index,* the AECOM Coping Scale, and others. An intensive clinical interview was conducted with each manager, and the spouse of each manager was also interviewed. Supervisory ratings of job functioning were also obtained.

When the scores on the eight ego defenses were correlated against the other measures it was found that managers who got high scores on most of the defenses tended to have many symptoms on the SCL-90 and evidence of high anxiety and depression. Managers who had high stress on the job and at home were found to have high scores on the defenses of projection, intellectualization, compensa-

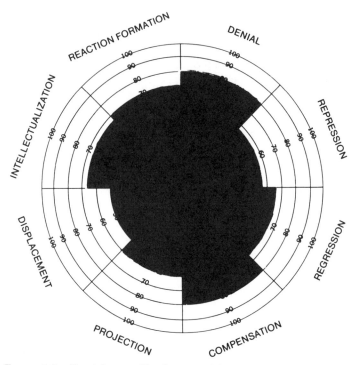

FIGURE 1.3.   Ego defense profile of a group of 29 hospitalized schizophrenics.

tion, and regression. Interestingly, managers with high scores on repression were found to have low stress at work, suggesting that they were able to ignore or avoid the experience of stress.

Two groups were identified, those with high stress and good adjustment, and those with high stress and poor adjustment. The pattern of ego defenses in these two groups was quite different. For example, the high stress–good adjustment managers were highest on denial and relatively low on reaction formation. In contrast, the high stress–poor adjustment managers were lowest on denial and highest on reaction formation.

Figure 1.3 is presented to provide some idea of the nature of the profile that results from use of the *Life Style Index*. As part of the study described by Plutchik et al. (1979), 29 hospitalized schizophrenic patients were asked to complete the *Life Style Index*. Their mean age was 32.8 years and all but eight were female. The profile represents percentiles based on a normal group of 130 college students. It is evident that the patients are higher on every dimension except one, and are particularly high on denial, compensation, and reaction formation. These elevated scores support the idea that ego defenses represent somewhat pathological ways of dealing with the stresses of everyday life. The high score on compensation may reflect a sense of dissatisfaction with oneself and with one's ability to deal effectively with life issues. The high reaction formation suggests a strong tendency to express the opposite of what one feels, while the high denial may be an attempt to shut out the unpleasant reality of life as a patient.

THE AECOM COPING SCALE

Ego defenses are assumed to be unconscious processes, of which an individual is normally not aware. This, of course, does not mean that an individual is not aware of the various aspects of his or her behavior that an observer may interpret as defensive behavior. Defenses are inferences made from overt behavior. The inferences are based upon verbalizations about preferences, motivations, feelings, and actions, the defensive significance of which the individual may not understand.

However, it is important to point out that defenses may be recognized by oneself or uncovered through comments by others or by interpreting one's own behavior. In such cases, an individual may continue to use certain defensive styles of interacting in a quite conscious and deliberate way. For example, the belief that other people are hostile, inconsiderate, and selfish may be a projection of one's own feelings. It is, however, possible to use *blame* of others for their apparent shortcomings as a conscious way to influence a situation for one's own ends.

As briefly stated earlier, it is therefore proposed that the transformation of unconscious defenses into conscious ways of interacting with others defines a new derivative domain of emotions, the domain of coping styles. Coping styles are general methods used by individuals to deal with problems, difficulties, and stresses. The model proposed here assumes that a different coping style exists as a kind of conscious parallel to each basic defense. For example, for the ego defense of repression, there exists a parallel coping style in which the individual deliberately inhibits certain classes of behavior in order to avoid anxiety and frustration. The term *suppression* is suggested as the conscious coping style for the unconscious mechanism of *repression*. Similarly, the unconscious mechanism of *denial* may be the precursor to a conscious coping mechanism that tries to minimize the significance of a stressful event. This coping style is therefore called *minimization*. The model of coping styles being proposed assumes that for each of the eight basic emotions there is a related ego defense and a derivative coping style. These relations are shown in Table 1.1. The various coping styles have been given the following names (with the related defenses listed in parentheses): *suppression* (repression), *minimization* (denial), *reversal* (reaction formation), *mapping* (intellectualization), *substitution* (displacement), *blame* (projection), *replacement* (compensation), and *help-seeking* (regression).

It is important to emphasize that these coping styles do not have any connotation of psychopathology, as do ego defenses. They are common, garden-variety methods all people use to varying degrees in order to deal with life problems. And they are general enough to be applicable to almost any problem an individual may encounter. Some, however, seem to work better than others, as will shortly be described.

THE CONSTRUCTION OF A SELF-REPORT COPING SCALE

A group of five clinicians met regularly to construct items that reflected the many different ways that people use to cope with problems. It became increasingly evident that the coping methods could be grouped into a relatively few categories. The schema proposed here of eight basic coping styles that correspond to eight basic ego defenses seemed to be both general and parsimonious.

After consensus had been arrived at among the members of the group, the items were then presented to an independent group of 10 psychiatrists, who were asked to indicate the extent to which each item adequately reflected each of the eight basic coping styles as defined by the theoretical model. On the basis of their responses, several items were dropped and the wording of others was changed.

The 95 items of the scale, labeled the AECOM Coping Scale, were incorporated into a format in which the respondent indicated how frequently, on a 4-point scale, he or she felt or acted in the ways described. For example, the coping style of *minimization* is reflected by such items as ''When something bothers me, I can ignore it'' and ''I feel that problems have a way of taking care of themselves.'' *Suppression* is expressed by such items as ''I try not to think about unpleasant things'' and ''I avoid funerals.'' *Help-seeking* is defined by such items as ''When I have a problem I try to get others to help me'' and ''I try to be associated with people who take charge of a situation.''

The AECOM Coping Scale has been administered to several normal as well as patient groups and has been modified so that the present version contains 87 items. Preliminary norms based on 120 college students are available. No sex differences have been found in coping styles in this college population. The internal reliabilities of the eight coping scales as measured by coefficient alpha varied from $+.58$ to $+.79$ with an average of $+.70$. The use of the scale as a teaching device in a series of workshops on professional burnout is described by Wilder and Plutchik (1982).

In a recent study, 199 prisoners in a Canadian penitentiary were asked to complete the AECOM Coping Scale along with several other instruments. A group of 76 Canadian college students also completed the same battery of tests. It was found that the college students were significantly higher than the prisoners on the coping styles of *minimization, replacement,* and *reversal,* and were significantly lower on *suppression, help-seeking,* and *mapping.* When these coping styles of the prisoners were correlated with parenting styles of their parents, it was found that high maternal rejection and depression were associated with the tendency of the prisoners to use *help-seeking* as a coping style for solving problems. The fathers' degree of *sociability* was found to be negatively correlated with the coping style of *suppression.* In other words, fathers who did not socialize warmly with their children tended to have children who *avoided* many social encounters (at least in this prison population) (Plutchik, Lange, & Picard, 1989).

In the study of middle managers cited earlier (Bunker, 1982), a number of correlations were found between coping scale scores and levels of stress, as well as other test data, based on 74 individuals. Those managers who were rated as having many psychological symptoms were significantly higher on the defense of *denial* and the coping style of *blame* than were those managers who had few psychological symptoms. They were also judged to be less effective managers. Managers evaluated as effective copers had relatively high scores on *mapping.* When the managers rated low on stress were compared to those rated high, it was found that the low-stress individuals were relatively lower on most of the coping styles, with the exception of *suppression* and *mapping,* while the high-stress individuals were high on everything except *reversal* and *help-seeking.* These patterns indicate that the presence of psychological symptoms and level of functioning on the job are related to patterns of coping.

A recently completed study compared 40 inpatient alcoholics on a detoxification ward with 40 controls who were patients from the same general social background but who came to an emergency room screening clinic for treatment of minor physical ailments. All patients took a battery of tests that included the coping scales.

Figure 1.4 shows the coping style profile of the 40 hospitalized alcoholics. It appears that they have a strong tendency to use *suppression* as a way of dealing with life stresses. They also are very likely to blame other people for their problems, and they have a strong tendency to seek help from others. (Perhaps this tendency is the basis for describing alcoholics as dependent personalities.) The alcoholics were significantly higher on these coping dimensions than were the matched controls (Conte, Plutchik, Picard, Galanter, & Jacoby, 1989).

The final study to be described that utilized the AECOM Coping Scale was concerned with the prediction of change in hospitalized schizophrenics after discharge. In this investigation a group of schizophrenic inpatients completed a battery of self-report questionnaires designed to measure dimensions of personality, affect, conflict, ego defenses, and coping styles. Similar ratings were made

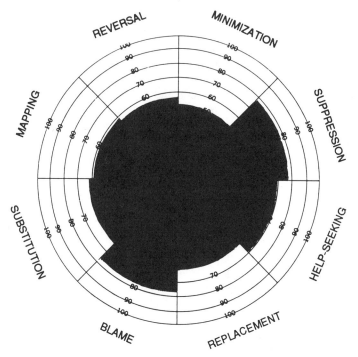

FIGURE 1.4.   Coping profile of a group of 40 hospitalized alcoholics.

by each patient's primary therapist. Those patients who were rehospitalized during the next 2 years were identified. It was found that the best predictors of readmission to the hospital included two ego defenses, *denial* and *displacement*, and the coping style of *suppression* (Conte, Plutchik, Schwartz, & Wild, 1983). This latter finding is consistent with the prisoner study in which the prisoners were also found to use *suppression* significantly more than did the controls.

CONCLUSIONS

This chapter has considered the issue of the measurement of emotion from a theoretical perspective. The point was emphasized that the most adequate kind of measure is one that is derived from theory so that the outcome of the measurement operations may contribute to the enhancement or modification of the theory. Theory-based measures also have a much wider nomological network than do purely empirical or arbitrary measures.

Given this perspective, the psychoevolutionary theory of emotion was described with particular attention being paid to the idea of derivatives of emotion. Since an emotion is a complex chain of events having behavioral homeostatic properties, aspects of the chain may be described through the use of many different "languages." For example, the language of personality traits such as *cheerful, gloomy,* and *quarrelsome* is conceptualized as the result of repeated expressions of transient emotional states such as *joy, sadness,* or *anger.* A test called the *Emotions Profile Index,* based on the theory, is described in detail and its application to a variety of issues is presented.

The point is made that the language of psychiatric diagnoses such as *depressed, passive,* and *manic* reflects extremes of emotional states and personality traits. Empirical evidence now reveals that such diagnostic terms share certain properties with emotions, for example, their circular similarity structure, or circumplex structure.

Data are presented demonstrating the interrelations between different emotion adjective checklists. What is especially interesting about the results are the relatively high correlations between basic emotion dimensions measured in different ways. In contrast, the history of adjective checklists reveals that purely empirical approaches to such measurement has led to a plethora of differently named scales of limited overlap.

Finally, attention is given to two important derivative domains, the areas of ego defenses and coping styles. Two new scales are described that are based directly on the psychoevolutionary theory. Each of the dimensions of the scales is related to the eight basic emotions in systematic ways, and empirical data are given to show the usefulness of these instruments in a variety of settings. Overall, the point that must be emphasized is that the measurement of emotion is a much broader issue than is the measurement of subjective feelings by means of adjective checklists. The field of emotion study comprises a vast array of phenomena, and the ideal measures of emotion and its derivatives are those that are diverse, theory based, and systematically related to these complex phenomena.

REFERENCES

Albrecht, E., & Brabender, V. (1983). Alcoholics in inpatient, short-term interactional group psychotherapy: An outcome study. *Group, 7,* 50–54.

Bendig, A. W. (1956). The development of a short form of the Manifest Anxiety Scale. *Journal of Consulting Psychology, 20,* 384–387.

Benjamin, L. S. (1974). Structural analysis of social behavior. *Psychological Review, 81,* 392–425.

Borgatta, E. I. (1961). Mood, personality, and interaction. *Journal of Psychology, 64,* 105–137.

Buckley, P., Conte, H. R., Plutchik, R., Wild, K., & Karasu, T. B. (1984). Psychodynamic variables as predictors of psychotherapy outcome. *American Journal of Psychiatry, 141,* 742–748.

Buirski, P., Plutchik, R., & Kellerman, H. (1978). Sex differences, dominance, and personality in the chimpanzee. *Animal Behaviour, 26,* 123–129

Bunker, K. A. (1982). Comparisons of marketing subjects high and low in psychological symptoms. Report No. CA2059, 114. New York: American Telephone & Telegraph Co. Assessment Center.

Clyde, D. J. (1963). *Manual for the Clyde Mood Scale.* Coral Gables, FL: University of Miami.

Conte, H., & Plutchik, R. (1974). Personality and background characteristics of suicidal mental patients. *Journal of Psychiatric Research, 10,* 181–188.

Conte, H. R., & Plutchik, R. (1981). A circumplex model for interpersonal personality traits. *Journal of Personality and Social Psychology, 40,* 701–711.

Conte, H. R., Plutchik, R., Picard, S., Galanter, M., & Jacoby, J. (1989). Personality and coping patterns in inpatient alcoholics. Submitted for publication.

Conte, H. R., Plutchik, R., Schwartz, B., & Wild, K. (1983). Psychodynamic variables related to outcome in hospitalized schizophrenics. Paper presented at the Convention of the American Psychological Association, Anaheim, CA.

Curran, J. P., & Cattell, R. B. (1975). *Manual for the eight state questionnaire.* Champagne, IL: Institute for Personality and Ability Testing.

Darwin, C. (1965). *The expression of the emotions in man and animals.* Chicago: University of Chicago Press (originally published in 1872 by Murray, London).

Edwards, M. E. (1980). Psychological factors and coronary heart disease. Ph.D. Dissertation, Microfilm No. 8027814. Ann Arbor, MI: Abstracts International.

Elias, N. (1977). *The civilizing process.* New York: Urizen.

Elizur, A., & Klein, M. M. (1974). Similarity, complementarity and difference of marital couples in problem and non-problem areas. *Israel Annals of Psychiatry and Related Disciplines, 12,* 145–155.

Fahs, H., Hogan, T. P., & Fullerton, D. T. (1969). An emotional profile of depression. *Psychological Reports, 25,* 18.

Fenichel, O. (1945). *The psychoanalytic theory of neurosis.* Boston: Routledge & Kegan Paul.

Fieve, R. R., Platman, S. R., & Plutchik, R. (1968). The use of lithium in affective disorders: I. Acute endogenous depression. *American Journal of Psychiatry, 125,* 487–491.

Fiorentino, D., Sheppard, C., & Merlis, S. (1970). Emotions Profile Index (EPI) pattern for paranoid personality types: Cross-validation and extension. *Psychological Reports, 26,* 303–308.

Fisher, G. A., Heise, D. R., Bohrnstedt, G. W., & Lucke, J. F. (1985). Evidence for extending the circumplex model of personality trait language to self-reported moods. *Journal of Personality and Social Psychology, 49,* 233–242.

Fitts, W. H. (1965). *The Tennessee Self Concept Scale.* Nashville, TN: Counselor Recordings & Tests.

Fracchia, J., Sheppard, C., & Merlis, S. (1972). Attitudes toward mental illness: Treatment unit profiles and personal adjustment patterns. *Diseases of the Nervous System, 33,* 645–648.

Fracchia, T., Sheppard, C., & Merlis, S. (1973). Personal adjustment of hospital staff and their attitudes about mental illness. *Journal of Psychiatry, 83,* 243–246.

Fracchia, J., Sheppard, C., & Merlis, S. (1974). Psychological characteristics of long-term mental patients: Some implications for treatment. *Comprehensive Psychiatry 15,* 495–501.

Frazier, S. H. (1975). *A psychiatric glossary.* Washington, DC: American Psychiatric Association.

Freedman, M. D., Leary, T. F., Ossorio, A. G., & Coffey, H. S. (1951). The interpersonal dimension of personality.*Journal of Personality, 20,* 143–161.

Grunert, B. K., Lynch, N. T., Erdmann, B. R., & Vasudevan, S. V. (1979). Low back pain: Use of the Emotions Profile Index to assess affective studies. *Archives of Physical Medicine and Rehabilitation, 60,* 541–547.

Hama, H., Matsuyama, Y., Hashimoto, E., & Plutchik, R. (1982). Emotion profiles of Japanese schizophrenics, neurotics, and alcoholics. *Psychologia: An International Journal of Psychology in the Orient, 25,* 144–148.

Hama, H., & Plutchik, R. (1975). Personality profile of Japanese college students: A normative study. *Japanese Psychological Research, 17,* 141–146.

Howarth, E., & Young, P.D. (1986). Patterns of mood change. *Personality and Individual Differences, 7,* 275–281.

Izard, C. E. (1972). *Patterns of emotion: A new analysis of anxiety and depression.* New York: Academic Press.

Kellerman, H. (1977). Shostram's mate selection model, pair attraction inventory, and Emotions Profile Index. *Journal of Psychology, 95,* 37–43.

Kellerman, H. (1979). *Group psychotherapy and personality: Intersecting structures.* New York: Grune & Stratton.

Kellerman, H. (1980). A structural model of emotion and personality: Psychoanalytic and sociobiological implications. In R. Plutchik & H. Kellerman (Eds.), *Theories and emotion.* New York: Academic Press.

Kellerman, H. (1987). Nightmares and the structure of personality. In H. Kellerman (Ed.), *The nightmare: Psychological and biological foundations.* New York: Columbia University Press.

Kellerman, H., & Plutchik, R. (1968). Emotion-trait interrelations and the measurement of personality. *Psychological Reports, 23,* 1107–1114.

Kellerman, H., & Plutchik, R. (1977). The meaning of tension in group therapy. In L. R. Wolberg, M. L. Aronson, & A. R. Wolberg (Eds.), *Group therapy 1977: An overview.* New York: Stratton.

Kellerman, H., & Plutchik, R. (1978). Personality patterns of drug addicts in a therapy group: A similarity structure analysis. *Group, 2,* 14–21.

Koukola, B. (1977). A method for determining personality traits and emotions. *Ceskoslovenska Psychologie, 21,* 131–135.

Lorr, M., & McNair, D. M. (1984). *Manual: Profile of mood states: Bipolar form.* San Diego, CA: Educational and Industrial Testing Services.

Lorr, M., & Youniss, R. P. (1986). *Interpersonal Style Inventory (ISI) manual.* Los Angeles: Western Psychological Services.

McNair, D. M., Lorr, M., & Droppleman, L. F. (1971). *Manual of the profile of mood states.* San Diego, CA: Educational and Industrial Testing Services.

McNair, D. M., Lorr, M., & Droppleman, L. F. (1981). *Manual of the profile of mood states.* San Diego, CA: Educational and Industrial Testing Services.

Perini, G., & Plutchik, R. (1981). The Emotions Profile Index of Plutchik and Kellerman: Theoretical bases and clinical applications. *Bollettino di Psicologia Applicata, 159,* 139–153.

Perini, G., & Plutchik, R. (1983). The Emotions Profile Index of Plutchik and Kellerman: Italian version and normative data. *Bollettino di Psicologia Applicata, 165,* 30–36.

Platman, S. R., Plutchik, R., Fieve, R. R., & Lawlor, W. G. (1969). Emotion profiles associated with mania and depression. *Archives of General Psychiatry, 20,* 210–214.

Plutchik, R. (1958). Outlines of a new theory of emotions. *Psychosomatic Medicine, 17,* 306–310.

Plutchik, R. (1962). *Emotions: Facts, theories, and a new model.* New York: Random House.

Plutchik, R. (1966). Multiple rating scales for the measurement of affective states. *Journal of Clinical Psychology, 22,* 423–425.

Plutchik, R. (1970). Emotions, evolution and adaptive processes. In M. Arnold (Ed.), *Feelings and emotions.* New York: Academic Press.

Plutchik, R. (1971). Personality and personal history differences between day hospital and ward patients. *Psychiatric Quarterly, 45,* 509–517.

Plutchik, R. (1980a). *Emotion: A psychoevolutionary synthesis*. New York: Harper & Row.

Plutchik, R. (1980b). A general psychoevolutionary theory of emotion. In R. Plutchik & H. Kellerman (Eds.), *Theories of Emotion* (Vol. 1). New York: Academic Press.

Plutchik, R. (1983). *Foundations of experimental research*. New York: Harper & Row.

Plutchik, R. (1984). Emotions: A general psychoevolutinary theory. In K. R. Scherer & P. Ekman (Eds.), *Approaches to emotions*. Hillsdale, NJ: Erlbaum.

Plutchik, R., & Conte, H. R. (1985). Quantitative assessment of personality disorders. In R. Michels, J. O. Cavenar, Jr., and H. K. H. Brodie (Eds.), *Psychiatry* (Vol. 1). Philadelphia: Lippincott.

Plutchik, R., & DiScipio, W. J. (1974). Personality patterns in chronic alcoholism (Korsakoff's syndrome), chronic schizophrenics, and geriatric patients with chronic brain syndrome.*Journal of the American Geriatrics Society, 22,* 514–516.

Plutchik, R., & Kellerman, H. (1974). *Emotions Profile Index manual*. Los Angeles: Western Psychological Services.

Plutchik, R., Kellerman, H., & Conte, H. R. (1979). A structural model of ego defenses and emotions. In C. E. Izard (Ed.), *Emotions in personality and psychology*. New York: Plenum.

Plutchik, R., & Landau, H. (1973). Perceived dominance and emotional states in small groups. *Psychotherapy: Theory, Research and Practice, 10,* 341–342.

Plutchik, R., Lange, R. A., & Picard, S. (1989). Child-rearing styles and parental conflict as predictors of coping styles and self-esteem in violent and sex offenders. Submitted for publication.

Plutchik, R., McCarthy, M., & Hall, B. H. (1975). Changes in elderly welfare hotel residents during a one year period. *Journal of the American Geriatrics Society, 23,* 265–270.

Plutchik, R., & Platman, S. R. (1977). Personality connotations of psychiatric diagnoses: Implications for a similarity model. *Journal of Nervous and Mental Disease, 165,* 418–422.

Plutchik, R., Platman, S. R., & Fieve, R. R. (1968). Repeated measurements in the manic depressive illness: Some methodological problems. *Journal of Psychology, 70,* 131–137,

Schaefer, E. S. (1959). A circumplex model for maternal behavior. *Journal of Abnormal and Social Psychology, 59,* 226–235.

Schaefer, E. S. (1961). Converging conceptual models for maternal behavior and for child behavior. In J. Glidewell (Ed.), *Parental attitudes and child behavior*. Springfield, IL: Thomas.

Schaefer, E. S., & Plutchik, R. (1966). Interrelationships of emotions, traits, and diagnostic constructs. *Psychological Reports, 18,* 399–410.

Scherer, K. R. (1984). Emotion as a multicomponent process: A model and some cross-cultural data. In P. Shaver (Ed.), *Review of personality and social psychology* (Vol. 5, pp. 37–63). Beverly Hills, CA: Sage.

Scott, J. P. (1980). The function of emotions in behavioral systems: A systems theory analysis. In R. Plutchik & H. Kellerman (Eds.), *Theories of emotion*. New York: Academic Press.

Sheppard, C., Fracchia, J., Collins, L., & Merlis, S. (1969). Comparison of emotion profiles as defined by two additional MMPI profile types in male narcotic addicts. *Journal of Clinical Psychology, 25,* 186–188.

Sheppard, C., O'Neill, C., & Fracchia, J. (1970). Levels of personal conflict derived from response to the Emotions Profile Index. *Journal of Psychology, 74,* 143–148.

Stacey, F. D. (1977). *Physics of the earth*. New York: Wiley.

Stern, G. G. (1958). *Activities index*. Syracuse, NY: Syracuse University Psychological Research Center.

Stevens, S. S. (1946). On the theory of scales of measurement. *Science, 103,* 677–680.

Stevens, S. S. (1959). Measurement, psychophysics, and utility. In W. W. Churchman and P. Ratoosh (Eds.), *Measurement: Definitions and theories*. New York: Wiley.

Unden, A. L., Orth, G. K., Edwards, M. E., & Hedling, B. (1985). Empirical studies: Social interaction and mortality: An 8 year followup study of 150 Swedish middle-aged men. *Stressfosknirgsrapporter, 6,* 76–87.

Vaillant, G. E. (1971). Theoretical hierarchy of adaptive ego mechanisms. *Archives of General Psychiatry, 24,* 107–118.

Vaillant, G. E. (1976). Natural history of male psychological health, V: The relation of choice of ego mechanism of defense to adult adjustment. *Archives of General Psychiatry, 33,* 535–545.

Wiggins, J. S. (1979). A psychological taxonomy of trait descriptive terms. The interpersonal domain. *Journal of Personality and Social Psychology, 37,* 395–412.

Wiggins, J. S. (1980). Circumplex models of interpersonal behavior. In L. Wheeler (Ed.), *Review of personality and social psychology* (Vol. 1, pp. 265–294). Beverly Hills, CA: Sage.

Wiggins, J. S., & Broughton, R. (1985). The interpersonal circle: A structural model for the integration of personality research. *Perspectives in Personality, 1,* 1–47.

Wilder, J. F., & Plutchik, R. (1982). Preparing the professional: Building prevention of burnout into professional training. In W. Payne (Ed.), *Job stress and burnout.* Beverly Hills, CA: Sage.

Wilson, E. O. (1975). *Sociobiology: The new synthesis.* Cambridge, MA: Harvard University Press.

Zuckerman, M., & Lubin, B. (1965). *Manual for the multiple affect adjective check list.* San Diego, CA: Educational and Industrial Testing Services.

Chapter 2

MODELS AND METHODS FOR MEASUREMENT OF MOOD

MAURICE LORR

ABSTRACT

The chapter begins with a proposed differentiation of states and traits. A review of 12 of the better known measures of mood or affect is next presented. The review reveals three major findings regarding the structure of mood. One group of investigators favors a multifactorial model that is composed of 6 to 10 mood dimensions. Another group associated with Tellegen argues for two orthogonal dimensions labeled Positive Affect and Negative Affect. A third group, which includes Plutchik and Russell, offers evidence for a circular two-dimensional ordering of affect variables. Since self-report measures are significantly influenced by response format and response bias, the five main response sets are described along with techniques for their control. The question of mood bipolarity is discussed both as a methodological problem and as a theoretical issue. The last section offers a discussion and description of two forms of dimensional analysis: factor analysis and multidimensional scaling. The circular order, or circumplex, is examined as a theoretical model for the understanding of mood.

INTRODUCTION

One of the goals of this chapter is to review presently available measures of mood or affect in order to acquaint the reader with the present state of assessment in this area. Following this an evaluation will be made of the principal findings of

37

factor analytic and scaling studies. In the process of review, various measurement problems become evident. It will be show that the two most important problems are rating response format and response bias. Accordingly, the four or five major response sets are described and methods for their control are discussed. Since these methodological difficulties lead to monopolar scales, the problems of bipolarity will be examined and discussed. The last section deals with structural models. Factor analysis and multidimensional scaling will be discussed and illustrated. The circumplex, or circular, ordering of attributes will be explained and various methods for testing the fit of data to the model will be suggested.

STATES AND TRAITS: DEFINITIONS

For a long time there has been confusion and conflict over the nature of states and traits (Allen & Potkay, 1981; Zuckerman, 1983). Typically, person attributes are viewed as more or less statelike or more or less traitlike. The two concepts are not sharply differentiated because they overlap in meaning. Terms denoting moods and feelings refer to brief and temporary experiences that are manifested sporadically and irregularly. In general, states are feelings and moods evoked by situational pressures, social–environmental conditions, or temporary physiological changes. Traits, in contrast, are viewed as stable, long-lasting, behaviors manifested in a variety of situations. Consequently, traits must be observed more frequently than states and across more situations before they are attributed to a person.

Recently it has been argued that the confusion arises from an Aristotelian either–or view of the two concepts. No explicit set of criteria is given for distinguishing states from traits. For example, terms such as *anxious* or *depressed* are classified depending on the views of the investigator. However, from this viewpoint the current conflict would be reduced if (1) these concepts were seen as fuzzy, overlapping categories, organized around a set of prototypical examples and (2) some specific criteria for determining the prototypicality of a term as a state rather than a trait were utilized. In the prototype model (Rosch & Lloyd, 1978), traits and states are viewed as fuzzy, overlapping categories organized around a core set of prototypic exemplars. Class membership is a matter of degree and there are no clear-cut boundaries separating categories.

CURRENT MEASURES OF MOOD

One of the earliest approaches to the description and assessment of mood was first reported by Nowlis and Nowlis (1956). Beginning about 1951, these authors became involved in studies of the effects of moderate dosages of commonly used drugs on the social, emotional, and motivational behavior of college men. They devised an adjective checklist of 100 or more adjectives to describe moment-to-moment states of conscious mood. Subjects read through the list rapidly and gave their first response to each word. Four options were permitted: (1) a double check if the word definitely defined the feeling, (2) a single check if it possibly described a feeling, (3) to skip the word if it probably did not apply, and (4) to cross out the word if it definitely did not apply. They postulated four bipolar dimensions of mood: (a) level of activation, (b) level of control, (c) social orientation (*agreeable–hostile*), and (d) hedonic tone (*joyful–depressed*). When Green and Nowlis (1957) later conducted a factor-analytic study of their adjectives, they failed to confirm the hypothesized bipolar structure. Instead, they identified eight unipolar dimensions. Borgatta (1961) selected 40 of the Nowlis adjectives to represent the eight factors. The short adjective checklist was administered before and after a battery of questionnaires to 180 male college students. Borgatta's factor analysis of item intercorrelations confirmed seven of the Green–Nowlis factors but only six were used for scoring. The six factors were labeled as follows: Lonely (depression), Warm hearted, Tired, Thoughtful, Defiant (aggression), and Startled (anxiety).

Plutchik (1962) formulated a comprehensive theory of primary emotions, which he viewed as adaptive devices that have played a role in individual survival. The basic prototypic dimensions of adaptive behavior and the emotions related to them are as follows: (1) *incorporation* (acceptance), (2) *rejection* (disgust); (3) *destruction* (anger), (4) *protection* (fear); (5) *reproduction* (joy); (6) *deprivation* (sorrow); (7) *orientation* (surprise), and (8) *exploration* (expectation). These eight primary emotions vary in intensity and interact to produce all the mixed emotions observed and reported in everyday life. The model presents the eight emotions in a circular order, whereas intensity represents the third dimension of a hypothetical cone. One measurement device constructed (1966) consists of eight affect terms of intermediate intensity that are rated on a 5-point rating scale. The scale points are (1) *do not feel,* (2) *feel slightly,* (3) *feel moderately,* (4) *feel strongly,* and (5) *feel very strongly.* When administered on the day of a scheduled examination, four of the eight affects showed significant changes.

The *Emotions Profile Index* (EPI; Plutchik & Kellerman, 1984) was developed on the basis of the Plutchik psychoevolutionary theory of emotion. The authors make the assumption that all interpersonal traits can be conceptualized as resulting from the mixture of two or more primary emotions. The EPI was developed initially by having 10 psychologists rate the primary components of a large number of traits. Twelve trait terms were selected on the basis of high interjudge consistency. These 12 traits were then paired in all possible combinations, yielding 66 pairs. Four pairs were dropped because they had identical scoring categories. The subject is asked to indicate which of the two paired words describes the person's *usual* mood. It should be recognized that many students of affect cannot accept the assumption made by these investigators. Furthermore, nearly all mood scales ask the subject to indicate his (or her) feeling *right now*. Trait ratings typically call for the subject's *usual* mode of responding.

Zuckerman and Lubin (1965) developed a Multiple Affect Adjective Check List (MAACL) designed to measure anxiety, depression, and hostility. The Anxiety Scale is composed of 21 adjectives, the Depression Scale is made up of 40 adjectives, and the Hostility Scale contains 28 adjectives. Each of the three scales contains both positive and negative adjectives. A total score is the sum of negative adjectives checked plus the sum of positive adjectives *not* endorsed. A recent factor analysis (Gotlib & Meyer, 1986) of data from a large sample yielded two large unipolar factors. One factor is defined only by negative adjectives, and the second is defined by positive adjectives from all three MAACL scales. A possible explanation for emergence of these two factors is the independence of positive and negative affect and the differential effects of response set (item checking tendency) on endorsement. Herron (1969), in his analysis, came to a similar conclusion. Negative items from all three MAACL scales load on Factor I, and positive affect items from all three scales load on Factor II. Thus the factor analyses do not differentiate among items from the three MAACL scales. Scores on the MAACL may reflect a response set in addition to measures of positive and negative affect.

In 1961, Lorr, McNair, Weinstein, Michaux, and Raskin, drawing on the Nowlis adjective checklist, designed a set of scales to assess the effect of various drugs on psychotherapy outpatients. The original form included 55 simple adjectives judged to be descriptive of six hypothesized mood states (McNair & Lorr, 1964). Each adjective was rated on a 4-point intensity scale: (1) *not at all,* (2) *a little,* (3) *quite a bit,* and (4) *extremely.* A factor analysis recovered five mood states. A revision of the scale included 57 adjectives, and a reanalysis yielded five factors again. The third form was enlarged to define Confusion and Friendliness and to broaden Anger. The factors identified were Tension–Anxiety, Depression–Dejection, Anger–Hostility, Vigor–Activity, Fatigue–Inertia, and Confusion. These studies led to the Profile of Mood States (POMS) (McNair, Lorr, & Droppleman, 1971). The published version of POMS consists of 65 adjectives to be rated on 5-point scales which measure six mood/affective states. An additional seven items constitute an unscored Friendliness Scale. The internal consistency reliabilities range from .84 to .95.

Thayer (1967) is responsible for an Activation–Deactivation Adjective Check List (AD-ACL). Thayer conceptualizes activation as a continuum ranging from extreme excitement to deep sleep. Beginning with some of Nowlis' mood study findings, the AD-ACL was constructed to obtain reports on a 4-point scale: (1) *Definitely feel,* (2) *Feel slightly,* (3) *Cannot decide,* and (4) *Definitely do not feel.* Data were collected on 28 activation adjectives and 21 nonactivation mood-descriptive adjectives. A factor analysis of the intercorrelations disclosed four factors. These were named General Activation (lively, active, full of pep, and energetic), High Activation (clutched up, jittery, stirred up, and intense), General Deactivation (at rest, still, leisurely, and quiescent), and Deactivation–Sleep (sleepy, tired, and drowsy). The set defining these four factors consists of 22 adjectives. The factors were shown to correlate substantially with physiological variables.

In a recent study Thayer (1986) sought to update his conception by comparing three types of rating scale formats with a smaller set of adjectives. The most recent version of the AD-ACL included 20 to 25 descriptive adjectives. The three rating formats compared were as follows. Scale A was defined by (1) *definitely feel*, (2) *feel slightly*, (3) *cannot decide*, and (4) *definitely do not feel*. Scale B replaced the third alternative by *do* not feel. Scale C was defined by (1) *extremely*, (2) *very much*, (3) *somewhat*, (4) *slightly*, and (5) *not at all*. The scales in the three formats were administered to substantial samples of men and women. Data collected by each format was intercorrelated and factored. Surprisingly, each analysis yielded four factors: General Activation, Deactivation–Sleep or Tiredness, High Activation or Tension, and General Deactivation or Calmness. The second and third factors were bipolar. Thus Thayer concluded that the factor structure remained the same with each rating scale format. This finding needs to be checked, since it is in conflict with the result of other investigators.

The Clyde Mood Scale (Clyde, 1963) was constructed to measure drug-induced changes in mood and behavior in psychiatric patients. Each adjective or phrase is rated on a 4-point scale: (1) *Not at all*, (2) *A little*, (3) *Quite a bit*, and (4) *Extremely*. For the analysis the 132 adjectives were subdivided into three sets of 44. Using a sample of 500 self-ratings, the three sets were separately intercorrelated and analyzed by principal components, and rotated to a Varimax solution. The 44 items with the highest factor weights were selected for a fourth analysis. The six factors isolated were labeled Friendly, Aggressive, Clear-Thinking, Sleepy, Unhappy, and Dizzy. A score consisted of the sum of weighted ratings. When observers are used to rate mood, the interrater reliabilities are high except for Sleepy and Dizzy.

Wessman and Ricks (1966) developed a set of rationally based Personal Feeling Scales. Each of the 16 bipolar scales is defined by 10 statements ranging in degree. Some of the scales are Elation versus Depression, Harmony versus Anger, Tranquility versus Anxiety, and Respect versus Contempt. Several scales represent relatively complex attitudes or traits such as Love and Sex, Impulse Expression versus Self Restraint.

The Differential Emotions Scale (DES) (Izard, 1972) is a self-report device that consists of 30 adjectives, three for each of the 10 unipolar "fundamental emotions" hypothesized. Each emotion is rated on a 5-point intensity scale: (1) *Not at all*, (2) *Slightly*, (3) *Moderately*, (4) *Considerably*, and (5) *Very Strongly*. Izard (1972), author of the scale, has a theory that specifies 10 monopolar fundamental emotions: *interest–excitement, enjoyment–joy, surprise–startle, distress–anguish, disgust–revulsion, anger–rage, shame–humiliation, fear–terror, contempt–scorn,* and *guilt–remorse.* An item factor analysis of the DES disclosed 10 factors: Interest, Enjoyment, Surprise, Distress, Anger, Disgust, Contempt, Fear, Shame/Shyness, and Guilt. Some of these factors could reasonably be interpreted as measures of attitude rather than affect and others as sets of adjectives grouped on the basis of similarity of meaning. Clearly additional criteria besides factor validity are needed to establish Izard's "fundamental emotions."

Curran and Cattell (1975) have constructed an Eight State Questionnaire (8SQ) designed to measure eight bipolar mood states. The eight scales are referred to as Anxiety, Stress, Depression, Regression (*confused, unorganized*). Fatigue, Guilt, Extraversion, and Arousal. The 8SQ consists of 96 statements to be rated as follows: (a) *very true,* (b) *fairly true,* (c) *fairly false,* and (d) *very false.* An example is "I'm feeling lively and bouncy." There are 12 items per scale, each scored 3, 2, 1, and 0. The various states have been demonstrated by factor analyses of change scores and by P-technique. The P-technique is a procedure in which the same set of items (adjectives or statements) is administered repeatedly to the same person over many occasions, such as each day for a month or longer. The items are then intercorrelated over the K occasions, are analyzed by principal components, and are rotated to some unique solution. The internal consistency of the eight scales is high and the retest stability coefficients are low.

The bipolar form of the Profile of Mood States (Lorr & McNair, 1984) was designed to measure six bipolar affective states. Each state is defined by a scale composed of 12 adjectives, of which 6 are positive and 6 are negative. The rating steps adopted are (1) *Much like this,* (2) *Slightly like this,* (3) *Slightly unlike this,* and (4) *Much unlike this.* A scale score is the sum of positive ratings minus the sum of negative ratings plus a constant to render all scores as positive. The six scales are Composed–Anxious, Agreeable–Hostile, Elated–Depressed, Confident–Unsure, Energetic–Tired, and Clearheaded–Confused. POMS-B1 was constructed with a rating scale designed to produce balanced rather than skewed response distributions. A series of factor-analytic studies provided supporting evidence for the bipolar nature of the mood factors and for the existence of the six mood states. These reports may be found in Lorr and Shea (1979) and Lorr, McNair, and Fisher (1982).

At this point it is useful to ask what can be concluded from the multifactor-analytic studies of the mood scales. Since some of the scales are bipolar and others are monopolar, a straightforward answer cannot be given. Nowlis–Borgatta, McNair–Lorr, and Clyde scales claim six monopolar factors while the Thayer scale finds only four. Izard finds 10 factors. Of the group finding bipolar mood states, the 8QS measures eight and POMS-B1 measures only six. These findings suggest the need for a more embracing study that would examine the problem of bipolarity as a central issue.

Another conception of affect has arisen out of studies by Zevon and Tellegen (1982) and by Watson and Tellegen (1985). They argue that all emotional experiences can be reduced to a two-dimensional framework of Positive Affect and Negative Affect. The high ends of each dimension represent a state of arousal and the low ends represent the absence of affective involvement. They see this two-factor conception as complementary to, rather than competitive with, multi-factor structures. A basic checklist of adjectives was assembled from available lists in order to assure broad representation of state variables. The list was constructed by selecting three adjectives from each of 20 categories, giving a total of 60 adjectives. Illustrative content categories are as follows: Excited, Strong, Joyful, Tired, Angry, Fearful, Jittery, and Content. Subjects rate each adjective on a 5-point scale presented as *Very slightly or not at all, A little, Moderately, Quite a bit,* and *Very much.*

In an initial study (Zevon & Tellegen, 1982), Tellegen applied a principal component analysis to the correlations among 60 adjectives rated by 284 subjects. This is called an R-analysis. Two broad dimensions of affect emerged. The Positive Affect factor was loaded positively by all the positive adjectives and negatively by *sleepy, sluggish, and tired.* The Negative Affect factor was defined by all the negative adjectives, However, certain adjectives (*content, at ease, and calm*) loaded negatively on this factor. In the second study they investigated the structure of intraindividual mood by P-factor analyses. Here 23 subjects rated their moods on the 60 adjectives during mornings, afternoons, and evenings for 90 days. The main analysis consisted of a series of P-factor analyses of each individual's response protocol, checking for the presence of two (positive and negative) affect dimensions. In the initial analysis it was found that the *surprise* content category (*astonished, surprised, amazed*) did not belong to either factor. To assess the 23 P-correlation matrices for the presence of Positive and Negative Affect, a quantitative comparison was made between the first two rotated factors of each subject and the first two factors obtained from the R-analysis of the 60 adjectives identified by Tellegen. Application of coefficients of congruence indicated a striking similarity of 20 of the individual two-factor structures. The multifactorial solutions derived for each subject yielded three positive mood factors (Joy, Physical Well Being, and Interest) and five negative mood factors (Guilt, Fear, Fatigue, Distress, Loneliness, and Surprise).

Seeking a consensus regarding the dimensional structure of affect, Watson and Tellegen (1985) reviewed published studies that would lend themselves to re-analyses and that were adequate in sample size. Included were studies by Thayer (1967), Hendrick and Lilly (1970), Borgatta (1961), McNair et al. (1971), Lebo and Nesselroade (1978), and Russell and Ridgeway (1983). These were compared with Zevon and Tellegen (1982) and with Japanese data collected by Watson, Clark, and Tellegen (1984) for a P-technique analysis of 18 subjects. An approximation to the original correlation matrices of eight studies was re-analyzed by principal factor analysis. Two large factors emerged in every case, each accounting for approximately one-half to three-quarters of the common variance. These were interpreted as representing Positive and Negative Affect. In addition, correlation coefficients were calculated between loadings on the factors obtained in each of the solutions. Overall, the pattern of results indicated considerable agreement. In addition, Watson and Tellegen (1985) demonstrated that Positive and Negative Affect emerge as second-order dimensions from analyses of correlations among the oblique primary factors. For example, Tellegen extracted 10 oblique factors from the Zevon and Tellegen (1982) R-data and then extracted two orthogonal second-order dimensions. Two second-order factors were also extracted from the McNair and Lorr data (1971) and from an analysis by Kotsch, Gerbing, and Schwartz (1982) from DES data for adolescents. The high ends of each dimension are interpreted as representing a state of arousal and the low ends as indicating the absence of affective involvement.

A CIRCULAR CONCEPTION OF MOOD STATES

Earlier in the chapter, Plutchik's (1962) theory of eight primary emotions was described. In 1966 Schaefer and Plutchik reported on interrelationships of emotions, traits, and diagnostic constructs. The universe of emotions was represented by words chosen as examples of each of eight primary emotions. The location of each emotion and trait within the two-dimensional spaces was found in terms of its angle from an arbitrary reference line. For example, *agreeable, kind,* and *cooperative* are found opposite to *dismayed, quarrelsome,* and *angry,* while *sad, pensive,* and *timid* are opposite *joyful* and *pleasureful.* Later Conte and Plutchik (1981) applied two methods to test the hypothesis of a circular order of traits and states. Similarity ratings were applied to 11-point bipolar scales for each trait term compared with three reference terms (*quarrelsome, cooperative,* and *withdrawn*). The hypothesized circular order was supported; terms most similar in meaning were located together while those opposite in meaning were located on opposite sides of the circle. The second method involved ratings of 40 trait terms selected from a longer set. These terms were rated by 10 judges on 23 unipolar semantic differential scales. The correlations among the trait terms were subjected to a principal component analysis. A plot of the factor coefficients on the first two components yielded a circular arrangement of trait terms. The correlation between the ordering of terms of the two procedures indicated essential equivalence.

Recently, Fisher, Heise, Bohrnstedt, and Lucke (1985) sought evidence for extending the circumplex model of personality trait language to self-reported moods. Because Conte and Plutchik's raters evaluated only the meaning of trait terms, one cannot be certain that their findings extend to self-ratings by subjects concerning themselves. They found that self-rating by 140 undergraduates on 17 items form a circumplex that closely agrees with the Conte–Plutchik (1981) circular order of trait terms. The state adjectives were rated on a 5-point scale anchored by *definitely describes my mood* to *does not describe my mood*. To locate the items, two principal components were extracted from the state correlation matrix. Multidimensional scaling (MDS) was also applied.

Russell (1979, 1980) also has explored the thesis that affective states are best represented by a circular arrangement of terms in a two-dimensional bipolar space. Supportive evidence that there are mainly two dimensions in the cognitive representation of emotions was obtained in a series of studies. A set of 28 adjectives was scaled in four different ways: (a) Ross' (1938) technique for a circular ordering of variables, (b) a multidimensional scaling procedure based on perceived similarity among terms, (c) a unidimensional scaling on hypothesized pleasure–displeasure and degree of arousal dimensions, and (d) a principal component analysis of 343 subjects' self-reports of their present affective states. The two axes are interpreted as bipolar dimensions of pleasure–displeasure and arousal–sleepiness. The hypothetical circular arrangement of affects is represented by the following terms in sequence: Arousal, Excitement, Pleasure, Contentment, Sleepiness, Depression, Misery, and Distress, followed by Arousal.

THE PROBLEM OF BIPOLARITY

At present, many consider the various mood states reported by normals and patients as monopolar. Yet semantics and common judgment suggest that each affect has a bipolar opposite. How did the viewpoint of monopolar mood states come to be dominant? As indicated earlier, Nowlis and Nowlis (1956) were among the first to utilize adjectives to assess the effect of drugs and films on mood. They postulated four bipolar dimensions, but a later factor analysis yielded eight monopolar factors. Borgatta (1961) confirmed six of these monopolar factors reported by Green and Nowlis (1957). Lorr et al. (1961), using other adjectives, also reported monopolar mood factors. In fact, studies that followed for the next 10 years reported monopolar dimensions. Meddis (1972) reported that his attention was drawn to the problem when he obtained a small number of bipolar factors while others found a large number of monopolar factors. Meddis attributed this result to his scaling format, which was symmetrical in that it offered as many positive as negative categories. It appeared that asymmetrical scales were suppressing negative correlations. The Meddis scale categories were (1) *Definitely feel,* (2) *Feel slightly,* (3) *Do not feel,* and (4) *Definitely do not feel.* The Nowlis' categories were (1) *Definitely feel,* (2) *Feel slightly,* (3) *Cannot decide,* and (4) *Definitely not.* Similarly, the McNair and Lorr (1964) categories were (1) *Not at all,* (2) *A little,* (3) *Quite a bit,* and (4) *Extremely.* Asymmetric scales result in skewed distributions while symmetric scales yield symmetric response distributions.

An analogous debate concerning bipolarity arose regarding the semantic differential (Osgood, Suci, & Tannenbaum, 1957). Osgood and his associates found that the affective meaning of concepts could be accounted for by three bipolar dimensions called Evaluation, Activity, and Potency. These dimensions were assessed by use of 7-point bipolar scales. Each dimension was represented by oppositional terms such as *good–bad, fast–slow,* and *strong–weak*. Green and Goldfried (1965) argued that the bipolar structure was built in by presenting subjects with polar-oppositional scales. To test the assumption of bipolarity they constructed a single adjective version of each scale and sought the expected high negative correlation between terms such as *good* and *bad*. They failed to find many such correlations and concluded that semantic space was not generally bipolar. Bentler (1969) had observed that rating scales were susceptible to acquiescence and extreme response bias. If the response bias was present, its effect would be to attenuate the potentially high negative correlations between polar oppositional terms. Bentler then constructed composite single adjective versions of the two polar ends of the three semantic differential scales. He partialled out a measure of acquiescence from the intercorrelations among the six adjective scales. When acquiescence was removed, the correlations between bipolar opposites became highly negative while cross-dimension correlations were small and positive. Thus the author concluded that semantic space was approximately bipolar

Russell (1979) conducted a study of self-report data ($N = 150$) on 11 affect scales and showed that response format and acquiescence response style significantly shifted correlations between hypothesized opposites away from showing bipolarity. When these biases were taken into account, pleasure was found to be the opposite of displeasure and arousal the opposite of sleepiness. To ensure an adequate sample of affect terms, items were chosen to represent *pleasure–displeasure, arousal–sleepiness,* and *dominance–submissiveness*. All adjectives from Thayer's four scales of activation were also included, as well as a set designed to assess depression. The 11 scales were defined by 58 items. Four response formats were employed: Meddis' (1972), Nowlis–Nowlis (1956) and Thayer's (1967), McNair–Lorr's (1964), and Yes–No. Altogether, each *S* responded four times, once to each of the four formats. The Meddis format resulted in a roughly symmetric distribution, and the Nowlis and Thayer format yielded a bimodal distribution, because subjects avoided *Cannot Decide*. The McNair–Lorr and Yes–No formats resulted in skewed distributions, because *Not at All* and *No* were model responses. In comparison with the Meddis format, the other patterns tended to shift correlations among items in a positive direction. Next Russell partialled out acquiescence from each pair of hypothesized opposites. In all but one case, partialling out acquiescence shifted the correlation between opposites, in the direction supporting bipolarity. Thus Russell concluded that affective space is bipolar.

In a third study (Lorr et al., 1982) the assessment device was the POMS (1972). Although not balanced as to the number of adjectives included to mark the two poles of each postulated mood, POMS adjectives cover both ends. A sample of 303 psychiatric patients completed the 72-adjective monopolar version of POMS. The adjectives were intercorrelated with each other and a measure of extreme response bias. Variance due to response bias was partialled out and the partial correlations were analyzed by the method of principal components. The rotated oblique solution revealed five bipolar factors: Elated–Depressed, Agreeable–Hostile, Energetic–Tired, Composed–Anxious, and Clear-thinking–Confused. These studies all support the notion that mood states are bipolar. Thus, it is important for the researcher to consider response format as well as response bias in measurement of affect.

THE CONTROL OF RESPONSE SETS

Response sets or styles are consistent ways of responding to test items regardless of content. There are several kinds of response sets that influence ratings as well as personality statements. First, there is the tendency to respond *yes* or *true,* that is, to agree to an item of self-descriptive, independent of the particular content of the item. This tendency, called *acquiescence,* represents an organized disposition to respond in a consistent manner across a variety of substantive domains. Partial control can be achieved by balancing the number of True and False keyed items. Another method for controlling acquiescence is called *paired choice* (Loevinger, 1962) in which each S must make the same number of responses. Each item presents two opposite views (e.g., happy vs sad) and all subjects respond to the same pair of alternatives.

A second response set is called *extreme response style* (ERS). This set is evoked by items requiring each S to respond along an intensity dimension such as *Not at all, A little,* or *Moderately* and *Extremely.* In responding, some persons tend to use the extreme alternatives. Hamilton (1968) reviewed the literature on extreme response style and found considerable evidence of the internal consistency of an ERS and of its stability over time. He also reports evidence for relationships between ERS and personality variables such as anxiety, as well as gender and age. The simplest and most common method for getting a measure of ERS is to count the number of responses in the extreme category at each end of the intensity continuum. ERS may also be measured independently by tests with items of a high degree of stimulus ambiguity. A list of such tests is given by Hamilton (1968, p. 194).

A third response set appears when checklists are used as measures of mood, personality, or attitude. Some subjects tend to check many items whereas others are disposed to check very few. The report by Herron (1969) on MAACL-Today described earlier illustrates the need to control this response bias of *item-checking tendency*. Three alternative approaches to control are to use a forced-choice format, a paired-choice procedure, or a balanced intensity scale that yields a symmetric distribution of responses. This is one reason why the Meddis scale format is often followed (i.e., *definitely feel, feel slightly, do not feel, or definitely do not feel*). Use of a Likert scale of agreement such as *strongly agree, agree, disagree,* or *strongly disagree* also represents a solution.

Another response set reflects *impression management* or role playing. To *fake bad,* the subject could endorse negative adjectives. To *fake good,* the person might endorse positive adjectives in order to impress the examiner. Tendencies to falsify self-reports by dissimulation, lying, or impression management is well known in personality measurement. If the researcher anticipates such responses, the widely used Marlowe–Crowne Social Desirability Scale could be used (Crowne & Marlowe, 1960) to detect their presence to an extreme degree.

The *social desirability* response set is defined as the tendency of subjects to attribute to themselves characteristics considered socially desirable in others. It can be shown that for True–False or Yes–No items, there is a high correlation between rated social desirability and the probability of endorsement. One approach to control is to delete items with endorsement rates .90 or higher or .10 or lower. If mood is evaluated on an intensity dimension, the item wording can be modified to reduce social desirability or to increase it if it is rated as socially undesirable. Fisher et al. (1985) found that measurement bias (social desirability) affects the shape of the circumplex circle. Item desirability influences mean responses and item intercorrelations.

It is well known that there are two opposed points of view regarding the importance of the acquiescent response set. One group believes the response set accounts for a large share of the content variance. The contrary viewpoint argued by Rorer (1965) and others is that acquiescence accounts for only a negligible proportion of (say Minnesota Multiphasic Personality Inventory) variance. In fact, the conflict between the opposed groups has subsided because it has become clear that stylish tendencies on personality tests are actually negligible. However, in mood scales, acquiescence and extreme response style result in skewed response distributions that, in turn, tend to reduce the potential negative intercorrelations that lead to bipolar factors.

DIMENSIONAL ANALYSIS

Two models have been used in the studies of mood states reported; dimensional analysis and the circumplex. The more common one is, of course, dimensional analysis. A dimension, as defined in the dictionary, is any measurable extent such as length, width, or depth. In psychology, the terms *attribute, dimension,* and *continuum* are often used more or less interchangeably. An attribute refers to a property of an object capable of further division. In contrast, a quality is a property of an object not capable of further division, such as *male* or *triangular.* The term *factor* refers to a dimension of individual differences, and as such represents a hypothetical scientific construct used to account for what is common to a set of attributes. One goal of factor or dimensional analysis is data reduction. A large group of measures is reduced to much smaller numbers with resulting economy. A second aim is the generation of hypotheses regarding the number and kinds of dimensions present in a block of data. A classification scheme is thereby created for easier conceptualization. A third goal of factor analysis is to test *a priori* hypotheses held by the investigator that can account for the relations among variables. Nowlis and Nowlis (1956), for example, sought to confirm his conception of the structure of mood as did Izard (1972).

The conceptual framework in a factor analysis can be uncorrelated (orthogonal) or correlated (oblique). If the correlations among the first-order factors are analyzed, several second-order factors can be isolated and identified. If the process is continued, even third-order dimensions can be found. In the cognitive domain Cattell (1971) has identified what he calls Fluid and Crystalized Intelligence. In the domain of personality Norman (1963), Goldberg (1981), and others have found five such higher-order dimensions: Extroversion–Introversion, Stability, Conscientiousness, Agreeableness, and Intellectance. In the field of affect the second-order dimensions appear to be Tellegen's Positive and Negative Affect or Pleasantness–Unpleasantness, and Arousal versus Sleepiness.

Multidimensional scaling (MDS) represents a third and very distinctive method for defining dimensions in a body of data. It was first proposed by Shepard (1962) and is available in several forms developed by others. Multidimensional scaling can be illustrated by considering a map of cities within a given state. If the task is to construct a table of distances between cities, it is easy to measure the distances and convert the ruler distance into actual distance using the scale of the map. MDS is a method for solving the reverse problem of producing the map from a table of distances between cities. In an actual problem it is not known beforehand whether two, three, or more dimensions are adequate for reproducing the map. In multidimensional scaling *proximities* among stimuli are used as input. A proximity is a number that indicates how similar or different two stimuli are perceived to be. In psychological problems a procedure for obtaining proximities is to ask subjects to judge directly the degree of closeness or psychological distance between stimuli. The output is a spatial representation or geometric configuration of points as on a map. Since each point in the geometric representation corresponds to one of the stimuli, the structure of the data is revealed. In an actual problem the dimensionality of a set of data is usually low (two or three).

Bush (1973) has reported a study on the dimensionality and structure of feelings. A test of 264 adjectives was partitioned into subsets of 20. The stimuli for each scaling consisted of all pairwise combinations of the 20 adjectives. Subjects judged the similarity or difference of pairs of feeling terms. Using the similarity judgments of 762 college students, the scaling method called INDSCAL was applied. Three dimensions were found and interpreted as Pleasantness–Unpleasantness, Level of activation, and Level of aggression (Outraged, Furious, Mad versus Needed, Sympathetic, and Heartened). The label *aggression* is probably not the most appropriate.

THE CIRCUMPLEX

The concept of a circular order derives from Guttman (1954). The basic hypothesis is that qualitatively different attributes in a given domain may have a rank order among themselves without beginning or end. A circle describes such an order. In a correlation matrix exhibiting a circular order, the highest correlations are next to the principal diagonal. Along any row (or column) the correlations decrease in size as one moves away from the main diagonal, and then increase again. Contiguous variables correlate positively while more distant variables correlate close to zero. If the attributes are bipolar the correlations may be negative. The circumplexity of a set of variables can be evaluated graphically by plotting the correlation of each variable (as ordinate) with other variables arranged in sequence (on the abscissa). A series of overlapping sine curves is generated. Another method for fitting data to a circumplex model may be tested by examining a plot of variables as a function of their coordinates on the first two principal components extracted from the intercorrelation matrix. A third procedure is to apply MDS and plot the relations among the variables. The more similar two variables are, the closer they will be located in space. Wiggins, Steiger, and Gaelick (1981) have developed a computerized procedure for fitting matrices that appear to conform to a circumplex. Guttman (1954) calls such a correlation matrix a "circulant matrix." As we have seen, good examples of a circumplex may be found in Conte and Plutchik (1981) and in Russell (1979, 1980). Wiggins (1979) has constructed an equally spaced interpersonal circle.

CONCLUSIONS AND QUERIES

The present review of measures of mood and affect, as well as models for their measurement, leads to a few conclusions. First, researchers and clinicians have a choice between a multiple factor conception of mood, a two-dimensional approach, and a circular ordering. In our judgment, a half dozen bipolar moods are most likely to have the greatest payoff for individual assessment. Another conclusion is that two problems remain unresolved. One is the question of whether all moods are bipolar. A second issue concerns the distinction between states and traits. What criteria differentiate the two? Are all traits really derived from states?

REFERENCES

Allen, B., & Potkay, C. R. (1981). On the arbitrary distinction between states and traits. *Journal of Personality and Social Psychology, 4*, 916–928.

Bentler, P. M. (1969). Semantic space is (approximately) bipolar. *Journal of Psychology, 71*, 33–40.

Borgatta, E. I. (1961). Mood, personality, and interaction. *Journal of General Psychology, 64*, 105–137.

Bush, L. E. (1973). Individual differences multidimensional scaling of adjectives denoting feelings. *Journal of Personality and Social Psychology, 25*, 50–57.

Cattell, R. B. (1971). *Abilities: Their structure, growth, and action*. Boston: Houghton Mifflin.

Clyde, D. J. (1963). *Manual for the Clyde Mood Scale*. Coral Gables, FL: University of Miami.

Conte, H. R. & Plutchik, R. (1981). A circumplex model for interpersonal personality. *Journal of Personality and Social Psychology, 40*, 701–711.

Crowne, D. P., & Marlowe (1960). A new scale of social desirability independent of psychopathology. *Journal of Consulting Psychology, 24*, 349–354.

Curran, J. P., & Cattell, R. B. (1975). *Manual for the eight state questionnaire*. Champaign, IL: Institute for Personality and Ability Testing.

Fisher, G. A., Heise, D. R., Bohrnstedt, G. W., & Lucke, J. I. (1985). Evidence for extending the circumplex model of personality trait language to self-reported moods. *Journal of Personality and Social Psychology, 49*, 233–242.

Goldberg, L. R. (1981). Language and individual differences: The search for universals in personality lexicons. In L. Wheeler (Ed.), *Review of personality and social psychology* (Vol. 2, pp. 141–165). Beverly Hills, CA: Sage.

Gotlib, I. H., & Meyer, J. P. (1986). Factor analysis of the multiple affect adjective check list: A separation of positive and negative affect. *Journal of Personality and Social Psychology, 50*, 1161–1165.

Green, R. F., & Goldfried, M. R. (1965). On the bipolarity of semantic space. *Psychological Monographs, 79*, No. 599.

Green, R. F., & Nowlis, J. (1957). A factor analytic study of the domain of mood with independent validation of the factors. *American Psychologist, 12*, 438.

Guttman, L. (1954). A new approach to factor analysis: The radex. In F. R. Lazerfeld (Ed.), *Mathematical thinking in the social sciences*. Glencoe, IL: Free Press.

Hamilton, D. L. (1968). Personality attributes associated with extreme response bias. *Psychological Bulletin, 69*, 192–203.

Hendrick, C., & Lilly, R. S. (1970). The structure of mood: A comparison between sleep deprivation and normal wakefulness conditions. *Journal of Personality, 38*, 453–465.

Herron, E. W. (1969). The multiple affect adjective check list: A critical analysis. *Journal of Clinical Psychology, 25*, 46–53.

Izard, C. E. (1972). *Patterns of emotions*. New York: Academic Press.

Kotsch, W. E., Gerbing, D. W., & Schwartz, L. E. (1982). The construct validity of the differential emotions scale as adapted for children and adolescents. In C. E. Izard (Ed.), *Measuring emotions in infants and children.* New York: Cambridge University Press.

Lebo, M. A., & Nesselroade, J. R. (1978). Intraindividual difference: Dimensions of mood change during pregnancy identified in five P-technique factor analyses. *Journal of Research in Personality, 12,* 205–224.

Loevinger, J. (1962). Measuring personality patterns of women. *Genetic Psychology Monographs, 65,* 53–136.

Lorr, M., & McNair, D. M. (1984). *Manual: Profile of mood states: Bipolar form.* San Diego, CA: Educational and Industrial Testing Service.

Lorr, M., McNair, D. M., & Fisher, S. (1982). Evidence for bipolar mood states. *Journal of Personality Assessment, 42,* 432–436.

Lorr, M., McNair, D. M., Weinstein, G. J., Michaux, W. W., & Raskin, A. (1961). Meprobamate and chlorpromazine in psychotherapy. *Archives of General Psychiatry, 4,* 381–389.

Lorr, M., & Shea, T. M. (1979). Are mood states bipolar? *Journal of Personality Assessment, 43,* 468–472.

McNair, D. M., & Lorr, M. (1964). An analysis of mood in neurotics. *Journal of Abnormal and Social Psychology, 69,* 620–627.

McNair, D. M., Lorr, M., & Droppleman, L. F. (1971). *Manual of the profile of mood states.* San Diego, CA: Educational and Industrial Testing Service.

Meddis, R. (1972). Bipolar factors in mood adjective checklists. *British Journal of Social and Clinical Psychology, 11,* 178–184.

Norman, W. T. (1963). Toward an adequate taxonomy of personality attributes. *Journal of Abnormal and Social Psychology, 66,* 574–583.

Nowlis, V., & Nowlis, H. H. (1956). The description and analysis of mood. *Annals of the New York Academy of Sciences, 65,* 345–355.

Osgood, C. E., Suci, C. J., & Tannenbaum, P. H. (1957). *The measurement of meaning.* Urbana, IL: University of Illinois Press.

Plutchik, R. (1962). *The emotions: Facts, theories and a new model.* New York: Random House.

Plutchik, R. & Kellerman, H. (1984). *Emotions Profile Index manual.* Los Angeles: Western Psychological Services.

Rorer, L. G. (1965). The great response-style myth. *Psychological Bulletin, 63,* 129–156.

Rosch, E., & Lloyd, B. B. (Eds.) (1978). *Cognition and categorization.* Hillsdale, NJ: Erlbaum.

Ross, R. T. (1938). A statistic for circular scales. *Journal of Educational Psychology, 29,* 384–389.

Russell, J. A. (1979). Affective space in bipolar. *Journal of Personality and Social Psychology, 37,* 345–356.

Russell, J. A. (1980). A circumplex model of affect. *Journal of Personality and Social Psychology, 39,* 1161–1178.

Russell, J. A., & Ridgeway, D. (1983). Dimensions underlying children's emotion concepts. *Developmental Psychology, 19,* 795–804.

Schaefer, E. S., & Plutchik, R. (1966). Interrelationship of emotions, traits, and diagnostic constructs. *Psychological Reports, 18,* 399–410.

Shepard, R. N. (1962). The analysis of proximities: Multidimensional scaling with an unknown distance function. *Psychometrika, 27,* 125–139, 219–246.

Thayer, R. E. (1967). Measurement of activation through self-report. *Psychological Reports, 20,* 663–678.

Thayer, R. E. (1986). Activation–deactivation adjective checklist: Current overview and structural analysis. *Psychological Reports, 58,* 607–614.

Veit, C. T., & Ware, J. E., Jr. (1983). The structure of psychological distress and well-being in general populations. *Journal of Consulting and Clinical Psychology, 51,* 730–742.

Watson, D., Clark, L. A., & Tellegen, A. (1984). A cross-cultural convergence in the structure of mood: A Japanese replication and a comparison with U.S. findings. *Journal of Personality and Social Psychology, 47,* 127–144.

Watson, D., & Tellegen, A. (1985). Toward a consensual structure of mood. *Psychological Bulletin, 98,* 219–235.

Wessman, A. E., & Ricks, D. R. (1966). *Mood and personality.* New York: Holt, Rinehart & Winston.

Wiggins, J. S. (1979). A psychological taxonomy of trait-descriptive terms: The interpersonal domain. *Journal of Personality and Social Psychology, 37,* 395–412.

Wiggins, J. S., Steiger, J. H., & Gaelick, L. (1981). Evaluating circumplexity in personality data. *Multivariate Behavioral Research, 16,* 263–286.

Zevon, M. A., & Tellegen, A. (1982). The structure of mood change: An ideographic/nomothetic analysis. *Journal of Personality and Social Psychology, 43,* 111–122.

Zuckerman, M. (1983). The distinction between trait and state scales is not arbitrary: Comment on Allen & Potkay's "On the arbitrary distinction between trait and state." *Journal of Personality and Social Psychology, 44,* 1083–1086.

Zuckerman, M., & Lubin, B. (1965). Manual for the multiple affect adjective check list. San Diego, CA: Educational and Industrial Testing Service.

Chapter 3

ASSESSING EMOTION BY QUESTIONNAIRE

HARALD G. WALLBOTT AND KLAUS R. SCHERER

ABSTRACT

We attempt to demonstrate the value of a questionnaire approach in assessing subjective emotional experience. Focusing on the subjective report of emotional experience, we compare questionnaire techniques to laboratory emotion induction and field observation. To illustrate the potential of questionnaire assessment we describe two types of questionnaires that were used in large-scale cross-national studies to assess various aspects of emotional experiences (e.g., nature of the situation eliciting an emotion, cognitive evaluation, physiological symptoms and verbal and nonverbal reactions, and control attempts). The empirical results indicate specific patterns of eliciting characteristics as well as specific symptom/reaction patterns for the different emotions studied (joy, sadness, fear, anger, disgust, shame, and guilt). We conclude that subjective experience constitutes an integral part of the emotion process, information accessible only through self-report. Questionnaires may be better suited to assess this emotion component than other self-report techniques. Furthermore, questionnaire data on emotional experience can provide important information for the design of laboratory induction experiments, or for field observation of emotional behavior.

THE NATURE OF EMOTIONAL EXPERIENCE

The major theoretical traditions in the history of psychology have not been kind to emotion research, particularly as far as the study of emotional experience is concerned. Behaviorism, which dominated psychology for many years,

55

focused on external, observable behavior, relegating emotion to the role of an arousal factor (e.g., intensifying overt behavior) or, at most, a signal (e.g., for danger). When the cognitive revolution began to challenge psychology in the 1960s, emotional experience was equally unfashionable: Whereas it was now legitimate to speculate about the inner workings of the black box, the concepts used had little affinity to affect or feeling. Phenomenological psychology emphasized introspection and understanding of subjective experiences such as *feeling,* but often limited itself to philosophizing rather than systematically assessing actual emotional experiences. Thus, we encounter a remarkable paradox—that all of us have firsthand personal knowledge of our own emotional experience but very little insight in terms of scientific description and measurement of such emotional experience across a large number of individuals. In this chapter it is proposed that questionnaire methods can be profitably used to study emotional experience empirically.

Let us first define what we mean by emotional experience. Emotion, as a psychological construct, is increasingly defined in terms of a syndrome by many theorists in psychology and related disciplines (Averill, 1980; Kleinginna & Kleinginna, 1981; Lazarus, Averill, & Opton, 1970; Plutchik, 1980). The components of such an emotion syndrome seem to be as follows: evaluation of an antecedent situation, physiological change, motor expression, motivational effects with prepared action tendencies, and subjective feeling state. Each of these components of emotion seems to have a specific functional significance and it can be argued that these components of the emotion process represent changes in functional subsystems of the organism (Scherer, 1984). Emotional *experience,* then, can be defined as the *conscious* representation of changes in the states of these subsystems that occurs in reaction to an emotion-eliciting situation. It should be noted that in this definition emotional experience is not synonymous with subjective feeling. The reflexive representation of subjective feeling state is only one aspect of emotional experience, which encompasses the experience of changes in all of the other emotion-related subsystems of the organism as well. Here is an example: A specific emotional experience could consist of the following report: "I have just listened to someone insulting me, I feel my muscles tensing and a hot feeling around my head and neck region, I noticed that I am gesturing with a clenched fist and that I am gritting my teeth, I have to hold myself back from hitting this other person, and I know that I am feeling angry. At the same time I feel that I should control myself rather than get carried away with anger."

Emotional experience of this sort can only be studied via the introspective report of an experiencing subject. Even if we were able to obtain physiological measurements and objective measures of expressive behavior, we would not be measuring emotional experience, since we have no way of analyzing the manner in which the subject experiences the physiological and expressive changes other than by self-report. Whereas we would expect a sizeable correlation between objective measures and self-report, the size of this correlation may vary with individuals and situations. Furthermore, the significance of particular aspects of the objectively occurring changes may be of great importance to understanding the total pattern of the emotional experience. Although in principle we can measure the objective underpinnings of emotional experience as far as physiological changes and expressive behavior are concerned, self-report is our only access to motivational changes and action tendencies as well as the subjective feeling state. Again, in many cases we might be able to infer these two components of the emotional experience on the basis of the nonverbal behavior, but we cannot be certain of the accuracy of our attribution, particularly in those cases where the subject succeeds in controlling expressive behavior. Finally, while we may be able to describe objectively the situational features that seem to have evoked the emotional experience, we might find it difficult to understand the patterns of evaluation that have led to the particular emotional response without having access to the subjects' self-report.

It seems rather obvious, then, that we need to use self-report techniques in order to study emotional experience in its own right. One can argue that such self-report approaches remain necessarily descriptive given that each person will show idiosyncratic profiles of emotional experience, particularly if one obtains self-reports of emotional situations that have happened to a particular individual. This is not necessarily true, however. It is possible that a large number of self-reports of emotional experience of many individuals and many different emotional situations will reveal a systematic pattern of relationships between patterns of situation evaluation, physiological response, expressive behavior, action tendencies and feeling states, as well as control attempts that transcend the level of individual introspection and allow the formulation of testable hypotheses of the following form: "If an individual of such and such type evaluates this particular situation in such and such manner, the following changes in physiology, behavior, motivation, and feeling will occur." Hypotheses of this nature would still be related to emotional experience. They would be tested by self-reports for those types or classes of individuals for whom one has made predictions. However, given that the experience of changes in the different emotion components is unlikely to be totally unrelated to the actual organismic changes during emotion, such systematic patterns of data might also be useful to generate hypotheses for more objective approaches to emotion research. We will briefly review some of the major questions in emotion research and the way in which self-report studies could help to advance research on these issues.

MAJOR QUESTIONS IN EMOTION RESEARCH

Many theories of emotion view the emotions as phylogenetically evolved adaptive responses to changing contingencies in the environment (see Plutchik,

1980). Consequently, the description of the situational patterns that evoke the different emotions is of major importance to understand the way in which specific emotional responses are adaptive. Whereas the description of situational invariants that tend to produce emotional responses of a particular kind may still be feasible for various species of animals for which the nature of the frequently occurring situational contingencies is limited, this has been found to be almost impossible for humans. Not only are there many more potentially emotion-inducing situations of a much more complex nature in terms of potentially significant features, in addition, in contrast to the animal case, one cannot assume that individuals will respond with a limited set of behavior patterns to situations with objectively similar features. The great difficulty of defining objective situation characteristics that can reliably be shown to produce particular emotions or behavior patterns is the basis of the rather unsatisfactory status of attempts to provide a taxonomy of the psychologically relevant features of situations (see Argyle, Furnham, & Graham, 1981; Magnusson & Stattin, 1982). As far as emotion is concerned, there have been some attempts to develop a classification of emotion-eliciting situations (Averill, 1980; Boucher, 1983; Magnusson & Stattin, 1981, 1982; McGrath, 1982; Plutchik, 1980; Schwartz & Weinberger, 1980; Sells, 1970).

The problem with most of these attempts has been that the actual situations to be used for the classification have not been gathered in an ecologically valid procedure in the sense of Brunswik (1956). In many cases, the investigators and their collaborators have imagined situations that they considered to be important emotion elicitors. The danger is that certain types of situations may have been overlooked, and others overly emphasized. Furthermore, to "imagine" emotion-producing situations implies that we know how to segment the behavioral stream in such a way as to reliably identify the beginning and end of emotion episodes. We may not yet have the insight required for such an operation.

It would seem reasonable, then, to obtain a large number of self-reports of situations that have evoked various kinds of emotions from a large number of individuals. Such a procedure might help to obtain a more solid information basis related to the range of potentially emotion-eliciting situations and the features that seem primarily implicated in emotion generation. In addition to obtaining information about the range and variety of situations, such a procedure would help to obtain an indication of frequency of particular types of situations—actuarial information, so to speak.

Apart from its significance for theory development, such data may be very useful for both the experimental study of emotions in the laboratory and systematic field observation of emotional behavior. Many writers have pointed out the difficulties of using experimental induction and field observation in the area of emotion research (Lang, 1979; Wallbott & Scherer, 1985). Experimental induction is not only limited by the inherent difficulty of manipulating very potent, ego-involving situation characteristics and events but also by ethical considerations, which have become increasingly strict in recent years. The observation and analysis of naturally occurring emotions are equally limited, particularly by the private nature of most emotions and the low predictability of emotion responses in public. However, a representative collection of self-reported emotion-inducing situations may well guide researchers in the selection of situational features for manipulation or field observation.

A second major issue in emotion research is the discussion concerning the existence of discrete fundamental emotions with highly differentiated response patterns (Izard, 1977; Plutchik, 1980; Tomkins, 1962, 1963), as compared to the view that emotional arousal may be rather undifferentiated in the physiological domain (with cognitive labels and culturally determined expressive signaling being responsible for a phenomenological differentiation; see, for example, Birdwhistell, 1970; Duffy, 1941; Schachter, 1970). In order to settle this debate, we would need extensive empirical data sets in which all of the components of emotion mentioned above were measured and in which the stability of a discrete patterning across these components for each of the postulated fundamental emotions could be shown (or these hypotheses would be rejected). While some attempts toward gathering such data have been made (Ekman, Levenson, & Friesen, 1983), it is unlikely that we can obtain sufficient evidence for many years to come. This is particularly true since many investigators tend to study only a limited subset of the emotion components, such as facial expression (Ekman & Oster, 1979; Izard & Buechler, 1979), vocal expression (Scherer, 1981a, 1981b, 1985, 1986b), or feeling state (Asendorpf, 1984; Izard, 1977; Schwartz & Weinberger, 1980). Given the difficulty of studying all of the emotion components simultaneously for a specific emotion episode in the same individual, it seems useful to approach the issue of the differentiatedness of emotional states via a self-report technique. In this case, e.g., by asking a person to report on the experience of changes in all emotion components for different emotions, one can attempt to provide better insight into the issue of differentiatedness and possibly generate a number of critical hypotheses that could be more economically studied in experiments.

A third issue which has long vexed researchers in the areas of emotion and stress is the great significance of individual differences in emotional response. We know from stress research that person specificity (which can be related to a large number of factors such as gender, age, personality, coping style, intelligence, etc.) explains much of the variance in stress experiments (for a review, see Scherer, Wallbott, Tolkmitt, & Bergmann, 1985). Although emotion researchers have been less sensitive to this problem in the past, presumably because of the smaller number of systematically controlled experiments in this area, it is evident that future research will have to take such individual differences and person specificity into account. Unfortunately, a systematic study of this problem requires a large number of subjects, and the possibility of assessing or even controlling for their background characteristics. This is hardly possible in expensive experimental studies with limited numbers of subjects or in field studies, where it is very difficult to observe many persons in similar emotion-producing situations.

Self-report studies can help to focus attention on those individual difference factors which are likely to be responsible for major differences in emotional responding. Given the relative ease with which self-reports can be obtained, it is possible to study a large number of subjects, obtain a fair amount of information concerning individual background factors, and use powerful statistics to determine the relative contribution of such individual characteristics in determining emotional experience.

Finally, a fourth major issue in emotion research is the control and regulation of emotional experience. The fact that emotional expression is subject to severe social control has been frequently mentioned in the emotion literature. Very early on, Aristotle (1941, p. 996) pointed out that the proper emotions have to be shown in an appropriate manner at the appropriate time in order for an individual to be accepted as a reasonably socially skilled person. Wundt (1905, p. 285) pointed out that civilized man tries to adapt his emotional expression to the expectations of those by whom he feels watched and increasingly attempts to control gestures and facial expression accordingly, trying to mask specific affects and to express others. Ekman (1972), stressing the prescriptive nature of social expectations in this respect, has used the term "display rules."

While these approaches have mainly focused on the control of expressive behavior, the regulation attempts may run much deeper. Hebb (1949) has claimed that it is the human ability to regulate emotion that forms the basis of human social organization and rationality (given that, according to him, man is the most emotional of all animals). Similarly, the sociologist Elias (1977) has described the development of civilization as a history of the control and regulation of emotion. While the control of expression is certainly one aspect, the examples given by Elias, as well as more recent attempts by sociologists to define the sociostructural role of emotion (see Hochschild, 1979; Kemper, 1978), show that the appropriateness of the complete syndrome of the emotional response, including all of the components, may be at stake. In other words, while it is true that we may sometimes attempt to control our emotional expression in a fairly strategic, conscious way, we may often be unaware of social constraints concerning our perception of the appropriateness of experiencing a certain emotion. Unconscious regulation attempts may serve to bring our emotional response in line with what can be socially justified in a particular situation. Obviously, such regulation attempts are very difficult to study objectively, by observation or physiological measurement, particularly when they are successful. While it is true that some of the regulation process occurs outside of awareness, we seem nevertheless capable of reporting on at least some of its aspects. Again, then, the use of self-report techniques to obtain information on the nature of emotional regulation attempts would seem highly promising.

POTENTIAL SETTINGS AND METHODS
FOR SELF-REPORT TECHNIQUES

In the preceding section of this chapter we tried to show that the use of self-report techniques is required for the study of conscious emotional experience and may help to provide interesting insights and leads for other, less subjective, approaches to the study of emotion. We will now turn to the question of which self-report technique to use and in which setting.

We will begin with the potential settings. These concern mainly the elicitation procedure, in particular, the type of event that motivates the self-report of emotional experience. There are three major types of such settings: induction of an emotion by the investigator, the natural occurrence of an emotional incident in the field, and the reproduction of past emotional incidents from memory.

INDUCTION

As has become painfully clear to many investigators in the past, the induction of real emotions, either in the laboratory or in the real world, is exceedingly difficult and fraught with problems. While researchers in social psychology have been successful in inducing in their subjects a variety of emotions, particularly anger and anxiety, but sometimes also shame or guilt, many of these studies have come under criticism concerning the ethics of strongly manipulating subject affect states. Given that strong emotions can only be obtained when events strongly related to a person's self are manipulated, it is inevitable that basic rights of protection of personal identity are often concerned. Even in cases where the self is not involved and the stimulation mainly consists in disgusting activities, such as the decapitation of mice in front of the subject (see Landis, 1924), such experiments would probably no longer pass human rights committees. Even if they did, major questions remain concerning the nature of the emotion that is elicited [see, for example, Ekman (1982), where the experiments by Landis are discussed]. The problem of knowing whether the intended emotion has really been elicited becomes all the more salient if fairly weak emotional stressors, such as showing unpleasant movies or slides, are being used. Many failures to find differentiated emotional responses or a correlation between objectively measured emotional arousal and subjective report (see Pennebaker, 1982) could be due to the fact that the emotions elicited were just not strong and/or specific enough to yield the predicted patterns.

One of the major shortcomings of the use of induction methods for self-report approaches to emotional experience is that one of the major questions, namely the nature of the eliciting situation, cannot be studied since knowledge of the eliciting factors is presupposed in order to induce the emotion. In a certain way, then, the question is short-circuited, preventing us from gaining further insight into the antecedent situational patterns that provoke certain types of emotional responses. Given these problems of what has been called the ''discrimination-validity dilemma'' (Asendorpf, 1984), the use of induction methods would seem of limited utility in this context.

A further problem is the fairly high expense of such research procedures. In general, subjects have to be studied individually in order to induce the emotion and for self-report to be elicited. This renders rather difficult the investigation of the third issue mentioned above, the role of individual differences, given that one would want to study a large number of individuals who systematically differ in terms of their background characteristics. Another disadvantage of the induction method is that the subject populations available for such induction are usually highly restricted, generally consisting of college students who are available for such laboratory studies as fulfillment of their study requirements.

Finally, emotion induction in the laboratory would also seem to offer little possibility for investigating the nature of social control and regulation of emotion. The laboratory, and even other induction settings, are generally fairly artificial social contexts with their special norms and expectations. It is unlikely that the social norms for emotion regulation will operate in an unhampered fashion in such settings. On the other hand, the special relationship between the subject and the experimenter creates quite particular norms of regulation and conformity [see the large body of literature on experimenter effects and experimental artifacts; e.g., Orne (1962) and Rosenthal (1966)].

REAL LIFE OBSERVATION

Clearly, this would be the ideal setting for a study of emotional experience. Practically, however, the difficulties would seem to be insurmountable. In order to do a systematic study, one would have to follow people around during their daily pursuits and wait for an emotional incident to happen in order to get a chance to obtain a self-report immediately after the event. To do this for a large number of persons in order to obtain a systematic sampling of the experience of several emotions would seem to be almost impossible. As soon as we do not have direct access to the emotional experience as it happens, we are approaching the third type of investigation, the use of memory.

RECALLING EMOTIONAL INCIDENTS

In this approach, the investigator trusts the subject to be able to fairly reliably recall emotional experiences from the past and to describe them in such detail as to provide information on a variety of the emotion components mentioned above. Several types of elicitation procedures can be used, such as asking subjects to write down self-reports as soon as something emotional happens to them (or to use a tape recorder for this purpose), as in the use of diary methods. A different approach consists in providing subjects with specific primes or elicitors, such as asking them for situations in which they experienced particular emotions or the last emotion they experienced before the request. Clearly, such procedures suffer from a multitude of methodological problems of their own, including effects of memory, retrieval heuristics (Nisbett & Ross, 1980; Tversky & Kahneman, 1974), and other factors related to the need to recall information from memory.

At the same time, this procedure offers quite a number of important advantages over the settings discussed previously. Most importantly, we gain access to the rich store of emotional experiences a person has lived through in the past weeks, months, or even years. We are likely to obtain a rather representative sampling of the kinds of situations that tend to elicit particular emotions. Furthermore, the emotions reported are likely to be strong, since otherwise they would not have remained in memory. Thus, one of the major problems with experimental and field observation approaches, the insufficient intensity of the emotions studied, would not seem to present a problem.

HOW TO ASSESS SELF-REPORT

The most flexible and comprehensive approach to obtaining self-reports on emotional incidents recalled from memory might be the in-depth interview in which the interviewer can explore the details of the recalled emotional incident by interactive questioning of the subject and by exploring the responses. Unfortunately, this method is very costly and time-consuming, since subjects have to be studied individually. Furthermore, and more seriously, it is quite possible that subjects may be less willing to report truthfully on a variety of emotional experiences than they would be in a more anonymous procedure. Many emotional experiences, particularly those related to negative emotions, may not reflect positively on the subject and may thus tend to be suppressed. This reluctance to respond might be somewhat reduced in situations in which the interviewer is a stranger and is not physically present. For example, in a telephone survey in which a professional telephone interviewer asked randomly selected respondents to report their latest emotional experience, 14% could not or would not comply (Scherer & Tannenbaum, 1986). Furthermore, it is possible that the questioning situation itself, in interaction with the material to be recalled and perhaps the person of the questioner, produces an emotional state which may affect the emotional experience to be recalled.

These potentially biasing factors can be avoided by the use of anonymous questionnaires. For example, in the studies in which we used questionnaires, the refusal rate was close to zero. As we shall show below, questionnaires can take a variety of forms but they all share the feature of requesting subjects to anonymously report in written form on their emotional experience.

Questionnaires are a staple method in the social and behavioral sciences. It is quite surprising that they have been so rarely used for research on emotion. Averill (1982) reviews the few studies that have used questionnaires. Most of these did not use the method to its full advantage and rarely acknowledged the methodological limitations. None of these studies has had a major impact and Averill concludes that "a healthy scepticism and caution about self-report have resulted in an unhealthy form of self-censorship in which psychologists have cut themselves off from some potentially useful sources of information" (1982, p. 150).

Clearly, a healthy skepticism as far as questionnaire assessment of emotional experiences is concerned is in order. We do know that such methods are susceptible to a number of serious artifacts, such as response distortion due to ego-defense tendencies, social desirability effects, or answer sets. In addition, it is quite possible that the responses obtained reflect social stereotypes, with subjects reproducing what they consider, consciously or unconsciously, as the proper response to give in a particular situation. However, most of these problems are not specific to questionnaire approaches but are inherent in any type of self-report assessment. What the researcher can do, however, is to attempt to reduce the potential for such artifacts to appear by designing a questionnaire on the self-report technique generally in such a way as to reduce possible biases. Such precautions include the safeguarding of complete anonymity, avoiding questionnaire formats that encourage stereotyped responses (e.g., using open-ended formats as much as possible), and trying to be as explicit as possible concerning the information required.

ILLUSTRATIVE EXAMPLES OF QUESTIONNAIRE STUDIES OF EMOTIONAL EXPERIENCE

In this chapter we cannot attempt to survey the entire body of literature on questionnaire approaches to emotion investigation. When we started this research in 1979, very few studies of this kind could be found in the literature. Most of the early studies are very ably reviewed by Averill (1982), who has conducted research very similar to ours, although limited to the emotion of anger.

In the meantime, a number of additional studies have appeared. Like our studies, quite a few of these studies were directed at gathering information about the types of situations or events that elicit specific emotions, in some cases with the idea of developing a classification or taxonomy of such situations. Only a few of these studies have been directed toward more than one emotion, however. In most cases, the eliciting events for specific types of emotion were investigated, for example, the causes of anxiety or fear (Bernstein & Allen, 1969; Geer, 1965; Hall, 1899; Magnusson & Stattin, 1981; Rose & Ditto, 1983; Stattin & Magnusson, 1983), stress situations (McGrath, 1982), jealousy (Hupka, 1981), anger (Averill, 1982), or shame (Wicker, Payne, & Morgan, 1983). Similar techniques for gathering information about situations and events that affect positive or negative mood or the well-being of a person have been extensively reported in the area of life event research (Bradburn, 1969; Dohrenwend & Dohrenwend, 1974; Warr & Payne, 1982).

Although respondents in most of these studies have been asked for events that they actually experienced, there are quite a few studies in which subjects were asked about stereotypical social situations that are likely to evoke certain emotions (e.g., Boucher & Brandt, 1981; Schwartz & Weinberger, 1980). In such studies, the major purpose was to assess to what extent subjects will report similar reaction patterns when asked to imagine that they experience similar situations.

Questionnaire approaches have also been used in recent years for the study of subjectively experienced physiological arousal (Pennebaker, 1982). In addition, a number of studies in the area of self-awareness and self-attribution may provide relevant material for interpreting the results reported in this chapter (see Cacioppo & Petty, 1982).

Furthermore, a number of research groups, particularly in the United States, have started using questionnaire methods to gather information about emotional experience (G. L. Clore & H. Ortony, personal communication; L. Roseman, personal communication; P. Shaver, personal communication; Smith & Ellsworth, 1985). Most of these researchers are interested in developing a taxonomy or classification of emotions and emotion-provoking situations on the basis of the cognitive factors involved in the elicitation of specific and discrete emotions.

THE "EMOTIONAL EXPERIENCE" QUESTIONNAIRES

Based on theoretical considerations when beginning our studies in 1979, we wanted to develop a questionnaire which would allow us to access characteristics of the emotion-arousing situation, characteristics of the experiencing person, characteristics of the subjective experience of emotion (such as intensity or

TABLE 3.1
FINAL VERSION OF THE OPEN-ANSWER QUESTIONNAIRE (STUDY 2)

Think of a situation in which you experienced. . .

Description of the situation
   Where did the situation occur?
   How long ago was it?
   Who was involved?
   What exactly happened?
   How long did the feeling last? Was it some minutes, hours, days?
   In what way did the situation end?

Description of your emotional reaction
   In your opinion, what words would best describe your emotion?
   How strongly did you feel this emotion? (Please circle the appropriate number)
     not at all   0 1 2 3 4 5 6 7 8 9   *very much*
   What did you say?
   What were your bodily reactions (for example, trembling or a churning stomach) and your
     nonverbal reactions (for example, specific facial expressions, voice qualities, or gestures)?

Control of emotion
   How strongly did you try to control what you said?
     not at all   0 1 2 3 4 5 6 7 8 9   *very much*
   What did you do?
   How strongly did you try to control your nonverbal reactions?
     not at all   0 1 2 3 4 5 6 7 8 9   *very much*
   How did you do that?
   What would you do differently, if you found yourself again in such a situation?

duration), characteristics of verbal, expressive, and physiological reactions, as well as control and regulation attempts of subjects. We did not want to use precoded questions, as the relevant knowledge to construct answer alternatives scarcely existed at that time. Instead, we developed open-ended questions that allowed subjects to describe their emotional experiences in detail.

The specific questions presented to subjects (in the slightly revised version of the questionnaire used in the subsequent study) are listed in Table 3.1. The questions finally used were based on pilot data from in-depth interviews with 20 subjects as well as on theoretical considerations. For most issues, open-ended cueing questions were used. For the assessment of the intensity of emotional experience and the strength of control attempts we used 9-point scales.

Using this questionnaire, four emotions—*joy, sadness, fear,* and *anger*—were studied. The selection of these emotions was guided by the fact that nearly all theories on emotion agree that these four emotions are basic or fundamental emotions. Only four emotions were studied in order to avoid putting too much strain on the responding subjects. Even with just four types of emotion to recall, it took subjects between 45 minutes and 2 hours to work through the questionnaire. Given the high degree of capacity for introspection as well as verbal encoding skill called for from subjects, in this as well as in the following studies, only student populations were used.

In the first study (see Scherer, Summerfield, & Wallbott, 1983, Study 1), the four emotions were introduced to subjects by using a pictorial representation of the typical facial expression and the labels *joy/happiness/pleasure, sadness/sorrow/grief, fear/fright/terror,* and *anger/bad temper/rage.* Equivalent forms of the questionnaire were developed in English, French, German, and Italian for the five participating countries, the Federal Republic of Germany, Switzerland, Great Britain, France, and Italy, using translation and back-translation. To allow quantitative access to the responses to the open-ended questions, extensive coding schemes were developed to code the emotion-eliciting situations reported (antecedent code). Additional characteristics of the situations reported, such as the other persons involved in the situation, the location, the amount of verbalization, and the duration of emotion, were also coded (modality code). An extensive coding scheme for the verbal and nonverbal behaviors reported, for the subjective sensations or feelings, and for the physiological symptoms mentioned by subjects (see Ellgring & Bänninger-Huber, 1986) was also developed. The development of these codes was guided primarily by the material collected in the questionnaires. Several attempts were made to check the comparability of the coding procedure in each of the participating laboratories. Reliability for the major codes (the antecedent code and the reaction/symptom code) reached about 80% on the average both within countries and between coders of different countries (see Scherer et al., 1983).

In the second study (Study 2), which is reported in detail by Scherer, Wallbott, and Summerfield (1986), a slightly revised questionnaire and a more extensive coding system for different aspects of the reported situations and of reported reactions and symptoms were employed. In this study the same four basic emotions were represented by only two verbal labels (the pictorial representations had not proved to be very efficient in the first questionnaire). Furthermore, samples from *eight* countries were collected (adding Israel, Belgium, and Spain). Instructions given to subjects were as follows:

The present study is concerned with the investigation of events and situations that provoke emotional arousal. We shall ask you to describe situations or events that have led to emotional reactions on your part. On the following pages you will find four emotions each illustrated with two different words. Please describe for each emotion one event or situation which, in the last few weeks, has resulted in your experiencing the respective emotion more or less intensely.

We should like you to give the following information for each event:

Where did it happen? Please describe the place where the event occurred. Did it happen in your living room, in a restaurant, in a public place, etc.?

How long ago was it?

Who was involved? Please indicate who else was involved in the situation and your relationship to these people.

What happened? Please describe the nature, cause, and development of the event.

How long did it last? Did the feeling continue for some minutes, hours or days?

We shall also be asking you some questions about what you said and how you otherwise reacted. Furthermore we shall ask a series of questions about your feelings and your behaviour during the event. You should not try to specify only extreme reactions, in which your emotional reactions were very strong and very obvious.

It is equally important to recall those events in which you reacted emotionally without anybody noticing it.

Perhaps you will have difficulties in recalling one event for each emotion right away. Try then, to recall the events that have happened during the last few weeks and try to think of an appropriate situation [Scherer et al., 1986, p. 257].

The questionnaire items, which were to a large degree identical to the items in the first study, are shown in Table 3.1. As in the first study, the questionnaire was followed by a personal background questionnaire, in which subjects were asked to report their age, their gender, their father's and mother's occupations, their field of study, and a number of other personal and socioeconomic characteristics. An overview of the categories developed to code the antecedent characteristics of the emotion-arousing situations is presented in Table 3.2 (for details see Scherer et al., 1986).

In a third study (see Wallbott & Scherer, 1986, Study 3), it was decided (for reasons of economy and comparability) to use a questionnaire with precoded answer alternatives rather than open-ended questions. We felt that the distribution over the coded answer categories that we had found in these two studies, with altogether about 1400 subjects from eight countries, provided sufficiently valid patterns to develop representative answer alternatives on a precoded questionnaire.

As in the previous studies, subjects had to remember and to describe a situation in which they had an emotional experience. After a free description of the situation, subjects had to answer a number of additional questions to assess different situation and reaction characteristics. Some of these questions were derived from the previous questionnaires and some were added to cover aspects of the emotional experience not assessed in the earlier studies. The selection of reaction and symptom categories, for instance, was determined by the results of the previous studies; symptoms and reactions were included only if they had proved to accompany differentially certain emotions or if they had been mentioned very frequently in general. Questions concerning situation evaluation characteristics were added to roughly check the plausibility of a new theory of emotion, the "component process model" (for details, see Scherer, 1984, 1986b). The questions used in this questionnaire are listed in Table 3.3. As in the previous studies, information about person characteristics was assessed via a background information questionnaire.

Whereas in the previous studies only four emotions were included, the answer alternative approach, which is much less time-consuming than answering open-ended questions, allowed us to include three additional emotions, namely

TABLE 3.2
ANTECEDENT CODING CATEGORIES USED IN STUDY 2

Category[a]	Description
1	News (immediate social context)
2	News (world news, mass media)
3	Relationships to friends and partners
4	Relationships to relatives
5	Relationships to groups
6	Temporary meeting/separation from friends, partners
7	Temporary meeting/separation from relatives
8	Permanent separation from friends (not relevant to *joy*)
9	Permanent separation from relatives (not relevant to *joy*)
10	Acquiring new friends/death of friends, partners
11	Acquiring new relatives (cf. birth)/death of relatives
12	Meetings/problems with strangers
13	Being alone
14	New, unknown experiences/end of positive experience
15	Success/failure in achievement situations
16	Acquiring/losing/destruction of objects
17	Traffic situations
18	Rituals
19	Noncultural pleasures/illness
20	Physical injury/pain (not relevant to *joy*)
21	General/unspecified

[a]Used for *joy, sadness, fear,* and *anger*; additional categories only relevant to one specific emotion include *joy* (cultural pleasures, non-material benefits/altruism); *fear* (supernatural events, conscious risk taking, phobic anxiety, external and natural forces); and *anger* (damage to public property/vandalism, unnecessary/unexpected inconvenience, injustice).

disgust, shame, and *guilt.* Furthermore, this study included not only samples from European countries but also samples collected from all over the world, restricted again to student populations within an age range of 18 to 35 years. So far, we have collected about 30 samples comprising about 2500 subjects, and there may be more samples to come.

SOME REPRESENTATIVE RESULTS FROM THE SERIES OF THREE STUDIES

We can only briefly describe some general results to illustrate the value of a questionnaire approach in measuring emotional experience. [For a more detailed account the reader is referred to Scherer et al. (1986) and to Wallbott and Scherer (1986).]

TABLE 3.3
FINAL VERSION OF THE ANSWER-ALTERNATIVE QUESTIONNAIRE (STUDY 3)

Emotion: . . . .

1. Please describe a situation or event—in as much detail as possible—in which you felt the emotion given above.

   _____

   _____

2. When did this happen?
   1. days ago / 2. weeks ago / 3. months ago / 4. years ago

3. How long did you feel the emotion?
   1. a few minutes / 2. an hour / 3. several hours / 4. a day or more

4. How intense was this feeling?
   1. not very / 2. moderately intense / 3. intense / 4. very intense

5. Below you find a list of bodily symptoms and reactions which often occur in such situations. Please make a check next to each one you experienced in the situation.

   Bodily symptoms

0. _____ Do not remember	6. _____ Feeling hot, cheeks burning	
1. _____ Lump in throat	7. _____ Heart beating faster	
2. _____ Change in breathing	8. _____ Muscles tensing, trembling	
3. _____ Stomach troubles	9. _____ Muscles relaxing, restful	
4. _____ Feeling cold, shivering	10. _____ Perspiring, moist hands	
5. _____ Feeling warm, pleasant	11. _____ Other symptoms	

   Expressive reactions

0. _____ Do not remember	7. _____ Abrupt bodily movements
1. _____ Laughing, smiling	8. _____ Moving towards people or things
2. _____ Crying, sobbing	
3. _____ Other changes in facial expression	9. _____ Withdrawing from people or things
4. _____ Screaming, yelling	10. _____ Moving against people or things, aggression
5. _____ Other changes in voice	
6. _____ Change in gesturing	11. _____ Other expressive reactions

   Verbal reactions

1. _____ Silence	5. _____ Speech melody change
2. _____ Short utterance	6. _____ Speech disturbances
3. _____ One or two sentences	7. _____ Speech tempo changes
4. _____ Lengthy utterance	8. _____ Other verbal reactions

6. Did you try to hide or to control your feelings so that nobody would know how you really felt?

   1. not at all / 2. a little / 3. very much / 0. not applicable

7. Now please think back to the situation or event that caused your emotion. Did you expect this situation to occur?

   1. not at all / 2. a little / 3. very much / 0. not applicable

(*continued*)

TABLE 3.3—*Continued*

8. Did you find the event itself <u>pleasant or unpleasant</u>?

   1. pleasant / 2. neutral / 3. unpleasant / 0. not applicable

9. How <u>important</u> was the event for your <u>goals, needs, or desires</u> at the time it happened? Did it <u>help</u> or <u>hinder</u> you to follow your plans or to achieve your aims?

   1. it helped / 2. it didn't matter / 3. it hindered / 0. not applicable

10. Would you say that the situtation or event that caused your emotion was <u>unjust</u> or <u>unfair</u>?

   1. not at all / 2. a little / 3. very much / 0. not applicable

11. Who do you think was <u>responsible</u> for the event in the first place? Check one, the most important, of the following:

0.	_____ Not applicable		6.	_____ Authority figures
1.	_____ Yourself		7.	_____ Natural forces
2.	_____ Close relatives		8.	_____ Supernatural forces
3.	_____ Close friends		9.	_____ Fate
4.	_____ Colleagues/acquaintances		10.	_____ Chance
5.	_____ Strangers			

12. How did you evaluate your <u>ability to act on or to cope with the event and its consequences</u> when you were first confronted with this situation? Check one, that most appropriate, of the following:

   1. _____ I did not think that any action was necessary
   2. _____ I believed that I could positively influence the event and change the consequences
   3. _____ I believed that I could escape from the situation or avoid negative consequences
   4. _____ I pretended that nothing important had happened and tried to think of something else
   5. _____ I saw myself as powerless and dominated by the event and its consequences

13. If the event was caused by your own or someone else's behavior, would this behavior itself be judged as <u>improper</u> or <u>immoral</u> by your acquaintances?

   1. not at all / 2. a little / 3. very much / 0. not applicable

14. How did this event affect your <u>feelings about yourself</u>, such as your <u>self-esteem</u> or your <u>self-confidence</u>?

   1. negatively / 2. not at all / 3. positively / 0. not applicable

15. How did this event change your <u>relationships</u> with the people involved?

   1. negatively / 2. not at all / 3. positively / 0. not applicable

TABLE 3.4
PERCENTAGE FREQUENCY OF ANTECEDENT GROUPS BY EMOTION[a]

Factor	Joy	Sadness	Fear	Anger
News	9.9	9.5	2.4	4.6
Relationships	29.4	27.1	4.6	38.5
Social institutions	4.7	3.1	1.5	1.8
Temporary meeting/separation	19.6	6.5	1.0	.6
Permanent separation	—	8.9	.8	.4
Death/birth	8.3	22.2	6.5	.8
Body/mind centered	12.8	10.1	7.2	2.1
Interactions with strangers	2.3	.9	14.9	19.9
Achievement	16.0	7.2	11.7	6.7
Supernatural	—	—	3.9	—
Risky situations/natural forces	—	—	11.2	—
Traffic	—	—	20.0	—
Unknown, novel situations	—	—	14.5	—
Injustice	—	—	—	20.9
Inconvenience	—	—	—	8.5

[a]Based on 779 subjects; data do not add up exactly to 100% because of some "uncodeable" situation descriptions and double coding. Adapted from Scherer, Wallbott, & Summerfield (1986, p. 71).

One major aim of our approach was to study emotion-eliciting situations, in particular the question whether there are typical situation configurations eliciting the different emotions. In Table 3.4, percentage frequencies for the major groups of antecedent categories from Study 2 averaged across country samples are listed (for details, see Scherer et al., 1986).

For *joy* we find *relationships* (e.g., falling in love) and *temporary meetings* to be by far the most frequent antecedents for pleasurable experiences. These are followed by achievement-related success experiences (which, given the fact that our subjects were students, for the most part reflect success in examinations or courses) and body-related joy experiences such as food, drink, and sex. For *sadness*, the major eliciting category is also *relationships* (deterioration of a marriage), closely followed by *death* of close persons. The third most important category for sadness is *body/mind-centered* events, especially illnesses and other harmful events happening to close persons.

For *anger,* too, personal relationships were by far the most important elicitor. Such relationships incidents are often provoked by the negligence of others, especially of close relatives or friends. The second most important elicitor of anger is the feeling of being *treated unjustly.* This is in line with the findings by Averill (1982), who found that the violation of normative standards is at the root of most anger experiences. This violation of implicit or explicit normative standards also accounts for the high frequency of relationship problems and the feeling of injustice found in our study. The next most frequent category eliciting anger was *interactions with strangers,* which often consisted of situations in which the respondents witnessed willful damage to property, or vandalism. *Unnecessary inconvenience* also was a fairly consistent contribution to anger experiences. Here situations are described where subjects encounter a frustration which is unexpected and appears unjustified. Whereas for *joy, sadness,* and *anger* the especially relationship-centered situations elicit these emotions, the picture is rather different when looking at fear experiences.

Joy, sadness, and *anger* are very *social* emotions with respect to eliciting conditions; fear, on the other hand, is rather *nonsocial.* The most important fear-eliciting categories are dangerous situations encountered while driving, for example, suddenly realizing that the brakes of a car do not function properly or that fog impairs vision. Second in importance are *interactions with strangers,* where quite often situations are described that center around a subject being followed by dangerous-looking people or unknown persons in the dark. Other important elicitors of fear are novel, unknown situations and achievement situations. These results, which closely replicate the results found in Scherer et al. (1983), suggest that there are differential situational configurations that elicit the different emotions. Joy to a large degree is elicited by encounters with known and liked persons; sadness, by severe losses (either terminated relationships or death); anger, by norm violations; and fear experiences, by situations which involve an actual or imagined danger to body or mind.

The differences between emotions were rather stable when comparing European countries, but the picture changed drastically when we compared the European sample with samples from the United States and Japan. Japanese subjects in particular reported rather different emotion-eliciting situations. *Death,* for instance, was rarely a cause of sadness in Japan compared to both Europe and the United States, which may be due to different religious and social orientations (for details, see Scherer, Wallbott, Matsumoto, & Kudoh, 1988).

Another aspect we looked at were characteristics of the emotional experience such as its intensity or its duration. We will focus here on the duration of emotional experiences as an example. Figure 3.1 presents the deviations from the general mean (adjusted for different scale formats used in the different studies) for the emotions in all three studies. The data clearly indicate that there are highly significant differences between emotions in terms of duration. Furthermore, these differences are replicated in all three studies. Sadness and joy are relatively long-lasting emotions whereas anger and especially fear are relatively short-lived experiences. For the three emotions, *disgust, shame,* and *guilt,* included in the third study, *shame* and especially *disgust* are also rather short-lived but *guilt* is reported to be a longer lasting emotional experience. Statistically, Newman–Keuls' post hoc comparisons in the third study indicate the

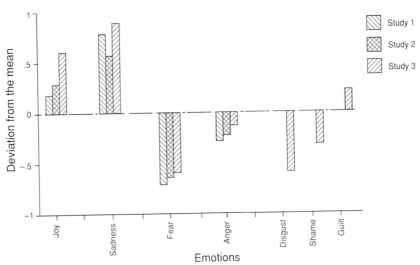

FIGURE 3.1. Differences in the duration of emotions in the three studies. Values indicate deviations from the grand mean of the respective scale in each study. Because scales of different length were used in the different studies, deviations are adjusted according to scale length.

following succession of emotions with respect to duration: *sadness* > *joy* > *guilt* > *anger* > *shame* > *disgust* = *fear*.

Another major issue we wanted to answer with the questionnaire approach was the question of whether there are differentiated response patterns for the different emotions. Table 3.5 presents the number of samples from the third study, in which at least 25% of respondents mentioned the respective reaction or symptom for a specific emotion. The pattern found (which again replicates the other two studies to a large degree) indicates that there are indeed differential reaction and symptom patterns for the emotions. The temperature sensations *feeling cold, feeling warm,* and *feeling hot,* for instance, systematically distinguish between emotions. While *joy* is experienced as being *warm, fear* and *sadness* are reported to be *cold* emotions, and *anger* and *shame* are experienced as being *hot.* Muscle symptoms differentiate positive (i.e., *joy*) from all negative emotions. On the other hand there are some symptoms and reactions which seem to indicate general arousal processes not typical for certain emotions but which are an integral part of the arousal process involved in all emotional experiences, such as changes in respiration or faster heartbeat.

Of the expressive reactions studied, *laughing* and *smiling* are reported for *joy* in all samples, while *crying* and *sobbing* accompany *sadness.* Changes in facial expression are frequently mentioned for all negative emotions. Most likely, these

TABLE 3.5
SYMPTOMS/REACTIONS DESCRIBED IN N SAMPLES[a]

Symptom/reaction	Joy	Fear	Anger	Sadness	Disgust	Shame	Guilt
Physiological symptoms							
Lump in throat	2	17	10	26	9	15	17
Change in breathing	9	26	24	15	4	7	3
Stomach trouble	—	7	—	2	6	—	—
Feeling cold	—	22	—	16	3	—	1
Feeling warm	27	—	—	—	—	—	—
Feeling hot	3	1	23	—	—	20	4
Heart beat faster	26	27	26	19	12	23	19
Muscles tensing	—	27	24	17	12	12	13
Muscles relaxing	15	—	—	—	—	—	—
Perspiring	1	27	9	2	2	12	2
Other symptoms	1	2	2	6	6	2	3
Nonverbal reactions							
Laughing, smiling	27	—	—	—	—	—	—
Crying, sobbing	—	1	2	27	—	—	—
Changed facial expression	2	21	24	16	22	21	16
Screaming	—	—	14	—	—	—	—
Changes in voice	2	8	20	11	7	5	3
Change in gesturing	5	3	16	2	3	4	1
Abrupt movements	—	7	11	—	—	—	—
Moving toward	25	—	—	3	—	—	—
Withdrawing	—	4	2	22	11	17	14
Moving against	—	—	16	1	1	—	—
Other reactions	2	8	2	4	6	1	1
Verbal behavior							
Silence	—	27	15	27	25	27	27
Short utterance	3	10	5	6	7	9	5
One/two sentences	—	—	1	—	1	1	—
Lengthy utterance	21	—	20	—	3	—	1
Speech melody change	18	1	13	4	1	1	2
Speech disturbances	1	1	3	2	—	3	3
Speech tempo change	11	—	16	1	—	—	1
Other verbal reactions	3	—	1	—	1	—	—

[a]Based on 27 country samples with 2235 subjects; criterion was that 25% of the subjects in the sample mention symptom/reaction for a specific emotion.

reported changes should be different ones for the different emotions. The same is true for changes in voice, which are mentioned especially often accompanying anger. A distinctive pattern between emotions also emerges when one compares the three action tendencies *moving toward, withdrawing,* and *moving against* (Horney, 1937; compare also the ethological concepts of bonding, flight, and attack). When experiencing joy, subjects tend to move toward other persons,

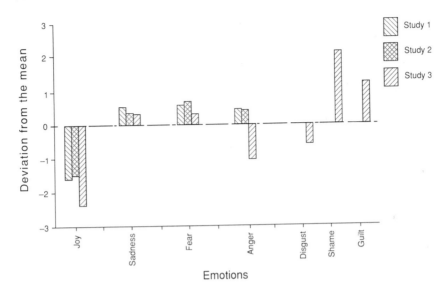

FIGURE 3.2. Differences in the amount of control of emotional reactions in the three studies. Values indicate deviations from the grand mean of the respective scale in each study. Because scales of different length were used in the different studies, deviations are adjusted according to scale length.

when experiencing sadness and to some lesser degree shame and guilt, subjects tend to withdraw from other people, and when experiencing anger, subjects tend to be aggressive.

Verbal reactions were reported less often than both the nonverbal and the physiological reactions. In general, copious verbal reactions distinguish joy and anger from the other, more silent, emotions. This indicates that joy and anger are more *active* emotions with respect to verbal and expressive behavior, while the others are more *passive* [again a replication of Scherer et al. (1986)]. It is interesting to note that by far the most often-mentioned verbal reaction is silence. Except for joy and anger, where subjects report lengthy utterances accompanying the emotional experience, the other emotions are most often accompanied by silence. That indicates that during emotional experiences people either talk a lot or they do not talk at all.

Finally, we reproduce some data on the amount of control or regulation of emotional experience and expression that subjects reported in the different studies. The deviations from the mean for all three studies (again adjusted for different scale lengths) are depicted in Figure 3.2. The results are again very similar across studies. Joy as a positive emotion is controlled to a much lesser degree than all negative emotions. Sadness and fear are controlled slightly more than average, while especially shame and guilt (not assessed in the first two studies) are controlled to a high degree. One interesting difference between the three studies was found for the control of anger reactions and experiences. In the first two studies within Europe, anger was controlled more than average, but in the third worldwide study anger was reported to be controlled less than average. It may well be that social norms or display rules (Ekman, 1972) call for a high amount of control of anger expressions within Europe, but that in other countries anger expressions are much less sanctioned.

USING TELEPHONE SURVEY METHODOLOGY

Scherer and Tannenbaum (1986) have used a survey approach to study emotional experiences in everyday life. In a study conducted as part of a larger omnibus telephone survey, a random sample of residential telephone subscribers in the San Francisco Bay area (California), respondents were asked to remember the last time they had something happen to them, either good or bad, that affected them emotionally. Interviewers used an automated computer-assisted telephone interview schedule developed at the Survey Research Center at the University of California, Berkeley. Respondents were encouraged to describe in a sentence or two the situational event that had last aroused strong feelings in them; the statements were entered verbatim by the interviewer into the computer response file. At the same time, the interviewer coded the emotional tone (negative or positive) as well as the content characteristics of the antecedent situation. In addition, the respondents were questioned about a number of physiological and nonverbal responses that they might have had in the situation as well as about the verbal labels that they would give the experience. About 85% of the respondents reported an emotional situation and provided detailed information about the responses.

Whereas the studies described above required respondents to find at least one situation for each of the emotion labels provided, in this setting the respondents were required to report the last significant emotional incident without any specification as to type. Clearly, this procedure, which attempts to get at the last important emotional experience, is better suited to obtain actuarial information about the frequency and nature of specific emotional events.

Results showed that the majority of the situations reported evoked negative emotions and that most of the emotion antecedent events were connected to relationships with family and friends or to work-related situations. The large majority of the feeling states reported consisted of affect blends, particularly *anger/sadness* and *sadness/fear*. The symptoms and nonverbal behaviors reported for these emotional incidents again replicated the general pattern found in the questionnaire studies reported above.

CONCLUSIONS

In the present context, we could present only some illustrative results from the three huge intercultural data sets on the experience of emotion that we have collected using a questionnaire approach. However, we hope that these few results may have exemplified the potential value of this approach. It was not only possible to demonstrate the existence of rather specific antecedent situation patterns for the different emotions (which we could only briefly mention here), but also differential reaction and symptom patterns accompanying the emotions. Emotions also differed in the strength of control attempts. Finally, we were able to establish the influence of person characteristics on emotional experience. Furthermore, the worldwide study allows speculation on the potential universality of such situation and symptom/reaction patterns as proposed by biologically oriented researchers in emotion following Darwin's lead (Darwin, 1965). The data analyzed so far suggest a high degree of generality, especially of symptom/reaction patterns across countries, though there are cultural differences in other aspects of the emotion experience, such as the reported duration or intensity (see Wallbott & Scherer, 1986). The analysis of such cross-cultural differences in emotional experience seems to be a promising topic for cross-cultural psychology.

Although the high degree of generality found for many variables does not allow us to rule out the possibility that subjects reported stereotypes, the fact that in the many culturally different countries all over the world converging results were found makes it at least implausible that our results reflect only stereotypes of emotion. Obviously, the results found in questionnaire studies do not eliminate the need to conduct laboratory experiments or field studies within a cross-cultural framework. In fact, the results call for such approaches, since the data collected allow us to specify further which experimental situations might be useful to induce different emotions. Furthermore, the data on physiological symptoms and nonverbal reactions reported might give researchers some hints on where to look when objectively measuring physiological and nonverbal behaviors as components of the emotion process. The differences with respect to temperature sensations, for instance, indicate that it is essential to measure peripheral blood flow changes or skin temperature changes of subjects who are experiencing different emotions.

As was pointed out earlier,

> It is essential for future studies to obtain respondent populations that represent a broader sampling of the people in a society and at the same time provide a better representation of the life events that are likely regularly to evoke emotional reactions . . . It will also be essential to be more specific about our predictions concerning the differences between the various kinds of social groups being studied, as well as about cultural effects on emotional experience. This can be done fruitfully only when we have a

better grasp of the way in which individuals evaluate events that are of central importance to them. Thus, while we clearly need more data, we also urgently need more theory [Scherer, 1986a, p. 189].

We do not want to claim that the questionnaire methods advocated in this chapter do not present a certain number of methodological problems. The recall procedure used is certainly beset by a number of potential artifacts, such as response bias, stereotypical notions, or defense strategies. On the other hand, we do not believe that recall of emotional experience from memory is totally unrelated to the nature of the actual emotion process as experienced in the situation. Also, as we have argued, a number of components of the emotion process can only be obtained via self-report, which makes it impossible to avoid facing these methodological difficulties. It may be useful to try to assess some of the cognitive processes that may be involved in recalling and reporting emotional experience. In particular, general inference tendencies or strategies such as the *availability, representativeness,* and *vividness* heuristics may be relevant here (see Nisbett & Ross, 1980; Tversky & Kahneman, 1974). In general, it would certainly be useful to intensify research on the nature of memory storage and retrieval of emotional experience.

In conclusion, we feel that in spite of the inherent limitations of this methodology, the use of questionnaires can significantly contribute to the research arsenal available for the study of emotional experience.

REFERENCES

Argyle, M., Furnham, A., & Graham, J. A. (1981). *Social situations.* Cambridge, England: Cambridge University Press.
Aristoteles (1941). Ethica Nicomachea. In R. McKeon (Ed.), *The basic works of Aristoteles.* New York: Random House.
Asendorpf, J. B. (1984). Lassen sich emotionale Qualitäten im Verhalten unterscheiden? *Psychologische Rundschau, 35,* 125–135.
Averill, J. R. (1980). A constructivist view of emotion. In R. Plutchik & H. Kellerman (Eds.), *Emotion, theory, research, and experience* (Vol. 1, pp. 305–339). New York: Academic Press.
Averill, J. R. (1982). *Anger and aggression: An essay on emotion.* New York: Springer.
Bernstein, D. A., & Allen, G. J. (1969). Fear Survey Schedule II: Normative data and factor analysis based upon a large college sample. *Behavior Research and Therapy, 7,* 403–407.
Birdwhistell, R. L. (1970). *Kinesics and context.* Philadelphia: University of Pennsylvania Press.
Boucher, J. D. (1983). Antecedents to emotions across cultures. In S. H. Irvine & J. W. Berry (Eds.), *Human assessment and culture factors* (pp. 407–420). New York: Plenum.
Boucher, J. D., & Brandt, M. E. (1981). Judgment of emotion: American and Malay antecedents. *Journal of Cross-Cultural Psychology, 12,* 272–283.
Bradburn, N. M. (1969). *The structure of psychological well-being.* Chicago: Aldine.
Brunswik, E. (1956). *Perception and the representative design of psychological experiments.* Berkeley: University of California Press.

Cacioppo, J. T., & Petty, R. E. (1982). *Perspectives in cardiovascular psychophysiology*. New York: Guilford.

Darwin, C. (1965). *The expression of the emotions in man and animals*. Chicago: University of Chicago Press (originally published in 1872 by Murray, London).

Dohrenwend, B. S., & Dohrenwend, B. P. (1974). *Stressful life events: Their nature and effects*. New York: Wiley.

Duffy, E. (1941). An explanation of "emotional" phenomena without the use of the concept "emotion." *Journal of General Psychology, 25*, 283–293.

Ekman, P. (1972). Universals and cultural differences in facial expressions of emotion. In J. K. Cole (Ed.), *Nebraska Symposium on Motivation, 1971* (pp. 207–283). Lincoln, NE: University of Nebraska Press.

Ekman, P. (1982). Methods of measuring facial action. In K. R. Scherer & P. Ekman (Eds.), *Handbook of methods in nonverbal behavior research* (pp. 45–90). Cambridge, England: Cambridge University Press.

Ekman, P., Levenson, R. W., & Friesen, W. V. (1983). Autonomic nervous system activity distinguishes between emotions. *Science, 221*, 1208–1210.

Ekman, P., & Oster, H. (1979). Facial expressions of emotion. *Annual Review of Psychology, 30*, 527–554.

Elias, N. (1977). *The civilizing process*. New York: Urizen.

Ellgring, J. H., & Bänninger-Huber, E. (1986). The coding of reported emotional experiences: Antecedents and reactions. In K. R. Scherer, H. G. Wallbott, & A. B. Summerfield (Eds.), *Experiencing emotion: A cross-cultural study* (pp. 39–49). Cambridge, England: Cambridge University Press.

Geer, J. H. (1965). The development of a scale to measure fear. *Behavior Research and Therapy, 3*, 45–53.

Hall, G. S. (1899). A study of anger. *American Journal of Psychology, 10*, 516–591.

Hebb, D. O. (1949). *The organization of behavior*. New York: Wiley.

Hochschild, A. R. (1979). Emotion work, feeling rules, and social structure. *American Journal of Sociology, 3*, 551–575.

Horney, B. (1937). *The neurotic personality of our time*. New York: Norton.

Hupka, R. B. (1981). Cultural determinants of jealousy. *Alternative Lifestyles, 4*, 311–356.

Izard, C. E. (1977). *Human emotions*. New York: Plenum.

Izard, C. E., & Buechler, S. (1979). Emotion expressions and personality integration in infancy. In C. E. Izard (Ed.), *Emotions in personality and psychopathology* (pp. 447–472). New York: Plenum.

Kemper, T. K. (1978). *A social interactional theory of emotions*. New York: Wiley.

Kleinginna, P. R., & Kleinginna, A. M. (1981). A categorized list of motivation definitions, with a suggestion for a consensual definition. *Motivation and Emotion, 5*, 263–291.

Landis, C. (1924). Studies of emotional reactions: II. General behavior and facial expression. *Journal of Comparative Psychology, 4*, 447–509.

Lang, P. J. (1979). A bio-informational theory of emotional imagery. *Psychophysiology, 16*, 495–512.

Lazarus, R. S., Averill, J. R., & Opton, E. M., Jr. (1970). *Towards a cognitive theory of emotion. Feelings and emotions* (pp. 207–232). New York: Academic Press.

Magnusson, D., & Stattin, H. (1981). *Situation-outcome contingencies: A conceptual and empirical analysis of threatening situations*. Report No. 571. Stockholm, Sweden: Department of Psychology, University of Stockholm.

Magnusson, D., & Stattin, H. (1982). Methods for studying stressful situations. In H. W. Krohne & L. Laux (Eds.), *Achievement, stress, and anxiety* (pp. 317–331). Washington, DC: Hemisphere.

McGrath, J. E. (1982). Methodological problems in research on stress. In H. W. Krohne & L. Laux (Eds.), *Achievement, stress, and anxiety* (pp. 19–50). Washington, DC: Hemisphere.

Nisbett, R., & Ross, L. (1980). *Human inference: Strategies and shortcomings of social judgment.* Englewood Cliffs, NJ: Prentice-Hall.

Orne, M. T. (1962). On the social psychology of the psychological experiment. *American Psychologist, 17,* 776–783.

Pennebaker, J. W. (1982). *The psychology of physiological symptoms.* New York: Springer.

Plutchik, P. (1980). *Emotion: A psycho-evolutionary synthesis.* New York: Harper & Row.

Rose, R. J., & Ditto, W. B. (1983). A developmental-genetic analysis of common fears from early adolescence to early adulthood. *Child Development, 54,* 361–368.

Rosenthal, R. (1966). *Experimenter effects in behavioral research.* New York: Appleton-Century-Crofts.

Schachter, S. (1970). The assumption of identity and peripheralist–centralist controversies in motivation and emotion. In M. B. Arnold (Ed.), *Feelings and emotions: The Loyola symposium* (pp. 111–121). New York: Academic Press.

Scherer, K. R. (1981a). Speech and emotional states. In J. Darby (Ed.), *Speech evaluation in psychiatry* (pp. 189–220). New York: Grune & Stratton.

Scherer, K. R. (1981b). Vocal indicators of stress. In J. Darby (Ed.), *Speech evaluation in psychiatry* (pp. 171–187). New York: Grune & Stratton.

Scherer, K. R. (1984). On the nature and function of emotion: A component process approach. In K. R. Scherer & P. Ekman (Eds.), *Approaches to emotion* (pp. 293–318). Hillsdale, NJ: Erlbaum.

Scherer, K. R. (1985). Vocal affect signaling: A comparative approach. In J. Rosenblatt, C. Beer, M. C. Busnel, & P. J. B. Slater (Eds.), *Advances in the study of behavior* (Vol. 15, pp. 198–244). Orlando, FL: Academic Press.

Scherer, K. R. (1986a). Emotion experiences across European cultures: A summary statement. In K. R. Scherer, H. G. Wallbott, & A. B. Summerfield (Eds.), *Experiencing emotion: A cross-cultural study* (pp. 173–189). Cambridge, England: Cambridge University Press.

Scherer, K. R. (1986b). Vocal affect expression: A review and a model for future research. *Psychological Bulletin, 99,* 143–165.

Scherer, K. R., Summerfield, A. B., & Wallbott, H. G. (1983). Cross-national research on antecedents and components of emotion: A progress report. *Social Science Information, 22,* 355–385.

Scherer, K. R., & Tannenbaum, P. (1986). Emotional experiences in everyday life: A survey approach. *Motivation and Emotion, 10,* 4.

Scherer, K. R., Wallbott, H. G., Matsumoto, D., & Kudoh, T. (1988). Emotional experience in cultural context: A comparison between Europe, Japan, and the USA. In K. R. Scherer (Ed.), *Facets of emotion: Recent research* (pp. 5–30). Hillsdale, NJ: Lawrence Erlbaum.

Scherer, K. R., Wallbott, H. G., & Summerfield, A. B. (Eds.).(1986). *Experiencing emotion: A cross-cultural study.* Cambridge, England: Cambridge University Press.

Scherer, K. R., Wallbott, H. G., Tolkmitt, F., & Bergmann, G. (Eds.).(1985). *Die Stressreaktion: Physiologie und Verhalten* (pp. 195–205). Göttingen, FRG: Hogrefe.

Schwartz, G. E., & Weinberger, D. A. (1980). Patterns of emotional responses to affective situations: Relations among happiness, sadness, anger, fear, depression, and anxiety. *Motivation and Emotion, 4,* 175–191.

Sells, S. B. (1970). On the nature of stress. In J. E. McGrath (Ed.), *Social and psychological factors in stress.* New York: Holt, Rinehart & Winston.

Smith, C. A., & Ellsworth, P. C. (1985). Patterns of cognitive appraisal in emotion. *Journal of Personality and Social Psychology, 48,* 813–838.

Stattin, H., & Magnusson, D. (1983). *Outcome classes of anxiety-provoking situations.* Report No. 597. Stockholm, Sweden: Department of Psychology, University of Stockholm.

Tomkins, S. S. (1962). *Affect, imagery, consciousness* (Vol. 1). *The positive affects*. New York: Springer.

Tomkins, S. S. (1963). *Affect, imagery, consciousness* (Vol. 2). *The negative affects*. New York: Springer.

Tversky, A., & Kahneman, D. (1974). *Judgment under uncertainty: Heuristics and biases*. New York: Springer.

Wallbott, H. G., & Scherer, K. R. (1985). Differentielle Situations- und Reaktionscharakteristika in Emotionserinnerungen: Ein neuer Forschungsansatz. *Psychologische Rundschau, 36*, 83–101.

Wallbott, H. G., & Scherer, K. R. (1986). How universal and specific is emotional experience? Evidence from 27 countries on five continents. *Social Science Information, 25*, 763–795.

Warr, P., & Payne, R. (1982). Experiences of strain and pleasure among British adults. *Social Science and Medicine, 16*, 1691–1697.

Wicker, F. W., Payne, G. C., & Morgan, R. D. (1983). Participant descriptions of guilt and shame. *Motivation and Emotion, 7*, 25–39.

Wundt, W. (1905). *Grundzüge der physiologischen Psychologie* (Vol. 3). Leipzig, GDR: Engelmann.

Chapter 4

MEASURES OF EMOTION

JAMES A. RUSSELL

ABSTRACT

This chapter is about self-report questionnaires, rating scales, behavioral or physio-logical indexes, and other measures of emotion that rely, directly or indirectly, on such everyday English words as anger, fear, happiness, anxiety, *or* stress. *These measures are typically constructed and interpreted on the assumption that people use each such word as if it were independent of all other emotion words that are not its synonym. Considerable evidence suggests otherwise: people use emotion words as it they were highly and system-atically interrelated. Interpretation of any measure that relies on emotion words requires that we take these interrelationships into account. The key is to realize that saying someone is, for example,* anxious *is not independent of saying that he or she is* happy, sad, *etc. Implications of this thesis are discussed for topics such as the use of mood questionnaires in a psychological clinic, research on the causes and consequences of emotion, research on the meaning of facial expressions, and theories of emotion in which labeling is thought to play a central role.*

INTRODUCTION

This chapter is about measures of emotion that rely on ordinary English words, such as *happiness, anxiety, anger,* and *fear.* One example would be a self-report questionnaire that includes an item such as ''I am afraid.'' Another would be a response scale on which an observer assigns each of a set of facial expressions to

83

EMOTION
Theory, Research, and Experience
Volume 4

one of six categories labeled *happiness, surprise, fear, anger, disgust,* or *sadness.* A less obvious example would be a physiological or behavioral index that is claimed to be a measure of, say, anxiety, when that claim is validated by its correlation with an affect adjective checklist consisting of words such as *anxious* and *nervous.*

Such measures sometimes involve a single emotion term. They sometimes involve a list of emotion terms. In either case, a psychologist will typically assume that the emotion named is a discrete entity and that the corresponding term can therefore be treated as independent of all other emotion terms that are not its synonym. Two scales with nonsynonymous labels are therefore thought to correspond to two different emotions. Unfortunately, emotion terms are far from independent. When used in such contexts, they are highly and systematically interrelated.

I shall try to illustrate here how a failure to consider these interrelationships can lead to misinterpretation of empirical results and misunderstanding in our theories of emotion and its role in human activities. I shall discuss the implications of these interrelationships for verbal self-report scales, biological indexes of emotion, nonverbal behavioral signs of emotion, and research on the causes and consequences of emotional states. Finally, I shall discuss their implications for those psychological theories of emotion, such as that proposed by Schachter and Singer (1962), in which labeling is thought to play a key role.

IMPLICIT EMOTION TAXONOMY

The person on the street is an amateur psychologist. People have an informal and implicit "naive theory" of emotion, which they use when they anticipate, identify, communicate about, and try to influence the emotional states of others. Everyday emotion words are labels for the categories of an informal and implicit naive taxonomy of emotional states, a taxonomy that is part of the folk theory. It is only because these notions and categories are largely shared within a language community that verbal communication about emotion is possible. As professional psychologists, we rely on this shared folk taxonomy when we ask subjects, clients, or trained observers to use the various verbal scales now available. The resulting ratings of how happy or angry or anxious someone is must therefore be interpreted in light of the entire system of shared emotion categories on which those ratings depend.

This implicit folk taxonomy must be sharply distinguished from the more formal and explicit taxonomies of emotion developed by professional scholars. Neither the content nor the form of a scholarly taxonomy of emotions necessarily tells us about the informal and implicit taxonomy that underlies our everyday words. The emotion taxonomies given historically by philosophers such as Aristotle, Aquinas, Descartes, Hobbes, Spinoza, and Kant were all in the form of a list of discrete emotions. Lists have also been compiled by influential psychologists, including Watson, McDougall, and, more recently, Tomkins (1962–1963), Ekman (1972), and Izard (1977). The idea that emotions are discrete and independent entities has naturally led some psychologists to treat emotion *labels* as discrete and independent of one another. Much psychological research thus presupposes that people categorize emotions in terms of a list of discrete and independent (or even mutually exclusive) categories. For example, in clinical, personality, and social psychological studies, emotion is often assessed with mood adjective checklists such as those developed by Izard (1971), McNair, Lorr, and Droppleman (1971), Nowlis (1965), or Zuckerman and Lubin (1965). These checklists purport to measure a list of discrete emotions, each one assessed by a cluster of alleged synonyms and thought of as independent of other discrete emotions.

However psychologists come to classify emotional states scientifically, more is required than a list of separate categories if we are to represent the layman's everyday emotion taxonomy. A list rarely suffices to represent everyday taxonomies. Conceivably, a list suffices in some domains: perhaps we can do nothing more than list human needs (such as need for water, food, and air) and certain psychological disorders (such as anorexia nervosa and infantile autism). But, for most domains, the categories of our everyday taxonomies are *related* to one another. Thus while the English language may seem to suggest two discrete categories by the discrete words *hot* and *cold,* a description of human perception would be incomplete without specifying that these two categories are related: underlying their use is a single bipolar dimension of temperature. This is so even though separate physiological mechanisms are involved in the perception of hot and cold. To take another example, blue, yellow, red, green, and other hues can be listed as discrete entities. But we also know that hues are interrelated such that they can be represented as a circle, which is definable by *two* underlying bipolar dimensions. The color circle graphically represents certain properties of the perception of color that would be lost if hues were simply listed. An adequate understanding of everyday emotion categories likewise requires their representation in a way that specifies the relationships among the categories. Such a representation is called a structural model.

A CIRCUMPLEX MODEL

The specific structural model of everyday emotion categories I shall advocate is depicted in Figure 4.1. The structure is in the form of a circle, around which names for categories (much like hues around the color circle) blend into one

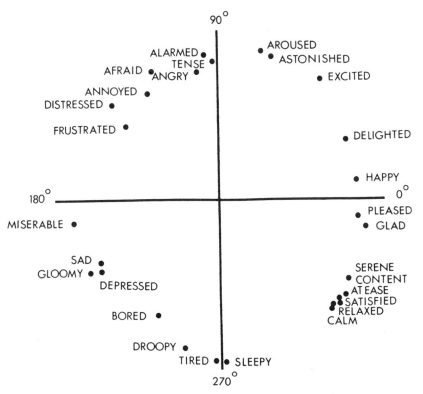

FIGURE 4.1. Circumplex model of emotion-related categories.

another in a continuous form without beginning or end. Terms closer to being synonyms (*happy* and *delighted*) are closer together on the circle; antonyms (*happy* and *sad*) are opposite on the circle. A circular structural model of emotion categories was first proposed by Schlosberg (1952), and variants have appeared thereafter (e.g., Daly, Polivy, & Lancee, 1981; Plutchik, 1958, 1962, 1970, 1980; Russell, 1980). Unlike a list of emotions, a circumplex model specifies the degree to which emotion-related categories are interrelated: The correlation between any two categories in Figure 4.1 equals the cosine of the angle between them (e.g., cos 45° = .707, cos 90° = 0, and cos 180° = −1.00).

Although the circumplex of Figure 4.1 is defined by the interrelationships among the categories, two bipolar dimensions can also be seen to underlie the taxonomy represented. Whereas the categories shown there are named by everyday lay terms, the underlying dimensions need not be named in English, nor even interpretable. Mathematically, any rigid rotation of the axes would define the space equally well. [Plutchik (1980) proposed a circumplex in which the axes are not interpreted.] Nevertheless, the obvious interpretation of the horizontal dimension in Figure 4.1 as pleasure–displeasure relates this model to the long tradition of thinking of pleasure and its opposite as primary ingredients of our emotional lives. The equally obvious interpretation of the vertical axis as a continuum ranging from sleep to states of high arousal (whether positive or negative) relates the model to another tradition, one mainly within psychology, in which activation or arousal is thought of as a primary ingredient in emotion (Duffy, 1957; Lindsley, 1951; Mandler, 1984; Schachter & Singer, 1962).[1]

The space of Figure 4.1 also captures other features of our implicit taxonomy not captured by a list: we feel we can divide states into broader or narrower groups. Sometimes a simple division into pleasant and unpleasant states suffices—which corresponds to slicing Figure 4.1 in half. A division into quarters gives us four quadrants: I, pleasure/high arousal (excitement); II, displeasure/high arousal (distress); III, displeasure/low arousal (depression); and IV, pleasure/low arousal (relaxation). Finer divisions can be made to suit specific purposes. Moreover, emotion fades gradually into non-emotion (Fehr & Russell, 1984).

The center of Figure 4.1 can be thought of as an adaptation level, a neutral point on all the bipolar dimensions (Russell & Fehr, 1987; Russell & Lanius, 1984). Each emotion label can be thought of as a vector originating from the center of the circle, with its length representing intensity (extremity or saturation). Degree of arousal (the vertical axis) is thus conceptually distinct from intensity (see Daly et al., 1981). A person could describe an intense, low-arousal state (extreme serenity, extreme sadness) as well as a mild, high-arousal state (mild surprise). For convenience, only 28 categories are shown in Figure 4.1, but any emotion-related category would be defined similarly. The English language provides hundreds of emotion words—the number has been estimated at between 500 (Averill, 1975) and 2000 (Wallace & Carson, 1973). The assumption of the circumplex model is that they all have their place within Figure 4.1.

SOME CONSIDERATIONS FAVORING THE CIRCUMPLEX

My principal aim in this chapter is to illustrate the heuristic value of a structural model, but first it may help to elaborate why I believe the circumplex is the best specific model for this purpose and why it, or something similar, is a necessary complement to a list of emotions as a representation of our everyday implicit taxonomy. Let me begin by considering the problems encountered in attempting to formulate an adequate list.

---

[1] I mean to point out that these theorists *conceptualized* emotional states as varying along a single arousal dimension, not to deny that, physiologically, there are multiple and at best loosely connected arousal responses. The pleasure–displeasure and arousal–sleep concepts are used here to refer to perceptual dimensions. It is tempting to hypothesize that both are, in fact, also related to physiological mechanisms, a possibility I discuss later in this chapter.

The most justifiable list would consist of all emotion-denoting terms, but a list of upward of 2000 entries is unwieldly. The difficulty arises when trying to group various items together to shorten the list. The basic problem is that a list, in principle, only allows two alternatives: as we construct the list each new word we encounter must be classified either as a genuinely new type of emotion or as a synonym for an item already on the list. Various writers have published such lists, but the lists do not match and suffer from similar difficulties. Words clustered together are not really synonyms. For example, Izard (1977) lists *shame* and *shyness* as being in the same cluster (as referring to the same emotion). Second, different clusters are not equally dissimilar to each other. Some clusters are obviously more similar to each other than to some other clusters. Izard lists *shame, guilt,* and *joy* as three separate clusters. Yet shame and guilt are clearly more similar to each other than they are to joy. A list is incapable of representing this property. These two problems suggest that similarity between emotion terms is not an all-or-none matter. Rather, similarity is a matter of degree. As a consequence, there are many reasonable ways to group emotion terms together and it is not surprising that different writers group them differently. Even 8-year-old children can divide terms into two groups, three groups, or whatever number of groups you ask for (Russell & Ridgeway, 1983). If so, no natural boundaries separate discrete clusters of synonyms. And no principled method exists for deciding whether a particular word is to be considered a genuinely new type of emotion or merely a synonym for an emotion already on the list.

If similarity between emotion categories is a matter of degree, we can use multidimensional scaling (MDS) to represent the interrelationships among the categories. MDS uses distance in a "space" to represent similarity and is therefore ideally suited to continuous variation and avoids arbitrary groupings. By now, a number of such studies have been carried out and the result is straightforward. Preliminary scalings of small samples of emotion terms yielded a small number of dimensions, with the first two dimensions interpretable as *degree of pleasure* and *degree of arousal,* or as some rotation of these two (e.g., Fillenbaum & Rapoport, 1971; Lundberg & Devine, 1975; Stone & Coles, 1970). A much more adequate sample of terms, 264 adjectives denoting feelings, was scaled by Bush (1973), but again only two dimensions were reliable and interpretable: *pleasure* and *arousal.* Similar results have now been found in various languages (Russell, 1983) and with subjects as young as 8 years (Russell & Ridgeway, 1983).

More than two dimensions can be obtained through multidimensional scaling, and three-, four-, or *n*-dimensional structural models of people's implicit emotion taxonomy are possible (Russell, 1978; Smith & Ellsworth, 1985). The two-dimensional model I advocate is, nevertheless, a very good first approximation. It accounts for most of the variance and will serve the purposes of this chapter by illustrating the uses of a structural model. Third and higher dimensions account for only a tiny proportion of the variance and are limited to subsamples of emotion words. And, when these dimensions are interpreted, they fail to appear to be emotional in nature. They appear instead to refer to (beliefs about) the cause of the emotional state, its outcome, its importance, its temporal course, and the like.[2]

Figure 4.2 is an MDS solution for the 28 emotion-related words given in Figure 4.1 (Russell, 1980). Our intuition that emotions are independent entities may have led some readers to be skeptical when I first presented the circumplex model of Figure 4.1, because what are called discrete emotions were not represented as independent but as closely related. It is important then to bear in mind one fact: Figure 4.2, which matches Figure 4.1 almost perfectly, is an *empirical* solution, based on subjects' judgments of how these categories are interrelated.

Figure 4.2 is a semantic structure. It is based on words, and many readers will automatically put the word *merely* in front of the word *semantic*. Indeed, a question should be raised whether this semantic structure tells us anything about how people make actual judgments about emotions. I shall consider this question in two contexts: the way in which people report their own emotional states and the way they describe the emotions of others, as exemplified in the case of seeing another's facial expression.

If, as the circumplex suggests, emotion words are not independent, then we can expect to find correlations between self-report scales purported to measure different types of emotion. And this is what is found. In one study, correlations were calculated among 42 mood scales commonly used in clinical, personality, and social psychology (Russell and Mehrabian, 1977b). The 42 scales were substantially intercorrelated. As just one example, consider the Nowlis Sadness Scale, and note the diverse labels on scales with which it correlated: .88 with Thayer's (1967) Deactivation Scale and .52 with Thayer's (1967) High Activation Scale, .70 with Zuckerman and Lubin's (1965) Anxiety Scale, .60 with

---

[2]Smith and Ellsworth (1985) refer to these higher order dimensions as aspects of the appraisal process preceding an emotion. Fehr and Russell (1984) suggest they are features of the prototypical script for each emotion category. It is our thinking in terms of prototypes (rather than the entire range of application) that probably explains our intuition that emotion categories are not as interchangeable as is implied by Figure 4.1. For example, in the *prototypical* case of fear, we fear a future event; in the *prototypical* case of anger, we are angry about something that already happened. Most actual cases of emotion, however, probably involve considerations of past, present, and future, and thus are eligible for categorization as both *fear* and *anger*. The circumplex model advocated here does not deny the possibility of an emotional state being classified as only *anger,* only *fear,* etc. It asserts that most emotional states classified as *anger* will also be classified as *fear*—the correlation between them is high, not perfect. An emotional state classified only as *anger* is probably the prototypical state of anger, a state in which the cause, the outcome, the temporal course, and so on correspond precisely to the prototypical case of anger. The point to remember is that words such as *fear* and *anger* are, in fact, used in many nonprototypical occasions.

FIGURE 4.2.   Multidimensional scaling of emotion-related words. Figure taken from Russell (1980).

Izard's (1971) Fear Scale, .58 with Izard's (1971) Contempt Scale, .64 with Izard's (1971) Disgust Scale, .86 with Izard's (1971) Distress Scale, and .65 with McNair et al.'s (1971) Anger–Hostility scale. The overall structure among the 42 scales was close to that predicted by a circumplex model: A pleasure factor and an arousal factor each accounted for large and independent amounts of variance. Together, these two dimensions pretty much sufficed to define any emotion scale. From scores on the bipolar dimensions of pleasure–displeasure and arousal–sleep, excellent predictions were obtained for scores on almost all 42 scales studied, once response style was accounted for.

Factor analysis has been applied in many studies to correlations among emotion scales in order to reveal the structure underlying their use. Results from the early studies had been interpreted in terms of independent, unipolar (lacking a bipolar opposite) factors—the factor–analytic equivalent of a list. With methodological improvements, however, results from later studies have tended to be interpreted more in line with a bipolar system (Meddis, 1972; Plutchik, 1980; Russell, 1979; Svensson, 1978)—the factor–analytic equivalent of the kind of structure I am advocating. Indeed, support for the unipolar lists appears to be waning: Thayer, who had reported evidence for unipolar factors in 1967, reported evidence for a bipolar structure in 1978. Elsewhere, I offer evidence that a circumplex model adequately accounts for the structure of self-report data (Russell, 1980). Again, dimensions beyond pleasure and arousal can be found; nevertheless, they account for a small proportion of variance and appear to be interpretable as aspects of events surrounding the emotion, dimensions such as dominant versus submissive status (Russell, 1980) or social orientation (Svensson, 1978).

The circumplex is also richly supported in studies of how people categorize facial expressions of emotions. It was Woodworth (1938) who first noticed that subjects' "errors" in emotion recognition were quite systematic—that some were "more wrong" than others. Woodworth and Schlosberg (e.g., 1954, pp. 124–129) used these errors to discover which emotion words were always used interchangeably, which were occasionally so used, and which were never so used. From this analysis, Schlosberg found that emotion categories formed a circle in a two-dimensional space. One dimension was clearly degree of plea- sure. Schlosberg (1952) initially favored attention–rejection as the interpretation of the second dimension, but subsequent evidence favored degree of arousal (Abelson & Sermat, 1962; Cliff, & Young, 1968; Green & Cliff, 1975; Royal & Hays, 1959; Russell & Bullock, 1985, 1986; Shepard, 1962).

In summary, available evidence shows that people do not use emotion catego- ries as if they are independent or mutually exclusive. Rather, emotion categories are systematically and highly interrelated. A structural model attempts to repre- sent these interrelationships and is required if we are to understand what people mean when they respond to a verbal rating scale. I believe that a circumplex is the most useful structural model proposed to date. Evidence favoring something very like a circumplex has appeared in three separate lines of evidence: direct judgments of the similarity between emotion terms, verbal self-report data, and judgments of facial expressions of emotion. The circumplex structure is thus not limited to semantic judgments, to co-occurrences of self-reported emotions, or to similarities in the appearance of facial expressions (cf. Boucher & Ekman, 1965). It occurs whenever people categorize emotions. If intuition leads us to suppose that people use *fear, anger, sadness,* and other emotion words as if they were independent of one another, then the set of relationships summarized in the circumplex are a genuine, counterintuitive finding. And, as I shall discuss next, it is a finding that raises serious questions about our common methods of obtain- ing and interpreting verbal ratings of emotion.

Before discussing the implications of all this for the measurement of emotion, let me repeat that the circumplex is only an approximation of the actual network of interrelationships among emotion categories. Better models may be found. Nevertheless, the circumplex will provide the discussion to follow with a simple, convenient, graphic summary of that network. The implications to be discussed next do not depend on the precise details of the circumplex model, but only on the existence of the network of interrelationships it represents.

IMPLICATIONS

VERBAL SELF-REPORT SCALES: AFFECT
ADJECTIVE CHECKLISTS

In psychological laboratories and clinics, people are sometimes given an affect adjective checklist or some other sort of a paper-and-pencil test said to measure specific moods or emotions. How are scores from such tests to be interpreted?

Consider an individual who scores high on a scale labeled *anxiety*. Let us first ask how that person would score on scales of other types of emotion. If we think of anxiety as separate and discrete, then a high score on the anxiety scale should tell us nothing about scores on scales of other separate and discrete emotions. According to the circumplex, in contrast, a high anxiety score should tell us much about scores on other scales. Figure 4.3 gives some data on this issue from 57 subjects who scored one standard deviation or more above the mean on the Nowlis (1965) Anxiety Scale. Figure 4.3 gives their average standard score on 49 commonly used verbal self-report emotion scales. As can be seen at a glance, these "anxious" subjects scored substantially above or below the mean on most of the scales they filled out. Moreover, their high and low scores form a visible pattern because the scales are ordered as they would fall along the perimeter of the circumplex.

One way to understand these results is to consider a person who is unhappy. This person will probably score above the average on *any* scale of an unpleasant emotion, whether the label on that scale is *stress, anxiety, hostility, depression,* or whatever. That same person will probably score below average on any scale of a pleasant emotion, whether the label is *elation, relaxation,* or whatever. Conversely, a person who is happy will obtain the opposite pattern on all these scales. What follows is that a high score on an anxiety scale, or any scale with a negative label, could mean nothing more than unhappiness.

The sorts of results seen in Figure 4.3 are not specific to anxiety, but are typical of emotion scales. Far from being mutually exclusive or independent, emotion scales are highly interrelated in self-report data. Someone with a high score on any one scale would likely obtain a high score on scales of emotion categories nearby in the circular order. This is the implication of the correlations among verbal self-report scales with undoubtedly different labels. A score on any such single emotion scale should therefore probably be interpreted more broadly than is commonly done. The label placed on the typical self-report scale does not pinpoint a person's emotional state to the degree advertised.

To take a specific example relevant to a clinical setting, consider Zuckerman and Lubin's (1965) widely used Multiple Affect Adjective Check List (MAACL), which consists of three separate scales claimed to measure hostility, anxiety, and depression. A clinician might administer the anxiety scale to patients and assume

Standard score

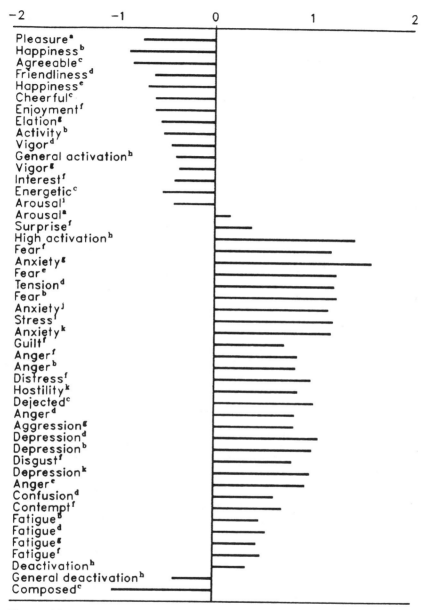

Figure 4.3. Mean standard scores on 49 self-report emotion questionnaires for anxious students. Data are from a study of 343 college students; *anxious* students were those ($n = 57$) scoring at least one standard deviation above the mean on the Nowlis (1965) Anxiety Scale. a, Mehrabian and Russell (1974); b, Ryman, Biersner, and La Rocco (1974); c, Lorr and Shea (1979); d, McNair and Lorr (1964); e, Jacobs, Capek, and Meehan (1959); f, Izard (1972); g, Nowlis (1965); h, Thayer (1967); i, Mackay, Cox, Burrows, and Lazzerini (1978); j, Spielberger, Gorsuch, and Lushene (1970); k, Zuckerman and Lubin (1965).

that patients scoring high have the specific problem of anxiety. This was the goal in developing the three scales. And, on the assumption that hostility, anxiety, and depression, are discrete emotions, Zuckerman and Lubin (1965) expected their three scales to be uncorrelated. But the evidence says otherwise: reported correlations among the three scales range from .67 to .90 (Gotlib & Meyer, 1986; Herron, 1969; Herron, Bernstein, & Rosen, 1968; Lubin & Zuckerman, 1967; Russell & Mehrabian, 1977b). The clinician's interpretation of that high anxiety score should therefore take into account that the same person would very likely receive high scores on the other two scales as well. To a psychologist, the terms *hostility*, *depression*, and *anxiety* each have rather specific psychological meaning. *Hostility* might be associated with aggressive motivation; *depression*, with psychiatric disorders that include insomnia, loss of appetite, and suicidal motivation; and *anxiety*, with various psychophysiological symptoms. Yet a high score on a verbal self-report scale need not imply any of these things. It is a mistake for a clinician to believe that he or she is dealing with separate problems of anxiety, hostility, and depression because there are three separate scales. It is a mistake for a researcher to believe he or she is studying separate states by using separate scales.

SELF-REPORT: DIMENSIONAL RATINGS

Psychologists sometimes describe mood or emotional state in terms of bipolar dimensions rather than discrete categories. The most frequently considered dimension is *pleasure–displeasure*, although often this is under an alias: positive–negative quality, valence, hedonic tone, affect, dysphoria–euphoria. *Arousal–sleepiness* is occasionally considered, but rarely in conjunction with *pleasure–displeasure*. The circumplex model of Figure 4.1 suggests that we should ask about both components of the person's feeling simultaneously. Failure to do so could challenge the interpretation of the particular measure used.

To illustrate why this is important, consider Maslach's (1979a, 1979b) attempt to replicate the famous Schachter and Singer (1962) experiment on labeling of unexplained arousal. Maslach had questioned whether unexplained arousal was really just as likely to be labeled positively as negatively. She suspected that a negative label was more likely. As one of her measures of the positive–negative quality of their emotional state, Maslach (1979a, 1979b) asked subjects to verbally rate their current state on the following eight bipolar items: *tense–relaxed*, *apprehensive–confident*, *anxious–calm*, *irritated–not irritated*, *annoyed–serene*, *angry–peaceful*, *sad–happy*, and *closed–open*. With the exception of the last two, these items contrast distress states with relaxation states. Rather than the horizontal *pleasure–displeasure* dimension, distress versus relaxation would be a diagonal in Figure 4.1. It is that dimension in which high arousal is associated with displeasure and low arousal is associated with pleasure. Aroused subjects will thus score on the negative side of this scale of distress, because arousal is part of the meaning of these particular negative terms. It is thus not surprising that Maslach found just such a positive correlation between arousal and a composite score on these items. Support of her hypothesis was built into this particular self-report measure.[3]

Turner (1986) was also interested in measuring the positive–negative quality of subjects' emotional states. His measure was a single semantic differential-type item labeled *low* at one end and *high* at the other end. I have no evidence on this, but I suspect this measure corresponds more to the *depression–excitement* diagonal of Figure 4.1 than to the horizontal *pleasure–displeasure* dimension. On this measure, high arousal is associated with pleasure, low arousal with displeasure.

For the sake of argument, let me exaggerate and say that Maslach's scale measured precisely the *distress–relaxation* diagonal and that Turner's scale measured precisely the *depression–excitement* diagonal. These two scales are each highly saturated with *pleasure–displeasure* and therefore serve as approximate measures of *pleasure–displeasure*. But, each would also measure (although in opposite directions) degree of arousal and the two measures could be uncorrelated with each other. It is not hard to imagine the confusion that would be generated trying to compare and to integrate results from studies that used these different scales, both claiming to be measures of the positive–negative component of emotion.

Occasionally, psychologists try to measure a person's feelings along the *arousal–sleep* dimension. Thayer (1967, 1978) provided four scales purported to assess arousal, but problems exist in Thayer's scales analogous to those seen in Maslach's (1979a, 1979b) and Turner's (1986): Each of Thayer's scales is confounded with *pleasure* or *displeasure* (Russell, 1979).

When I want to measure the *pleasure–displeasure* or *arousal–sleepiness* dimensions, I use either the scales described in Table 4.1, which were constructed to be independent of each other, as well as independent of how dominant the person feels, or the Affect Grid (Russell, Weiss, & Mendelsohn, in press).

BIOLOGICAL INDEXES OF EMOTION

The problem in the interpretation of self-report scales can also affect the interpretation of nonverbal measures of emotion. To take just one example, consider Frankenhaeuser's (1979) argument for a certain biochemical index as a

---

[3]Fortunately, she also examined the results item by item, and found that scores on *happy–sad* supported her hypothesis. This is fortunate because happy–sad would be biased against her hypothesis and thus provided strong support for it. In addition, she employed other measures not subject to this problem.

TABLE 4.1

PRINCIPAL COMPONENTS OF MEHRABIAN AND RUSSELL'S (1974) SCALES OF EMOTIONAL STATE[a]

State	Factor		
	I	II	III
Pleasure			
Annoyed–pleased	**.86**	−.06	.03
Dissatisfied–satisfied	**.86**	−.07	.01
Unhappy–happy	**.85**	.02	.09
Bored–relaxed	**.84**	.13	−.13
Melancholic–contented	**.80**	−.09	.04
Despairing–hopeful	**.68**	.11	.06
Arousal			
Sluggish–frenzied	−.15	**.77**	.01
Unaroused–aroused	.39	**.75**	−.11
Sleepy–wide awake	.26	**.71**	−.04
Calm–excited	−.40	**.70**	.05
Relaxed–stimulated	−.12	**.68**	.14
Dull–jittery	.07	**.68**	−.05
Dominance			
Submissive–dominant	.07	.19	**.72**
Influenced–influential	.00	−.10	**.65**
Controlled–controlling	.22	−.10	**.61**
Guided–autonomous	.10	−.03	**.57**
Cared for–in control	−.17	.12	**.56**
Awed–important	−.06	−.07	**.54**

[a]$N = 323$. Factor I correlated .10 with Factor II, and .25 with Factor III; Factor II correlated .18 with III. Taken from Russell, Ward, and Pratt (1981). In actual administration, items are intermixed in random order, half in reverse direction, and presented in a 9-point semantic-differential format. With each item scored −4 to +4, the total *pleasure–displeasure* score varies potentially from −24 to +24, similarly for the *arousal–sleepiness* scale.

measure of stress. She claimed that "our psychoendocrine approach is well suited for identifying the stressful aspects of daily commuting by train" (1979, p. 137). Part of her argument is based on two studies. One study showed that crowding on a train (number of fellow passengers) was positively correlated with adrenaline secretion rate (assessed through analysis of urine samples). The other study showed that adrenaline secretion rate was positively correlated with verbal self-ratings of *stress*.

The question is whether adrenaline secretion rate is specific to reports of stress. The thrust of the evidence we have seen so far suggests otherwise—a suggestion supported by evidence from a study in which high rates of adrenaline secretion were found in subjects shown various movies that were annoying, frightening, or even amusing (Levi, 1965). We see Frankenhaeuser's study of train passengers in a different light when we realize that her crowded passengers might have been amused. More generally, this range of results suggests that adrenaline secretion rate might be an index of arousal (the vertical dimension of Figure 4.1). If so, adrenaline secretion rate might be positively correlated with verbal reports of anything from *angst* to *zest*.

I must emphasize that I am using the term *stress* here as an everyday word, just as Frankenhaeuser's subjects must have done. It is not always clear in the literature just how the word *stress* is being used. At times, it is used as a shorthand label for the scientific construct of the General Adaptation Syndrome, which Selye (e.g., 1952) defined as a syndrome of physiological reactions to toxins, diseases, injuries, and similar harmful agents. Defined as Selye's scientific construct, *stress* requires appropriate physiological measurement, for which subjects' self-report on a scale labeled *stress* may or may not be a substitute. Defined as a dimension of self-report, *stress* must be analyzed like any other everyday emotion-related word, and it may or may not bear much relationship to the General Adaptation Syndrome.

RECOGNITION OF NONVERBAL EXPRESSIONS OF EMOTION

Research on how well one person can recognize the emotion expressed in another person's face has a history of controversy. One of the problems has been and continues to be a failure to take into account how labels for categories of emotion are interrelated.

In the early decades of this century, subjects were shown photographs of various posed or spontaneous facial expressions. When subjects were asked to name the emotion in the face, they could not agree. So many "errors" occurred that psychologists concluded that emotion could not be recognized from a facial expression (Bruner & Tagiuri, 1954). There are many problems with this research (Ekman, Friesen, & Ellsworth, 1972), but at least one problem was the criterion for deciding which labels were correct and which were errors. What might have been going on is shown with a slight change in procedure: rather than ask subjects to select a single label, ask them to rate how applicable *each* category label is. Figure 4.4 shows the mean of such ratings from 20 subjects who were shown what, according to Ekman and Friesen's (1976) research, is a prototypical expression of surprise. *Surprise* received the highest rating, but the important point is this: other category labels were found somewhat appropriate as well. Ordering the categories as they would fall around the circumplex predicts the degree of category applicability. This kind of result is not peculiar to this particular stimulus, but has been found with photographs of even the most prototypical facial expressions of what have been called basic emotions (Russell

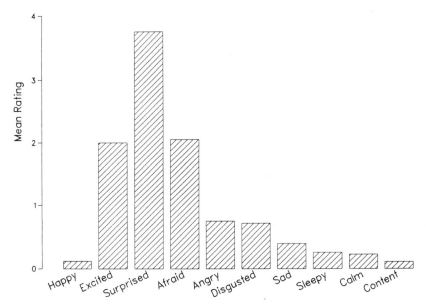

FIGURE 4.4. Mean ratings for a prototypical expression of surprise. Subjects were 20 volunteers from the University of British Columbia, who were shown photograph number M01-14 from Ekman and Friesen's (1976) collection. This was a 3-inch by 5-inch black and white print. Subjects viewed the photograph for as long as they wanted and then rated each of the 10 categories on the 0–4 scale, which was labeled *not at all, slightly, moderately, very much,* and *extremely.*

& Bullock, 1986): The degree of applicability of each emotion category label predicts the proportion of subjects who select that label when they are forced to choose a single label. If only one category label is counted as correct, subjects selecting nearby labels will be thought to have made an error. In short, consistency in subjects' behavior may have been overlooked because the interrelatedness of emotion category labels was overlooked.

In more recent studies, consistency may have been *overestimated.* Subjects are now typically given a set of highly selected facial expressions, a short pre-specified list of emotion categories, and instructions to assign each expression to one and only one category. With this procedure, near perfect agreement was found and psychologists concluded that specific categories of emotion could be recognized from facial expressions (Ekman et al., 1972). Now, when almost all subjects place a particular expression in the same category, it is tempting to say that the face *is,* in fact, expressing just that category of emotion. Correctness is inferred from consensus. A little trick illustrates one problem in this thinking.

I showed one of Ekman and Friesen's (1976) photographs to two groups of subjects (see Table 4.2). In one condition, 93% picked *sad* as the correct category. In the other condition, no one picked *sad.* Which consensus is correct? Even

TABLE 4.2
PERCENTAGE OF SUBJECTS JUDGING THE SAME PHOTOGRAPH
AS EXPRESSING A PARTICULAR EMOTION[a]

Options available:	Sad	Upset	N
	0%	100%	30
Options available:	Sad	Happy	N
	93%	7%	30

[a]Subjects were 60 volunteers from the University of British Columbia, who were shown Photograph Number 53 (MF-2-07) from Ekman and Friesen's (1976) collection. This is a black and white 35-mm slide. Subjects viewed the slide for as long as they wanted and then judged which of the two options available best described the emotional state of the woman shown.

though *sad* was an option available to both groups, its use varied dramatically. The difference between the conditions was the list of emotion categories provided to the subjects: *sad* and *happy* for the first group, *sad* and *upset* for the second group. Simply put, consensus varies with the specific list of options given the subjects to choose from. (By the way, Ekman and Friesen found that 100% of their subjects labeled this same photograph as *anger*, when the options available were a list of six categories. With the results of Table 4.2 in mind, the reader might be cautious in interpreting this high interrater agreement.)

My demonstration works because categorization is not an absolute phenomenon; rather, a person can pick the best option available. The list of categories I provided my subjects in this demonstration was greatly impoverished, and the shorter the list the easier it may be to obtain high interrater agreement on the best category label available (however bad it may be in an absolute sense). The history of the study of interpretation of facial expressions reveals just such a trend. The early researchers had allowed subjects to use any name they wanted or to choose from a relatively long list of emotion categories [Buzby (1924), for example, provided 18 items]. And they concluded that emotion could not be read from the face. Later investigators gave subjects shorter lists, found greater agreement, and concluded that emotion could be read from the face (Ekman et al., 1972).

The problem of inappropriate response scales in this research tradition is compounded by use of *selected*, rather than randomly sampled, facial expressions. When subjects agree with one another in assigning each selected facial expression to one emotion category, it is tempting to assume that the subjects must know more than simply how much *pleasure–displeasure* and *arousal–sleep* is expressed in the face. That might be true, but the current evidence does not warrant that conclusion. To see the problem with this assumption, consider a case that we would all agree involves a single dimension rather than independent categories: our judgments of how tall or short someone is. If a researcher were to use selected stimuli (adult targets of 3', 5'3", 6'3", and 8') and a categorical response scale (*midget, short, tall, giant*), subjects might achieve close to 100% agreement among themselves in recognizing four categories of height. We should nonetheless be reluctant to agree that there are four discrete categories of height—even though researchers have used the same procedure to suggest that there are a certain number of discrete categories of emotion expressed in the face.[4]

THE CAUSES OF EMOTIONAL CHANGE

When verbally rated emotion is treated as a dependent variable, problems can arise, no matter how proper the experimental design. For example, to understand the mood-altering effects of a drug (or anything else) requires more than experimental evidence that differences in scores on a verbal scale of, say, anxiety are attributable to the drug. As the reader might anticipate by now, each drug seems to produce changes in most of the self-report emotion scales that happen to be included in the experiment (Russell & Mehrabian, 1975, 1977a). Researchers are thereby forced to list all the emotion scales showing reliable differences due to the drug. Some researchers have analyzed their results item by item and then listed all those items showing reliable changes due to the drug. It is not surprising that despite years of research, the mood-altering effects of even alcohol cannot be clearly stated (Freed, 1978).

The situation is further complicated because subjects' moods are influenced not only by the drug but by the experimental setting and by their own prior mood. To illustrate, suppose that a particular drug simply increases arousal. Depending on setting and prior mood, subjects taking the drug would report a wide range of emotions. A subject with a pleasant prior mood or in a pleasant setting would report feeling happy, euphoric, excited, delighted, and the like. A subject with an unpleasant prior mood or in an unpleasant setting would report feeling upset, anxious, afraid, angry, and the like. By focusing exclusively on the labels applicable to the final mood, researchers would face a vast number of seemingly disparate effects of a drug that, by hypothesis, simply alters how aroused people feel.

As an alternative approach, drug researchers could focus on the change in the

---

[4]The purpose of this exercise was to illustrate how people use emotion labels and to question the standard interpretation of high interrater agreement from forced-choice rating data. High interrater agreement is not the only basis on which investigators such as Ekman, Friesen, and Ellsworth (1972) infer emotions from facial expressions. Part of their reasoning, for example, concerns the neuromuscular basis, the cross-cultural consistency, and the evolutionary history of facial expressions.

basic dimensions of mood that is brought about by a drug. A clearer picture of what is going on might emerge if pretest scores and posttest scores, both for the drug group and for the placebo group, were taken directly on measures of *pleasure–displeasure* and *arousal–sleepiness*. Plotting these scores in the space shown in Figure 4.1 would not solve all problems, but it should display the basic mood-altering effect of the drug. Once this is done, we could then begin to sort out effects due to setting, cognitive set, prior mood, and so on, particularly if they interact with the drug (Russell & Bond, 1980).

THE EFFECTS OF EMOTION

Two lines of research focus on the effects of emotion. In one line, psychologists have tried to study the effects of emotion on behaviors, cognitions, or other psychological processes. Techniques devised to induce the emotion have included the reading of self-referent elation statements (Velten, 1968) or hypnotic instruction to feel a certain way (Bower, 1981). In the other line, psychologists have been concerned with accounting for the relationship between environment and behavior by reference to a mediating emotional state: An environmental change produces a change in emotion, which causes the observed change in behavior. In either sort of study, a key question is how the emotional state is described and measured.

Describing the emotional state along a single dimension, such as positive–negative, may be insufficient. For example, "good mood" has been shown to promote helping. Batson, Coke, Chard, Smith, & Taliaferro (1979) offered evidence that "good mood" does so by acting as a general activator of all behavior. The circumplex model of Figure 4.1 would suggest that we should also ask about the arousal level of the subjects in Batson et al.'s experimental group. If good mood is induced through a pleasant surprise—an unexpected gift or finding money—then the experimental subjects might also be somewhat aroused. If so, it would not be surprising if their emotional state was a general activator. The problem is that not all good moods involve high arousal. With a different mood-altering treatment, we might be able to show that "good mood" serves as a general *deactivator*. We would just have to think of a way to induce "good mood" that was also calming (i.e., 315° around the circle). How about gentle music, soft light, and a brandy?

More often, the researcher claims to have induced a specific category of emotion. Dutton and Aron (1974) found that male subjects were more sexually attracted to a female when they met her on a bridge suspended 230 feet above a canyon floor than were males who met the same female on a bridge only 10 feet above a shallow rivulet. Dutton and Aron (1974) explained their result as due to the mediating emotion of "high anxiety." However, in the laboratory, Kenrick,

Cialdini, and Linder (1979) tried four times to replicate this aphrodisiac effect of anxiety but failed.

Manipulation checks were included in these studies: a single self-report scale labeled *fear* in the Dutton and Aron (1974) study and a scale labeled *anxiety* in the Kenrick et al. (1979) studies. But, as we have seen, greater *fear* and *anxiety* scores are likely to coexist with a range of other category labels. Experimental subjects feeling anything from distress to excitement could score higher on fear or anxiety scales than would control subjects who were bored, calm, or sleepy.

Light might have been shed on this controversy if the emotional states of the subjects were assessed in a slightly different way. Rather than be given a single label such as *anxiety*, subjects could be assessed so that their mood could be plotted in Figure 4.1. Of course, there is no way to know now what emotional states subjects in either study would actually have reported. But, for the sake of argument, let us suppose that Dutton and Aron's (1974) subjects, vacationers who had paid to walk across a suspension bridge over a beautiful canyon, were at 45° in the circumplex, near the word *excited*. Let us suppose that Kenrick et al.'s (1979) subjects, who were in a laboratory being threatened with electric shock, were closer to 135° in the circumplex, near the word *distress*. This possibility is illustrated in the left half of Figure 4.5, which shows a simplified version of the circumplex of Figure 4.1. We see that the two groups might fall 90° apart. Even though both groups might be described as *anxious*, their emotional states might still be orthogonal to one another. It is not surprising if they fail to behave in exactly the same way.

Another possible explanation for controversies in this literature lies in the control groups. The emotional states of subjects in the control conditions are *equally important* in determining the results obtained. The observed result is really the *difference* between the experimental and control groups. Consider two hypothetical experiments in which the experimental subjects are induced to feel anxious. Indeed, imagine that exactly the same emotional state is induced in the experimental subjects in the two experiments. But then let us further suppose that in Experiment A, control subjects feel excited [for example, in the Dutton and Aron (1974) study, the control subjects were picnickers in a park]. Suppose that in Experiment B, control subjects feel bored [in the Kenrick et al. (1979) study, control subjects were waiting for a psychology experiment to begin]. This possibility is illustrated in the right half of Figure 4.5. The difference between the emotional states of experimental and control subjects in Experiment A would mainly be a difference along the *pleasure–displeasure* dimension. In Experiment B, the difference would mainly be along the *arousal–sleep* dimension. If so, there would be little reason to expect similar results in the two experiments, since they would again be dealing with orthogonal dimensions.

Polivy (1981) reviewed the literature on mood induction studies and un-

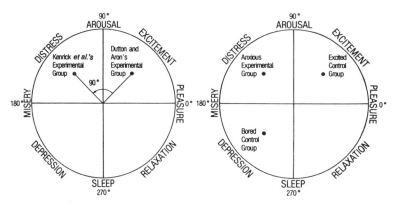

FIGURE 4.5. Possible emotional self-reports from experimental and control subjects.

covered what appears to be a serious problem. She first observed that "attempting to induce one particular emotion may actually result in arousal of several affects. . . . Even naturally occurring emotions seem to occur in clusters rather than singly" (p. 803). For example, when Roth and Kubal (1975) checked on the success of their attempt to induce depression, they found that their subjects reported not only depression but anxiety and anger as well. This phenomenon is readily predictable from Figure 4.1 and previous authors had noted its occurrence (Izard, 1972; Zuckerman, 1980), but it remained for Polivy to point out that it undermines the rationale and interpretation typically given in such studies—a rationale based on the assumption that a single discrete emotion has been induced. She pointed out that we cannot attribute a change in behavior to, say, depression when depression is only one among other possible antecedent emotions.

Polivy considered various explanations of the "multiple moods" phenomenon. Perhaps one emotion can elicit another. Perhaps emotions spontaneously change in nature. But each such explanation perpetuates the assumption that each emotion scale corresponds to a separate emotion. I suggest a simple alternative interpretation: rather than multiple moods, multiple words apply to the same mood. When three emotion scales show elevated scores, it might seem reasonable to infer three different moods, but what about 50 emotion scales? The number of moods found may only be limited by the number of verbal scales included. The alternative view suggested by Figure 4.1 is that a person is said to be in *one* state and that emotion words vary in how accurately they describe that state. Many words will be quite accurate and many will not. The data reported earlier predict that Polivy's evidence is only the tip of the iceberg, that mood-induction techniques will be found to induce changes in most of the mood scales included.

THEORIZING ABOUT EMOTION

Theorizing about emotion is also permeated with the everyday language of emotion. Let us consider Schachter and Singer's (1962) theory of emotion.[5] Probably the most novel aspect of their theory was their restriction of the role of physiological processes in emotion to the occurrence of a state of high physiological arousal. All remaining aspects of the emotion were held to be determined, not physiologically but cognitively, by the label chosen on the basis of the social situation. The circumplex model suggests a number of problems with this notion.

First, consider their assumption that high arousal is necessary for emotion. Schachter and Singer (1962) discuss (and tried to create in their laboratory) situations where subjects were aroused and would label themselves either *angry* or *euphoric*. According to Figure 4.1, *anger* and *euphoria* are both high-arousal terms and therefore reasonable labels of high-arousal states. Their choice of these particular labels with which to illustrate their theory was thus a wise one. The top half of the circumplex of Figure 4.1 suggests other good candidates. On the other hand, Schachter and Singer (1962) might have a harder time convincing us that highly aroused subjects would choose *depression, sorrow, boredom, sadness, calm, serenity, contentment,* or other labels in the bottom half of the circumplex. Schachter and Singer's account is thus restricted to those labels containing a component of high arousal. In everyday thought, the best exemplars, or prototypical cases, of the concept *emotion* are just such high-arousal states as *anger, fear,* or *euphoria*. A theory based on prototypical emotions would be expected to have intuitive appeal, but still may not be applicable to all emotions. [See Leventhal's (1974) discussion of the necessity and sufficiency of arousal for emotion.]

Of course this may just be quibbling about the definition of *emotion*. Besides, we can easily generalize Schachter and Singer's idea. We could propose that, to use their language, people can label any degree of arousal. Now, as a thought

---

[5]Maslach (1979a, 1979b) presented a detailed empirical and theoretical critique of Schachter and Singer's (1962) notion that emotion is a person's label for unexplained arousal. Maslach (1979b) questioned whether unexplained arousal would ever be experienced as pleasant. She wrote "the concept of unexplained arousal is very close to the clinical definition of 'free-floating anxiety,' which is always characterized by negative emotional affect" (p. 470). Despite the merits of Maslach's critique, this part of her argument might be misleading. As shown in Figure 4.1, arousal is close to anxiety (which falls in the distress quadrant), and indeed, anxiety is negative. But it does not follow that arousal is negative. After all, arousal is also close to excitement, which is positive. Moving around the circle shown in Figure 4.1, one might be led into agreeing that distress is close to displeasure, which is close to depression, which is close to low arousal, which is close to relaxation. But distress and relaxation are opposites! The emphasis in Maslach's statement must thus be on the lack of explanation for the arousal, rather than on arousal per se.

experiment, let us surreptitiously put subjects into a state of low arousal by means of an appropriate drug. Put half of the subjects into a pleasant condition and the other half into an unpleasant condition. Subjects should label themselves *calm* in the first case and *depressed* in the second.

Next consider the problem of speaking of arousal in strictly physiological terms. Implicit in Schachter and Singer's (1962) theory, arousal must have a mental counterpart—because the physiological arousal must be perceived before it is explained. Therefore, perceived arousal, rather than physiological arousal, is the *immediate* precursor to emotional labeling. Besides, there is ample evidence that physiological arousal is no unitary phenomenon but rather a host of separate processes. It becomes unitary when perceived.

Once we see arousal in this light, we are in the realm of affective experience, and we must ask about the other major dimension of reported affective experience: *pleasure–displeasure*. The circumplex and all the evidence on which it is based points to the importance of *pleasure–displeasure* and to its independence from arousal.

Schachter and Singer's (1962) experimental procedure did attempt to manipulate arousal physiologically (through epinephrine) and to manipulate *pleasure–displeasure* situationally (through the euphoria or anger situation). However, the way in which Schachter and Singer chose to manipulate these factors should not be confused with the necessary, or even the typical, role they play in emotion. One could manipulate arousal through situational differences. (Arousal varies with, for example, the intensity, novelty, and complexity of environmental stimulation.) One could also manipulate *pleasure–displeasure* chemically. Partially for reasons outlined above, the emotion-altering effects of drugs are not known precisely. Anecdotal evidence suggests that cocaine induces a state of high pleasure and high arousal (euphoria), whereas heroin and related opium derivatives induce a state of high pleasure and somewhat lowered arousal (serenity) (Snyder, 1974). Research with β-endorphin suggests the possibility of a purely chemical means to alter pleasure (e.g., Gerner, Catlin, Gorelick, Hui, & Li, 1980). We might suppose, then, that when examined closely there will be some drug with which *pleasure–displeasure* can be manipulated.

Someone could propose a theory complementary to Schachter and Singer's: Emotion occurs when the physiological counterpart of pleasure or displeasure changes. The person seeks a label for this change in state and the label is chosen to be consistent with, among other things, the arousing quality of the situation. To test this theory in another thought experiment, let us surreptitiously create a state of displeasure in a group of subjects by giving them an appropriate drug. Put half of the subjects in an arousing (stimulating, intense, novel, or complex) situation, the other half in an unarousing one. Subjects would be predicted to label the displeasure as *distress* in the arousing situation and as *depression* in the nonarousing one. In another thought experiment, we create a state of pleasure in our subjects. In this case, subjects should label the pleasure as *excitement* in the arousing condition and as *relaxation* in the nonarousing condition.

The phenomenon just described may occur naturally. Among the major affective disorders is endogenous depression. Patients who suffer from this disorder report extreme unhappiness, which is apparently brought about by biochemical abnormalities and is thus unexplainable to the victims. They label themselves not only as depressed, but as *sad, anxious, panicked, nervous,* and so on, presumably depending on the particular situation.

All these considerations suggest, to me, that there is no more reason to speak of arousal as strictly physiological and pleasure–displeasure as strictly mental than there is to express it the other way around. Let me propose then that *pleasure–displeasure* be treated in the same way we treat *arousal–sleepiness.* Both presumably have some physiological basis, although in neither case is this basis well understood. Both may be quite complex physiologically—they become simple dimensions on the mental side. Both can be manipulated (indirectly) either chemically or through changes in the environment or the information given to a person. Both emerge as fundamental and independent dimensions of emotional state. Both appear as primary components of the labels used to describe emotional states.

From this perspective, Schachter and Singer may have described not a general account of emotion but a particular phenomenon: the emotional consequences of unexplained increases in physiological arousal. Other phenomena occur: There are emotional consequences of unexplained decreases in arousal, and of both increases and decreases in the physiological counterpart of pleasure–displeasure. No one of these exhausts the range of emotions.

Combining the psychometric approach of this article with Schachter and Singer's social psychological approach, we might imagine that the typical course of an emotion goes like this: Some event or combination of events, either internal or external, produces a noticeable change in our internal state. A person automatically perceives this change in state in terms of *pleasure–displeasure* and *arousal–sleep.* This core affective state, which I call *mood state* (Russell & Snodgrass, 1987), is likely to be primitive and preverbal. When the person seeks to label this state, these two dimensions are the main determinants of which words are applicable and which are not. Many words for mood denote nothing more than combinations of pleasure and arousal: excitement is *high pleasure/high arousal;* depression is *displeasure/low arousal;* distress is *displeasure/high arousal;* serenity is *high pleasure/low arousal.*

At this point, psychologists have traditionally asked how people distinguish between the various possible emotions. First, people differentiate between categories of emotion much less than psychologists commonly assumed. People judge many labels as reasonably descriptive of their emotional state and the applicability of any label can be reasonably predicted from the pleasure and arousal quality of the emotional state. For example, if a combination of displeasure and high arousal occurs in about equal parts, *anger, fear, frustration, anxiety* and other labels from the distress quadrant of Figure 4.1 would all be somewhat applicable—much more applicable than *calm* or *happy*. In some cases all these labels might be equally applicable, but at times one label may be more appropriate than the others. Which category is most applicable depends on the social situation, the person's behavior, the person's intentions, and so on. *Anger* would be more appropriate if the eliciting situation involved some offense and if the motive to aggress was elicited; *fear* would be more appropriate if the eliciting situation involved threat and if the motive to escape was elicited. In other words, we now come across the role played by the third, fourth, fifth, and higher dimensions of emotion uncovered in scaling studies (Russell, 1978; Smith & Ellsworth, 1985). Different dimensions come into play to distinguish between terms.

SUMMARY

Too little attention has been focused on just what people mean when they use words to label emotional states, their own or those of others. Schachter and Singer (1962), for example, implicitly assumed that an emotional person, after consulting his or her level of physiological arousal and the nature of the immediate situation, chooses a single appropriate label. The emotion denoted by that label is then present, all other emotions absent. Ekman and Friesen (1976) implicitly assumed that one person, on seeing facial signs of emotion in another, chooses a single appropriate label (or in the case of blends, two labels). The response scales and checklists used by psychologists typically force subjects into just such a pattern.

Words do not mean whatever we psychologists want them to mean. When we ask a man how anxious he feels, or a woman how stressed she feels, their answers depend on what they take the words *anxiety* and *stress* to mean. Like any English word, an everyday word for an emotion is embedded in a cognitive network of beliefs and concepts. In constructing and interpreting verbal measures of emotion, we need to consider this network, the implicit folk taxonomy of emotion. And that is what the circumplex is all about.

Through selected cases, I have tried to show in this chapter how an instrument claiming to measure independent discrete unipolar emotions can be misleading—because everyday emotion categories are not mentally represented as independent or mutually exclusive. Rather, they are related to one another in a manner roughly described in the circumplex. As an alternative measurement strategy, therefore I would suggest that whenever a verbal measure of emotion is needed you follow a simple procedure: include scales of *pleasure–displeasure* and *arousal–sleepiness*. In other words, scale a person's emotion or an emotional stimulus within the space of Figure 4.1. In many studies this measure alone would suffice. If you are also interested in a specific category of emotion, I would suggest assessing pleasure and arousal, that specific category, plus a range of other category labels. And, rather than ask the subject to select the single best category label, allow the subject to rate each label for its applicability. Interpretation of the resulting ratings can be made easier by arranging the categories as they are ordered in the circumplex (as they are, for example, in Figure 4.2) and interpreting the category ratings in conjunction with the results from the pleasure and arousal ratings.

REFERENCES

Abelson, R. P., & Sermat, V. (1962). Multidimensional scaling of facial expressions. *Journal of Experimental Psychology, 63,* 546–554.

Averill, J. R. (1975). A semantic atlas of emotional concepts. *JSAS Catalogue of Selected Documents in Psychology, 5,* 330 (Ms. No. 421).

Batson, C. D., Coke, J. S., Chard, F., Smith, D., & Taliaferro, A. (1979). Generality of the "glow of goodwill": Effects of mood on helping and information acquisition. *Social Psychology Quarterly, 42,* 176–179.

Boucher, J., & Ekman, P. (1965). *A replication of Schlosberg's evaluation of Woodworth's scale of emotion.* Paper presented at a meeting of the Western Psychological Association.

Bower, G. H. (1981). Mood and memory. *American Psychologist, 36,* 129–148.

Bruner, J. S., & Tagiuri, R. (1954). The perception of people. In G. Lindzey (Ed.), *Handbook of social psychology* (Vol. 2, pp. 634–654). Reading, MA: Addison-Wesley.

Bush, L. E., II (1973). Individual differences multidimensional scaling of adjectives denoting feelings. *Journal of Personality and Social Psychology, 25,* 50–57.

Buzby, D. E. (1924). The interpretation of facial expressions. *American Journal of Psychology, 35,* 602–604.

Cliff, N., & Young, F. W. (1968). On the relation between unidimensional judgments and multidimensional scaling. *Organizational Behavior and Human Performance, 3,* 269–285.

Daly, E. M., Lancee, W. J., Polivy, J. (1983). *A conical model for the taxonomy of emotional experience. Journal of Personality and Social Psychology, 45,* 443–457.

Duffy, E. (1957). The psychological significance of the concept of arousal or activation. *Psychological Review, 64,* 265–275.

Dutton, D., & Aron, A. (1974). Some evidence for heightened sexual attraction under conditions of high anxiety. *Journal of Personality and Social Psychology, 30,* 510–517.

Ekman, P. (1972). Universals and cultural differences in facial expressions of emotion. In J. K. Cole (Ed.), *Nebraska Symposium on Motivation, 1971.* Lincoln, NE: University of Nebraska Press.

Ekman, P., & Friesen, W. V. (1976). *Pictures of facial affect.* Palo Alto, CA: Consulting Psychologists Press.

Ekman, P., Friesen, W. V., & Ellsworth, P. (1972). *Emotion in the human face.* New York: Pergamon.

Fehr, B., & Russell, J. A. (1984). Concept of emotion viewed from a prototype perspective. *Journal of Experimental Psychology: General, 113,* 464–486.

Fillenbaum, S., & Rapoport, A. (1971). *Structures in the subjective lexicon.* New York: Academic Press.

Frankenhaeuser, M. (1979). Psychoneuroendocrine approaches to the study of emotion as related to stress and coping. In H. E. Howe, Jr., & R. A. Dienstbier (Eds.), *Nebraska Symposium on Motivation, 1978.* Lincoln, NE: University of Nebraska Press.

Freed, E. X. (1978). Alcohol and mood: An updated review. *International Journal of the Addictions, 13,* 173–200.

Gerner, R. H., Catlin, D. H., Gorelick, D. A., Hui, K. K., & Li, C. H. (1980). Beta-endorphin: Intravenous infusion causes behavioral change in psychiatric inpatients. *Archives of General Psychiatry, 37,* 642–647.

Gotlib, I. H., & Meyer, J. P. (1986). Factor analysis of the Multiple Affect Adjective Check List: A separation of positive and negative affect. *Journal of Personality and Social Psychology, 50,* 1161–1165.

Green, R. S., & Cliff, N. (1975). Multidimensional comparisons of structures of vocally and facially expressed emotions. *Perception & Psychophysics, 17,* 429–438.

Herron, E. W. (1969). The Multiple Affect Adjective Check List: A critical analysis. *Journal of Clinical Psychology, 25,* 46–53.

Herron, E. W., Bernstein, L., & Rosen, H. (1968). Psychometric analysis of the Multiple Affect Adjective Check List: MAACL-today. *Journal of Clinical Psychology, 24,* 448–450.

Izard, C. E. (1971). *The face of emotion.* New York: Appleton-Century-Crofts.

Izard, C. E. (1972). *Patterns of emotions.* New York: Academic Press.

Izard, C. E. (1977). *Human emotions.* New York: Plenum.

Jacobs, A., Capek, L., & Meehan, J. P. (1959). The development of an adjective check list to measure affective states. *Psychological Newsletter, 10,* 115–118.

Kenrick, D. T., Cialdini, R. B., & Linder, D. E. (1979). Misattribution under fear-producing circumstances: Four failures to replicate. *Personality and Social Psychology Bulletin, 5,* 329–334.

Leventhal, H. (1974). Emotions: A basic problem for social psychology. In C. Nemeth (Ed.), *Social psychology: Classic and contemporary integrations.* Chicago: Rand McNally.

Levi, L. (1965). The urinary output of adrenaline and noradrenaline during pleasant and unpleasant emotional states. *Psychosomatic Medicine, 27,* 80–85.

Lindsley, D. B. (1951). Emotion. In S. S. Stevens (Ed.), *Handbook of experimental psychology.* New York: Wiley.

Lorr, M., & Shea, T. M. (1979). Are mood states bipolar? *Journal of Personality Assessment, 43,* 468–472.

Lubin, B., & Zuckerman, M. (1967). Affective and perceptual–cognitive patterns in sensitivity training groups. *Psychological Reports, 21,* 365–376.

Lundberg, U., & Devine, B. (1975). Negative similarities. *Education and Psychological Measurement, 35,* 797–807.

Mackay, C., Cox, T., Burrows, G., & Lazzerini, T. (1978). An inventory for the measurement of self-reported stress and arousal. *British Journal of Social and Clinical Psychology, 17,* 283–284.

Mandler, G. (1984). *Mind and body: Psychology of emotion and stress.* New York: Norton.

Maslach, C. (1979a). Negative emotional biasing of unexplained arousal. *Journal of Personality and Social Psychology, 37,* 953–969.

Maslach, C. (1979b). The emotional consequences of arousal without reason. In C. E. Izard (Ed.), *Emotions in personality and psychopathology.* New York: Plenum.

McNair, D. M., & Lorr, M. (1964). An analysis of mood in neurotics. *Journal of Abnormal and Social Psychology, 69,* 620–627.

McNair, D. M., Lorr, M., & Droppleman, L. F. (1971). *Manual of the Profile of Mood States*. San Diego, CA: Educational and Industrial Testing Services.

Meddis, R. (1972). Bipolar factors in mood adjective checklists. *British Journal of Social and Clinical Psychology, 11*, 178–184.

Mehrabian, A., & Russell, J. A. (1974). *An approach to environmental psychology*. Cambridge, MA: MIT Press.

Nowlis, V. (1965). Research with the Mood Adjective Check List. In S. S. Tomkins & C. E. Izard (Eds.), *Affect, cognitive, and personality*. New York: Springer.

Plutchik, R. (1958). Outlines of a new theory of emotion. *Transactions of the New York Academy of Sciences, 20*, 394–403.

Plutchik, R. (1962). *The emotions: Fact, theories, and a new model*. New York: Random House.

Plutchik, R. (1970). Emotions, evolution, and adaptive processes. In M. Arnold (Ed.), *Feelings and emotions*. New York: Academic Press.

Plutchik, R. (1980). *Emotion: A psychoevolutionary synthesis*. New York: Harper & Row.

Polivy, J. (1981). On the induction of emotion in the laboratory: Discrete moods or multiple affect states? *Journal of Personality and Social Psychology, 41*, 803–817.

Roth, S., & Kubal, L. (1975). The effects of noncontingent reinforcement on tasks of differing importance: Facilitation and learned helplessness effects. *Journal of Personality and Social Psychology, 32*, 680–691.

Royal, D. C., & Hays, W. L. (1959). Empirical dimensions of emotional behavior. *Acta Psychologica, 15*, 419.

Russell, J. A. (1978). Evidence of convergent validity on the dimensions of affect. *Journal of Personality and Social Psychology, 36*, 1152–1168.

Russell, J. A. (1979). Affective space is bipolar. *Journal of Personality and Social Psychology, 37*, 345–356.

Russell, J. A. (1980). A circumplex model of affect. *Journal of Personality and Social Psychology, 39*, 1161–1178.

Russell, J. A. (1983). Pancultural aspects of the human conceptual organization of emotions. *Journal of Personality and Social Psychology, 45*, 1281–1288.

Russell, J. A., & Bond, C. R. (1980). Individual differences in beliefs concerning emotions conducive to alcohol use. *Journal of Studies on Alcohol, 41*, 753–759.

Russell, J. A., & Bullock, M. (1985). Multidimensional scaling of emotional facial expressions of emotion: Similarity from preschoolers to adults. *Journal of Personality and Social Psychology, 48*, 1290–1298.

Russell, J. A., & Bullock, M. (1986). Fuzzy concepts and the perception of emotion in facial expressions. *Social Cognition, 4*, 309–341.

Russell, J. A., & Fehr, B. (1987). Relativity in the perception of emotion in facial expressions. *Journal of Experimental Psychology: General, 116*, 223–237.

Russell, J. A., & Lanius, U. (1984). Adaptation level and the affective appraisal of environments. *Journal of Environmental Psychology, 4*, 119–135.

Russell, J. A., & Mehrabian, A. (1975). The mediating role of emotions in alcohol use. *Journal of Studies on Alcohol, 36*, 1508–1536.

Russell, J. A., & Mehrabian, A. (1977a). Environmental effects on drug use. *Environmental Psychology and Nonverbal Behavior, 2*, 109–123.

Russell, J. A., & Mehrabian, A. (1977b). Evidence for a three-factor theory of emotions. *Journal of Research in Personality, 11*, 273–294.

Russell, J. A., & Ridgeway, D. (1983). Dimensions underlying children's emotion concepts. *Developmental Psychology, 19*, 795–804.

Russell, J. A., & Snodgrass, J. (1987). Emotion and the environment. In D. Stokols & I. Altman (Eds.), *Handbook of environmental psychology*. New York: Wiley.

Russell, J. A., Ward, L. M., & Pratt, G. (1981). The affective quality attributed to environments: A factor analytic study. *Environment and Behavior, 13,* 259–288.

Russell, J. A., Weiss, A., & Mendelsohn, G. A. (in press). The Affect Grid: A single-item scale of pleasure and arousal. *Journal of Personality and Social Psychology.*

Ryman, D. H., Biersner, R. J., & La Rocco, J. M. (1974). Reliabilities and validities of the mood questionnaire. *Psychological Reports, 35,* 479–484.

Schachter, S., & Singer, J. E. (1962). Cognitive, social, and physiological determinants of emotional state. *Psychological Review, 69,* 379–399.

Schlosberg, H. (1952). The description of facial expressions in terms of two dimensions. *Journal of Experimental Psychology, 44,* 229–237.

Selye, H. (1952). *The story of the adaptation syndrome.* Montreal, Quebec, Canada: Acta.

Shepard, R. N. (1962). The analysis of proximities: Multidimensional scaling with an unknown distance function. *Psychometrika, 27,* 125–139, 219–246.

Smith, C. A., & Ellsworth, P. C. (1985). Patterns of cognitive appraisal in emotion. *Journal of Personality and Social Psychology, 48,* 813–838.

Snyder, S. H. (1974). *Madness and the brain.* New York: McGraw-Hill.

Spielberger, C. D., Gorsuch, R. L., & Lushene, R. E. (1970). *Manual for the State–Trait Anxiety Inventory.* Palo Alto, CA: Consulting Psychologists Press.

Stone, L. A., & Coles, G. J. (1970). Correlational similarity: The basis for a new revised method of similarity analysis. *Studia Psychologica (Bratislava), 12,* 258–265.

Svensson, E. (1978). Mood: Its structure and measurement. *Goteborg Psychological Reports, 8,* 1–19.

Thayer, R. E. (1967). Measurement of activation through self-report. *Psychological Reports, 20,* 663–678.

Thayer, R. E. (1978). Toward a psychological theory of multidimensional activation (arousal). *Motivation and Emotion, 2,* 1–34.

Tomkins, S. S. (1962–1963). *Affect, imagery, consciousness* (2 vols.). New York: Springer.

Turner, C. K. (1986). *Validity and artifact in the measurement of self-induced mood.* Unpublished Ph.D. dissertation. Los Angeles: University of California.

Velten, E. (1968). A laboratory task for the induction of mood states. *Behavior Research and Therapy, 6,* 473–482.

Wallace, A. F. C., & Carson, M. T. (1973). Sharing and diversity in emotion terminology. *Ethos, 1,* 1–29.

Woodworth, R. S. (1938). *Experimental psychology.* New York: Holt.

Woodworth, R. S., & Schlosberg, H. (1954). *Experimental psychology* (rev. ed.). New York: Holt, Rinehart & Winston.

Zuckerman, M. (1980). To risk or not to risk. In K. R. Blankstein, P. Pliner, & J. Polivy (Eds.), *Assessment and modification of emotional behavior.* New York: Plenum.

Zuckerman, M., & Lubin, B. (1965). *Manual for the Multiple Affect Adjective Check List.* San Diego, CA: Educational and Industrial Testing Services.

Chapter 5

THE DICTIONARY OF AFFECT IN LANGUAGE

CYNTHIA M. WHISSELL

ABSTRACT

This chapter examines the Dictionary of Affect in Language, *one of many acceptable routes to the measurement of emotion, in terms of research conducted with the dictionary and in terms of a framework of metameasurement that includes the question of concept definition and a consideration of the state–trait distinction. The* Dictionary of Affect *contains over 4000 words and each word in the dictionary is accompanied by a score along the affective dimensions of Evaluation and Activation. In use, the dictionary can be applied to any verbal material, ranging from freely produced text to lists of words and passages of literature. Significant effects associated with scores, which are based on the dictionary, are summarized, the reliability and validity of the instrument are discussed, and some potential limitations are suggested. In conclusion, the role of the dictionary and its potential for future development are considered.*

A GENERAL APPROACH TO THE PROBLEM OF MEASUREMENT

The question "Can we measure emotion?" cannot be answered by a simple "yes" or "no," since both a positive and a negative answer would have to be qualified in terms of the existing research that deals with the concept. In this chapter, the positive answer ("Yes, we can measure emotion") is put forward

113

EMOTION
Theory, Research, and Experience
Volume 4

and some of its limitations are discussed. One possible approach to the measurement of emotion is then proposed and its limitations and applications are specified in terms of the qualifications of the general positive answer. This approach is based on the affective tone of English-language words: it is a logical extension of previous theoretical work (Russell, 1978; Osgood, 1969) and its bipolar ruler is *A Dictionary of Affect in Language* (Whissell, Fournier, Pelland, Weir, & Makarec, 1986).

CONCEPT DEFINITION

Attempts to define the concept *emotion* (feeling, aesthesis, passion) originated in the domains of religion and philosophy. Such attempts are historically much older than the science of psychology, of which the first emotion-defining theorist is generally recognized to be William James, whose "What Is an Emotion?" appeared in *Mind* in 1884 (see James, 1967). Within psychology, attempts to define emotion have been of three kinds: theoretical, encyclopedic, and definition by example. Highly structured theories, such as those of Freud, Cannon, or James, postulate what emotion should be and the adherents of the theory then rigorously assimilate all instances of *emotion* into the theory. A wide range of theories, introduced by their proponents, is found in the first volume of this series (Plutchik & Kellerman, 1980). Accommodation characterizes encyclopedic definitions of emotion, where all instances of the concept name are collected noncritically in an attempt to formulate the concept definition. For example, Whissell (1984) defined emotion in terms of a literature search of the *Psychological Abstracts* for the descriptor *emotion*. Definition by example is the main recourse of psychology's standard "naive" population: first- and second-year university students define emotion either by synonym or by example. Examples are offered as definitions in statements such as "emotion is like seeing a bear in the forest" or "emotions are feelings like love and hate." Psychoanalysis incorporated examples in the form of case studies, while James unashamedly used "a dark moving form in the woods" and "the heart-swelling and lachrymal effusion" which occurs when we listen to "heroic narrative" as examples for his concept of emotion.

Theoretical definitions, because of their nature, are most likely to fail in convincingly incorporating all instances which employ the label *emotion* into a single theory. Encyclopedic definitions are sufficiently inclusive but are simultaneously guilty of fuzziness—the lack of a clear rule system of inclusion, which is especially important for determining boundary instances of the concept. Definition by example communicates specific instances with empathetic clarity, but fails to address either the rules or the boundaries of the concept. Fehr and Russell (1984) espouse definition by example (in their words, "prototype") precisely *because* they considered emotion to be a fuzzy concept. In such a case, definition by example becomes a powerful technique for the description of an entity without clear limits rather than a naive response equating concept with example.

DEFINITION AS A PRECONDITION OF MEASUREMENT

The entire body of research in emotion, from James' day to the present (over 900 abstracts were keyed with the descriptor *emotions* in the *Psychological Abstracts* in the last 10 years) is the evidence which we may use to conclude that scientists have been addressing the question of the measurement of emotion for over a century in the absence of a definition that is universally accepted.

Researchers holding that the most important characteristic of measurement is its *reliability* (represented by the *replicability* and *objectivity* requirements of the scientific method) rely on operational definitions of emotion, which are communicable but not necessarily exhaustive with respect to the concept. For those whose first requirement is equated with the *validity* of measurement, no claim to measurement can be made unless the concept is first defined and then connected in a satisfactory manner to the measure under consideration. Members of this second group who are convinced that there must be some set of events whose membership distinguishes the concept of *emotion* from the concept of *green vegetables,* or, more problematically, concepts such as *stress,* have tried to establish a definition of emotion which can then become a yardstick for the validity of measurement.

Theorists are restricted by the requirement of validity with respect to their theory, and the measures which they use must clearly reflect this requirement [as, for example, do the various scales included by Plutchik (1980) in his appendices, or by Izard (1972) in his discussion of the Differential Emotion Scale].

THE STATE–TRAIT DICHOTOMY

In addition to the fact that humans frequently report the experience of a number of different emotions in rapid succession, we have evidence of responses, labeled as emotional reactions (such as skin conductance, which is controlled by the autonomic nervous system), whose latency and duration combined are less than 5 seconds. At the other extreme of the continuum, humans have reported the constant presence of emotions such as depression and anxiety, which govern their "style of life," and psychosomatic patterns of autonomic nervous system reactivity can be characteristic of individuals on the same time scale (Grings & Dawson, 1978). In a detailed treatment of the state–trait distinction, Allen and Potkay (1981) deal with the implicit but not necessarily defensible assumption underlying the use of state–trait terminology in a dichotomous manner. Allen and Potkay argue that the state–trait distinction is arbitrary (1981, p. 917), and that dramatic differences in the duration factor between variables lead to an insufficient treatment of problems such as the classification of short-duration/high-frequency-of-occurrence variables.

Mood scales (e.g., the Multiple Affect Adjective Check List) are used by Allen and Potkay to illustrate their claim that "one person's trait is another person's state" (1981, p. 919). The dire "consequences of uncritical acceptance" of the state–trait distinction, which include a reliance on post hoc explanations of the results of personality research, are stressed as well (1981, p. 925). In their conclusions, the authors note that uncritical acceptance of the state–trait distinction encourages the researcher to ignore his duty: When he should be defining his variables in terms of factors such as frequency, latency, duration, and autocorrelation, he opts for a binary label with limited meaning. The repudiation of a state–trait distinction redirects the emphasis of the description of various measures from binary labeling to the accurate description of variables in terms of several time factors.

Although it would be tempting to equate mood scales with state measures, and personality inventories with trait measures, even the most cursory examination of existing materials brings some problems to light. Depression, for example, appears as a score in both kinds of instruments [Nowlis' Mood Adjective Check List (Nowlis, 1965), as well as the Minnesota Multiphasic Personality Inventory], and anxiety is transformed from a state into a trait by a minor modification in test instructions (State–Trait Anxiety Inventory). Also, mood instruments such as Plutchik's 1980 *Mood Profile Index* have been known to employ trait-oriented language (the subject's *usual* mood is asked for, and the word usual is italicized). An alternative way to consider the state–trait issue is to assume that measures of emotion are distributed within a multidimensional space whose two most important dimensions are duration and frequency.

VISCERAL ACTIVITY AND FACIAL EXPRESSION

Is some measure of visceral activity necessary to the measurement of emotion? This question arises for at least five reasons. First, a reference to visceral activity is the lowest common denominator for encyclopedic definitions of emotion [the dictionaries of Chaplin (1968) and English & English (1958) both include visceral activity in their definitions of the term *emotion*]. Second, theoretical definitions of emotion generally recognize the visceral component, although they do not all emphasize it to the same degree. Third, the theories of emotion most frequently cited at the introductory psychology level, as exemplified by the contents of textbooks designed for such courses, include what is referred to as the "James–Lange" theory of emotion (Cannon, 1927), whose reported emphasis is visceral. Though James emphasized skeletal reactions, and Lange emphasized vascular ones, the portion of their theories that has been perpetuated at this level is predominantly visceral. Fourth, the common usage of the English language includes many visceral references to emotional experience ("gut feelings" and fear "in the pit of" one's stomach). Fifth, the continued popularity of autonomic nervous system (ANS)-related measures as indicators of emotions suggests that such measures are indispensible to the measurement of emotion. Although the measures taken by a polygraph (heart rate, breathing rate, and galvanic skin response) are not taken in the pit of the stomach or in the intestines, they reflect the activity of the same controlling system—the ANS.

However, each of the arguments for the inclusion of visceral activity in the measurement of emotion is associated with a counterargument that supports a negative answer. First, encyclopedic definitions are not exclusively visceral (cognitive elements are also frequently referred to). Second, theories that recognize the presence of visceral activity do not necessarily assign a primary role to it. Cannon's critique of James' theory suggests that although we may be viscerally active during the experience of an emotion, such activity is too slow (long latency) and too diffuse and undifferentiated to be the crucial determinant of the experience (Cannon, 1927). Third, the James–Lange theories were, as stated above, more than visceral theories, each admitting to cognitive responses as well as bodily responses as part of the total emotional syndrome. Fourth, the common usage of the English language refers to *vague feelings* as indicators of an emotional experience, and is not limited to viscerally descriptive language. Finally, the popularity of a response measure is not always a direct linear function of its validity.

Measures reflecting the activity of the autonomic nervous system have enjoyed great popularity for a number of years. In the present research literature on emotion, facial expression has been frequently employed both as a stimulus (Lanzetta & Kleck, 1970) and as a response (Ekman, Friesen, & Ancoli, 1980). The fact that facial expression can communicate affect (as well as inducing it in the person who holds the expression) has been established in a variety of studies reviewed by Laird (1984) and again by Whissell (1985). However, there are documented cases where facial expression has not affected emotional experience and cases where emotional experiences have occurred in the absence of measurable differences in facial expression. On the basis of this data, Whissell (1985) has argued that the role of facial expression is that of "one of many" measures of emotion and that facial expression (or its measurement) is not indispensible to the concept of emotion.

THE MEASUREMENT OF EMOTIONAL STIMULI
AND EMOTIONAL RESPONSES

THE S–O–R MODEL

The Stimulus–Organism–Response (S–O–R) model is not completely descriptive of emotional responding. In use, it would probably lead mainly to errors of omission because even multiple S–R chains are not complex enough to describe the interactions between the many processes that may be involved in emotion. The endocrine system, the visceral ANS, the higher levels of the ANS (the hypothalamus and the limbic system), and the frontal lobes of the cortex are not interconnected in a direct linear fashion, and their interactions cannot be sufficiently well approximated by a model of successive linear stimuli and responses, regardless of how many recursions the model allows. In spite of this limitation, the body of research in emotion has tended to follow (explicitly or implicitly) the model in which a stimulus leads to a response, or an independent variable (IV) produces changes measured in terms of a dependent variable (DV). In use, the S–O–R model does not preclude the existence of interactions—it simply focuses measurement. Thus, while Klinnert, Campos, Sorce, Emde, and Svejda (1983) are perfectly correct in suggesting that interactive models are an advancement on linear ones, and that differences between dependent and independent variables become blurred in an interactive model, the S–O–R model (which is not satisfactory as a final answer to the question of ''what is emotion?'') serves as a satisfactory pragmatic approach to measurement.

Within this model, the description and measurement of stimuli and responses is an important prerequisite. A random selection of 25 abstracts of research on emotion that have been included in the *Psychological Abstracts* in the last 10 years was used to generate the sample of stimuli and responses listed in Table 5.1. It is obvious from this table that some stimuli, such as facial expressions, and some responses, such as the identification of emotions, are more commonly studied than others. However, neither this list nor any other list in existence at present provides an exhaustive coverage of potential stimuli for emotional responding, or potential responses.

Some of the research with quantified emotional stimuli has stressed the innate tendency of an organism to respond to particular stimuli in particular ways. This view of emotion may be traced back to Darwin's classic, *The Expression of the Emotions in Man and Animals* (1872), and it is extended in more recent treatments of the role of evolution (Plutchik, 1980) and the role of facial expression (Ekman, 1973) in emotion.

In his studies of facial expression, Ekman (1982) has suggested that learning and culture are *not* important determinants of the ability to respond to facial expression. When loud noises and/or loss of support fail to produce a startle

TABLE 5.1
STIMULI AND REPONSES FROM 25 RANDOMLY SELECTED ABSTRACTS
BEARING THE DESCRIPTOR *Emotion*[a]

	Stimulus	Response
1.	Training in positive social–emotional behavior	Rate of emission of the behavior
2.	Images of faces expressing emotion, masked, and highlighted by white spots at key positions	Recognition of the emotion
3.	Emotional faces presented to a right-hemisphere lesion patient	Recognition of facial expression
4.	Mood of characters in a story	Imperative nature of verbal statements attributed to each character (is the character giving orders?)
5.	Orienting, emotional, and aversive stimuli	Amplitude and recovery time for skin conductance R
6.	Emotion expressed vocally	Identification of the emotion
7.	Emotional labels	Ranking of importance
8.	Rorschach cards	"Affective pull" (pleasant, unpleasant)
9.	Descriptions of emotional situations	Attribution of causality of the emotion (kindergardeners)
10.	Questionnaires	"Affective profiles" of psychotic vs general patients
11.	Questionnaires	"Personal orientation" after participation in "feeling therapy"
12.	Schizoid pathology	Experience of emptiness
13.	Disasters	Emotions of the survivors (e.g., guilt, anxiety)
14.	Head injury	"Loss of pleasure" syndrome
15.	Intrafamilial emotional expression	Schizophrenic relapse
16.	Expression of remorse by a violator	Evaluative judgment of violator's character
17.	Facial expression of emotion	Recognition
18.	Facial expression of emotion	Recognition in left and right visual field
19.	Verbal conditioning	Self-referenced statements of affect
20.	Past emotional experiences	Ratings along cognitive dimensions
21.	Geographic distance	Emotional involvement (degree)
22.	Vocal expression of emotion in an unknown language	Recognition of emotion
23.	Teaching of a mental health unit on "affect"	Self-awareness
24.	Facial expression	Recognition by normal and emotionally disturbed children
25.	Senders of truthful and nontruthful messages	Segments of output (from speech and videotape)

[a]Abstracts of experimental reports were sampled, regardless of language. Dissertations and theoretical articles were omitted from the population. The abstracts used appeared between 1976 and 1985, inclusive.

response in a neonate, the failure to respond is interpreted as an indicator of neurological pathology, because the stimuli do not have to be learned (conditioned) in order to be effective. At the other extreme of the continuum, emotional responses to written text or linguistic stimuli (such as science fiction or soap operas) depend heavily on the acquisition of language. Responses to a mood questionnaire are also dependent on acquired linguistic skills.

PROBLEMS WITH THE MEASUREMENT OF
EMOTION IN DEVELOPING ORGANISMS

There are dramatic changes in an infant's repertoire of emotional responses, and an equally dramatic differentiation among the stimuli to which the infant will respond within the first year of his life (Murphy, 1983). The appearance of smiling (within 2 months), laughter (within 5 months), attachment to mother (second half of the first year), and fear of strangers (also in the second half of the first year) all illustrate the existence of age-related changes that are dependent on innate factors, on maturation, and, to some extent, on learning. Pouting and frowning (two easily identifiable facial expressions of emotion) appear during the second year of life, and the response of fear is prompted by an increasingly complex series of stimuli (loud noises, absence of mother, the dark, monsters, and failure in school are sources of fear that appear successively between birth and 7 years). Changes in the direction of increasing complexity are clearly observable across time from birth to adolescence, but not so clearly observable thereafter.

Cognitive development follows a similar path, and many theories (emotional and/or cognitive) have misleadingly limited their predictions of age-related changes to the age range of 0 to 12 or 16 years [Erikson's theory is an exception (Erikson, 1968)]. A *middle-aged crisis*, or an attack of *death anxiety* may occur anywhere from a person's thirtieth to their final year of life. Both of these age-related reactions have strong emotional components. At no point in the age continuum is it safe to assume that the human organism will remain emotionally stable and that this can be assessed (quantified, measured) in a consistent way with an invariant set of instruments. This is especially true if the stimulus or response being measured involves language (there is plentiful evidence that language acquisition and verbal intelligence continue to increase well beyond adolescence).

The emotional response of *fear* is activated by different stimuli at different stages of maturational development. The same stimulus (a drawing of a monster) might lead to different responses from subjects at different stages of development. A neonate would respond to the optical characteristics of the picture, such as contrast, contour, and color. A 4-year old might respond with fear, and a 12-

year-old might respond with amusement to the same picture. Among others, Murphy (1983) has commented on the problem of "adulto-morphism" in the understanding of infant emotions. The corresponding problem at the other extreme of the age scale could be termed "jejeunomorphism"—the attempt to describe the emotions of mature adults in terms of theories based on the behavior of young adults and adolescents. Given that age-related differences may always be assumed to exist (whether they are based on maturation or learning), the researcher is obliged to exercise some care in employing a measure of emotion that is suitable to the age and learning history of his subjects, and further must expect that an "individual error" component will generally modify even such carefully selected measures.

LANGUAGE AS A BASIS FOR EMOTIONAL MEASUREMENT

LINGUISTIC AND NONLINGUISTIC COMMUNICATION OF EMOTION

Many experimental reports illustrate the importance of channels other than language in specific experimental situations. For Wilson, Hull, and Johnson (1981), self-report of internal states (a linguistic communication) is an adjunct to behavioral changes in a self-attribution task. According to Apple and Hecht (1982), verbal communication of affect is not always as effective as vocal communication (where a voice is heard, but semantic content is disguised). In an experiment reported by Krauss, Apple, Morency, Wenzel, and Winton (1981), the verbal channel was the one most communicative of evaluative judgments, but other channels were communicative as well. In comparing the relative accuracy of face, body, and speech judgments of personality and emotion, Ekman, Friesen, O'Sullivan, and Scherer (1980) concluded that the most informative channel varied according to the type of attribute being judged.

Although the reports quoted above illustrate the effectiveness of alternative channels of communication, most of them incorporate evidence for the effectiveness of language as a communicator. For Wilson et al. (1981), verbal information was transmitted when subjects were "induced" to describe internal states. In the experiment reported by Apple and Hecht (1981), semantic content was important to the identification of the emotion *sadness*. For Krauss et al. (1981), the verbal channel was the single most effective channel, while in the report of Ekman et al. (1980), the verbal channel most accurately communicated the distinction *expressive–unexpressive*.

Language is not the only channel suitable to the communication of emotion: it is, however, one of the "cheapest" stimulus or response measures available, because it is easily obtained and does not require an extensive support technology. In addition, the language response is insensitive to certain artifacts that plague other potential measures of human emotion (muscle movements obscure responses in both polygraphic and electroencephalographic recordings, while angle of facial presentation is a problem for pupilography and for the scoring of facial expression).

Verbal responding can be measured for emotional content in a number of different ways, ranging from the frequency of self-references (use of the word *I*) by psychotics and neurotics (Lorenz & Cobb, 1954) to a scoring of *tension* based on the dimensions of the semantic differential (Anderson & McMaster, 1982). Naturally, a cheap measure is only valuable if it is theoretically and ecologically valid, as well as sufficiently reliable to satisfy the requirements of science. Measures of emotion based on language have shown evidence of reliability and validity in a number of different research situations (Anderson & McMaster, 1982; Heise, 1965; Lorenz & Cobb, 1954; Whissell et al., 1986).

INTERRELATEDNESS OF MULTIPLE MEASURES OF THE SAME CONCEPT

Like the concept *arousal* (with which it shares several problems), the concept *emotion* admits to a large population of acceptable measures. Although each measure is in some way tied to the concept, the interrelationships among measures can be strong, weak, positive, negative, nonlinear, or even nonexistent. Russell (1978) identifies two independent bipolar dimensions of emotion in his model of "affective space." Although both Evaluation and Activation are measures of the same concept, their correlation is by definition zero. Russell discusses possible additional dimensions of affect, all of which would also, by definition, be independent of the first two dimensions and of each other. Osgood's three factors (Evaluation, Activation, and Potency) are independent of each other. Although Buck (1983) notes that, in some contexts, "the simplest and perhaps most common way to eliminate the dilemmas posed by the complex relationships between various measures of emotion is to choose and analyze a single measure" (p. 270), he does not argue in favor of this solution.

THE DICTIONARY OF AFFECT IN LANGUAGE

It *is* possible to provide quantitative data with respect to the concept *emotion;* the use and understanding of such data is, however, subject to the limitations and qualifications described in this chapter. Any measure claiming to reflect the concept of emotion may be deemed to do so appropriately if it is understood that the concept itself is not fully defined, that the measure has to be accompanied by proof of reliability and at least partial validity, that the measure should be described in terms of time-dependent factors, that it is not a unique or exclusive measure of the concept, that it is not independent of the characteristics of the subjects being measured, and that is need not be highly correlated to other quantifications of the same concept. One measure of emotion that may be viewed within this framework is the *Dictionary of Affect in Language* (Whissell et al., 1986).

The *Dictionary of Affect* includes approximately 4000 English words. Words used by different experimenters (Conte & Plutchik, 1981; Russell, 1980; Whissell, 1981) and common English words with affective connotations (culled from West, 1953) are included in the list. Each word is described in terms of a score along the dimension of Activation (or Arousal, mean = 4.00; standard deviation = 1.00; range 1–7) and a second score along the dimension of Evaluation (or Pleasantness, mean = 4.00; standard deviation = 1.00; range 1–7); both scores are based on ratings provided by subjects. Any verbal materials, including those produced by subjects and those designed by the experimenter to be administered to subjects, can be scored in terms of the dimensions of the *Dictionary of Affect.*

The most recent version of the dictionary is discussed by Whissell et al. (1986) and evidence for reliability (full test–retest and test–retest of a random subsample) and validity [concurrent validity evaluated against word scores from the original experiments by Russell (1980), Conte and Plutchik (1981), and Whissell (1981) and construct validity of the list in use] is provided. In addition, some problems and limitations of the dictionary, such as a lower reliability for the Activation dimension, and the importance and/or usefulness of words which are close to the mean for both dimensions, are also discussed. In use, the dictionary works best when applied to passages or lists (as opposed to single words), because it allows for the evaluation of the affective tone of the entire passage or list. The mean score for the passage along each dimension, the variability of the scores on each dimension, and the frequency of occurrence of words at either extreme of each dimension are all emotional measures that may be generated by the dictionary (Whissell & Dewson, 1986; Whissell et al., 1986). A sample of some listings from the dictionary is found in Table 5.2, and an example of the scoring procedure is given in Table 5.3. According to the results described in Table 5.4, the passage from I Corinthians (*Good News Bible,* 1976) is quite positive (4.73) and moderately aroused (4.25). Variability is comparable to that of the dictionary list (i.e., 1). The most commonly appearing group of words is the one that is high in both dimensions (*pleasant* and *active, n* = 14)—a group that includes the key word of this passage (*love;* Evaluation = 6.2, Activation = 5.5).

Ratings from an earlier version of the dictionary were used to score free-form passages written by subjects in response to imaginary situations distinguished by

TABLE 5.2

A Sample of 107 Words from the *Dictionary of Affect* with Scores along the Dimensions of Evaluation and Activation[a]

Word	Activation	Evaluation	Word	Activation	Evaluation
Adventurous	4.3	5.9	Distrustful	3.8	2.8
Affectionate	4.7	5.4	Eager	5.0	5.1
Afraid	4.9	3.4	Ecstatic	5.2	5.5
Aggressive	5.9	2.9	Embarrassed[b]	4.4	3.1
Agreeable	4.3	5.2	Empty	3.1	3.8
Amazed	5.9	5.5	Enthusiastic	5.1	4.8
Ambivalent	3.2	4.2	Envious	5.3	2.0
Amused	4.9	5.0	Furious	5.6	3.7
Angry	4.2	2.7	Gleeful	5.3	4.8
Annoyed	4.4	2.5	Gloomy	2.4	3.2
Antagonistic	5.3	2.5	Greedy	4.9	3.4
Anticipatory[b]	3.9	4.7	Grouchy	4.4	2.9
Anxious	6.0	2.3	Guilty	4.0	1.1
Apathetic	3.0	4.3	Happy	5.3	5.3
Ashamed	3.2	2.3	Helpless	3.5	2.8
Astonished	5.9	4.7	Hopeful[b]	4.7	5.2
Attentive	5.3	4.3	Hopeless	4.0	3.1
Bashful	2.0	2.7	Hostile	4.0	1.7
Bewildered	3.1	2.3	Impatient	3.4	3.2
Bitter	6.6	4.0	Impulsive	3.1	4.8
Boastful	3.7	3.0	Indecisive	3.4	2.7
Bored	2.7	3.2	Intolerant	3.1	2.7
Calm	2.5	5.5	Irritated	5.5	3.3
Cautious	3.3	4.9	Jealous	6.1	3.4
Cheerful	5.2	5.0	Joyful	5.4	6.1
Confused	4.8	3.0	Loathful[b]	3.5	2.9
Contemptuous[b]	3.8	2.4	Lonely	3.9	3.3
Content	4.8	5.5	Meek	3.0	4.3
Contrary	2.9	3.7	Nervous	5.9	3.1
Cooperative[b]	3.1	5.1	Obedient	3.1	4.7
Critical	4.9	2.8	Obliging	2.7	3.0
Curious	5.2	4.2	Outraged[b]	4.3	3.2
Daring	5.3	4.4	Panicky[b]	5.4	3.6
Defiant	4.4	2.8	Patient	3.3	3.8
Delighted	4.2	6.4	Pensive	3.2	5.0
Demanding	5.3	4.0	Pleased	5.3	5.1
Depressed	4.2	3.1	Possessive	4.7	2.8
Despairing	4.1	2.0	Proud	4.7	5.3
Disagreeable[b]	5.0	3.7	Puzzled	2.6	3.8
Disappointed	5.2	2.4	Quarrelsome	4.6	2.6
Discouraged	4.2	2.9	Rebellious	5.2	4.0
Disgusted	5.0	3.2	Rejected	5.0	2.9
Disinterested	2.1	2.4	Remorseful	3.1	2.2
Dissatisfied	4.6	2.7	Resentful	5.1	3.0

TABLE 5.2   (*Continued*)

Word	Activation	Evaluation	Word	Activation	Evaluation
Sad	3.8	2.4	Surprised	6.5	5.2
Sarcastic	4.8	2.7	Suspicious[b]	4.4	3.0
Satisfied	4.1	4.9	Sympathetic	3.6	3.2
Scornful	5.4	4.9	Terrified	6.3	3.4
Self-controlled[b]	4.4	5.5	Trusting	3.4	5.2
Serene	4.3	4.9	Unaffectionate	3.6	2.1
Sociable	4.8	5.3	Unfriendly	4.3	1.6
Sorrowful	4.5	3.1	Wondering	3.3	5.2
Stubborn	4.9	3.1	Worried[b]	3.9	2.9
Submissive	3.4	3.1			

[a]From Plutchick's (1980, p. 170) population of emotional terms.

[b]The score given represents a close semantic equivalent (e.g., panic instead of panicky).

TABLE 5.3

AN EXAMPLE OF THE SCORING SYSTEM FOR THE *Dictionary of Affect*[a]

4.2/5.2   3.4/5.0   3.5/4.7   5.5/6.2 3.2/3.9
I may be able to speak the languages of men and even of angels, but if I have no love my speech is
            5.3/3.3   4.9/5.0   3.1/4.2
no more than a noisy gong or a clanging bell. I may have the gift of inspired preaching; I may have all
                  3.4/5.0   2.5/4.9 5.1/4.1   3.5/4.7
knowledge and understand all secrets; I may have all the faith needed to move mountains—but if I
    5.5/6.2   2.3/4.1   3.4/5.0   3.2/3.9 4.6/4.8
have no love I am nothing. I may give away everything I have and even give up my body to be
4.5/3.1 3.5/4.7   5.5/6.2   4.0/5.6 3.8/5.1 5.5/6.2 3.3/3.8   4.5/6.2   6.1/3.4
burned—but if I have no love this does me no good. Love is patient and kind; it is not jealous or
        4.7/5.3 5.5/6.2   3.4/2.9   5.1/2.9 5.5/6.2
conceited or proud; love is not ill-mannered or selfish or irritable; love does not keep a record of
3.2/3.3 5.5/6.2   5.3/5.3   4.8/1.5   5.3/5.3   4.7/5.7 5.5/6.2   3.2/3.9 4.7/5.2
wrongs; love is not happy with evil, but is happy with the truth. Love never gives up; and its hope,
2.5/4.9 3.0/4.4   3.6/2.8
faith, and patience never fail.

[a]Text from I Corinthians, Chapter 13, verses 1–7, (*Good News Bible*, 1976); scored by the circumplicial version of the dictionary that includes only words distant from the origin (4, 4) by one or more units. The first number represents Activation and the second represents Evaluation. Scores appear above the words to which they apply.

TABLE 5.4

VARIABLES GENERATED ON THE BASIS OF DICTIONARY SCORES FOR THE EXAMPLE IN TABLE 5.3

Hit rate = 29% scored words

Evaluation: M = 4.73; SD = 1.07
Activation: M = 4.25; SD = 1.04
Dictionary parameters: $\mu = 4$; $\sigma = 1$

Distribution of scored words according to quartiles from the entire dictionary:

		Evaluation			
		Lowest quartile	Middle 50%	Highest quartile	
	Lowest quartile	1	7	2	10 (23%)
Activation	Middle 50%	3	0	11	14 (33%)
	Highest quartile	3	2	14	19 (42%)
		7 (16%)	9 (21%)	27 (63%)	

their outcome ("A" grade, failing grade) and their locus of causality (internal, external). A more positive evaluation was evident for subjects responding to the hypothetically positive outcome and greater activation was evident for subjects responding to externally caused situations (Sweeney & Whissell, 1984). From ratings included in the early version of the dictionary, it was possible to show differences (some of which were predicted *a priori*) in the emotional content of responses to a set of imaginary situations such as job promotion and *not being taken seriously* (Whissell & Charuk, 1985); both Evaluation and Activation means were higher for the former situation. The complete dictionary was also used to score subjects' self-descriptions, which were produced in the form of a list of 10 or 20 words, and to score the descriptions of famous (i.e., popular) television characters produced in the same format. The Evaluation and Activation scores of self-descriptive lists were related to scores from a personality test, and clear differences in Evaluation and Activation characterized the famous roles that were rated by subjects (Whissell et al., 1986).

The dictionary has also been used as the basis of word selection for a dichotic listening task, where memory for words was found to be a joint function of the type of word (defined in terms of Evaluation and Activation) and the personality of the respondent. Existing passages of text were analyzed according to the dictionary (Whissell & Dewson, 1986), and differences in overall Evaluation and Activation were clearly evident both in terms of passage means and in terms of the use of words with extreme scores along either dimension. In recent (as yet unpublished) work, the *Dictionary of Affect* has discriminated between the headline text of three different newspapers in terms of the affective content of the headline material; *sensationalism* is operationally defined, in view of these data, as the use of words with a high level of Activation and words with a low level of Evaluation. When they were scored using our dictionary, titles of articles from the journal *Psychological Reports* satisfied the first criterion of sensationalism (they yielded a high mean for Activation), but were more positive than headlines from the North American newspapers (the mean for Evaluation for the titles was also high, whereas for newspaper headlines it was low).

In use, the *Dictionary of Affect* is capable of being applied to both short-term and long-term responses (mood description, personality description, reaction to immediate situations, and analysis of texts or diaries). Words having extreme scores along either dimension, or those distant from the origin of an Evaluation–Activation space, have proved to be more useful in the scoring of affect, whereas words close to the origin have been effectively used as controls in other situations (Whissell et al., 1986). The classification of words as *emotional* words has also been shown to be related to their distance from the origin (Whissell & Berezowski, 1986). Various circumplicial theories of affect (Plutchik, 1980; Russell, 1980) have already made the point that words close to the origin in a two-dimensional space are probably devoid of emotional connotations. A compact version of the *Dictionary of Affect* lists some 3000 words that are at least one unit (equal to one standard deviation) away from the origin in Evaluation–Activation space. The words listed in Table 5.2 are a subset of those proposed by Plutchik (1980, p. 170) as a "population of emotion terms." Of a total of 142 words, 119 were included in the *Dictionary of Affect*. Of these 119, 107 were at least one unit away from the origin in Evaluation–Activation space, while 12 were not; 23 words were not in this dictionary.

The first of two major advantages associated with the use of the *Dictionary of Affect* as an instrument for the measurement of emotion comes from the fact that subjects' responses are not restricted to a small set of choices in terms of ratings or in terms of yes–no responses to an inventory. Books, speeches, newspaper text, diaries, and freely produced oral or verbal materials may be analyzed using this dictionary because it includes a large population of affectively "loaded" words. This dictionary has been shown to have discriminative power in the scoring of such materials. The second advantage associated with the use of the *Dictionary of Affect* lies in its assessment of affect via the connotative rather than the denotative meaning of words: the importance of the affective connotations which underly language has been addressed at length by Osgood (e.g., 1969). The dictionary's first advantage is also, by extension, its first limitation. Although the scores that it produces will discriminate between subjects, situations, and texts, an appreciable portion of words in scored materials does not appear in this dictionary. This proportion has ranged from .15 to over .75 in different applications. Further research is in progress that was designed to identify additional words which should be included in the dictionary. Any word potentially occupying a position more than one unit distant from the origin in Evaluation–Activation space should be a candidate for inclusion in the list, since it conveys affective information.

CONCLUSIONS

When the *Dictionary of Affect,* which is a source of measurement for the concept *emotion,* is considered in the light of the points discussed in this chapter, the following specifications can be made:

Like any single source of measurement, the dictionary cannot be considered as a complete measure of the concept *emotion.* Measures provided by the dictionary are valid with respect to the definition of emotion provided by theorists such as Russell (1978, 1980) and Osgood (1969). This dictionary could be used in conjunction with measures of facial expression or measures of ANS activity, as all three are valid measures of a complex (and nonunitary) concept.

The *Dictionary of Affect* may be used to score verbal reports of short-duration responses (such as brief mood changes or short-term emotional responses to specific situations), and it may also be used to score verbal descriptions of long-duration responses (such as personality descriptions). In the traditional language of the dichotomy, both "states" and "traits" could be scored by the Dictionary method if these were described verbally.

Verbal stimulus material (instructions, word lists for memory tasks, or descriptions of hypothetical individuals) can also be scored using the *Dictionary of Affect.* Such scoring may have the purpose of ensuring that materials are emotionally neutral, or it might be designed to select stimulus materials with predetermined emotional tone. Both of these uses of the dictionary have been reported by Whissell et al. (1986). The *Dictionary of Affect* can quantify (measure) both stimulus and response materials, although in most applications to date it has been used for scoring the latter.

Scores reported by the *Dictionary of Affect* were produced by a group of adults, most of whom were young adults (between 20 and 25 years of age). The use of the dictionary is therefore most appropriate to material produced for or by that age group. The extent to which the dictionary may be applied validly to the measurement of responses from other age groups has yet to be established. Analyses of some data support the conclusion that younger subjects will not be familiar with some of the words that are included in the dictionary, but that they will respond similarly to the affective content of the words with which they are familiar.

In addition, computer programs can easily be designed to score verbal materials according to the *Dictionary of Affect*,[1] making the dictionary easier to apply and more attractive from a cost–benefit point of view.

The *Dictionary of Affect in Language* is a measure of emotion in the early stages of its development. The psychometric characteristics of the measure have been promising, and its theoretical underpinnings have historic significance in the research area. It has not often been possible to provide a method for the objective scoring of open-ended (or subjectively produced) materials, so that the dictionary's early successes have been interpreted as an encouragement to further research in the same vein.

REFERENCES

Allen, B. P., & Potkay, C. R. (1981). On the arbitrary distinction between states and traits. *Journal of Personality and Social Psychology, 41,* 916–928.

Anderson, C. W., & McMaster, G. E. (1982). Computer assisted modeling of affective tone in written documents. *Computers and the Humanities, 16,* 1–9.

Apple, W., & Hecht, K. (1982). Speaking emotionally: The relation between verbal and vocal communication of affect. *Journal of Personality and Social Psychology, 42,* 864–875.

Buck, R. (1983). Emotional development and emotional education. In R. Plutchik & H. Kellerman (Eds.), *Emotion: Theory, research, and experience* (Vol. 2). New York: Academic Press.

Cannon, W. B. (1927). The James-Lange theory of emotions: A critical examination and an alternative theory. *American Journal of Psychology, 39,* 106–124.

Chaplin, J. P. (1968). *Dictionary of psychology.* New York: Dell.

Conte, H. R., & Plutchik, R. (1981). A circumplex model for interpersonal personality traits. *Journal of Personality and Social Psychology, 40,* 701–711.

Darwin, C. (1872). *The expression of the emotions in man and animals.* London: Murray.

Ekman, P. (Ed.) (1973). *Darwin and facial expression.* New York: Academic Press.

Ekman, P. (Ed.) (1982). *Emotion in the human face.* New York: Cambridge University Press.

Ekman, P., Friesen, W. V., & Ancoli, S. (1980). Facial signs of emotional experience. *Journal of Personality and Social Psychology, 39,* 1125–1134.

Ekman, R., Friesen, V. W., O'Sullivan, M., & Scherer, K. (1980). Relative importance of face, body, and speech in judgments of personality and affect. *Journal of Personality and Social Psychology, 38,* 270–277.

English, H., & English, A. (1958). *A comprehensive dictionary of psychological and psychoanalytical terms.* New York: McKay.

Erikson, E. H. (1968). *Identity: Youth and crisis.* New York: Norton.

Fehr, B., & Russell, J. A. (1984). Concept of emotion viewed from a prototype perspective. *Journal of Experimental Psychology, General, 113,* 464–486.

Good News Bible (1976). Toronto, Ontario, Canada: Canadian Bible Society.

Grings, W. W., & Dawson, M. E. (1978). *Emotions and bodily responses.* New York: Academic Press.

---

[1]M. Dewson has adapted LOTUS 123 to this purpose and has written a scoring program in BASIC (Whissell & Dewson, 1986).

Heise, D. R. (1965). Semantic differential profiles for 1000 most frequent English words. *Psychological Monographs, 79*, No. 601.

Izard, C. E. (1972). *Patterns of emotions: A new analysis of anxiety and depression.* New York: Academic Press.

James, W. (1967). What is an emotion? In K. Dunlap (Ed.), *The emotions.* New York: Hagner (originally published in *Mind*, 1884).

Klinnert, M. D., Campos, J. J., Sorce, J. F., Emde, R. N., & Svejda, M. (1983). Emotions as regulators: Social referencing in infancy. In R. Plutchik & H. Kellerman (Eds.), *Emotion: Theory, research, and experience* (Vol. 2). New York: Academic Press.

Krauss, R. M., Apple, W., Morency, N., Wenzel, C., & Winton, W. (1981). Verbal, vocal, and visible factors in judgments of another's affect. *Journal of Personality and Social Psychology, 40*, 312–320.

Laird, J. D. (1984). The real role of facial response in the experience of emotion: A reply to Tourangeau and Ellsworth and others. *Journal of Personality and Social Psychology, 47*, 909–917.

Lanzetta, J. T., & Kleck, R. E. (1970). Encoding and decoding of nonverbal affect in humans. *Journal of Personality and Social Psychology, 16*, 12–19.

Lorenz, M., & Cobb, S. (1954). Language patterns in psychotic and psychoneurotic subjects. *AMA Archives of Neurology and Psychiatry, 72*, 665–673.

Murphy, L. B. (1983). Issues in the development of emotion in infancy. In R. Plutchik & H. Kellerman (Eds.), *Emotion: Theory, research, and experience* (Vol. 2). New York: Academic Press.

Nowlis, V. (1965). Research with the Mood Adjective Check List. In S. S. Tompkins & C. E. Izard (Eds.), *Affect, cognition and personality.* (pp. 352–388.) New York: Springer.

Osgood, C. E. (1969). On the whys and wherefores of E, P, and A. *Journal of Personality and Social Psychology, 12*, 194–199.

Plutchik, R. (1980). *Emotion: A psychoevolutionary synthesis.* New York: Harper & Row.

Plutchik, R., & Kellerman, H. (Eds.) (1980). *Emotion: Theory, research, and experience* (Vol. 1). New York: Academic Press.

Russell, J. A. (1978). Evidence of convergent validity on the dimensions of affect. *Journal of Personality and Social Psychology, 36*, 1152–1168.

Russell, J. A. (1980). A circumplex model of affect. *Journal of Personality and Social Psychology, 39*, 1161–1178.

Sweeney, K., & Whissell, C. M. (1984). A dictionary of affect in language: I. Establishment and preliminary validation. *Perceptual and Motor Skills, 59*, 695–698.

West, M. (1953). *A general service list of English words.* New York: Longmans & Green.

Whissell, C. M. (1981). Pleasure and activation revisited: Dimensions underlying semantic responses to fifty randomly selected ''emotional'' words. *Perceptual and Motor Skills, 53*, 871–874.

Whissell, C. M. (1984). Emotion: A classification of current literature. *Perceptual and Motor Skills, 59*, 599–609.

Whissell, C. M. (1985). The role of the face in human emotion: First system or one of many? *Perceptual and Motor Skills, 61*, 3–12.

Whissell, C. M., & Berezowski, H. (1986). A dictionary of affect in language: V. What is an emotion? *Perceptual and Motor Skills, 63*, 1156–1158.

Whissell, C. M., & Charuk, K. (1985). A dictionary of affect in language: II. Word inclusion and additional validation. *Perceptual and Motor Skills, 61*, 65–66.

Whissell, C. M., & Dewson, M. R. J. (1986). A dictionary of affect in language: III. Analysis of two biblical and two secular passages. *Perceptual and Motor Skills, 62*, 127–132.

Whissell, C. M., Fournier, M., Pelland, R., Weir, D., & Makarec, K. (1986). A dictionary of affect in language: IV. Reliability, validity, and applications. *Perceptual and Motor Skills, 62,* 875–888.

Wilson, T. D., Hull, J. G., & Johnson, J. (1981). Awareness and self-perception: Verbal reports on internal states. *Journal of Personality and Social Psychology, 40,* 53–71.

Chapter 6

INFORMATION INTEGRATION APPROACH TO EMOTIONS AND THEIR MEASUREMENT

NORMAN H. ANDERSON

ABSTRACT

Emotion and affect are considered in terms of a general theory of information integration, which embodies a functional, goal-directed perspective. From this perspective, emotion and affect are considered information, with biosocial functions of guiding thought and action. The basic theme of information integration *reflects the theoretical focus on studying how thought and action are constructed through joint action of multiple determinants. This integration theme makes it axiomatic that nonaffective, cognitive determinants are fundamental in emotion. This theme also leads to a distinction between unconscious and conscious emotion. Integration theory is not a promissory principle, but a working reality, for integration has been found to follow exact algebraic rules in diverse domains. This* cognitive algebra *provides a new approach to emotion theory. It allows fractionation of emotion into affective and nonaffective determinants. It allows measurement of both conscious and unconscious emotion on true psychological scales. And it is useful for analysis of certain problems of attention, memory, inference, and decision. Empirical applications are discussed for phobias, recognizing emotion, social affect, pain, and cerebral organization.*

INTRODUCTION

The themes of this chapter are defined in two phrases, *information integration* and *functional measurement*. These themes of the present theory of information

133

integration need preliminary discussion in relation to emotion. The basic theme of integration arises because emotional experience and behavior seldom result from a single cause. Multiple causes or determinants typically act together: how they are integrated to produce emotional experience and behavior is a fundamental problem.

The functional theme arises from the focus on goal-directed thought and action. Emotions are considered to have functional roles as information to guide goal-directed behavior. This informational approach to emotions follows naturally from the general theory. Equally naturally, it follows that emotions are considered integral to cognition. Emotion is information not despite but because of its affective character.

The final theme, that of measurement, reflects a necessity for general analysis of multiple determination. Even an adding rule, almost the simplest way in which multiple stimuli can determine a response, can hardly be tested without measurement of individual subjective values. Physical values of the stimuli will not do, for psychophysics has shown that physical values generally differ from subjective, psychological values. And the base fact of individual differences, nowhere greater than in the affective realm, underscores the need for measurement of individual values.

The foregoing themes have been considered by previous writers on emotion. A functional perspective underlies the evolution-oriented approaches adopted by Emde (1980), Plutchik (1980), and Scott (1980). The importance of cognition in emotion has been discussed by Arnold (1960), Frijda (1969), Janis and Mann (1977), Konečni (1975), Lazarus, Averill, and Opton (1970), Leventhal (1980), and Mandler (1984), among others. Some relations with these and other theories of emotion are noted in a later section.

The basic difference between information integration theory and other approaches to emotion concerns multiple determination. Although integration is considered common in emotional reactions by virtually all writers, few have attempted to determine the nature of the integration process. Many have claimed that cognitive factors influence emotional reactions, for example, but go no farther than showing that one or another experimental manipulation affects the behavior. Integration theory goes farther to study the form and structure of integration processes that underlie all emotional reactions. Significant progress has been made, as is summarized in the following four-point preview.

- Many integration tasks obey simple rules whose structure can be exactly determined.
- Integration rules make it possible to measure emotional experience for individuals on true psychological scales.
- Integration rules can be used in reverse, to fractionate out the determinants of observed emotional responses. The contributions of affective and non-affective factors to emotional experience can thus be separated.

- Emotion can be measured at both conscious and unconscious levels.

INFORMATION INTEGRATION DIAGRAM

This section gives a brief conceptual overview of the theory of information integration (Anderson, 1981, 1982). Three kinds of processing are basic to the theory, namely, *valuation, integration,* and *action.* These are shown in the simplified integration diagram of Figure 6.1. The organism is considered to reside in a field of information, in which observable stimuli, denoted by S_i, impinge on the organism to produce some observable response, denoted by R. The three kinds of processing appear as successive though unobservable operations within the organism.

Also represented in the integration diagram is the goal. The goal controls all three processing operations, as indicated in the following three subsections. The goal directedness of thought and action is thus explicitly incorporated in the integration diagram.

VALUATION

Valuation gives stimuli their meaning and value. Psychophysical valuation may be important, as with stimuli for pain or tactile interaction. Human emotion, however, is predominantly interpersonal and social and is heavily dependent on memory knowledge, especially in the form of attitudes. In the schematic of

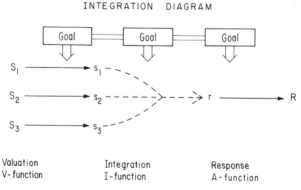

FIGURE 6.1. Information integration diagram. Chain of three linked operators, V, I, and A, leads from observable stimulus field, $\{S_i\}$, to observable response, R. Valuation operator, V, transforms observable stimuli, S_i, into subjective representations, s_i. Integration operator, I, transforms subjective stimulus field, $\{s_i\}$, into implicit response, r. Action operator, A, transforms implicit response, r, into observable response, R. (After Anderson, 1981.)

Figure 6.1, the valuation operation transforms the observable stimuli, S_i, into their subjective counterparts, denoted by s_i. This view stresses the commonality of affective and nonaffective values, for both typically involve similar valuation processes.

Valuation is goal directed. The same stimulus may have different values, depending on the operative goal. Valuation thus depends on and represents motivational state. For the same reason, valuation is contextual, since the meaning of a stimulus usually depends on the context.

Valuation is also individual. This is required, of course, by the fact of individual differences. Cognitively, this reflects the role in valuation of the experiential background, stored in memory, of the individual organism.

INTEGRATION

Multiple determination is represented by the integration function, I, in Figure 6.1. Following valuation, the several operative stimuli, s_i, are integrated to produce an internal response, r. Consider a snake presented to a snake phobic. The operative stimuli may include recognition of the snake, perception of its nearness, and a realization that it is loose. These distinct stimuli act jointly to produce an emotional feeling of fear and aversion. The emotional feeling is an integrated resultant of the several determinants.

This example illustrates further why affect is considered cognitive. The emotional reaction depends not only on the snake, but also on nonaffective factors of proximity and expectancy. Valuation of the snake, moreover, requires cognitive processes that refer to memory storage. From the standpoint of information integration theory, therefore, it is axiomatic that nonaffective, cognitive variables are important in affective reactions.

ACTION

In the third stage of processing, the implicit response, r, is transformed into an observable response, R. This may be a verbal report, a facial expression, or a physiological reaction. For some purposes, such overt behavior may have primary interest. For cognitive analysis, however, R is of interest mainly as a measure of the internal state, r.

Goal dynamics is not well represented in this simplified diagram. Feedback loops are common, so an integrated affective response may assume stimulus properties for further action, as when fear of the snake leads to withdrawal. The momentary information field, along with affective and motivational states, undergoes continuous evolution and change. These changes affect the operative goal, which in turn controls the three processing operations. The integration diagram of Figure 6.1 is thus only a momentary, static view of a dynamic process.

Goal dynamics is important in analysis of emotion and affect, for they constitute information that controls further action. In particular, positive affect usually leads to continuance of previous action; negative affect usually leads to discontinuance. From this informational perspective, emotion and affect become motivation and guide action. This is their biosocial function.

CONSCIOUS AND UNCONSCIOUS EMOTION

A conscious feeling state is often considered essential to human emotion. Integration theory entails a more complex view, in which emotion operates at different levels, both conscious and unconscious. This view is implicit in the integration diagram, which distinguishes between measurement of response and measurement of stimulus. What reaches consciousness is an emotional response that is an integrated resultant of multiple stimulus determinants. The subjective determinants, and indeed the integration operation, are often, perhaps typically, not accessible to consciousness.

An experimental illustration of the conscious–unconscious distinction is provided by the study of snake phobics shown in Figure 6.2. In this study, which is considered in more detail later, the plotted response represents the conscious

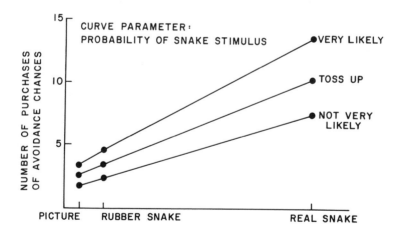

FIGURE 6.2. Expectancy × Valence rule is supported by linear fan pattern. Data are from snake phobics, who purchase chances (vertical axis) to avoid exposure to snake stimulus (horizontal axis). (From Anderson, 1981; after Klitzner, 1977.)

emotion. This conscious emotion, however, depends on two factors: the fearfulness of the snake stimulus (picture, rubber, or real snake listed on the horizontal axis) and the expectancy that the snake stimulus will actually be encountered (listed as curve parameter). The fearfulness of the snake stimulus is considered to represent an unconscious emotion, which reaches consciousness only after integration with expectancy. The conscious experience cannot ordinarily be fractionated to make conscious the separate determinants.

This distinction between conscious and unconscious emotion is basic. The cognitive character of emotion appears at both levels. The conscious experience is cognitive because it is a resultant of affective and nonaffective determinants. The unconscious emotion is cognitive because it is information that is integrated into the conscious experience. The distinction also illustrates a premise of integration theory, namely, that conscious experience is not primitive but is a constructed entity. These two theoretical implications are considered further in the next two subsections.

THE THREE UNOBSERVABLES

Three unobservable entities appear in the integration diagram of Figure 6.1, each associated with one of the processing operations. Although the physical stimuli, S_i, are observable, the corresponding psychological stimuli, s_i, are not observable. On the response side, similarly, the observable response, R, is distinguished from the unobservable feeling state, r. The integration function, I, which transforms the several s_i into r, is clearly unobservable.

This observable–unobservable distinction, although elementary, is important to keep in mind. Measurement must aim at psychological entities, s_i and r. Measurement at the observable level of S_i and R, although useful for many purposes, is not sufficient for general theory. In particular, the conscious feeling state, r, must be distinguished from its overt manifestation, R, a central point in the later discussion of response measurement [e.g., Eqs. (3) and (4), and Figure 6.5].

The three unobservables also illustrate the foregoing distinction between unconscious emotion, which corresponds to s, and conscious emotion, which corresponds to r. Integration theory makes this distinction determinate by providing methods for measuring both s and r on true psychological scales.

COGNITIVE ALGEBRA AND
FUNCTIONAL MEASUREMENT

The problem of the three unobservables is central to cognitive theory. It is clear, of course, that a solution to this problem must be derived from observable $S–R$ relations, but it may seem doubtful that such observable relations are sufficient to obtain a solution. That a solution is possible, sometimes even easy, has been shown by the work on information integration theory.

The cutting edge of integration theory is cognitive algebra. Extensive empirical studies have shown that integration tasks in many areas obey simple algebraic rules, collectively known as cognitive algebra (see Anderson, 1981, chap. 1). By establishing that the integration function, I, in Figure 6.1 is addition, say, or multiplication, it becomes possible to obtain true psychological scales of the unobservable s_i and r. Cognitive algebra thus provides a solution to the problem of the three unobservables.

To illustrate, the snake avoidance data of Figure 6.2 follow a multiplication rule, as will be shown later. It follows that the observable response, plotted on the vertical axis, is a veridical scale of the unobservable emotional response. A psychological scale of subjective fearfulness of the snake stimuli is also available. In fact, these psychological values are given by the spacing of the three stimuli on the horizontal axis in Figure 6.2. Establishing the form of the integration function can thus provide measurement scales of unobservable stimuli and unobservable responses.

The foregoing distinction between conscious and unconscious emotion becomes determinate through this solution to the measurement problem. Strictly speaking, the distinction should be made between emotion as stimulus and emotion as response, for these are what are measured. In some cases, emotion as stimulus may be accessible to consciousness, and in some cases the response may not become conscious. The need to consider emotion at more than one level is clear, however, as is the need to distinguish between conscious and unconscious levels of emotion.

Measurement based on cognitive algebra is called functional, in part because it depends on the integration function, in part because the measured stimulus values are those that were functional in the response. Measurement techniques are given by the parallelism theorem and the linear fan theorem. This technical development, however, is deferred to the later section on functional measurement. The following section takes up a number of conceptual issues in which the theory of information integration is compared and contrasted with other approaches to emotion.

COGNITIVE ISSUES

The theme of integration implies that emotional reactions are constructions. Conscious emotion is integrated, or constructed, from multiple determinants. The cognitive character of conscious emotion appears in its joint dependence on nonaffective determinants and preconscious emotion. The theme of integration also entails a functional conception of memory as a knowledge base for constructing implications and values. These cognitive issues are discussed here in relation to other theories of emotion.

FUNCTIONAL PERSPECTIVE

The present approach is one of the general class of functional theories, which are concerned with goal-oriented adaptive behavior. The classic functional essay on emotions, of course, is Darwin's 1872 conception of emotional expression as an evolution for social communication (see Darwin, 1965). More pertinent here is Scott's (1980) systems approach, which relates emotions to the action of nine behavioral systems, such as ingestion and sex, each concerned with one class of adaptive behavior. Plutchik's (1980) psychoevolutionary theory has a similar emphasis, and is worked out more extensively, with greater adherence to evolutionary continuity and with greater concern for human personality. Scott's approach seems more congenial to the present theory, however, because it relates emotions to action patterns that include the senses, on the one hand, and general affect, on the other.

Functional views often involve some conception of basic emotions, from which others are derived (e.g., Arnold, 1960; Ekman, 1984; Izard, 1977; Plutchik, 1980; Tomkins, 1984). This idea of basic emotions arises naturally from the distinct functions of different biological systems of adaptation. No classification has commanded wide assent, however, and all suffer from heterogeneity of categories, as well as nagging problems of borderline classification, not only among emotions, but also between emotions and sensory-affective reactions (such as pain), social-affective reactions (such as blame), and even mood. The quest for taxonomy remains attractive, nevertheless, because it seems to promise a conceptual foundation from which to make sense of the great diversity and complexity of emotional experience and behavior.

Because it rests on a conceptual foundation of multiple determination, information integration theory is not primarily concerned with basic emotions. Multiple determination provides a different base for theoretical issues. Analysis of multiple determination may be useful as a means for defining and measuring basic emotions, but the theory also applies to blends of emotions as molar units of stimulus or response. Hence integration theory can proceed to study pain, phobias, and social affect, for example, without waiting on uncertain taxonomic endeavors.

Functional views typically stress cognition. A major reason, no doubt, is the great influence of socialization processes in primate emotions (Averill, 1980; Bowlby, 1982; Emde, 1980; Harlow & Mears, 1983; Plutchik, 1980), although a parallel development appears in health psychology (Janis & Rodin, 1979; Leventhal, 1980). Few cognitive approaches to emotion, however, have been developed very far theoretically. They stress the importance of cognition, but they remain rudimentary in their treatment of cognitive processes of valuation, integration, attention, and memory.

This brief discussion of the functional perspective does not indicate the complicated lineage of ideas in the field of emotions (see Mandler, 1984; Plutchik, 1980; Strongman, 1978) and does not do justice to the value of previous work in writing this chapter. Besides the cited references, mention should be made of Leeper (1948, 1970) and Rogers (1951), early exponents of the beneficial, organizing properties of emotions, and especially of McDougall (1921, 1928), a pioneer of purposive behaviorism based on evolutionary concepts. McDougall's "instincts" fell into disrepute because they did not get beyond armchair analysis, but similar views have again become fashionable with recent interest in evolutionary and genetic conceptions. McDougall's instincts also derived from Darwin's theory, being similar to the biological systems and basic emotions already cited, and they explicitly recognized the fundamental role of learning and socialization in human emotion.

EMOTION AS INFORMATION

The present informational view of emotion is exactly the reverse of various arousal theories [most prominently that of Schachter (1964)], which claim that nonaffective, cognitive information is essential to define the phenomenal quality of emotional experience. A simple phenomenological argument supports the present view. Happiness and depression often seem to come naturally. We do not need to consult a list of reasons or labels to decide whether what we feel is happiness or depression. Our feeling of happiness is one aspect of a total bodily state, whose label follows the feeling. Our feeling of depression, similarly, may arise and persist despite reasons that should induce happiness. On this phenomenological argument, also invoked by Izard (1982), Schachter's claim seems hardly believable.

A second argument is biosocial: affective experience guides action. Far from requiring information to determine its nature, affective experience constitutes information that is utilized in goal-directed behavior. In its simplest form, this informational function is analogous to that of sensory experience and makes equal biological sense. Schachter's theory, by contrast, cannot recognize emotion in animals and young children (Berkowitz, 1982; Leventhal, 1980; Plutchik & Ax, 1967) because they lack the social language labels postulated as necessary to define emotional quality. The biosocial argument recognizes evolutionary continuity, while not neglecting the predominant influence of socialization in the development of emotional reactions in adult humans.

The biosocial argument parallels Darwin's conception of emotions as a means of social communication. The present focus, however, is on information flow within an individual organism. Emotion thus has a self-directing function, distinct from Darwin's other-directing social function. Whereas Darwin argued that social emotional expression evolved from "serviceable habits," the foregoing considerations look to an origin in affective processes utilized by the organism in guiding its own action.

That cognitive factors can influence emotional experience has long been recognized. What was novel in Schachter's (1964) theory was the extreme claim that such factors are essential. His theory rests on two assumptions: first, that physiological arousal is the basic, undifferentiated substrate of all emotion, and, second, that emotional specificity arises only through cognitive labeling induced by the social situation (see also Plutchik & Ax, 1967; Schachter, 1970). The two experiments presented to support these assumptions (Schachter & Singer, 1962; Schachter & Wheeler, 1962) generated extended controversy.

This controversy is surprising because Schachter's evidence had little value. In Schachter and Singer (1962), subjects were (1) injected with epinephrine or placebo, (2) informed, misinformed, or uninformed about symptoms produced by epinephrine, and (3) exposed to a confederate who role played euphoria or anger. The critical theoretical prediction concerns the epinephrine-uninformed and placebo conditions. Both were treated identically except for the injection.

Theoretically, the role playing of the confederate supplied a verbal label with which the epinephrine-uninformed subjects would explain their drug-induced arousal. Hence the critical theoretical prediction is that the epinephrine-uninformed subjects will feel more negative than the placebo subjects in the Anger condition, more positive in the Euphoria condition. Five separate tests of this prediction, involving both behavioral and self-report measures, were presented by Schachter and Singer. Only one was even marginally significant.

Other theoretical failures were also substantial. The first of these was the lack of significant differences in self-rating of emotion among the Anger conditions. Overall, in fact, the Anger conditions showed net happiness, virtually identical to the Euphoria conditions. This undercuts the basic theoretical assumption that the social labeling induced by these two conditions should determine opposite emotional experiences.

The other main dependable outcome was the repeated failure of the theoretical prediction of equivalence of placebo and informed conditions. This disconfirmed prediction, as Schachter and Singer (1962, p. 393) observed, raised "serious questions about our entire theoretical structure." Recourse was had to "internal analyses," which rested on post hoc selection of subjects, almost a third being eliminated according to Plutchik (1980, p. 38). With this, the pattern of data fell "neatly in line with theoretical expectations" (Schachter & Singer, 1962, p. 396).

It is not too surprising, therefore, that this work could not be replicated

(Marshall & Zimbardo, 1979; Maslach, 1979; see also Erdmann & Janke, 1978, cited by Marshall & Zimbardo, 1979, p. 985). Schachter and Wheeler (1962) suffer similarly from "internal analyses" (see reviews by Cotton, 1981; Manstead & Wagner, 1981; Reisenzein, 1983). It is not that Schachter's results had some alternative interpretation; there were essentially no results to interpret.

Ironically, Schachter's experiments were inherently inconclusive. Even had they succeeded, they logically could not have justified his basic claim that cognitive factors are essential for emotional specificity. That cognitive factors could partly influence emotional experience was not novel, of course, but Schachter's experiments did not demonstrate even this, much less his basic claim that emotional arousal per se is undifferentiated. The extensive influence of these experiments is thus a puzzle.[1]

AFFECT AS COGNITION

In the present informational view, affect is an organic component of cognition. Quality and intensity of an emotion both serve as information to guide further action. The classical trichotomy of affect–cognition–volition only defines three perspectives on one total response. The trichotomy has hindered inquiry by treating these perspectives as distinct, independent processes.

[1]Schachter's (1964) experiments are "classics," as they are often called, only as object lessons in poor science. It is worth asking why so many writers have spent so much time on so little substance. Part of the answer is indicated by Marshall and Zimbardo (1979, p. 985), who complain that Schachter and Singer (1962, 1979) "use their considerable literary talent to misdirect the reader's attention toward inadequately justified conclusions." This complaint is justified.

One illustration relates to the failure of the theoretical prediction about self-ratings of feeling in the Anger conditions. Indeed, the mean feeling in the Anger condition was actually positive, showing happiness virtually equal to that in the Euphoria condition. This contradicts Schachter's basic theoretical hypothesis.

This contradictory outcome for the Anger condition is dismissed with unfounded assertions: "The subjects, who had volunteered for the experiment for extra points on their final exam, *simply refused* to *endanger* those points by publicly *blowing up,* admitting their *irritation* to the experimenter's face or *spoiling* the questionnaire" (Schachter & Singer, 1962, p. 391, affective emphasis added). These statements are void of justification. The response in question was merely a mark on one of several questionnaire items. If the subjects felt irritated, they could easily and privately have expressed this by placing a mark one or two steps rightward on the rating scale. This is a far cry from "publicly blowing up" or even from "admitting their irritation to the experimenter's face." Nor was evidence presented that subjects were concerned about "spoiling the questionnaire" or felt that their points might be in danger. The only evidence actually presented is an oblique reference to the to-be-explained-away finding.

Scientific inquiry sometimes dictates exploration of what turn out to be sterile blind alleys. This blind alley, however, might well have been recognized as such and passed by. The inappropriate data analyses were there for all to see, and a sound critique that included important physiological considerations was given at an early date by Plutchik and Ax (1967). The matter may thus serve as an instructive case history for improving the payoff ratio of scientific inquiry.

This does not deny the possibility of noncognitive components, nor should the possibility that emotion may not require cognition, conscious or unconscious, be categorically dismissed. An emotional reaction might be produced by hormonal action, say, without any component that would be considered cognitive. That cognitive consequences should be lacking may seem unlikely, but should not be prejudged. Such a view has been proposed by Izard (1977), whereas Leventhal (1980) has argued for separate, parallel processing systems for affect and cognition. More immediately relevant here is Zajonc (1980), who has argued that affect has primacy and does not require cognition.

Some of Zajonc's evidence, however, seems misinterpreted. Of interest here is the two-memory representation of information integration theory (Anderson & Hubert, 1963), which Zajonc interpreted to imply independence of affect and cognition. The result in question concerned the failure of the then-standard verbal memory hypothesis, which asserted that attitudinal responses were based on the contents of verbal memory, as indexed by recallable stimuli. Contrariwise, Anderson and Hubert (1963) found that affective judgment of a person described by a list of personality adjectives was independent of recall of adjectives from that same list. This led to the two-memory representation, with different memory systems for the stimulus words and for the person memory based on those words. This finding about memory structure has been confirmed and extended [see Anderson, 1981 (Sect. 4.2), 1983a (Sect. A), in press-b; Hastie, 1981].

This two-memory hypothesis was taken by Zajonc [1980, 1984 (p. 264)] to imply that ''Appraisal and affect are often uncorrelated and disjoint.'' But Zajonc's interpretation only supports his position under two strong implicit assumptions: that the *affect,* which refers to the impression of the person, has no nonaffective component; and that its affective structure is in no sense *cognitive.* Both assumptions are doubtful. First, although the person was to be judged on an affective dimension, the person memory presumably contained nonaffective components; subjects typically have some idea of age and sex of the person, for example. Second, and more important, the affective evaluation should itself be considered cognitive. This evaluation rests on transformations that extract task-relevant meanings from the presented verbal input and integrate them to form the person impression, which is cognitive even in Zajonc's (1984, p. 261) definition.

A simple empirical test of Zajonc's claim is available. The two-memory representation is not limited to affective reactions. The same outcome should be obtained for nonevaluative judgments, about the age of the person, for example, which would undercut Zajonc's interpretation. Such demonstration of common process with affective and nonaffective judgments would demonstrate their common cognitive nature. Although there is little reason to doubt the outcome of this experiment, it has not actually been performed, so it provides a proper test of the two interpretations.

Not less important than the foregoing conceptual issue is the issue of strategy and tactics of investigation. Zajonc rightly criticizes mainstream cognitive theory for its neglect of affect and thereby has called attention to the importance of work by students of emotion. By attempting to demonstrate the primacy of affect, however, Zajonc goes to another extreme. Typically, *cognition* and *affect* act jointly. *Affect* cannot be tacked on to most current cognitive theories, nor can *cognition* be tacked on to affect. An integrated approach is needed, one that addresses problems of their joint action.

CONSTRUCTION PRINCIPLE

The constructive nature of cognition is an explicit premise of information integration theory. This construction principle appears in the integration diagram of Figure 6.1 for each of the three operations—integration, valuation, and action.

The integration operation is obviously constructive, for it constructs unitary responses from multiple determinants. The pervasive role of nonaffective determinants in affective reactions, illustrated in Figure 6.2, demonstrates the importance of the construction principle in emotion theory. Conscious emotional experience, accordingly, is considered a constructed entity. The example of Figure 6.2 goes farther, to show how the construction rule can be exactly determined.

The valuation operation is also constructive (Anderson, 1974b, pp. 88–90, in press-b). This follows from the goal directedness of thought and action. Stimulus values are not given constants, but goal-dependent parameters. Because goals depend on motivation and context, the same stimulus may have different values in different situations.

The constructive nature of action is clear in goal dynamics, as in constructing plans to attain specified goals. Action is not merely a matter of seeking goals, moreover, but of setting goals and revising them in the light of accumulating information.

The construction principle is not limited to emotion. Indeed, its role in the present theory originated in the psychophysical domain and in social attitudes. It may be useful, therefore, to comment briefly on both domains.

Construction of sensation in the psychophysical domain is nicely illustrated with the size–weight illusion, in which visual appearance affects conscious heaviness. The size of the object is considered to elicit a learned expectancy of heaviness, and this produces a contrast effect when compared to the kinesthetic information. Conscious sensation is thus influenced by a cognitive expectancy factor, one derived from another sense modality [Anderson, 1981 (Sect. 1.3.7)].

The foregoing distinction between emotion as stimulus and emotion as response is mirrored in the size–weight illusion. The proper sensory stimulus for heaviness is in the preconscious kinesthetic information. The conscious heaviness sensation is an integrated resultant of this preconscious heaviness and the expectancy. The methods of integration theory make it possible to fractionate conscious heaviness into its two stimulus determinants, especially preconscious heaviness [Anderson, 1981, 1982 (Note 3.1b)]. Similar methods apply in emotion theory, as already illustrated with the snake fear study of Figure 6.2.

In attitude theory, the construction principle appears in the distinction between attitudes and attitudinal responses (Anderson, 1976, 1981, in press-b). Attitudes are knowledge systems, whereas attitudinal responses are constructions based on the knowledge system in relation to some particular situation and goal. Most relevant for emotion theory are sociocultural attitudes, which embody cultural learning of right behavior, shame, blame, and so forth, and which typically have substantial affective content (see Figure 6.6).

This view of attitudes as systems differs from the predominant view in social psychology, which sees attitudes as one-dimensional entities with primary affective quality (see Berscheid, 1982; Cacioppo, Harkins, & Petty, 1981). The one-dimensional view only applies to certain attitudinal responses; the underlying knowledge system requires a quite different representation that includes multiple forms of memory storage as well as operators for utilizing memory storage for particular goals. Emotion and affect are organic components of such knowledge systems.

At bottom, the construction principle is inherent in the idea of stimulus integration, as noted in the earlier discussion of the integration diagram. Constructionist views have been considered by others, of course, the most relevant discussions being in the treatments of emotion by Izard (1977) and Mandler (1984). The advantage of integration theory lies in its development of concepts and methods for analysis of construction processes. The concepts and methods of cognitive algebra, in particular, illustrate how the general construction principle can be made into working theory.

CONSCIOUSNESS

It is a corollary of integration theory, as noted in the preceding subsection, that conscious feelings are generally constructions. This constructive nature of consciousness is illustrated in the size–weight illusion as well as in attitudinal responses: "People do not know their own minds. Instead, they are continually making them up" (Anderson, 1974b, p. 89).

From this construction principle, it follows that information integration theory rejects the *identity assumption* that conscious experience is a faithful mirror of preconscious structure. This identity assumption has dominated the concept of consciousness, not only in psychophysics (Anderson, 1975, p. 479), but throughout the history of psychology (Mandler, 1984, p. 91). But this identity assumption is inconsistent with the cited size–weight and snake fear experiments. The general implication for psychophysics is that "What does attain consciousness is often, perhaps always, a result integrated across different sense modalities at pre-conscious stages" (Anderson, 1981, p. 84). The same implication holds for emotion theory, as illustrated in the foregoing distinction between preconscious and conscious emotion.

Integration theory goes beyond the statement of general principle to provide effective methods to help analyze the construction of consciousness. One such method has already been illustrated with the snake fear experiment of Figure 6.2, in which the conscious emotion was fractionated into its separate determinants. This was accomplished by actually measuring the separate stimulus determinants, namely, the expectancy and the preconscious emotion.

In addition, the theory can provide validational criteria for conscious report. This also is illustrated in the snake fear experiment, which showed that the overt rating of fear was a true psychological scale of unobservable feeling (see later subsection on phobias, and also Figure 6.5). This solution to the problem of response measurement provides a beachhead on the study of emotion.

Consciousness can provide priceless information about emotion. The trouble is that conscious report is untrustworthy. The foregoing validity criteria provide ways to help determine when conscious report can be trusted. Other criteria are discussed in Anderson [1981 (Sects. 1.8, 3.2, 3.6, and 4.1)]. These criteria provide new methods for analysis of consciousness.

FUNCTIONAL MEMORY

The study of goal-directed behavior requires a *functional* as opposed to the traditional *reproductive* conception of memory. Recall is not generally sufficient; material stored in memory must generally be processed to extract implications and values relative to operative goals. Affective reactions, it is true, may have strong conditioned components, but most also depend on some cognitive analysis of the stimulus situation, performed by the valuation and integration operations. Memory is not merely reproductive, therefore, but productive, or functional (Anderson, 1983b, in press-b).

This functional conception of memory appears in the construction principle. Human emotion, whatever its biological base, is heavily determined by social learning. The diverse socialization processes that pervade everyday affective reactions are not stored merely as rote memory or conditioned responses, but as parts of knowledge systems. Knowledge systems operate in the valuation and integration operations to construct emotional reactions. Knowledge systems thus provide adaptive flexibility of cognitively based affect.

The contrast between functional and reproductive memory is epitomized in response measurement. Reproductive memory naturally relies on accuracy measures, whereas functional memory is more concerned with implications and values. The concern with accuracy began with Ebbinghaus' studies of rote learning and continues unabated even in the contemporary trend to study memory for meanings and ideas. Accuracy measures, however, have limited relevance to memory functioning in relation to value, affect, or emotion. Instead, a method of functional measurement is desired, as discussed in the next section.

FUNCTIONAL MEASUREMENT

Two basic tools of integration theory are the parallelism theorem and the linear fan theorem, which are presented in this section. These theorems have three functions: they allow empirical tests of addition and multiplication rules for integration; they provide a psychological scale of the response variable; and they provide psychological scales of the stimulus variables. These theorems are part of a functional measurement methodology (see Anderson, 1981, 1982).

MULTIPLE DETERMINATION

Emotions typically arise from joint action of multiple factors. The need for measurement stems from this fact of multiple determination, as with the simple adding model:

$$r = s_1 + s_2. \tag{1}$$

The obvious way to test this model is to measure r, s_1, and s_2, to check directly whether they add up. But they would not add up if they were measured, say, on a rank-order scale. Even for this simple case of multiple determination, linear (equal-interval) scales are essential.

Multiple determination has been largely avoided in contemporary research, owing to lack of measurement methodology capable of handling even the simple adding model. The obstacle lies in the unobservable, subjective nature of the quantities to be measured. This problem of unobservables requires further discussion, for it lies at the heart of psychological measurement theory.

THE THREE UNOBSERVABLES

Three basic problems underlie the study of multiple determination. Collectively, they are called the *problem of the three unobservables,* embodied in the symbolic equation from the integration diagram (Figure 6.1):

$$r = I(s_1, s_2, \ldots). \tag{2}$$

This equation seems formidable because the subjective stimulus values, s_i, the subjective response, r, and the integration function, I, are all three unobservable. Even the simple adding model of Eq. (1) requires true psychological scales of s_i and of r.

To solve Eq. (2) can only be accomplished with observable information, namely, about the dependence of the observable R on the observable S_i. Hence it may hardly seem possible to deduce all three unobservables at once. Traditional measurement theories, such as Thurstone's method of paired comparisons, attempt to divide and conquer: they focus on just one unobservable, namely, the scaling of the stimulus values, s_i. This strategy seems natural, much like that used in physical science. In psychological science, however, it has not worked very well.

Integration theory aims to determine all three unobservables at once. This inverts the traditional approach by making measurement depend on the structure of the integration function, I. The integration function provides the base and frame for obtaining true values of the unobservable stimuli and of the unobservable response. That this is possible, even simple, is shown by the parallelism and linear fan theorems that follow.

FACTORIAL DESIGN

A standard way to manipulate two (or more) stimulus variables is through *factorial design*. The variables are called *factors* and the chosen values of each variable are called its *levels*. A two-variable (two-way) factorial design can be represented as a rectangular row × column matrix, illustrated in Figure 6.3.

In Figure 6.3, the levels of the row factor are physical stimuli, denoted by S_{Ai}; the levels of the column factor are physical stimuli denoted by S_{Bj}. The experimental conditions are pairs of physical stimuli. Thus, cell ij of the design matrix corresponds to the experimental condition (S_{Ai}, S_{Bj}). The observed response to this stimulus combination is denoted by R_{ij}.

A *factorial graph* is obtained by placing the column stimuli, say, on the horizontal axis at some convenient spacing. The observed responses in each separate row of the design are then graphed as a separate curve (e.g., Figures 6.2, 6.4, and 6.6). The pattern in this factorial graph can reveal the three unobservables as shown by the two following theorems.

PARALLELISM THEOREM

An adding rule of integration can be diagnosed by a pattern of parallelism in the factorial graph. This follows from the parallelism theorem [see Anderson,

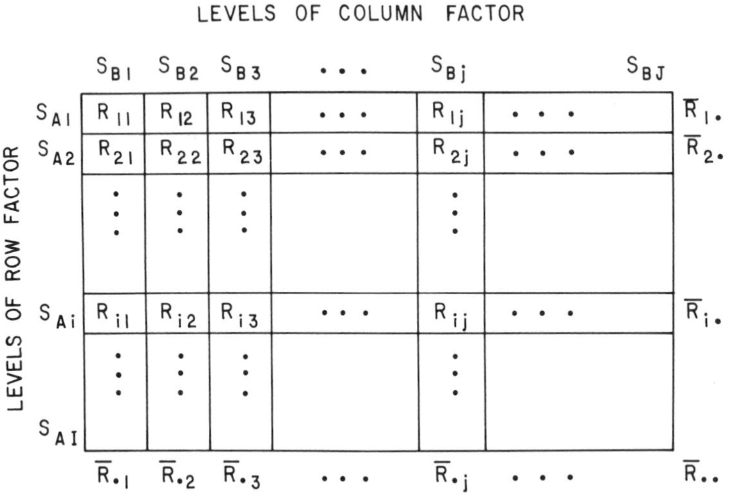

LEVELS OF COLUMN FACTOR

		S_{B1}	S_{B2}	S_{B3}	$\cdots$		S_{Bj}	$\cdots$		S_{BJ}
	S_{A1}	R_{11}	R_{12}	R_{13}	$\cdots$		R_{1j}	$\cdots$		$\bar{R}_{1\cdot}$
	S_{A2}	R_{21}	R_{22}	R_{23}	$\cdots$		R_{2j}	$\cdots$		$\bar{R}_{2\cdot}$
		$\vdots$	$\vdots$	$\vdots$			$\vdots$			
	S_{Ai}	R_{i1}	R_{i2}	R_{i3}	$\cdots$		R_{ij}	$\cdots$		$\bar{R}_{i\cdot}$
		$\vdots$	$\vdots$	$\vdots$			$\vdots$			
	S_{AI}									
		$\bar{R}_{\cdot 1}$	$\bar{R}_{\cdot 2}$	$\bar{R}_{\cdot 3}$	$\cdots$		$\bar{R}_{\cdot j}$	$\cdots$		$\bar{R}_{\cdot\cdot}$

LEVELS OF ROW FACTOR

FIGURE 6.3. Two-way $A \times B$ factorial design. S_{Ai} and S_{Bj} represent levels of stimulus variables, A and B, respectively. Cell entries R_{ij} denote observed response to stimulus pair (S_{Ai}, S_{Bj}) in cell ij. (After Anderson, 1981.)

1981 (Sect. 1.2)]. For two stimulus variables, with weights omitted for simplicity, the theorem may be stated thus:

PARALLELISM THEOREM. Suppose that an adding model holds, so that

$$r_{ij} = s_{Ai} + s_{Bj}, \tag{3a}$$

and that the observable response is on a linear (equal-interval) scale, so that

$$R_{ij} = c_0 + c_1 r_{ij}, \tag{3b}$$

where c_0 and c_1 are zero and unit constants. Then (1) the factorial graph will form a set of parallel curves and (2) the row means of the factorial design will be estimates of the subjective values of the row stimuli on linear (equal-interval) scales, and similarly for the column means.

Observed parallelism thus provides a remarkably simple and powerful tool. Observed parallelism supports the basic adding model; it also supports the other premise of the theorem, namely, that the observed response is a veridical linear scale of the unobservable response. If either assumption is incorrect, that will cause deviations from parallelism. There is, of course, a logical possibility that both assumptions are incorrect but just offset each other to yield net parallelism. Subject to this qualification, however, observed parallelism supports both assumptions and thereby accomplishes three simultaneous goals: (1) it supports the adding model, (2) it supports the linearity of the response scale, and (3) it provides linear scales of the subjective stimulus variables. These three goals correspond to the three unobservables just considered. The end has thus been achieved: a solution to the problem of the three unobservables.

LINEAR FAN THEOREM

A multiplying rule of stimulus integration can be diagnosed by a linear fan pattern. This follows from the linear fan theorem [see Anderson, 1981 (Sect. 1.4)].

LINEAR FAN THEOREM. Suppose that a multiplying model holds, so that

$$r_{ij} = s_{Ai} \times s_{Bj}, \tag{4a}$$

and that the observed response is on a linear scale, so that

$$R_{ij} = c_0 + c_1 r_{ij}. \tag{4b}$$

Then (1) the appropriate factorial graph will form a fan of straight lines and (2) the row means of the factorial design will be estimates of the subjective values of the row stimuli on linear scales, and similarly for the column means.

The linear fan theorem differs from the parallelism theorem in one important respect: the "appropriate" factorial graph requires that the column stimuli be spaced on the horizontal axis according to their subjective values. This might seem to vitiate empirical applications of the linear fan theorem, for these subjective values are not known. But the theorem shows that the column means provide these subjective values, if both premises are correct. Hence the observed column means may be used in this way provisionally to see if a linear fan does emerge.

By the same logic as with the parallelism theorem, therefore, an observed linear fan supports both assumptions of the theorem. This accomplishes three simultaneous goals: (1) it supports the multiplying model, (2) it supports the linearity of the response measure, and (3) it provides linear scales of the subjective stimulus variables. Here again is a solution to the problem of the three unobservables, for each listed goal corresponds to one of the three unobservables.

EMPIRICAL APPLICATIONS

The usefulness of these theorems may be illustrated with the snake fear experiment, already discussed in Figure 6.2. This factorial graph is not parallel, so the

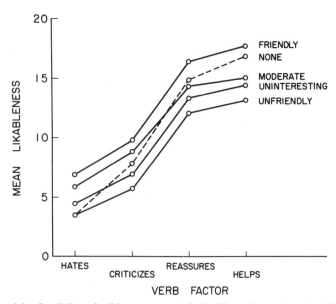

FIGURE 6.4. Parallelism of solid curves supports both adding and averaging rules. Crossover of dashed and solid curves eliminates adding rule and supports averaging rule. Subjects judged likableness of persons described by trait adjective (curve parameter) and behavior toward others (verb factor on horizontal axis). (After Anderson, 1981.)

adding model would be rejected. In fact, the factorial graph shows a linear fan pattern, and so supports the Expectancy × Valence multiplying rule that was originally hypothesized. This fan pattern also implies that the observable response, R, is a linear scale of the unobservable fear, r, thereby validating the measure of conscious report (see later subsection on phobias). Moreover, by virtue of the second conclusion of the theorem, the spacing of the snake stimuli on the horizontal axis provides a linear scale of their fearfulness. Together, these two scales measure the conscious and preconscious emotion.

An illustrative application of the parallelism theorem is given in the study of person cognition summarized in Figure 6.4. In this experiment, subjects made affective judgments of hypothetical persons described by adjective–predicate sentences of the form

The *adjective* man *verbs* people

where adjectives and verbs were combined according to the 4 × 4, Adjective × Verb factorial design indicated in Figure 6.4.

The theoretical hypothesis at issue is that the adjective and verb information in each sentence are added. This hypothesis seems plausible. The adjective *friendly*, for example, and the predicate *reassures people* give information of similar quality, so they could be meaningfully added. The problem, however, is not to make the hypothesis but to test it. This requires a solution to the measurement problem—which is provided by the parallelism theorem.

The four solid curves in Figure 6.4 are essentially parallel. This parallelism supports the hypothesis that adjective and predicate are integrated by an adding-type rule. The parallelism also implies that the rating response was a true linear scale. The scale of adjective values, although not of special interest in this experiment, is given by the vertical spacing of the solid curves in Figure 6.4. In short, the observed parallelism provides a solution to the problem of the three unobservables.

Both theorems have been useful in numerous experiments across diverse areas of psychology. Illustrative applications are given in Anderson (1981), for adding-type models (in Sects. 1.3.1–1.3.8) and for multiplying models (in Sects. 1.5.1–1.5.7). The two theorems are developed in Sects. 1.2 and 1.4, respectively, and chapter 5 gives a comparative discussion of psychological measurement theory.

It may seem odd that such a simple, powerful method should not have been recognized and exploited long ago. Two difficult obstacles blocked the way. Each obstacle relates to the empirical validity of one premise of the theorem, and both require comment.

One premise is that the observable response, R, is a linear scale of the unobservable response, r. This is not generally true, as is discussed later (see especially Figure 6.5). But without a linear response scale, the theorems will fail even when the models are correct. Functional measurement succeeded through the development of certain experimental procedures to yield linear response measures (see later subsection on rating methodology).

The other premise is that the models hold empirically. The multiplying model has done surprisingly well, but this was only recognized after the linear fan theorem showed how to obtain the stimulus values needed to construct the linear fan graph.

The adding model, also surprisingly in light of its popularity, has done rather poorly. Many tasks have been found to exhibit parallelism, but turn out to obey the more complex averaging model. Development of cognitive algebra thus depended on establishing the averaging model, which is the subject of the next two subsections.

PARADOXICAL NONADDITIVITY

Adding positive information can have negative effects; a positive experience may actually decrease the net affective state. Adding negative information, similarly, can have positive effects. This paradoxical finding casts doubt on any kind of adding rule. Indeed, it seems to raise doubt about any simple rule of integration.

Actually, this paradoxical nonadditivity was predicted by the averaging hypothesis, and it has been verified in numerous experimental tests. One such test was included in the study of person cognition discussed in Figure 6.4. In this figure, the parallelism of the four solid curves supports the adding model, as already noted. There is, however, one other model that also predicts parallelism, namely, the equal weight case of the averaging model. This experiment included a critical test to distinguish between adding and averaging.

The critical test between adding and averaging is provided by the dashed curve, labeled *None* in Figure 6.4. The data points on this curve represent judgments based only on the predicate information, with no adjective being specified. The dashed curve crosses over the curve labeled *Moderate*. The crossover of these two curves eliminates the adding model and supports the averaging model.

The logic of this crossover test is straightforward. For both the *None* and *Moderate* curves, the judgment is based on the predicate information listed on the horizontal axis. The *None* curve contains no more information; the *Moderate* curve contains the added information that the man is moderate. Since this added information is moderately favorable, the *Moderate* curve would have to lie above the *None* curve at every point, according to a strict adding process. But in fact the two curves cross over. It cannot be argued that *Moderate* is slightly negative, for in that case the *Moderate* curve would have to lie below the *None* curve at every point. No contrast effect was involved, as shown by separate tests. The crossover thus rules out the strict adding model. Indeed, the crossover rules out a whole family of adding models, including those with diminishing returns and others that are not numerically additive.

The averaging hypothesis predicts the crossover. If *moderate* is averaged in, that will lower the response to the very positive *helps people*. Also, it will raise the response to the very negative *hates people*. The crossover thus requires consideration of an essentially new rule of integration, which is taken up next.

AVERAGING MODEL

The averaging model, with initial state included, may be written in the foregoing notation as

$$r_{ij} = (w_0 s_0 + w_{Ai} s_{Ai} + w_{Bj} s_{Bj})/(w_0 + w_{Ai} + w_{Bj}). \qquad (5)$$

Here s_{Ai} and s_{Bj} are the scale values of the two stimulus variables. The weights, or importance, of the stimuli are denoted by w_{Ai} and w_{Bj}. The subscript 0 refers to the *initial state,* or preexperimental information, an important construct but one that will not be considered here.

The numerator of Eq. (5) is just a weighted sum. Dividing by the sum of the weights in the denominator converts this weighted sum to a weighted average. This denominator is the source of the differences between the adding and averaging models.

One special case of the averaging model is the *equal weight* case, in which all levels of the A variable have equal weight, and similarly, for B: $w_{Ai} = w_A$ and $w_{Bj} = w_B$. In this special case, the denominator of Eq. (5) is constant and the averaging model is equivalent to an adding model. Hence the parallelism theorem applies to the equal-weight case of the averaging model.

This last point deserves emphasis. The foregoing discussion of the four solid curves in Figure 6.4 applies equally well to both the adding and the averaging models. Measurement scales of response and stimulus are the same regardless of which model lies behind the parallelism. The simplicity of this analysis means that equal weighting is often useful and worth seeking experimentally.

With unequal weighting, however, the averaging model no longer predicts parallelism. Unequal weighting may be produced by manipulating amount or reliability of information, for example, and this will cause predictable deviations from parallelism [see Anderson, 1981 (Sect. 4.4)]. The crossover of Figure 6.4 illustrates one such weight manipulation, based on amount of information.

A remarkable property of the averaging model is that it allows measurement of the weight parameters of qualitatively different variables on a ratio scale with a common unit [see Anderson, 1974a, 1982 (Sect. 2.3)]. Valid comparisons of importance of verbal and nonverbal information, for example, thus become possible. Also, the scale values of qualitatively different variables can be measured on a common scale with common unit. Verbal and nonverbal information can thus be compared in value as well as in weight.

Current methods for comparing importance of different variables are generally incorrect, as is noted in the later discussion of recognizing emotion. Current methods typically rest on some form of adding model, such as a regression model. But adding models do not generally allow identification of weights. The averaging model can resolve this problem.

The advantages of the averaging model come at a cost of complications in experimental design and statistical analysis [see Anderson, 1982 (Sect. 2.3)]. The estimation problems have become tractable with the user-friendly AVERAGE program developed by Zalinski and Anderson (1986, in press), but these technical issues are not of present concern.

COGNITIVE ALGEBRA

Empirical studies with the foregoing theory and methods have revealed a fairly general cognitive algebra. Considerable experimental work has been done in the areas of judgment–decision theory, psychophysics, learning-motivation, social cognition, and developmental psychology. Of special interest is the finding of exact algebraic rules in children even younger than 4 years. This suggests that cognitive algebra is a matter of biological maturation, for it is hard to see reinforcement contingencies in the environment that could produce this precision of behavior.

Besides its intrinsic interest, cognitive algebra provides a useful tool for cognitive analysis. It is the base for a general, practicable theory of psychological measurement. No less important is its role in analysis of functional memory, attention, comparison, and other cognitive processes.

MEASUREMENT ISSUES

Emotion theory, it seems fair to say, requires a general theory of measurement. Among the desiderata of such a theory are capabilities for (1) measuring both affective and nonaffective determinants of emotion, (2) measuring both conscious and unconscious emotion, (3) dealing with both verbal and nonverbal response, (4) analyzing general affective reactions, and (5) measurement for individual organisms. A number of topics relating to these desiderata are taken up in this section.

GENERAL MEASUREMENT THEORY

Measurement of emotion should be conceptualized as part of a more general theory of psychological measurement. One reason is multiple determination, for emotional reactions commonly depend on nonaffective as well as affective information. Expectancy of a phobic stimulus is as important as the phobic stimulus itself, as in the snake fear experiment of Figure 6.2. Measurement of both kinds of information is necessary for analysis of emotional reactions. A measurement theory with adequate breadth for emotion theory must also handle nonaffective determinants.

Furthermore, emotion must be measurable both as stimulus and as response. This point appeared in the earlier discussion of preconscious and conscious emotion, and a related point appears in goal dynamics. Goal dynamics implies that emotion functions not only as a response to initial stimulus conditions, but also as stimulus to subsequent action. Anger at a disparaging review, for example, may be a strong stimulus for action. The nature of this action, of course, also commonly depends on nonaffective factors. Perspectives that slight either kind of information are too narrow to handle emotions.

The dangers of narrowness appear in contemporary cognitive psychology, much of which literally has no place for emotion or affect. Studies of thinking

and problem solving typically concentrate on abstract tasks that have little relation to feelings and decisions of everyday life. Studies of memory are dominated
by the tradition of reproductive memory, which has little room for affect or even
functional memory. Decision theory, although taking values as a central concept,
shuns inquiry into the origin and nature of these values. Even social cognition,
heavily affective by nature, has usually been conceived as though cognition were
nonaffective (see Berscheid, 1982; Fiske, 1982; Zajonc, 1980).

This narrowness of current cognitive theory has been put succinctly in Simon's
(1982, p. 337) contrast between affect and cognition: "How can two languages
[of affect and cognition] that are so radically different, not only in vocabulary
and syntax, but in their very units of meaning, communicate with each other?"
The answer is that this is a false question that identifies cognition with Simon's
theory of problem solving. The Expectancy × Valence model of Figure 6.2
illustrates how affect and cognition can communicate with each other in common
measure.

Cognition needs to be construed on broader foundations. Emotion and affect
cannot be tacked on as afterthoughts; they need to be integrated from the beginning. Related views may be seen in certain of the cognitive theories of emotion
already cited, and this is reemphasized in the present focus on general theory of
psychological measurement.

VALIDITY OF CONSCIOUS REPORT

The validity of conscious report has been a central concern in integration
theory because the great majority of integration studies have relied on verbal
report. The question is whether such observable response gives veridical measures of unobservable conscious feeling. This question appears in the parallelism
and linear fan theorems, which assume that the observable R is a veridical or
linear function of the unobservable r.

How to obtain linear scales empirically has been a standing problem in psychology, most notably in psychophysics. Although the existence of subjective
metrics is intuitively clear for psychophysical sensations such as loudness and
grayness, different methods of measurement have yielded different results.

How sharply two methods can disagree appears in comparing the rating method with magnitude estimation. In rating, each stimulus is judged relative to two
standards, corresponding to the two end points of the rating scale. In the method
of magnitude estimation (Stevens, 1974), each stimulus is judged relative to a
single standard. If the standard were called 100, say, the subject would be
instructed to judge a given stimulus as 50, 75, or 200, according to whether it
seemed half, three-fourths, or twice the magnitude of the standard.

Rating and magnitude estimation are both easy to use. Subjects may use both

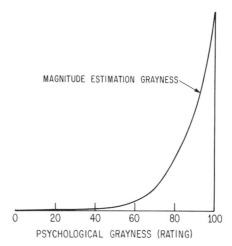

FIGURE 6.5.   Magnitude estimation of grayness disagrees sharply with rating of grayness. (After Anderson, 1982.)

methods in alternate sessions without any feeling that they are doing anything essentially different. But the two methods yield quite different results.

How different these methods can be is shown in Figure 6.5. Grayness of Munsell chips judged by magnitude estimation is plotted as a function of grayness judged by rating. If the two methods were equivalent, the graph would be a straight diagonal, from lower left to upper right. This is far from true. At least one method must yield a nonlinear scale of sensation.

How can the correct method be determined? The parallelism theorem provides a validational criterion. It is only necessary to choose an integration task that obeys an adding-type rule, for example, judging average grayness of two Munsell chips. The correct method is the one that yields parallelism.

Rating and magnitude estimation both have equal opportunity to satisfy the parallelism criterion, but not both can succeed. Figure 6.5 shows that at least one must yield nonparallelism. As it happened, the rating method succeeded and magnitude estimation failed (see Anderson, 1982, Fig. 1.3). Integration studies of other psychophysical tasks and dimensions have also generally supported the rating method. This makes it possible to determine the psychophysical law. A basic problem of classical psychophysics was thus resolved with integration psychophysics.

RATING METHODOLOGY

The rating method is subject to well-known biases. Functional measurement was successful with rating because experimental techniques were developed to eliminate these biases. Foremost among these techniques is the use of *end an-*

chors. These are special stimuli, a little more extreme than the regular experimental stimuli, that are used to define the ends of the rating scale. These end anchors, together with a few practice trials, set up a frame of reference that is essential for using a rating scale. Further detail is given in Anderson [1982 (chap. 1)]. These techniques cannot be taken for granted, as shown by the difficulties with loudness [Anderson, 1982 (Note 1.1.7c)]. Nevertheless, this form of rating method has provided linear scales in many domains, from psychophysics to social affect.

The graphic rating format has substantial advantages over the 1–10-type numerical format [Anderson, 1982 (Sect. 1.1)]. The subject sees a line, 10 or 20 cm in length, say, and marks or points to some location on this line to indicate the magnitude of the given stimulus relative to the two end anchors. Being typically unmarked, except for the two ends, this graphic format reduces number preferences. The graphic format also reduces memory effects when a succession of judgments is required of some changing affective state. Being nonverbal, moreover, the graphic format is usable with young children.

The key problem, of course, was to find how to eliminate the several biases to which all rating formats are subject. This was only possible with a validational criterion to assess response linearity, a validational criterion that was provided by the parallelism theorem and similar methods of functional measurement theory.

SCALE TYPE

The main scale types in functional measurement are *monotone, linear,* and *ratio*. For a linear scale, the observable measure R is a linear function of the unobservable r, as defined in the parallelism theorem. For a monotone scale, it is only required that R and r have the same rank order, so that R is a monotone function of r. The monotone and linear scales correspond to the customary *ordinal* and *interval* scales (Stevens, 1974), but they have a clearer conceptual definition in terms of the functional relation between the observable and the unobservable. The ratio scale is a linear scale with a known, natural zero.

Monotone scales are adequate for the majority of empirical investigations, for example, to test whether one treatment for phobics is more effective than another or whether the intensity of some emotion may be affected by the intensity of some stimulus variable. There is a lingering misconception that analysis of variance is not permissible with monotone scales; in fact, a monotone (ordinal) scale may actually be statistically superior to a linear (interval) scale [Anderson, 1982 (Sects. 1.1.9 and 5.4)]. For many important questions, response linearity is not needed.

For certain questions, however, linear scales are essential. A correct adding model, for example, will generally fail the parallelism test unless the response measure is linear. Similar questions sometimes arise in disguised form. Current methods of comparing the relative importance of verbal, nonverbal, and other kinds of information, for example, are seldom meaningful because of uncertainty about scale linearity (Anderson, 1982, Sect. 6.1.4). The interpretation of *interaction* terms in analysis of variance may also depend critically on possession of linear response measures [Anderson, 1982 (Sects. 7.10 and 7.11)].

Knowledge of an affective zero is necessary for certain questions. To illustrate the problem, a decrease from 40 to 30°C cannot properly be called a 25% decrease when the equivalent decrease from 104 to 86°F is 17%. The problem arises because the Celsius and Fahrenheit scales both have arbitrary zero points. A psychological example appears in the claim that placebos reduce clinical pain in double-blind tests by 50% as much as the analgesic being tested—both for strong and weak analgesics (Evans, 1974). The very same placebo is thus much less effective when aspirin is being tested than when morphine is being tested. The interpretation, which has achieved considerable currency, is that the physician's belief about the potency of the analgesic is somehow communicated through the double-blind procedure to the placebo patients to produce a proportionate effect. This interpretation reflects Evans's position on the importance of placebo effects.

The claim, however, seems not meaningful. It rests on the assumption that pain was measured on a ratio scale, for which there is neither evidence nor likelihood. The "seven reviewed studies" (Evans, 1974) that formed the basis for the morphine–placebo comparison are not identified or referenced and almost no detail is presented. There is a suggestion that patients rated pain on a 4- or 5-point rating scale, but this would surely not provide a ratio scale. The claim thus appears to reflect a measurement misconception lacking any empirical support.

The parallelism and linear fan theorems require only linear scales; knowledge of zero points is unnecessary. This is a notable advantage for ease and generality of application. The averaging model also requires only a linear response, but it can go farther to provide information on stimulus zeros as noted earlier.

Some tasks involve categorical response measures, or nominal scales, as in recognition studies of emotion faces and in applications of signal detection theory to pain research (Clark & Yang, 1983; Rollman, 1977). Extensions of functional measurement ideas to handle categorical data have been made for signal detection [Anderson, 1982 (Sect. 3.10)] and in an impressive body of work on a ratio model for speech perception by Massaro (1979, 1985; Oden & Massaro, 1978). These extensions, however, lie outside the scope of this chapter [see Anderson, 1982 (Sects. 1.1.9, 7.8, 7.10, 7.11, Note 5.2c, and chap. 5)].

Finally, it should be pointed out that the assumptions of linear response in the parallelism and linear fan theorems is a convenience, not a necessity. If only a monotone, rank-order scale is available, it is possible in principle to transform it into a true linear scale. Empirical illustrations appear in psychophysical bisection [Anderson, 1981 (Sect. 1.3.8)] and neural integration of brain stimulation

(Hawkins, Roll, Puerto, & Yeomans, 1983). The statistical analysis is practicable, though not simple [see Anderson, 1982 (chap. 5)]. At bottom, therefore, functional measurement rests solely on the algebraic structure of the integration function.

NONVERBAL RESPONSE

The parallelism and linear fan theorems may be applied to behavioral and physiological variables—both as response and as stimulus. As response variables, nonverbal reactions may be analyzed in accord with these theorems [see, e.g., Anderson, 1981 (Sects. 1.3.8, 1.5.2, 1.5.5, and 1.5.7)]. As stimulus variables, moreover, functional scales of behavioral and physiological variables may be derived even from a rating response, by virtue of the second conclusion of the theorems. An interesting application would be to ratings of facial expressions of very young children (see Beuchler & Izard, 1983, pp. 309–311).

Nonverbal response measurement is clearly necessary for emotion theory, as with children and animals and in behavioral or physiological investigations. Analysis is simplest if the raw response is a linear scale, as with the snake avoidance data of Figure 6.2. However, monotone (ordinal) scales can be transformed into true linear scales, as indicated in the previous subsection. True psychological scales of behavioral and physiological response, such as amount of vocalization, frequency of facial movements, and measures of arousal, are thus potentially obtainable.

STATES AND TRAITS

The customary state–trait distinction may reasonably be summarized by saying that traits are considered average states, the average being taken over some set of situations or contexts. The fact of multiple determination, together with the variability of the environment, implies that traits will be weakly related to actual behavior because traits average out contextual effects.

The low predictiveness of traits has been emphasized in current interactionist and contextualist views in personality theory (e.g., Magnusson, 1981; Mischel, 1968; Sarbin, 1977). These views typically go farther and criticize the usefulness and validity of trait conceptualizations.

This criticism is partially justified. Trait measures can be useful, as illustrated later in Kaplan's (1971a, 1971b, 1971c) studies of personality disposition, but they are often reified in one-dimensional form. This reification is implicit in measurement methodologies that impose some kind of homogeneity, for example, that items and subtests must be intercorrelated to measure the same "thing." This practice expresses the implicit assumptions that proper test items make contact with some graded quality and serve to measure how much of it is there.

In the functional measurement view, traits are conceptualized as knowledge systems for dealing with the environment. Traits are like attitudes, therefore, not average states. Trait measures, correspondingly, are like attitudinal responses, being the functional expression of the knowledge system in some test setting. In general, trait-based responses are goal-oriented adaptations to the momentary situation. Different persons may express the same trait in different ways; low and high levels may be represented in different action patterns. Two test items may thus measure the same trait even though they have zero intercorrelation. Trait theory, accordingly, requires measurement directed at function (see also Benjamin, 1984; Janke, 1983; Sjöberg, 1982).

The contextualist and interactionist views rightly emphasize the joint roles of person, situation, and their interaction. These views have remained largely programmatic, however, owing to lack of theory of multiple determination. In a few useful cases, person and situation might follow an averaging model, as in the later discussion of mood, but such simple integration rules can hardly have much generality. The primary loci of person–environment interaction are in valuation and action, especially in goal setting. Little is known about goal dynamics, however, and new theoretical models are required.

PROCESS GENERALITY AND
OUTCOME GENERALITY

Generalizations may be sought at the level of *outcome* or at the level of *process*. These two goals usually entail different considerations of design and procedure and are to some degree incompatible (Anderson, 1981, 1982, 1986). Among other differences, outcome studies usually involve between-subject design, with different subjects in each treatment condition. Process studies, in contrast, ideally use within-subject design, with each subject in multiple treatment conditions.

Experimental studies of phobic cases, for illustration, usually seek outcome generality, hoping that the treatment that is more effective with one sample of patients and therapists will generalize to others. Large samples are necessary because of large individual differences in responsiveness to therapy, and different subjects are usually required in each treatment condition. True phobic subjects also seem essential, for Emmelkamp's (1982) review indicates that treatments effective with everyday fears seldom generalize to clinical populations. Because of the concern with changing behavior, moreover, treatment conditions tend to include anything and everything that might help, with secondary concern about confounding of cognitive process. These procedures are appropriate for outcome generality, but they are undesirable for process generality.

Within-subject design is typical of integration studies. In the snake phobic study of Figure 6.2, for example, each subject served in all nine experimental conditions. This provides greater precision and power in the data analysis than would be obtained from between-subject design [Anderson, 1982 (Sect. 1.3.1)]. This greater power is important, sometimes essential, to obtain worthwhile tests of integration rules. Once established, the integration rule can be used in further process analysis, as in delineating the role of unconscious emotion in the conscious reaction.

SINGLE-SUBJECT DESIGN AND PERSONAL DESIGN

Single-subject design and personal design are used to study single cases. Each separate subject would constitute a complete experiment that could be analyzed by itself. Single-subject design is a straightforward extension of within-subject design, requiring only that each subject serve in more than one replication of the factorial design. For process analysis, whether cognitive or clinical, single-subject design is an ideal, for process has its locus in the individual. Illustrative examples from person cognition are given in Anderson [1981 (Sect. 2.2.1), 1982 (Fig. 6.3)].

Personal design carries this individualization one step further to tailor stimulus materials and procedure to the individual (see Anderson, in press-c; Anderson & Armstrong, 1989). Different phobics, for example, fear different objects or situations. Hence stimulus materials would often need to be selected individually. The stimulus levels of each variable would thus be relevant and meaningful to the individual. The same general design may thus be personalized to each of several individuals. Unconscious emotion could thus be measured at the individual level in the same way as previously indicated for group data in Figure 6.2.

One potential application is to projective tests. Projective tests rest on the idea that unconscious impulses, ordinarily repressed, may manifest themselves in reactions to ambiguous stimuli that do not trigger ego defenses. This idea could be incorporated in an integration design, by including stimuli that elicit low levels of the unconscious impulses to be integrated with other stimulus factors in the design. The unconscious impulses are thus incorporated into the conscious response, from whence they could be fractionated using functional measurement. This application is speculative, for it depends on development of appropriate integration tasks. Within the realm of repressed affect, however, it suggests a rigorous supplement to the method of psychoanalysis (Brenner, 1980).

EXPERIMENTAL PARADIGMS

This section considers experimental analysis, to illustrate specific ways that information integration theory may help in the study of emotions. The integration approach provides a base for conceptual and experimental issues that is not predicated on formal taxonomy of emotions. The following applications, accordingly, include some affective reactions, such as pain and social affect, in which emotional components are important but perhaps not central. Some of these applications are based on existing studies, as with phobias, blame, and recognizing emotion. Others are more speculative, as with clinical pain and divided visual fields.

PHOBIAS

Phobias offer an interesting empirical domain for the study of emotion. Phobics come with living emotions that are subject to some degree of experimental manipulation. Fear of specific objects and situations can be manipulated by proximity and other stimulus characteristics. More general fears, such as social anxiety and agoraphobia, are amenable to similar manipulation (Emmelkamp, 1982; Marks, 1969). Such experimental manipulations are possible within socially acceptable frameworks and can facilitate the study of cognitive process in phobias.

In an experimental study with everyday snake phobics [Klitzner, 1977; reported by Anderson, 1981 (Sect. 1.5.5)], subjects could purchase chances to avoid a picture, rubber, or real snake, with the probability that the snake stimulus would actually be avoided varied over three levels on different trials. They also rated fearfulness of each of these experimental conditions. Both responses, however, depend not only on the fear valence of the snake stimulus, but also on the subjective expectancy set up by the probability stimulus. The integration of these affective and nonaffective determinants was hypothesized to obey the multiplying rule

$$\text{Fear Behavior} = \text{Expectancy} \times \text{Valence}$$

The avoidance data, shown earlier in Figure 6.2, had a near perfect linear fan pattern; an analogous fan pattern was obtained with the ratings of fear. This fan pattern supports the Expectancy × Valence rule, by virtue of the linear fan theorem. The verbal equation is thus transformed into a true cognitive equation with functional measurement methodology (Anderson, 1978; Klitzner & Anderson, 1977).

This cognitive equation goes beyond showing that cognitive expectancy factors influence emotional response to determine the rule of influence. The integration rule was the same for the avoidance behavior and the conscious report, moreover, which provides mutual support for the validity of both measures of fear.

At the same time, this analysis fractionates the observed emotional response into a cognitive expectancy component and an emotional valence component. Both unobservable stimulus determinants thus become measurable. By the second conclusion of the linear fan theorem, the slopes of the lines give the expectancy values. Similarly, the valences of the three snake stimuli are proportional to their spacing on the horizontal axis.

This fractionation of the response into its two subjective stimulus determinants illustrates the distinction between conscious and unconscious emotion discussed in the introductory section. Also, it underscores the theme of multiple determination: Observable behavior cannot be well understood without conceptual and methodological analysis of stimulus integration.

The analysis also implies that the conscious report is a veridical measure of the unobservable conscious fear, as noted in the subsection on consciousness. A further implication is that expectancy and valence are proper cognitive units, for otherwise an exact fan pattern would be unlikely. This illustrates two ways in which algebraic models can winnow truth from everyday language.

Cognitive process in clinical phobias could be studied in a similar manner, with personal design for individual patients. What characterizes phobics is their nonnormal expectancies and valences; yet these nonnormal values are as basic to their cognition as everyday fears are to everyday cognition. Once phobics' values are taken into account, much of their cognitive process, especially their integration rules, may be quite normal.

The essential idea of personal design, as previously described, is to embed the integration task within the knowledge system of the individual. Personal design is congruent with the emphasis on *in vivo* or contextual therapy (DuPont, 1982; Emmelkamp, 1982), which seeks treatment within the specific everyday settings that elicit each patient's phobic reactions. Integration analysis may then facilitate study of cognitive process for individual cases. For example, the observation of Hardy (1982) and Flaxman (1982) that phobics are prone to always-or-never valuation could be put to test with personal design to determine its degree of truth and its generality beyond the phobic system. Further discussion of the potential of personal design within therapy situations is given in Anderson and Armstrong (1989).

The present approach, of course, is mainly concerned with cognitive analysis. Therapy entails different design considerations, as noted under process-outcome generality. Work on phobic reactions has been dominated by a search for outcome generality, and cognitive process is virtually terra incognita. Despite general recognition of the importance of multiple determination, for example, no other study of integration rules in phobic thinking was found.

RECOGNIZING EMOTION

One facet of the integration problem has been considered in studies of emotion recognition, namely, what kind of information is more important. Typical are attempts to compare the relative importance of verbal and nonverbal information, for example, or facial expression and voice quality. Perhaps without exception, these studies rest on invalid methods of measurement. A reasonably complete analysis has been obtained with functional measurement [Anderson, 1981 (Sect. 4.4), 1982 (Sects. 2.3, 6.1, 7.9, and Notes 6.1.4c,d)].

The question of relative importance depends squarely on measurement theory. To illustrate, consider the case of verbal (V) and nonverbal (NV) information with an adding rule of integration:

$$R = w_V s_V + w_{NV} s_{NV}.$$

What is usually intended by the term "importance" is the weight parameter, w. The value parameter, s, is not generally appropriate because it will differ for different information items of the same type. The s value of a verbal item, for example, could be large or small, depending on its content. Opposite conclusions about relative importance could thus be obtained, depending on an arbitrary choice of information items. Importance thus ordinarily refers to the type, or channel, of information, independent of particular channel content.

But the w parameter cannot generally be measured with the adding model. Each weight is inextricably confounded with the unit of the corresponding value scale. Except in special cases, therefore, valid comparison of weight parameters for different types, or channels, of information is mathematically impossible with an adding model.

It follows that the popular regression method is inappropriate, for it embodies an adding model. Regression weights are not valid measures of importance because of the cited unit confounding. Standardizing the weights merely changes the locus of the confounding. Interpretations based on regression weights, such as the oft-cited conclusion of Mehrabian (1972) that facial expression is more important than voice quality, are seldom meaningful. Such data simply have no bearing on the conclusion (Anderson, 1982, pp. 275–276).

Similar considerations apply to various studies by Ekman and his collaborators (e.g., Ekman, Friesen, & Ellsworth, 1972; Ekman, Friesen, O'Sullivan, & Scherer, 1980; O'Sullivan, Ekman, Friesen, & Scherer, 1985). Ekman has criticized other workers for using artificial situations and for limited samples of stimuli, but the measurement problem is more basic. In Ekman et al. (1980), for example, importance was measured by the correlation between the judgment based on each single information channel and the judgment based on all information channels considered together. This involves an implicit shift in the definition of importance, from a weight concept to a magnitude concept involving scale values [Anderson, 1982 (Sect. 6.1)]. Moreover, the sizes of these correlations depend on the ranges of stimulus values for the several channels. Since these ranges are typically arbitrary, so also are the conclusions (Anderson, 1982, Sect. 7.9).

The problem of measurement depends on the operative integration model.

This may be illustrated with Frijda's (1969) relative shift ratio for comparing importance of face (F) and context (C) in judging emotion: $|R_{FC} - R_F|/|R_{FC} - R_C|$, where R_F, R_C, and R_{FC} denote the judgments based on face alone, context alone, and face and context together. This ratio seems to provide a direct, empirical index of relative importance based on the two relative change scores in the numerator and denominator. Adding context to face changes the response by $|R_{FC} - R_F|$; adding face to context changes the response by $|R_{FC} - R_C|$. When these two changes are equal, context and face would seem equally important, reflected in a ratio of 1. By similar reasoning, ratios greater or less than 1 reflect greater or lesser importance of context.

Measurement analysis, however, shows that this ratio has one meaning under the adding model, a different meaning under the averaging model without initial state, and no simple meaning under the averaging model with initial state [Anderson, 1976 (Sect. 7.3.8), 1982 (pp. 276–277)]. Without knowledge of the operative integration rule, importance is not generally determinate (Anderson, 1982, Notes 6.1.4c,d).

The averaging model, as indicated previously, does allow proper measurement of weights. What is not possible with adding models or regression-correlation models becomes possible with the averaging model, owing to its different algebraic structure. Since the averaging model has substantial empirical validity, valid comparisons of importance in recognizing emotion seem attainable.

Relative importance, it should be added, may not have much outcome generality. The weight parameter is not a fixed property of each given piece of information, as noted in the discussion of valuation. The same piece of information will have different importance, depending on situation, context, and goal, so little outcome generality can be expected. Of course, study of such dependencies can be useful in analysis of cognitive process.

The functional measurement analysis shows that the concept of importance is essentially theoretical, not empirical. Everyday language makes it seem empirical, a determinate matter of fact, which is not correct. Everyday language does contain an important intuition in distinguishing between scale value and weight. This intuition is an invaluable beginning for cognitive theory, but it is only a beginning and needs to be clarified and corrected. In general, everyday language and phenomenology need to be clarified and corrected, which requires a deeper base for analysis (Anderson, 1981, pp. 84–85). As this example of the concept of importance shows, cognitive algebra can contribute to this endeavor.

MOOD

A central problem in the study of mood is how it influences judgment and action. Several ways are indicated by the integration diagram of Figure 6.1. Mood may be conceptualized as an active assemblage that can operate in valuation, integration, action, and goal setting. In valuation, for example, mood would influence the w–s parameters of other given information. However, mood effects may be obtained more directly by integration of the w–s parameters of the mood state. This question of mood integration is the main concern here.

Mood integration has been studied in two theories of interpersonal attraction, one based on information integration theory, the other based on the reinforce- ment-conditioning model of Byrne (1969; Clore & Byrne, 1974). Both theories were tested in a systematic series of studies on personality disposition and mood in interpersonal attraction by Kaplan (1971a, 1971b, 1971c).

Kaplan's main purpose was to test the hypotheses that personality disposition and mood state can both be considered internal stimuli that are integrated with other, given information. An adjective checklist was used to assess subjects' dispositions toward others, considered as a stable trait rather than a temporary mood state. Positive, negative, or neutral mood was induced by a simulated radio broadcast, presented incidentally during an initial period while the subjects were waiting for the experimenter to appear. When the experimenter did appear, subjects were given descriptions of various persons and judged them on interper- sonal liking and attraction.

Personality disposition and mood were both found to follow an exact averag- ing rule. In Kaplan's interpretation, disposition and mood affected the initial state, an internal stimulus represented by the w_0–s_0 parameters in Eq. (5). Although disposition could not be manipulated, it could be assessed through the model by manipulating other, given information. A variety of such tests, involv- ing value and amount of information, source reliability, and induced mood, provided notable support, both qualitative and quantitative, for the averaging model [see summary in Anderson, 1981 (Sect. 4.3.1)].

Other mood studies that have addressed the integration problem have been conducted within the framework of Byrne's (1969; Clore & Byrne, 1974) rein- forcement-conditioning theory of interpersonal attraction. Mood was induced with neutral or aversive temperature by Griffitt (1970), for example, and with happy or sad films by Gouaux (1971). Both mood manipulations evidently had an additive effect with other information about hypothetical persons, as may be inferred from their parallelism analyses. This agrees with the averaging rule. Neither study, however, discriminated between Byrne's reinforcement theory and the theory of information integration. Kaplan, who did use discriminative tests, found clear superiority for the informational view of interpersonal attrac- tion [see Anderson, 1981 (Fig. 4.13)].

The foregoing mood effects may be interpreted in terms of a *general integra- tion propensity* to form integrated wholes, even with ostensibly irrelevant con- textual stimuli [Anderson, 1981 (Sect. 4.1.8)]. Mood may thus have direct effects on judgment and action, in accord with the conceptualization of affect as cognition. It is not necessary to assume that mood effects are mediated by some other process, for mood per se may be integrated into the response.

This implication differs from prevailing views, which generally assume some mediating process to account for mood effects. This assumption of mediating process appears in memory interpretations of mood, as by Bower and by Isen. Bower (1981; Bower & Cohen, 1982) postulates a basic set of emotions that correspond to specific nodes in a network of associative memory. This form of memory representation stems from traditional reproductive memory, which seems appropriate for the reproductive tasks, recall and recognition, with which Bower was primarily concerned. Judgment and action, however, require a rather different conception of functional memory.

Isen's memory interpretation, based on interesting studies of everyday behavior in natural settings (e.g., Isen, Means, Patrick, & Nowicki, 1982; Isen, Shalker, Clark, & Karp, 1978), rests on the assumption that induced mood acts as a retrieval cue for memories with similar affective tone. This retrieval assumption has some affinity with the present representation of mood as an assemblage activated by the mood induction. Isen, however, sees this as a two-stage process, in which mood is initially represented as a feeling state and this feeling state then elicits material from memory. This memory retrieval is assumed to be the causal agent in the mood effects.

But the present view would allow the feeling state to act directly, without requiring mediation through memory retrieval. In particular, feeling state may be integrated directly into the response, by virtue of the general integration propensity. The very same interpretation would apply to various of Isen's findings, for example, that receiving a small gift caused subjects to think better of their cars and TV sets (Isen et al., 1978). The memory retrieval interpretation was apparently considered necessary because the possibility of direct effects of feeling state was not recognized. Whether there is any evidence that actually requires a retrieval assumption, beyond that involved in assemblage of the mood state itself, is outside the scope of this discussion.

A related issue arises in interpreting effects of mood on memory-based judgments. Eich, Reeves, Jaeger, and Graff-Radford (1985), for example, found that pains were remembered as more or less intense than those recorded in diaries, according to whether present pain level was more or less intense. Similar effects were obtained by Bower (1981, p. 133) for judgments of emotional intensity of past diary incidents. In both cases, present mood should theoretically be integrated with the memorial information. This represents the *positive context effect* of integration theory, for the present mood will color the memory-based judgments—without necessarily affecting memory itself [Anderson, 1981 (Sect. 4.1, in press-b)]. Memory effects will be important in various situations, of course, and the present discussion may help unify the study of judgment and memory.

Mood has been attractive to many investigators, for simple experimental manipulations can have substantial effects on diverse affective responses. However, two complexities have also been emphasized. First, a single mood manipulation may induce not (only) mood, but nonaffective *side effects,* such as activity level or social pressure, that confound interpretation of observed results. Second, mood can have similar effects through different processes, as illustrated in the foregoing discussion of memory effects. Both complexities go beyond the scope of this chapter, but the problem of goal dynamics deserves brief discussion.

The informational view implies that emotion and affect have motivational properties. Positive affect is not merely a feeling state, therefore, but a signal for action whose consequences tend to perpetuate positive affect. Good mood will beget good mood because integration of the mood state will automatically raise the affective tone of subsequent judgments and activities. Feeling good, moreover, will not merely cause other persons to seem more likeable, but will also tend to elicit more positive social action, complimenting a colleague, for example, which may be self-reinforcing (Berkowitz, 1972) or which may elicit positive social feedback (Isen et al., 1982; Nowlis & Nowlis, 1956), both of which would augment good mood. Also at the action stage, good mood may lead to selection of more pleasant activities, deciding to play some music, for example, or simply pausing to admire the sights and sounds of the moment, which also would tend to perpetuate good mood. Mood thus becomes motivation.

Bad mood tends to beget bad mood by many of the same mechanisms just considered for good mood. Good–bad symmetry appeared in Kaplan's mood study, but symmetry should not be expected in general, for many bad moods tend to be avoided, whereas good moods tend to be sought. A curious complication that deserves investigation is that not all bad moods are avoided. Some bad moods apparently serve goal functions, as in blaming, envy, and other strong negative affects that often accompany the ubiquitous factions of social life.

SOCIAL AFFECT

Affective reactions pervade social life; friendship and love are on the positive side, blame, envy, and jealousy are on the negative side; other affective reactions include pride, showing off, and even confidence. Experimental analysis, however, has been hobbled by the sharp traditional separation between affect and cognition. On the one hand, standard cognitive psychology has been at a loss when faced with the facts of affective life (see e.g., Norman, 1980; Reykowski, 1982; Simon, 1982; Zajonc, 1980). On the other hand, social-psychological studies of affect have, with a few notable exceptions, largely neglected or avoided cognition (see Berscheid, 1982; Fiske, 1982).

The concept of attitude, considered by many to be the foundation concept of social psychology, illustrates the inappropriateness of the affective–cognitive dichotomy. Whereas the standard view in social psychology sees attitudes as one-dimensional affective reactions (see Berscheid, 1982; Cacioppo et al., 1981), integration theory conceptualizes attitudes as knowledge systems that function in goal-directed activity. This entails a concept of functional memory, rather than reproductive memory, together with cognitive operators that subserve goal-directed activity (see Figure 6.1). Attitudes thus manifest themselves as attitudinal responses in relation to particular goals. Goal directedness often imposes a one-dimensional affective character, in terms of approach or avoidance, on attitudinal responses. It is these attitudinal responses that are taken as attitudes in the standard view. In the present view, in contrast, attitudinal responses cannot be well understood without reference to the underlying attitude, which forms a cognitive–affective knowledge system.

Similar need for a unified treatment of affect and cognition appears in recognition of emotion and, more generally, in social attribution, in which states or traits are attributed to people to explain their behavior. Recognition of emotion, although ordinarily studied as a matter of objective accuracy, rests basically on attribution. Apple (1979), who used integration methods to study the role of nonverbal voice and gesture cues in recognition of emotion, obtained evidence for an adding-type model. These results extend work on person cognition, and point to the operation of a general cognitive algebra of social attribution (Anderson, 1974b).

Blaming, as another example, typically rests on some judgment of intention, or social responsibility, which is an attribution to the person rather than an observable property of the person. Blame itself may be considered an attribution. Kelley's (1972) attribution theory, however, disallows affect. Hence it cannot handle blame or numerous other social affects, and so is too narrow to represent social reality. An alternative theory that includes affect as part of social attribution is given in Anderson (1974b, 1976, in press-a), and an application to blame is taken up next.

BLAME SCHEMA

"Who's to blame?" and "It's not my fault" are almost reflex reactions when things go awry. They illustrate the pervasiveness of social conditioning as well as the controlling role of cognition in expression of social affect. People are generally open, moreover, not repressed, about blaming and avoiding blame, a further advantage for experimental analysis.

One line of investigation is based on the blame schema:

$$\text{Blame} = \text{Intent} + \text{Harm}$$

This schema asserts that blame for some harmful act is an integration of the intent attributed to the actor and the harm caused by the act (which may include insult, humiliation, and other ego-noxious effects). This schema has been found to follow an averaging rule in several experiments (e.g., Anderson, 1976, 1983a; Hommers & Anderson, 1985; Leon, 1980, 1984; Surber, 1982).

Leon's (1984) remarkable study of mother–son similarity in blame judgments illustrates how the blame schema can be determined exactly. Thirty-two mothers and their 7-year-old sons assigned blame to a story child for an action with specified intention (curve parameter) and harm (horizontal axis). Individual analyses of the mothers' data revealed three integration rules; their sons followed the same rule in virtually every case.

The parallelism in the top left panel of Figure 6.6 shows that 18 mothers followed a simple averaging rule; exactly the same pattern of parallelism was found in their sons' data, shown in the right side of the panel. The pattern in the center panel reflects an accident-configural rule: the lowest curve represents accidental harm, and its flatness means that degree of harm had little effect when it was accidental; but the other two curves show that harm was averaged in when any degree of intent was involved. Here again, these 10 mothers and their 10 sons show similar blame schemas. Finally, the bottom panel shows mother–son similarity for the four cases that gave zero weight to intent, judged only on the basis of harm.

Leon's study illustrates an approach that can provide quantitative results within individual families. This suggests a new line of inquiry about social learning and emotional development.

OTHER ALGEBRAIC MODELS

A striking sex difference in judgments of emotion has been claimed by Leventhal and Cupchik (1975): males average but females add. Subjects rated funniness of cartoons under one of several conditions of canned audience laughter. The cartoon and the audience laughter constitute two pieces of information that are integrated to produce the response. Previous work on integration theory would imply averaging for both sexes, contrary to the claim that females add.

Leventhal and Cupchik (1975, p. 379) rationalized the adding and averaging rules in term of a hypothesized sex difference in type of processing. Males were assumed to follow an objective integration process, in which the separate pieces of stimulus information are "stored as distinct attributes prior to making judgment." Females were assumed to follow an emotional integration process, in which the separate pieces of stimulus information "are grouped in a gestalt-like, subjective register."

The reported sex difference is notable, for it involves a qualitative difference in information processing. It is also notable because Leventhal (1980) is almost alone in his attempts to go beyond isolated demonstrations and generalities about the role of cognition in emotion to attempt a detailed, specific theory. The data

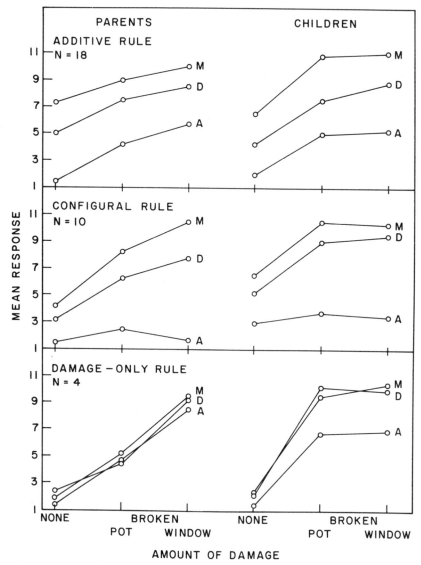

FIGURE 6.6. Mothers and sons use the same rules for integrating intent and damage information in judging punishment; see text. M, malice; D, displacement; A, accident. (From Leon, 1984, p. 2109.)

and reasoning of Leventhal and Cupchik (1975; Cupchik & Leventhal, 1974) are not easy to follow, however; the parallelism and crossover tests of Figure 6.4 would give simpler and stronger tests of their two hypothesized sex rules.

The second related study concerns the Expectancy–Valence formulation tested in the snake fear experiment of Figure 6.2. Price and Barrell (1984; Price, Barrell, & Barrell, 1985) have suggested that the Expectancy–Valence formulation represents a general law of human emotion. They emphasize the conceptual distinction between such experiential laws and psychophysical laws, paralleling the distinction between the integration and valuation functions of the integration diagram of Figure 6.1. Their analyses, unfortunately, suffer serious limitations so no test of deviations from the model is possible [see Anderson, 1982 (Sects. 4.1 and 6.2)]. However, their attempts to test the formulation in actual life situations deserve to be pursued.

Finally, functional measurement may provide exact tests of Simonov's (1970, p. 145) formula for negative emotions: "Negative emotions constitute a special nervous mechanism thrown into action when a living being lacks the information necessary and sufficient for organizing the actions that will satisfy a need." Formally, the (negative) emotion E is given by

$$E = -N(I_n - I_a),$$

where I is information and N is the need; $I_n - I_a$ is the "difference between the prognostically necessary and available information."

This formula might seem merely symbolic, not mathematical, owing to lack of methods for measuring need and information. Functional measurement can transform this symbolic formula into a true equation. It is only necessary to vary the three variables in a factorial design and measure the resulting emotion. The parallelism theorem implies that the factorial plot of $I_n \times I_a$ will exhibit parallelism. The linear fan theorem implies that the factorial plots for $N \times I_n$ and $N \times I_a$ will both exhibit linear fan patterns. Prior measurement of these three stimulus variables is not necessary. With monotone analysis [Anderson, 1982 (chap. 5), moreover, only a rank-order response scale is needed, for the algebraic structure of the model provides a base and frame for psychological measurement.

PAIN

"How much does it hurt?" is an intensely practical question that underscores the need for psychological measurement. Adults can readily use category scales (*moderate, severe*, etc.) or rate pain on a 1–10 scale, but different scales can yield very different results. How different they can be has already been shown in the comparison of graphic rating and magnitude estimation in Figure 6.5. Some questions in pain research require linear or even ratio scales, as noted in the subsection on scale types, so some criterion is needed to determine whether a given pain response measure is a true linear scale. Functional measurement can provide such a validity criterion, as with the parallelism and linear fan theorems.

The following discussion is aimed mainly at the affective, or distress, dimension of pain, although similar considerations apply to the sensory, intensity dimension. Pains differ also in quality, as with dull aches and sharp shooting pains, which can to some degree be represented in task instructions. A good overview of this fascinating field is given by Melzack and Wall (1983) and discussions of measurement are given in Bromm (1984) and Melzack (1983).

Pioneering applications of functional measurement by Jones (1980) and Jones and Gwynn (1984) found parallelism for ratings of average or combined intensity of two successive electric shocks. The most important implication, for present purposes, is that their rating scale was a true linear function of the unobservable pain response. The parallelism theorem also shows how to obtain linear scales of each separate stimulus variable. In short, pain becomes measurable.

Supportive results have been obtained by Gracely and Wolskee (1983), with a sensory–semantic integration involving electrical tooth-pulp stimulation and verbal pain descriptors. Their averaging task is interesting because the averaging model can put the pain stimuli and the verbal descriptors on a common scale with common unit. Of special interest is the careful study of cross-modal integration of painful noise and shock by Algom, Raphaeli, and Cohen-Raz (1986), which provides a more natural kind of integration. Algom et al. also argue for a functional theory of pain, based on central integration of sensory signals according to algebraic rules. This approach is reminiscent of Goldscheider's (1894, cited by Melzack & Wall, 1983) idea of central summation and contrasts with the gate-control theory of Melzack and Wall (1983).

Two other methods of quantitative response have also been used in attempts to obtain linear pain scales. The visual analog scale (see Huskisson, 1983) is similar to the graphic rating procedure developed in functional measurement. Both require certain precautions to eliminate known biases. The few foregoing functional measurement studies support the validity of the rating method, but more systematic work is desirable, especially with a variety of pain qualities.

The method of magnitude estimation, on the other hand, appears to contain inherent bias, in the form of a law of diminishing returns in the use of numbers, that produces systematic nonparallelism. Thus, Algom et al. (1986), who did use magnitude estimation, were forced to apply a transformation to obtain parallelism. Unfortunately, some pain researchers have taken Stevens' (1974) claims about magnitude estimation at face value, not realizing that neither the power law nor cross-modal matching constitutes a proper validity criterion [Anderson, 1974a, 1981 (Sect. 5.4); Hall, 1981]. A clever attempt to break through this validity barrier was made by Price, McGrath, Rafii, and Buckingham (1983), who coupled a power function fit for graphic ratings (visual analog scale) of heat-induced cutaneous pain with a fractionation procedure. The two agreed quite well, which would seem to constitute a validity check. Regrettably, their application suffers a fatal objection, for it yielded a zero point of 34°C, which implies that higher cutaneous temperatures would feel painful. Since normal body temperature is 37°C, their result implies that a finger in the mouth would feel painfully hot. The parallelism and linear fan theorems can provide proper validity criteria for power functions.

The most important direction in pain research, from the present point of view, is more extensive development of integration tasks, especially to bridge between experimental and clinical pain. Spatial integration has special interest, for it is characteristic of much clinical pain and lends itself to experimental analysis with radiant heat, bone pressure, and certain other stimulation methods. Factorial designs may be obtained by stimulation at two or more sites, allowing easy application of the parallelism theorem to test adding-type rules. Spatial integration has both clinical and physiological interest and has some likelihood of yielding simple integration rules.

Temporal integration can provide information on the dynamics of pain, including pain memory. The successive time points of stimulation would be the variables in the factorial design, following the theoretical analysis for serial integration (Anderson, 1982, Sect. 3.6). This has been studied by Jones (1980) and Jones and Gwynn (1984), who relate the time order effects to individual differences in pain intensity. Temporal integration is also characteristic of much clinical pain, and this may explain some of the substantial differences from experimental pain, which usually has short duration.

Integration of different sources of pain may contribute to structural analysis of pain. There are many types of pain and any one type may have multiple qualities (see Melzack, 1983). The noise-shock study of Algom et al. is a model that deserves extension with diverse methods of pain induction, especially those that are more characteristic of clinical pain (Wolff, 1983). This approach could be helpful in studying the structure of pain as well as interaction among types of pain.

Cognitive factors are important in pain experience and an obvious area for integration studies is that of placebo effects. A more interesting possibility would be to use phobics, say, with anxiety manipulated by proximity to the phobic stimulus and pain manipulated experimentally. Anxiety and depression are widely believed to be important causal factors in clinical pain, but the evidence is largely correlational. Although speculative, the use of phobics has the attraction of allowing experimental manipulation of anxiety with substantial realism.

Attention, which is widely recognized to be important in pain, may perhaps be represented in terms of the weight parameter of an averaging process. Equation (5) implies that placing greater weight on one stimulus necessarily decreases the *relative* weight of any other stimulus. This might help explain the beneficial effects observed from distraction. Attentional manipulations might accordingly be used in conjunction with experiments on spatial integration.

Of exceptional interest is the prospect of incorporating experimental pain within clinical cases (Chapman, 1983; Rollman, 1983). A simple integration study would overlay a two-factor design of experimental pain on a clinical pain, thereby yielding an effective three-variable integration of overall pain or distress. Component judgments of each separate pain would also be desirable for information on pain interaction. One purpose of the two-factor design is to allow validation of the response scale on an individual basis, thereby obtaining a proper measure of the clinical pain. In addition, the experimental and clinical pains might be measurable on a common scale.

Ideally, clinical pain could be manipulated as one factor of a joint clinical–experimental, personal design. This might not be impossible with hypnosis used to control the clinical pain alone. An alternative would be to capitalize on temporal trends in acute clinical pain or temporal fluctuations in chronic pain, incorporating these as a nominal temporal variable in the design. The difficulty, of course, is that such temporal changes might affect sensitivity to the experimental pain. The same objective pain stimulus might thus be psychologically different across the time variable. This would be empirically interesting, however, and it might be handled theoretically through a sensitivity parameter in a more general integration rule.

CEREBRAL ORGANIZATION

Integration theory may be useful in studying cerebral organization by adapting the divided visual field paradigm to integration tasks. Work with divided visual fields has shown that the left cerebral hemisphere is specialized for language production, whereas the right hemisphere is often superior on holistic and perceptual tasks (see Beaumont, 1982a). In particular, despite conflicting results (see Davidoff, 1982; Davidson, 1984; Thompson, 1983, 1985; Tucker, 1981), the right hemisphere seems to have a major role in emotional processes. The guiding theme in all this work has been to use tasks that, at least ideally, involve only one hemisphere.

An alternative approach is to use tasks that explicitly study joint action of both hemispheres. To illustrate the idea with psychophysical integration, consider the finding that a spot of light seems brighter in the left visual field (for right handers; see Davidoff, 1982). A simple integration task would present two spots of light, one to each visual hemifield, and the subject would judge the average or difference in brightness. The brightness of each spot would be varied in a symmetrical factorial design, in effect making the design factors the cerebral hemispheres themselves. Functional measurement methods may then be applied, as outlined in the earlier discussion of the parallelism and linear fan theorems.

Relative effects of the two hemispheres would appear directly in the main effects of the two factors. Quantitative statements that the right hemisphere contributed 72%, say, of the brightness sensation would become possible. The pattern of the data, moreover, would provide information on the rule of hemisphere integration. A pattern of parallelism, in particular, would imply cross-hemisphere adding or averaging. Deviations from parallelism could point to a prebrightness intensity integration. Further useful information could be expected by varying duration of each light spot and the temporal relation between them.

Emotion tasks could be studied the same way. The two spots of light could be replaced with bilateral pictures of a phobic object, for example, with brightness and/or duration varied independently in each visual hemifield. Alternatively, two phobic objects could be presented so the subject sees a scene whose aversiveness depends on an integration of the two values. Two emotion faces could be presented similarly, with the subject judging combined or average affective intensity. Such emotion responses could be treated exactly as the judgments of brightness in the psychophysical task. A natural expectation is that the emotional reaction will obey an adding-type rule, thereby allowing the analyses associated with the parallelism theorem.

The experimental leverage of the foregoing integration design comes from the joint independent manipulation of stimulation to the two hemispheres, with tasks that allow or require integrated responses to both sources of stimulation. This approach could also be used with integration across sense modalities, including touch (Sperry, 1984) and hearing (Berlin, 1977). Bilateral stimulation has been used in divided visual field studies (Beaumont, 1982b, pp. 72–75), but with different, independent tasks for each hemifield.

Within-hemisphere integration is also of interest. This could be studied with factorial presentation of information to one hemisphere at a time. In a two-factor design, each factor could contain information congruent to the specialization of one hemisphere. The factorial plot could then reveal how the relative contribution of each type of information depended on each hemisphere. This could be extended to joint within–between hemisphere integration.

Integrations tasks represent a natural mode of functioning. Although the two hemispheres may share the work on some either–or basis, it seems a reasonable hypothesis that both cooperate in normal processing. Even a stimulus presented in the right visual field, although projecting initially only to the left hemisphere, is quickly transmitted in some form to the right hemisphere via the corpus callosum and other cerebral commissures in the normal brain. Little seems to be known, however, about what form of information is transmitted or about joint action of the two hemispheres. Asymmetric results with left versus right presentation point to gross cerebral localization but are not very specific. The integration mode may help reduce the ambiguity and provide a useful new tool for analysis of cerebral organization.

A number of observations on cross-hemisphere integration in split-brain patients are noted by Gazzaniga (1985), and some discussion of hemisphere interaction processes is given by Denenberg (1981) and commentators. The emotion study of Safer and Leventhal (1977) comes close to the present approach. Using short paragraphs, they varied verbal content and voice quality over three levels each (positive, neutral, and negative), and subjects categorized each of the nine stimulus combinations as positive, neutral, or negative. When stimuli were presented to the left ear, most subjects seemed to rely more on tone of voice; when stimuli were presented to the right ear, the two cues were about equally effective. This outcome was interpreted to reflect right hemisphere specialization for processing of emotional information (voice quality) and left hemisphere specialization for processing of objective information (verbal content). These laterality results are notable because each ear has some minor projection to the ipsilateral hemisphere and because of the 10-second duration of the paragraph stimuli. Unfortunately, the accuracy measure used by Safer and Leventhal precludes any integration analysis. The accuracy data cannot even rule out the possibility that subjects did not integrate, but relied solely on one or another cue. A rating of overall affective value would have allowed quantitative assessment of how much each hemisphere relied on each kind of cue.

The integration approach, although applicable to the threshold-level identification and recognition tasks that are standard in divided visual field studies, has an affinity for more complex and meaningful tasks, both in terms of stimulus and of response. This, however, entails longer exposures, which is generally considered undesirable, barring special contact lenses or continuous monitoring of eye movements. Young (1982) recommends exposure durations under 180 milliseconds to avoid eye movements and ensure that the initial stimulation is only to the specified hemisphere, but such durations, as a number of investigators have complained, are too short for all but very simple tasks. The eye movement problem may be lessened, however, with bilateral presentation that forms a unified percept. Of course, the eye movement problem may be overrated. As Klatzky and Atkinson (1971) note, any obtained laterality effects are diagnostic, regardless of exposure duration. It is possible, moreover, that hemispheric specialization will actually appear more strongly with more complex tasks that make greater processing demands.

Finally, integration tasks may tell about the nature of consciousness. Split-brain studies have been interpreted to mean that the right hemisphere is not conscious or at least not self-conscious (see Sperry, 1984). Sperry himself argues that the right hemisphere, even though unable to speak, has personality and social self-awareness very like that of the left hemisphere. Functional measurement methodology opens up the possibility of analyzing consciousness into its hemispheric determinants in the normal brain. This would go beyond testing Sperry's hypothesis to provide detailed specifications on the construction and operation of consciousness.

ACKNOWLEDGMENTS

This work was supported by National Science Foundation Grant BNS 82-12461 and by grants from the National Institutes of Mental Health to the Center for Human Information Processing, University of California, San Diego. I wish to thank R. Hastie and V. J. Konečni for helpful comments.

REFERENCES

Algom, D., Raphaeli, N., & Cohen-Raz, L. (1986). Integration of noxious stimulation across separate somatosensory communications systems: A functional theory of pain. *Journal of Experimental Psychology, Human Perception and Performance, 12,* 92–102.

Anderson, N. H. (1974a). Algebraic models in perception. In E. C. Carterette & M. P. Friedman (Eds.), *Handbook of perception* (Vol. 2, pp. 215–298). New York: Academic Press.

Anderson, N. H. (1974b). Cognitive algebra: Integration theory applied to social attribution. In L. Berkowitz (Ed.), *Advances in experimental social psychology* (Vol. 7, pp. 1–101). New York: Academic Press.

Anderson, N. H. (1975). On the role of context effects in psychophysical judgment. *Psychological Review, 82,* 462–482.

Anderson, N. H. (1976). *Social perception and cognition* (Tech. Rep. CHIP 62). La Jolla, CA: Center for Human Information Processing, University of California at San Diego.

Anderson, N. H. (1978). Measurement of motivation and incentive. *Behavior Research Methods & Instrumentation, 10,* 360–375.

Anderson, N. H. (1981). *Foundations of information integration theory.* New York: Academic Press.

Anderson, N. H. (1982). *Methods of information integration theory.* New York: Academic Press.

Anderson, N. H. (1983a). *Psychodynamics of everyday life: Blaming and avoiding blame* (Tech. Rep. CHIP 120). La Jolla, CA: Center for Human Information Processing, University of California at San Diego.

Anderson, N. H. (1983b). *Schemas in person cognition* (Tech. Rep. CHIP 118). La Jolla, CA: Center for Human Information Processing, University of California at San Diego.

Anderson, N. H. (1986). A cognitive theory of judgment and decision. In B. Brehmer, H. Jungerman, P. Lourens, & G. Sevón (Eds.), *New directions in research on decision making* (pp. 63–108). Amsterdam: Elsevier.

Anderson, N. H. (in press-a). Functional memory and on-line attribution. In J. N. Bassili (Ed.), *On-line cognition in person perception.* Hillsdale, NJ: Erlbaum.

Anderson, N. H. (in press-b). Functional memory and person cognition. In N. H. Anderson (Ed.), *Contributions to information integration theory.*

Anderson, N. H. (in press-c). Personal design and social cognition. In C. Hendrick (Ed.), *Review of Personality and Social Psychology* (Vol. 11). Beverly Hills, CA: Sage.

Anderson, N. H. (in press-d). Psychodynamics of everyday life: Blaming and avoiding blame. In N. H. Anderson (Ed.), *Contributions to information integration theory.*

Anderson, N. H., & Armstrong, M. A. (1989). Cognitive theory and methodology for studying marital interaction. In D. Brinberg & J. Jaccard (Eds.), *Dyadic decision making* (pp. 3–50). New York: Springer-Verlag.

Anderson, N. H., & Hubert, S. (1963). Effects of concomitant verbal recall on order effects in personality impression formation. *Journal of Verbal Learning and Verbal Behavior, 2,* 379–391.

Apple, W. L. (1979). Perceiving emotion in others: Integration of verbal, nonverbal and contextual cues. Unpublished Ph.D. dissertation. New York: Columbia University.

Arnold, M. B. (1960). *Emotion and personality* (Vol. 1). New York: Columbia University Press.

Averill, J. R. (1980). A constructivist view of emotion. In R. Plutchik & H. Kellerman (Eds.), *Emotion: Theory, research, and experience* (Vol. 1, pp. 305–339). New York: Academic Press.

Beaumont, J. G. (Ed.) (1982a). *Divided visual field studies of cerebral organization.* New York: Academic Press.

Beaumont, J. G. (1982b). Studies with verbal stimuli. In J. G. Beaumont (Ed.), *Divided visual field studies of cerebral organization* (pp. 57–86). New York: Academic Press.

Benjamin, L. S. (1984). Principles of prediction using structural analysis of social behavior. In R. F. Zucker, J. Aronoff, & A. I. Rabin (Eds.), *Personality and the prediction of behavior* (pp. 121–174). Orlando, FL: Academic Press.

Berkowitz, L. (1972). Social norms, feelings, and other factors affecting helping and altruism. In L. Berkowitz (Ed.), *Advances in experimental social psychology* (Vol. 6, pp. 63–108). New York: Academic Press.

Berkowitz, L. (1982). Aversive conditions as stimuli to aggression. In L. Berkowitz (Ed.), *Advances in experimental social psychology* (Vol. 15, pp. 249–288). New York: Academic Press.

Berlin, C. I. (1977). Hemispheric asymmetry in auditory tasks. In S. Harnad, R. W. Doty, L. Goldstein, J. Jaynes, & G. Krauthamer (Eds.), *Lateralization in the nervous system* (pp. 303–323). New York: Academic Press.

Berscheid, E. (1982). Attraction and emotion in interpersonal relations. In M. S. Clark & S. T. Fiske (Eds.), *Affect and cognition* (pp. 37–54). Hillsdale, NJ: Erlbaum.

Beuchler, S., & Izard, C. E. (1983). On the emergence, functions, and regulation of some emotion expressions in infancy. In R. Plutchik & H. Kellerman (Eds.), *Emotion: Theory, research, and experience* (Vol. 2, pp. 293–313). New York: Academic Press.

Bower, G. H. (1981). Mood and memory. *American Psychologist, 36,* 129–148.

Bower, G. H., & Cohen, P. R. (1982). Emotional influences in memory and thinking: Data and theory. In M. S. Clark & S. T. Fiske (Eds.), *Affect and cognition* (pp. 291–331). Hillsdale, NJ: Erlbaum.

Bowlby, J. (1982). *Attachment and loss* (Vol. 1, 2nd ed.). New York: Basic Books.

Brenner, C. (1980). A psychoanalytic theory of affects. In R. Plutchik & H. Kellerman (Eds.), *Emotion: Theory, research, and experience* (Vol. 1, pp. 341–348). New York: Academic Press.

Bromm, B. (Ed.) (1984). *Pain measurement in man: Neurophysiological correlates of pain.* Amsterdam: Elsevier.

Byrne, D. (1969). Attitudes and attraction. In L. Berkowitz (Ed.), *Advances in experimental social psychology* (Vol. 4, pp. 35–89). New York: Academic Press.

Cacioppo, J. T., Harkins, S. G., & Petty, R. E. (1981). The nature of attitudes and cognitive responses and their relationships to behavior. In R. E. Petty, T. M. Ostrom, & T. C. Brock (Eds.), *Cognitive responses in persuasion* (pp. 31–54). Hillsdale, NJ: Erlbaum.

Chapman, C. R. (1983). On the relationship of human laboratory and clinical pain research. In R. Melzack (Ed.), *Pain measurement and assessment* (pp. 243–249). New York: Raven.

Clark, W. C., & Yang, J. C. (1983). Applications of sensory decision theory to problems in laboratory and clinical pain. In R. Melzack (Ed.), *Pain measurement and assessment* (pp. 15–25). New York: Raven.

Clore, G. L., & Byrne, D. (1974). A reinforcement-affect model of attraction. In T. L. Huston (Ed.), *Foundations of interpersonal attraction* (pp. 143–170). New York: Academic Press.

Cotton, J. L. (1981). A review of research on Schachter's theory of emotion and the misattribution of arousal. *European Journal of Social Psychology, 11,* 365–397.

Cupchik, G. C., & Leventhal, H. (1974). Consistency between expressive behavior and the evaluation of humorous stimuli: The role of sex and self-observation. *Journal of Personality and Social Psychology, 30,* 429–442.

Darwin, C. (1965). *The expression of the emotions in man and animals.* Chicago: University of Chicago Press (originally published in 1872 by Murray, London).

Davidoff, J. (1982). Studies with non-verbal stimuli. In J. G. Beaumont (Ed.), *Divided visual field studies of cerebral organization* (pp. 29–55). New York: Academic Press.

Davidson, R. J. (1984). Affect, cognition, and hemispheric specialization. In C. E. Izard, J. Kagan, & R. B. Zajonc (Eds.), *Emotion, cognition, and behavior* (pp. 320–365). New York: Cambridge University Press.

Denenberg, V. H. (1981). Hemispheric laterality in animals and the effects of early experience. *The Behavioral and Brain Sciences, 4,* 1–49 (includes peer commentary).

DuPont, R. L. (Ed.) (1982). *Phobia: A comprehensive summary of modern treatments.* New York: Brunner/Mazel.

Eich, E., Reeves, J. L., Jaeger, B., & Graff-Radford, S. B. (1985). Memory for pain: Relation between past and present pain intensity. *Pain, 23,* 375–379.

Ekman, P. (1984). Expression and the nature of emotion. In K. R. Scherer & P. Ekman (Eds.), *Approaches to emotion* (pp. 319–343). Hillsdale, NJ: Erlbaum.

Ekman, P., Friesen, W. V., & Ellsworth, P. (1972). *Emotion in the human face.* New York: Pergamon.

Ekman, P., Friesen, W. V., O'Sullivan, M., & Scherer, K. (1980). Relative importance of face, body, and speech in judgments of personality and affect. *Journal of Personality and Social Psychology, 38,* 270–277.

Emde, R. N. (1980). Levels of meaning for infant emotions: A biosocial view. In W. A. Collins (Ed.), *Minnesota Symposium on Child Psychology* (Vol. 13, pp. 1–37). Hillsdale, NJ: Erlbaum.

Emmelkamp, P. M. G. (1982). *Phobic and obsessive–compulsive disorders.* New York: Plenum.

Erdmann, G., & Janke, W. (1978). Interaction between physiological and cognitive determinants of emotions: Experimental studies on Schachter's theory of emotions. *Biological Psychology, 6,* 61–74.

Evans, F. J. (1974). The placebo response in pain reduction. In J. J. Bonica (Ed.), *Advances in neurology* (Vol. 4, pp. 289–296). New York: Raven.

Fiske, S. T. (1982). Schema-triggered affect: Applications to social perception. In M. S. Clark & S. T. Fiske (Eds.), *Affect and cognition* (pp. 55–78). Hillsdale, NJ: Erlbaum.

Flaxman, N. J. (1982). The correlation between quantity of fears and the ability to discriminate among similar items. In R. L. DuPont (Ed.), *Phobia: A comprehensive summary of modern treatments* (pp. 121–125). New York: Brunner/Mazel.

Frijda, N. H. (1969). Recognition of emotion. In L. Berkowitz (Ed.), *Advances in experimental social psychology* (Vol. 4, pp. 167–223). New York: Academic Press.

Gazzaniga, M. S. (1985). *The social brain.* New York: Basic Books.

Gouaux, C. (1971).Induced affective states and interpersonal attraction. *Journal of Personality and Social Psychology, 20,* 37–43.

Gracely, R. H., & Wolskee, P. J. (1983). Semantic functional measurement of pain: Integrating perception and language. *Pain, 15,* 389–398.

Griffitt, W. (1970) Environmental effects on interpersonal affective behavior: Ambient effective temperature and attraction. *Journal of Personality and Social Psychology, 15,* 240–244.

Hall, W. (1981). On ''Ratio scales of sensory and affective verbal pain descriptors.'' *Pain, 11,* 101–107.

Hardy, A. B. (1982). Phobic thinking: The cognitive influences on the behavior and effective treatment of the agoraphobic. In R. L. DuPont (Ed.), *Phobia: A comprehensive summary of modern treatments* (pp. 93–98). New York: Brunner/Mazel.

Harlow, H. F., & Mears, C. E. (1983). Emotional sequences and consequences. In R. Plutchik & H.

Kellerman (Eds.), *Emotion: Theory, research, and experience* (Vol. 2, pp. 171–197). New York: Academic Press.

Hastie, R. (1981). Schematic principles in human memory. In E. T. Higgins, C. P. Herman, & M. P. Zanna (Eds.), *Social cognition* (pp. 39–88). Hillsdale, NJ: Erlbaum.

Hawkins, R. D., Roll, P. L., Puerto, A., & Yeomans, J. S. (1983). Refractory periods of neurons mediating stimulation-elicited eating and brain stimulation reward: Interval scale measurement and tests of a model of neural integration. *Behavioral Neuroscience, 97,* 416–432.

Hommers, W., & Anderson, N. H. (1985). Recompense as a factor in assigned punishment. *British Journal of Developmental Psychology, 3,* 75–86.

Huskisson, E. C. (1983). Visual analogue scales. In R. Melzack (Ed.), *Pain measurement and assessment* (pp. 33–37). New York: Raven.

Isen, A. M., Means, B., Patrick, R., & Nowicki, G. (1982). Some factors influencing decision-making strategy and risk taking. In M. S. Clark & S. T. Fiske (Eds.), *Affect and cognition* (pp. 243–261). Hillsdale, NJ: Erlbaum.

Isen, A. M., Shalker, T. E., Clark, M. S., & Karp, L. (1978). Affect, accessibility of material in memory, and behavior: A cognitive loop? *Journal of Personality and Social Psychology, 36,* 1–12.

Izard, C. E. (1977). *Human emotions.* New York: Plenum.

Izard, C. E. (1982). Comments on emotion and cognition: Can there be a working relationship? In M. S. Clark & S. T. Fiske (Eds.), *Affect and cognition* (pp. 229–240). Hillsdale, NJ: Erlbaum.

Janis, I. L., & Mann, L. (1977). *Decision making: A psychological analysis of conflict, choice, and commitment.* New York: Free Press.

Janis, I. L., & Rodin, J. (1979). Attribution, control, and decision making: Social psychology and health care. In G. C. Stone, F. Cohen, & N. E. Adler (Eds.), *Health psychology—A handbook* (pp. 487–521). San Francisco, CA: Jossey-Bass.

Janke, W. (1983). Response variability to psychotropic drugs: Overview of the main approaches to differential pharmacopsychology. In W. Janke (Ed.), *Response variability to psychotropic drugs* (pp. 33–65). New York: Pergamon.

Jones, B. (1980). Algebraic models for integration of painful and nonpainful electric shocks. *Perception & Psychophysics, 28,* 572–576.

Jones, B., & Gwynn, M. (1984). Functional measurement scales of painful electric shocks. *Perception & Psychophysics, 35,* 193–200.

Kaplan, M. F. (1971a). Dispositional effects and weight of information in impression information. *Journal of Personality and Social Psychology, 18,* 279–284.

Kaplan, M. F. (1971b). The effect of evaluative dispositions and amount and credibility of information on forming impressions of personality. *Psychonomic Science, 24,* 174–176.

Kaplan, M. F. (1971c). The effect of judgmental dispositions on forming impressions of personality. *Canadian Journal of Behavioral Science, 3,* 259–267.

Kelley, H. H. (1972). Causal schemata and the attribution process. In E. E. Jones, D. E. Kanouse, H. H. Kelley, R. E. Nisbett, S. Valins, & B. Weiner (Eds.), *Attribution* (pp. 151–174). Morristown, NJ: General Learning Press.

Klatzky, R. L., & Atkinson, R. C. (1971). Specialization of the cerebral hemispheres in scanning for information in short-term memory. *Perception & Psychophysics, 10,* 335–338.

Klitzner, M. D. (1977). Small animal fear: An integration-theoretical analysis. Unpublished Ph.D. dissertation. San Diego, CA: University of California.

Klitzner, M. D., & Anderson, N. H. (1977). Motivation × expectancy × value: A functional measurement approach. *Motivation and Emotion, 1,* 347–365.

Konečni, V. J. (1975). The mediation of aggressive behavior: Arousal level versus anger and cognitive labeling. *Journal of Personality and Social Psychology, 32,* 706–712.

Lazarus, R. S., Averill, J. R., & Opton, E. M., Jr. (1970). Towards a cognitive theory of emotion.

In M. B. Arnold (Ed.), *Feelings and emotions* (pp. 207–232). New York: Academic Press.

Leeper, R. W. (1948). A motivational theory of emotion to replace "emotion as disorganized response." *Psychological Review, 55,* 5–21.

Leeper, R. W. (1970). The motivational and perceptual properties of emotions as indicating their fundamental character and role. In M. B. Arnold (Ed.), *Feelings and emotions* (pp. 151–168). New York: Academic Press.

Leon, M. (1980). Integration of intent and consequence information in children's moral judgments. In F. Wilkening, J. Becker, & T. Trabasso (Eds.), *Information integration by children* (pp. 71–97). Hillsdale, NJ: Erlbaum.

Leon, M. (1984). Rules mothers and sons use to integrate intent and damage information in their moral judgments. *Child Development, 55,* 2106–2113.

Leventhal, H. (1980). Toward a comprehensive theory of emotion. In L. Berkowitz (Ed.), *Advances in experimental social psychology* (Vol. 13, pp. 139–207). New York: Academic Press.

Leventhal, H., & Cupchik, G. C. (1975). The informational and facilitative effects of an audience upon expression and the evaluation of humorous stimuli. *Journal of Experimental Social Psychology, 11,* 363–380.

Magnusson, D. (Ed.) (1981). *Toward a psychology of situations.* Hillsdale, NJ: Erlbaum.

Mandler, G. (1984). *Mind and body.* New York: Norton.

Manstead, A. S. R., & Wagner, H. L. (1981). Arousal, cognition and emotion: An appraisal of two-factor theory. *Current Psychological Reviews, 1,* 35–54.

Marks, I. M. (1969). *Fears and phobias.* London: Heinemann Medical Books.

Marshall, G. D., & Zimbardo, P. G. (1979). Affective consequences of inadequately explained physiological arousal. *Journal of Personality and Social Psychology, 37,* 970–988.

Maslach, C. (1979). Negative emotional biasing of unexplained arousal. *Journal of Personality and Social Psychology, 37,* 953–969.

Massaro, D. W. (1979). Reading and listening (tutorial paper). In P. A. Kolers, M. Wrolstad, & H. Bouma (Eds.), *Processing of visible language* (pp. 331–354). New York: Plenum.

Massaro, D. W. (1985). *Speech perception by eye and ear: A paradigm for psychological inquiry.* Santa Cruz, CA: University of California.

McDougall, W. (1921). *An introduction to social psychology* (14th ed.). Boston: Luce.

McDougall, W. (1928). Emotion and feeling distinguished. In M. L. Reymert (Ed.), *Feelings and emotions: The Wittenberg Symposium* (pp. 200–205). Worcester, MA: Clark University Press.

Mehrabian, A. (1972). *Nonverbal communication.* Chicago: Aldine-Atherton.

Melzack, R. (Ed.) (1983). *Pain measurement and assessment.* New York: Raven Press.

Melzack, R., & Wall, P. D. (1983). *The challenge of pain.* New York: Basic Books.

Mischel, W. (1968). *Personality and assessment.* New York: Wiley.

Norman, D. A. (1980). Twelve issues for cognitive science. *Cognitive Science, 4,* 1–32.

Nowlis, V., & Nowlis, H. H. (1956). The description and analysis of mood. *Annals of the New York Academy of Sciences, 65,* 345–355.

Oden, G. C., & Massaro, D. W. (1978). Integration of featural information in speech perception. *Psychological Review, 85,* 172–191.

O'Sullivan, M., Ekman, P., Friesen, W., & Scherer, K. (1985). What you say and how you say it: The contribution of speech content and voice quality to judgments of others. *Journal of Personality and Social Psychology, 48,* 54–62.

Plutchik, R. (1980). *Emotion: A psychoevolutionary synthesis.* New York: Harper & Row.

Plutchik, R., & Ax, A. F. (1967). A critique of *Determinants of Emotional State* by Schachter and Singer (1962). *Psychophysiology, 4,* 79–82.

Price, D. D., & Barrell, J. J. (1984). Some general laws of human emotion: Interrelationships between intensities of desire, expectation, and emotional feeling. *Journal of Personality, 52,* 389–409.

Price, D. D., Barrell, J. E., & Barrell, J. J. (1985). A quantitative–experiential analysis of human emotions. *Motivation and Emotion, 9,* 19–38.

Price, D. D., McGrath, P. A., Rafii, A., & Buckingham, B. (1983). The validation of visual analogue scales as ratio scale measures for chronic and experimental pain. *Pain, 17,* 45–56.

Reisenzein, R. (1983). The Schachter theory of emotion: Two decades later. *Psychological Review, 94,* 239–264.

Reykowski, J. (1982). Social motivation. *Annual Review of Psychology, 33,* 123–154.

Rogers, C. R. (1951). *Client-centered therapy; its current practice, implications, and theory.* Boston: Houghton-Mifflin.

Rollman, G. B. (1977). Signal detection theory measurement of pain: A review and critique. *Pain, 3,* 187–211.

Rollman, G. B. (1983). Measurement of experimental pain in chronic pain patients: Methodological and individual factors. In R. Melzack (Ed.), *Pain measurement and assessment* (pp. 251–258). New York: Raven.

Safer, M. A., & Leventhal, H. (1977). Ear differences in evaluating emotional tones of voice and verbal content. *Journal of Experimental Psychology, Human Perception and Performance, 3,* 75–82.

Sarbin, T. R. (1977). Contextualism: A world view for modern psychology. In J. K. Cole and A. W. Landfield (Eds.), *Nebraska Symposium on Motivation, 1976* (pp. 1–41). Lincoln, NE: University of Nebraska Press.

Schachter, S. (1964). The interaction of cognitive and physiological determinants of emotional state. In L. Berkowitz (Ed.), *Advances in experimental social psychology* (Vol. 1, pp. 49–80). New York: Academic Press.

Schachter, S. (1970). The assumption of identity and peripheralist–centralist controversies in motivation and emotion. In M. B. Arnold (Ed.), *Feelings and emotions* (pp. 111–121). New York: Academic Press.

Schachter, S., & Singer, J. E. (1962). Cognitive, social, and physiological determinants of emotional state. *Psychological Review, 69,* 379–399.

Schachter, S., & Singer, J. E. (1979). Comments on the Maslach and Marshall–Zimbardo experiments. *Journal of Personality and Social Psychology, 37,* 989–995.

Schachter, S., & Wheeler, L. (1962). Epinephrine, chlorpromazine, and amusement. *Journal of Abnormal and Social Psychology, 65,* 121–128.

Scott, J. P. (1980). The function of emotions in behavioral systems: A systems theory analysis. In R. Plutchik & H. Kellerman (Eds.), *Emotion: Theory, research, and experience* (Vol. 1, pp. 35–56). New York: Academic Press.

Simon, H. A. (1982). Comments. In M. S. Clark & S. T. Fiske (Eds.), *Affect and cognition* (pp. 333–342). Hillsdale, NJ: Erlbaum.

Simonov, P. V. (1970). The information theory of emotion. In M. B. Arnold (Ed.), *Feelings and emotions* (pp. 145–149). New York: Academic Press.

Sjöberg, L. (1982). Beliefs and values as attitude components. In B. Wegener (Ed.), *Social attitudes and psychophysical measurement* (pp. 199–217). Hillsdale, NJ: Erlbaum.

Sperry, R. (1984). Consciousness, personal identity and the divided brain. *Neuropsychologia, 22,* 661–673.

Stevens, S. S. (1974). Perceptual magnitude and its measurement. In E. C. Carterette & M. P. Friedman (Eds.), *Handbook of perception* (Vol. 2, pp. 361–389). New York: Academic Press.

Strongman, K. T. (1978). *The psychology of emotion* (2nd ed.). New York: Wiley.

Surber, C. F. (1982). Separable effects of motives, consequences, and order of presentation on children's moral judgments. *Developmental Psychology, 18,* 257–266.

Thompson, J. K. (1983). Visual field, exposure duration, and sex as factors in the perception of emotional facial expressions. *Cortex, 19,* 293–308.

Thompson, J. K. (1985). Right brain, left brain: Left face, right face: Hemisphericity and the expression of facial emotion. *Cortex, 21*, 281–299.

Tomkins, S. S. (1984). Affect theory. In K. R. Scherer & P. Ekman (Eds.), *Approaches to emotion* (pp. 163–195). Hillsdale, NJ: Erlbaum.

Tucker, D. M. (1981). Lateral brain function, emotion, and conceptualization. *Psychological Bulletin, 89*, 19–46.

Wolff, B. B. (1983). Laboratory methods of pain measurement. In R. Melzack (Ed.), *Pain measurement and assessment* (pp. 7–13). New York: Raven Press.

Young, A. W. (1982). Methodological and theoretical bases of visual hemifield studies. In J. G. Beaumont (Ed.), *Divided visual field studies of cerebral organization* (pp. 11–27). New York: Academic Press.

Zajonc, R. B. (1980). Feeling and thinking: Preferences need no inferences. *American Psychologist, 35*, 151–175.

Zajonc, R. B. (1984). On primacy of affect. In K. R. Scherer & P. Ekman (Eds.), *Approaches to emotion* (pp. 259–270). Hillsdale, NJ: Erlbaum.

Zalinski, J., & Anderson, N. H. (1986). AVERAGE: A FORTRAN program for parameter estimation for the averaging model. La Jolla, CA: University of California at San Diego.

Zalinski, J., & Anderson, N. H. (in press). Parameter estimation for averaging theory. In N. H. Anderson (Ed.), *Contributions to information integration theory*.

Chapter 7

PROJECTIVE MEASURES OF EMOTION

HENRY KELLERMAN

ABSTRACT

Rorschach measures have been widely used to define two broad personality and affect dimensions, labeled as extratensive and introversive. Extratensive profiles are defined by such characteristics as lability, expansiveness, impulsivity and emotional dyscontrol. Introversive profiles are characterized by the qualities of control, constriction, rigidity, and guardedness. This basic dichotomy is described in detail and related to a theoretical model of emotions, which assumes that specific emotions are the precursors or bases for specific diagnostic conditions. Illustrations of such emotion–diagnosis connections are joy–mania, anger–aggression, fear–passivity, and disgust–paranoia. The projective measures described reveal an inherent systematic organization of Rorschach scoring categories that becomes apparent when considered within this theoretical model of emotions and diagnoses.

INTRODUCTION

In the early part of the twentieth century, Hermann Rorschach experimented with ambiguous forms and developed the Form Interpretation Test—later to be called the Rorschach. This test and his discussion of interpretations of personality dispositions were published in 1924 (Rorschach & Oberholzer, 1924). More specifically, Rorschach was interested in creating a link between one's response

187

EMOTION
Theory, Research, and Experience
Volume 4

to ambiguity in the form of ink blots and what such responses could mean in terms of their implications for psychoanalysis.

The publication of Rorschach's *Psychodiagnostics* in 1942 became one of the foundation blocks in the burgeoning field of clinical psychology. In retrospect, it is clear that the Rorschach was the first major projective test purporting to measure the inner life. The Rorschach test became for clinicians the single most important technology for the gathering of data on the nature of individual psychopathology, diagnosis, and personality, as well as the emotional life of a person. Thus, other than the psychoanalytic method—especially as it applied to the understanding of dreams—the Rorschach test became the cornerstone of projective psychology.

The 1940s became a decade of ferment in the development of projective psychology. In 1943 Henry A. Murray published the *Thematic Apperception Test* (TAT). This test was reported in the literature by Morgan and Murray as early as 1935, but it was not until the middle to late 1940s that the TAT became the second standard test joining the Rorschach in comprising the two basic projective measures used by psychologists.

The Thematic Apperception Test was designed as a method for investigating fantasies, needs, and issues of *press,* that is, motivations. Subjects were presented with a largely representational picture, although the content and setting of the picture were ambiguous. The TAT required subjects to generate a story from the stimulus each picture presented. The psychologist would then be able to evaluate the person's inner life on the basis of what was imagined by the patient to have preceded the stimulus event, what was occurring in the stimulus event, and the projected result. Psychologists were instructed to understand the subject's responses in terms of the person's need system. However, in actual clinical use, psychologists, through experience with the test, began to utilize the TAT more as a means of understanding fantasies and thought processes and how these fantasies and thinking are affected by the emotions. The TAT was thus transformed through a natural clinical evolution from a test to assess motivations to one that assesses the person's fantasies and needs as grounded in emotional and interpersonal life.

The Rorschach was the projective measure that seemed to address a person's emotional life with respect to intrapsychic or intrapersonal considerations; that is, the Rorschach assessed inner life with respect to the nature of impulses and controls, level of anxiety, state of reality testing, and so forth—basically, issues of personality structure and intrapsychic conflict. In contrast, the TAT was the projective measure of a person's emotional life within an interpersonal framework. In this interpersonal framework, a person's fantasies could reveal, for example, interpersonal style, typical attitudes, relationship with parental or authority figures, and other such interpersonal needs.

The third major projective measure that, when combined with the Rorschach and the TAT, became for clinicians the decisive clinical standard projective battery was Karen Machover's Figure Drawing Test, published in 1949 (Machover, 1949). Machover developed her analysis of figure drawings based upon research and rich clinical experience. Although Schilder (1935) and others had utilized figure drawings well before the 1940s, it was Machover who systematized the psychological meanings of the figure drawings, relating both intrapsychic and interpersonal interpretations to the categories of measurement that she applied to the drawings. Machover was also vitally interested in a person's emotional life and how the emotions were connected to defenses and diagnoses.

These three projective tests, the Rorschach, TAT, and Machover Figure Drawing Test have for almost 50 years comprised the clinicians' core projective assessment technology for the distillation of information on the infrastructure of emotions, personality, and thinking. Although clinicians have also utilized other tests, such as word association, the Bender Gestalt, and animal metaphors, to fill out the basic battery, these other tests have been used quite selectively. Simply by the power of their clinical usefulness, the Rorschach, TAT, and Machover became the tacitly agreed upon basic projective battery. It was observed that, together, these tests could, by projective means, elicit a picture of a person's emotions, defenses, psychodynamic arena of conflict, personality configuration. or type, unique psychopathology, symptoms, and diagnostic state. In addition, the power of this projective battery generated a proliferation of interest in the development of projective psychology generally, as well as in the development of other tests.

The configuration of psychodynamic psychology in its applied form, with its hoped-for scientific base, to an important degree rested on the use and validation especially of these three projective tests. It can even be claimed that projective psychology was born with the advent of the Rorschach, but that projective psychology, as an aspect of clinical work with a purported scientific foundation, was crystallized more fully with the amalgamation in clinical use of the Rorschach, TAT, and Machover Figure Drawing tests.

Through use, these three tests began to generate a wealth of clinical data. The clinical use of this basic projective battery led to the gradual surfacing of the test subjects' emotional landscape in greater detail. This emotional landscape also included aspects of personality, cognitive processes, and diagnostic considerations.

Scoring systems exist for each test. For example, the use of the Psychogram on the Rorschach (Klopfer, Ainsworth, Klopfer, & Holt, 1954) separates the introversive or controlled person from the extratensive or labile or dyscontrolled one. Although such scoring systems are clinically useful, they do not relate to broader issues of theory. What could be additionally useful with respect to projective measures is a category system that has a systematic relation to a theory of emotion, personality, or both. The following sections present such an attempt to develop some hypotheses and new approaches that may help relate projective scoring categories to emotions and personality in a systematic way.

A CIRCULAR STRUCTURE OF EMOTIONS, DIAGNOSES, AND RORSCHACH CATEGORIES

In this section, an attempt will be made to connect the various standard measures of the Rorschach with the structural theory of emotional organization developed by Plutchik (1962, 1980, 1984). In addition, these standard projective measures of the Rorschach also will be related to specific aspects of personality that have been shown by Kellerman (1979, 1980, 1987) and by Plutchik and Kellerman (1974) to be connected intrinsically with, and even derived from, the emotions. It will be suggested that an inherently cohesive similarity structure and internal consistency of these Rorschach scoring categories exists; that is, such scoring categories follow a predictable pattern when considered in relation to emotions and diagnoses. For example, the Rorschach scoring category, usually believed to indicate lability in the personality—the sum of the color responses (ΣC)—consistently correlates with those diagnostic states and emotions that contain strong labile components. By strong labile components is meant that there are certain diagnostic types whose personality is generally characterized by impulsivity, gregariousness, impetuousness, expansiveness, and an overall action orientation. Such persons may experience inner pressure to engage in social activity, may be compulsive talkers, or may tend to show agitated or acting-out behaviors.

Of the eight emotions postulated by Plutchik as basic, four seem to be characteristic of this labile category. These four emotions are *joy, acceptance, anger,* and *surprise.* In a number of papers Plutchik and Kellerman have proposed that certain diagnoses are associated with emotions. The rationale for associating the basic emotions with these specific diagnostic states has been elaborated in many of the studies that establish theoretical connections between the domains of emotions and diagnostic states (Kellerman, 1979, 1980, 1983, 1987; Kellerman & Plutchik, 1977, 1978; Plutchik, 1980, 1983, 1984, this volume; Plutchik, Kellerman, & Conte, 1979).

This connection between emotion and diagnosis is elaborated in Figure 7.1. It shows the emotions and diagnoses that are assumed to be related, arranged according to similarity. Those categories that are closest to one another on the circle are more similar and those located further apart are more dissimilar. If one dichotomizes the circle in Figure 7.1, the top half contains the more expansive diagnoses of *manic, hysteric, aggressive,* and *psychopathic.* These diagnoses are assumed to represent various degrees of dyscontrol. The lower half of the circle consists of the diagnoses of *depressed, paranoid, passive,* and *obsessive*—a grouping that clinically implies containment or control.

Similarly, Rorschach scoring categories have almost universally also been dichotomized between those projective measures that imply *expansive, labile,* and *dyscontrolled* propensities of the personality and others that imply more

EXTRATENSIVE

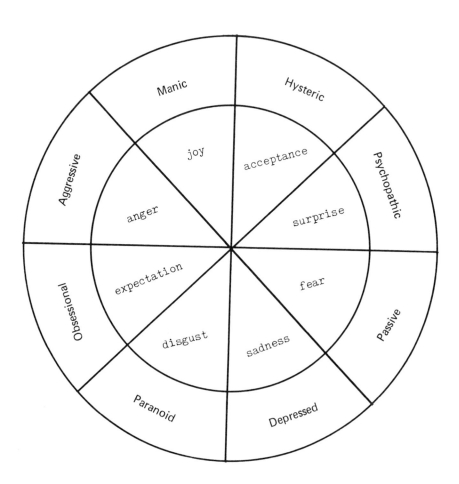

INTROVERSIVE

FIGURE 7.1. A circular model of the basic emotion system showing corresponding diagnostic states. The upper half of the circle contains emotions and diagnoses that are assumed to reflect the extratensive personality, while the lower half encompasses emotions and diagnoses reflecting the introversive personality.

constricted or controlled personality features. In fact, Rorschach (1942) conceived of personality structure generally as roughly dichotomized between the extratensive type—labile and dyscontrolled—and the introversive type—constricted and controlled. As such, Rorschach's studies generated measures that can identify the more controlled as well as the more dyscontrolled types.

In Figure 7.1, the emotion–diagnostic states of *joy–manic, acceptance–hysteric, anger–aggressive,* and *surprise–psychopathic* are hypothesized to correspond to Rorschach's extratensive-labile types while *fear–passive, sadness–depressed, disgust–paranoid,* and *expectation–obsessional* are hypothesized to correspond to Rorschach's introversive–controlled types. In the following sections, various projective measures will be defined and their hypothetical relations to emotion–diagnostic states will be described.

THE RORSCHACH SCORING CATEGORIES

An important Rorschach conceptualization broadly conceives of the person as one who is engaged in managing or attempting to balance internal needs for control as well as needs for expression. This balance between impulse and control corresponds to Hermann Rorschach's conception of the experience balance composed of extratensive and introversive personality dispositions. In fact, Rorschach scoring categories are for the most part divided into those that reflect aspects of the ink blot, purporting to identify impulses in the personality, and those scoring categories that purport to measure control features of the personality.

The Rorschach scoring categories that address the issue of lability in the personality and correspond to the extratensive type include a large number of responses to the color aspects of the blots, a large number of animal movement responses, a high percentage of animal responses offered, fast reaction time to the blots, and a greater frequency of response to the colored cards (in contrast to the noncolored cards). Each of these Rorschach measures shall be more specifically considered in the following sections.

THE EXTRATENSIVE PROFILE

THE COLOR SCORE

Rorschachers derived three ways of understanding the influence of color on a subject's response. The first was the subject's response, in which the form of the blot determined the percept but the presence of color also seemed important. Yet, it was discovered that the same response from the subject would be elicited even if the blot was achromatic. This form-determined measure is designated FC (F for Form dominant, and C for Color). The second way that Rorschachers utilized scores to reflect the contribution of color to a subject's perception is called the color-determined response. Here subjects would not necessarily have responded with the same percept to an achromatic rendering of a given colored blot, and yet Rorschachers generally recognized that the form of the blot was nevertheless useful to the subject in determining the response. Such a response was considered a color-dominated response. This color-dominated response is designated in Rorschach language as a CF response (or C for Color dominant, and F for Form). A third color response is the pure color (or C) response in which considerations of form are absent and only the response to the color of the blot determines the subject's percept. When the form-dominated color responses are added to the color-dominated responses in designated proportions, then a new score reflecting the overall influence of color of the blots emerges. This new score is called the sum of the color responses (or ΣC) and high scores are generally considered the core reflection of an extratensive labile personality.

THE ANIMAL MOVEMENT RESPONSE AND TOTAL PERCENTAGE OF ANIMAL RESPONSES

Closely allied with a preponderance of color responses is the animal movement response. This response, a representation of a form-determined response of an animal in motion, is designated FM (F for Form and M for Motion). Rorschach interpretation considers a high frequency of such responses—in addition to the presence of many animal contents (A%) per se—to indicate an action orientation in the personality along with corresponding poor delay capacity or poor frustration tolerance. Such responses in adults imply immaturity, especially since in the protocols of children, animal movement responses dominate the record. A high FM suggests that there are strong impulses in the personality pressing for immediate gratification. Thus, along with a high percentage of animal responses (or A%) in the entire Rorschach protocol, this pair, high FM and high A%, resembles primarily the protocol seen in children, and, at least, points toward an action orientation and lability of the personality and, in the extreme, to a tendency to act out. The A% score on Rorschach protocols is usually greater than the FM because subjects will perceive animals in motion as well as animal percepts not in motion.

REACTION TIME AND NUMBER OF RESPONSES TO CHROMATIC CARDS

The labile extratensive type, in addition to exhibiting a high ΣC, high FM, and high A%, tends to have a quicker reaction time to each ink blot as well as a greater number of responses offered to the chromatic or color cards relative to the number of responses offered to the black and white blots.

High scores on these five Rorschach scoring categories—the ΣC, FM, A%, Reaction Time (Chromatic versus Achromatic), and Number of Responses to the Chromatic Cards—represent a sample of projective measures of the Rorschach indicative of an extratensive labile profile.

In the following section a sample of Rorschach projective measures will be defined that reveal a profile of the introversive or more controlled personality.

THE INTROVERSIVE PROFILE

THE FORM RESPONSE

The form response (or F%) on the Rorschach may be considered to be the cornerstone of Rorschach's central assumption; that is, that good form reflects good reality testing and that poor form correspondingly suggests the presence of psychopathology. Form is implied in most of the scoring determinants, whether percepts involve human or animal movement, form-dominated color responses, shading responses, or a host of contents such as inanimate objects. Such form responses may be assessed in terms of whether the form is well articulated, so that persons other than the subject would readily agree that the perceived form does, in fact, look like what the subject says it does. In contrast, sometimes the perceived object reflects a form level that is questionable—that is, one would have to make allowances to agree that the subject's response actually resembles what the percept is purported to be. Finally, in the extreme, F minus (F−) responses, or poor form, are responses in which the articulated form cannot be seen by others, and, when delineated by the subject, cannot be justified as representing what the subject claims it to be.

When the form level is good and the F%—that is, pure form responses in relation to all other responses—is high, Rorschachers consider this to reflect the importance that the subject gives to internal controls. This focus on the control aspect of the personality in most cases also means that the need to curb impulses in such a person is correspondingly strong. When the F% is extremely high— close to 100%—the record would be one in which hardly any of the other determinants are used, so that the subject is understood to be a person who carefully controls and monitors qualities such as spontaneity, empathy, emotionality, expression of anxiety, and so forth. Such persons are considered to be investing in the operation of defenses designed to control tension and emotion, and to be withholding and even rigid. Generally, this high F% represents the basis of the existence of an introversive profile.

THE HUMAN MOVEMENT RESPONSE (M)

According to typical Rorschach interpretation, seeing the human object in good form perception on the blots corresponds to positive considerations of object relatedness. Human movement—that is, people in motion (walking, running, and gesticulating, for example)—is assumed to reflect healthy control and also implies a capacity for empathy. The M response is considered to be the main counterbalance of the ΣC response and Rorschachers are usually interested in ascertaining what is referred to as the nature of the subject's *experience balance* in any given protocol. Thus, the M response in general can reflect introversive tendencies while ΣC can reflect extratensive urges—a counterbalance.

The experience balance is the contrast between the number of human movement (M) responses on the test protocol and the sum of the color responses (ΣC). Another way Rorschach originally conceived of this balance was to consider the M to ΣC comparison as one between introversive qualities and extratensive ones. It is this ratio, $M : \Sigma C$, that constitutes a major construct of Rorschach analysis and will be discussed further in a following section. Basically however, the M score was appreciated as a derivative estimate of control needs in the personality while the ΣC was understood to be a reflection of emotionality and impulsivity.

Rapaport, Gill, and Schafer (1970) indicate that the well-perceived or well-articulated M—reflecting excellent form level—as a measure of control is assumed to reflect a mature ego that can tolerate primitive impulses. This sort of response suggests that the ego is strong enough to permit the experience of such primitive impulses and even can utilize such impulses as a source of creative energy.

TOTAL NUMBER OF RESPONSES AND
OVERALL REACTION TIME

On the introversive side of the experience balance, two further measures of the Rorschach are assumed to reflect the control feature of the personality. One is the amount of time it takes for any person to offer a first response to the presentation of a blot. This score is designated as reaction time. Usually, in the introversive personality, for example, in the depressed or passive states, the reaction time measure will be at best moderate, and for the most part, slow. This slow to moderate reaction time occurs because the introversive personality is usually less impulsive. Normally such types are more thoughtful and are given to analysis and control. When introversive types show more pathological experience they can become withdrawn, rigid, and overcontrolled and may even exhibit what is clinically called psychomotor retardation. Thus, for the most part, introversive persons will be more likely to produce reaction times slower than subjects who are generally impulsive and more extratensive.

Another scoring category of the Rorschach that reflects a profile of the introversive or controlled type is that of the overall number of responses offered by the subject to the entire Rorschach test. For the introversive type, this number is usually lower in contrast to extratensive types, for which such a score tends to be higher. Large numbers of responses in the overall record are produced by labile persons while relatively fewer responses are offered by introversive types.

The differences between the extratensive and introversive personalities are also portrayed by special ratios of the Rorschach scoring categories, especially with respect to the experience balance (M : ΣC), the relationship between human movement and animal movement (M : FM), and the relation between responses to the chromatic blots versus the achromatic ones.

M : ΣC—HUMAN MOVEMENT RELATIVE TO THE SUM OF THE COLOR RESPONSES

Generally, when the M : ΣC ratio is 2 : 1, an introversive pattern is interpreted. When this ratio is reversed (1 : 2), the personality is considered to be extratensive. Further, during stressful and even psychopathological periods in the experience of the introversive person, the M : ΣC ratio can also become flattened on both sides of the equation, reflecting a personality withdrawal, a schizoid episode, or some other extremely controlled condition.

M : FM—HUMAN MOVEMENT TO ANIMAL MOVEMENT

An M : FM ratio of 1 : 2 is consistent with an extratensive disposition. On the other hand, when the M : FM ratio is more than 2 : 1, the subject is considered to possess good delay responses and impulses that are subordinate to controls.

The M : ΣC and M : FM ratios will usually correspond to the person's experience balance. For example, on the extratensive side, protocols where ΣC is higher than the M values also exhibit FM scores that are higher than the M values. When M : ΣC and M : FM are supported by a ratio of higher chromatic to achromatic responses, these three Rorschach measures are considered to comprise the core measures with respect to the person's experience balance.

NUMBER OF ACHROMATIC TO CHROMATIC RESPONSES

Because of the controlled nature of introversive types, the total number of responses is reduced for both achromatic and chromatic blots. In contrast, for extratensive personalities, the responses to achromatic and chromatic blots are fewer for achromatic blots and much greater for chromatic blots.

Thus, the $M : \Sigma C$, the $M : FM$, and the ratio of number of responses to the achromatic versus the chromatic blots are usually consistent and will form the basis for the overall assessment and diagnosis of either the introversive or extratensive disposition.

In the following section these projective measures will be related to the basic emotion and diagnostic system portrayed in Figure 7.1.

THE EXTRATENSIVE AND INTROVERSIVE EMOTION-DIAGNOSTIC STATES AND CORRESPONDING RORSCHACH MEASURES

The extratensive states of *aggressive, manic, hysteric* and *psychopathic* all contain elements of expansiveness, lability and dyscontrol. The introversive states of *passive, depressed, paranoid,* and *obsessive* all contain features of constriction and control. Thus, in a broad sense, the emotion-diagnostic circle seen in Figure 7.1 is dichotomized. The basic emotion-diagnostic categories either fall within the extratensive or introversive arc of the circle in Figure 7.1.

In this chapter, the emotion-diagnostic states encompassed within either of the two broad categories, introversive or extratensive, are not assessed with regard to their respective differences. Rather, these emotion-diagnostic states are separated only with respect to the dichotomy of introversive–extratensive. In future studies and theoretical work other measures of the Rorschach can be introduced in order to make further distinctions between the emotion-diagnostic categories. Such distinctions in individual profiles may be able not only to distinguish introversive from extratensive states, but also to discriminate emotion-diagnostic states among the introversive or extratensive categories, respectively, for example, in providing profiles that show the difference between the extratensive manic and aggressive types.

In practice, clinicians are able to do this kind of specific discrimination by the introduction of a fuller complement of projective measures and by observation of various clinical and diagnostic indicators. This present model contributes to the hypothesis concerning unity of personality domains by proposing that a sample of projective measures of the Rorschach can be related to a similarity structure of emotion- and derivative-diagnostic conditions.

In the analysis that follows, this hypothetical sample of projective measures of the Rorschach is presented with respect to how such measures correspond to the emotion-diagnostic dichotomy between the introversive and extratensive arcs of the circle portrayed in Figure 7.1.

TABLE 7.1

A Comparison of Introversive and Extratensive Emotion-Diagnostic Categories and
Corresponding Differences of the M : ΣC Ratio According to the Proposed Model

Emotion	Diagnostic category	M	ΣC	Description
Introversive personality				
Expectation	Obsessive	High	Low	Controlled, constricted, guarded, with-
Disgust	Paranoid	Low	Low	held, inhibited
Sadness	Depressed	Low	Low	
Fear	Passive	Low	Low	
Extratensive personality				
Surprise	Psychopathic	Low	High	Labile, expansive, impulsive, acting
Acceptance	Hysteric	Low	High	out, emotional, immature, dys-
Joy	Manic	Low	High	controlled
Anger	Aggressive	Low	High	

THE M : ΣC

In Table 7.1, the M : ΣC ratios (or propensity for control in contrast to lability)
for each of the introversive and extratensive types are given based on the emotion-diagnostic model. It should be noted that in Rorschach usage clinicians
understand the general indication of low, medium, and high levels, even though
within each category of low, medium, or high scores may not be identical.

In Table 7.1, the extratensive diagnoses of *psychopathic, hysteric, manic,* and
aggressive show a consistent finding in which, in all cases, the control side of the
M : ΣC ratio is low and the labile side is high. In a general sense, it is proposed
that, in all of these extratensive states, subjects are labile, expansive, impulsive,
emotionally expressive, and dyscontrolled, and may be, in addition, immature
and given to acting out. In contrast, the introversive types of obsessive, paranoid, depressed, and passive also show consistent trends. Except for the obsessive type, Rorschach experience indicates a low production of M responses as
well as a low production of ΣC. This attenuated M : ΣC is usually interpreted to
mean that individuals in the introversive states are guarded types who show a
conscious control over responses, constriction of spontaneity, and an overall
inhibition of expressive responses.

The one exception is the obsessive type, who shows a high M output. One
explanation for this glaring difference in the obsessive as compared to the other
introversive types concerns the nature of control mechanisms of the obsessive
character. The manifestation of control, constriction, and guardedness in the
obsessive is attained paradoxically through an overproduction of responses (see
later, Table 7.4). Thus, the obsessive also utilizes the smaller details of the blot,

choosing to endlessly search for fragments of the ink blot that might qualify as good form responses. In this sense of looking for detail, the obsessive is likely to produce many more responses than the average subject and among these responses are likely to emerge several M responses. Yet, it should be noted that were these fragmentary and smaller detail responses subtracted from the total number of responses offered by the obsessive subject, and were only responses that refer to the whole blot or a very large detail of the blot to be counted, then it is likely that the high proportion of M responses would be considerably reduced. What would remain would be an inhibited and controlled picture of the obsessive—a pattern more like the other introversive states with respect to the attenuated nature of the $M : \Sigma C$ ratio.

THE M : FM

In Table 7.2 is presented the M : FM ratio (human movement to animal movement ratio). This ratio concerns the tendency for action-orientation as represented by the FM score. When combined with the ΣC score, the FM forms an

TABLE 7.2

A COMPARISON OF INTROVERSIVE AND EXTRATENSIVE EMOTION-DIAGNOSTIC CATEGORIES
AND CORRESPONDING DIFFERENCES OF THE M : FM RATIO AND A% ACCORDING TO
THE PROPOSED MODEL

Emotion	Diagnostic category	M	FM	A%	Description
Introversive personality					
Expectation	Obsessive	High	Low	Low	A guarded profile is in-
Disgust	Paranoid	Low	Low	Low	dicated. Increased re-
Sadness	Depressed	Low	High	High	sponse of the obses-
Fear	Passive	Low	Low	Moderate	sive reflects control
					attempts, while higher
					FM in the depressive
					presumably represents
					suicidal implications
					rather than typical ex-
					pansiveness.
Extratensive personality					
Surprise	Psychopathic	Low	High	Moderate	The tendency for action
Acceptance	Hysteric	Low	High	Moderate to high	orientation and poor delay capacities with
Joy	Manic	Low	HIgh	Moderate to high	a trend toward imma- turity in these extra-
Anger	Aggressive	Low	HIgh	Moderate to high	tensive types

important part of the lability or extratensive picture. In this table, as in Table 7.1, the extratensive diagnoses of *psychopathic, hysteric, manic,* and *aggressive* show a consistent finding in which in all cases the control side of the M : FM ratio is low and the more labile action-oriented side is high. Within the extratensive category there is an increased probability of acting out and perhaps an overall immaturity. In contrast, the introversive types of obsessive, paranoid, depressed, and passive show a more mixed trend insofar as the usual clinical findings are less consistent. Yet, other than the inflated high M of the obsessive (as discussed above), low scores on both sides of the equation imply a general guardedness for such types.

The major exception is with the depressive personality, who shows a high number of animal responses (or A%). In most cases, high A% correlates with high FM or animal movement. Here, the lability in the higher FM and A% of this introversive depressive type, is manifested as a high score along the dimension of action orientation. However, clinicians would probably expect some action orientation in the depressive profile because of the suicidal implications usually associated with depressive conditions, including the action orientation of suicidal acts as expressions of self-aggression. Such action orientation in all likelihood would be indeed correlated to suicidal potential and not be at all considered a bona fide lability or expansiveness trait.

TOTAL RESPONSES, REACTION TIME, AND THE ACHROMATIC TO CHROMATIC RATIO

In Table 7.3, similar clinical observations are reported that largely support the findings of Tables 7.1 and 7.2. Here, the extratensive diagnoses of *psychopathic, hysteric, manic,* and *aggressive* show a consistent trend in which in all cases total numbers of responses are high, reaction times are quick, and chromatic responses are greater in number while the achromatic responses are fewer. In contrast, on the introversive side the diagnoses of *obsessive, paranoid, depressed,* and *passive* show somewhat of a mixed picture. Except for the higher total responses of the obsessive (discussed earlier), total numbers of responses are lower for the remaining introversive states while reaction times are either slow or slow to moderate. In no case is reaction time quick, as it is in each diagnostic state of the extratensive profile.

The obvious discrepancy in Table 7.3 is in the greater number of responses to the achromatic blots for the depressed diagnosis. However, in the analysis of Rorschach protocols of depressed persons it is frequently the case that a relatively greater number of responses to the achromatic blots is obtained. These responses are frequently offered as color responses to the black and white of the blot and indicate a typical depressive subject who essentially shows an absence of response to the color cards, and instead points to the black areas of the blot as constituting color determinants. This use of black and white as color is usually

TABLE 7.3

ADDITIONAL RORSCHACH MEASURES DISTINGUISHING INTROVERSIVE AND EXTRATENSIVE
EMOTION-DIAGNOSTIC STATES ACCORDING TO THE PROPOSED MODEL

Emotion	Diagnostic state	Total no. of Rs	Reaction time	Achromatic responses	Chromatic responses
Introversive personality					
Expectation	Obsessive	High	Slow to moderate	Few	Few
Disgust	Paranoid	Low	Slow to moderate	Few	Moderate
Sadness	Depressed	Low	Slow	Many	Few
Fear	Passive	Low	Slow	Few	Few
Extratensive personality					
Surprise	Psychopathic	High	Quick	Few	Many
Acceptance	Hysteric	High	Quick	Few	Many
Joy	Manic	High	Quick	Few	Many
Anger	Aggressive	High	Quick	Few	Many

not observed in nondepressed persons. Thus, in Table 7.3, the depressive diagnosis in fact actually would be expected to correlate with a greater frequency of responses to the achromatic blots.

The theoretical and clinical rationale of these few exceptions in Table 7.3 seems to be consistent with the overall profile of introversive personality qualities, and findings listed in Table 7.3 actually seem to discriminate quite well between those emotion-diagnostic states considered introversive and those of the extratensive type.

F%—FORM RESPONSES

In Table 7.4, the F%, reflecting the general level of control in the personality, again expresses the overall theme proposed throughout this chapter concerning the nature of the introversive versus the extratensive diagnoses. In the extratensive diagnoses of *psychopathic, hysteric, manic,* and *aggressive,* the F% level is low, while in the introversive types of *obsessive, paranoid, depressed,* and *passive,* the level of F% is moderate to high.

CONCLUSION

A variety of projective Rorschach measures have been considered in terms of the differences between introversive and extratensive emotion-diagnostic states.

TABLE 7.4
F% as a Measure of Control in the Introversive and Extratensive Types
According to the Proposed Model

Emotion	Diagnostic category	F%	Description
Introversive personality			
Expecation	Obsessive	High	Introversive types, in their need for control,
Disgust	Paranoid	High	for restricting urges, and for maintaining a
Sadness	Depressed	Moderate	kind of rigidity, typically show moderate
Fear	Passive	Moderate	to high F%
Extratensive personality			
Surprise	Psychopathic	Low	Extratensive types, who are labile, action
Acceptance	Hysteric	Low	oriented, and somewhat immature in their
Joy	Manic	Low	need to seek immediate satisfaction, typ-
Anger	Aggressive	Low	ically show a low F%

It was concluded that the introversive types generally express control needs while the extratensive types show lowered control capacities and higher proclivities toward liability, as well as a general action orientation.

The approach discussed in this chapter and the findings regarding a sample of Rorschach scoring categories suggest that a similarity organization exists in the infrastructure of the Rorschach and that this similarity organization of measures parallels the similarity structure of the system of emotions and diagnostic states in predictable ways. This overall similarity structure seems to dichotomize the basic emotion-diagnostic system into introversive and extratensive types very much the way in which Rorschach first conceived of this dichotomy. Thus, the application of a theory of emotion to Rorschach projective measures has revealed a unity between emotion, personality, and diagnosis that becomes more visible through the resulting Rorschach profile.

REFERENCES

Kellerman, H. (1979). *Group psychotherapy and personality: Intersecting structures*. New York: Grune & Stratton.

Kellerman, H. (1980). A structural model of emotion and personality: Psychoanalytic and sociobiological implications. In R. Plutchik & H. Kellerman (Eds.), *Emotion: Theory, research, and experience* (Vol. 1). New York: Academic Press.

Kellerman, H. (1983). An epigenetic theory of emotions in early development. In R. Plutchik & H. Kellerman (Eds.), *Emotion: Theory, research, and experience* (Vol. 2). New York: Academic Press.

Kellerman, H. (1987). The nightmare and the structure of personality. In H. Kellerman (Ed.), *The *nightmare: Psychological and biological foundations* (pp. 271–360). New York: Columbia University Press.

Kellerman, H., & Plutchik, R. (1977). The meaning of tension in group therapy. In L. R. Wolberg, M. L. Aronson, and A. R. Wolberg (Eds.), *Group therapy 1977—An overview*. New York: Stratton International Medical Book Corp.

Kellerman, H., & Plutchik, R. (1978). Personality patterns of drug addicts in a therapy group: A similarity structure analysis. *Group, 2,* 14–21.

Klopfer, B., Ainsworth, M. D., Klopfer, W. G., & Holt, R. R. (1954). *Developments in Rorschach technique* (Vol. 1). New York: Harcourt Brace World.

Machover, K. (1949). *Personality projection in the drawing of the human figure.* Springfield, IL: Thomas.

Morgan, C. D., & Murray, H. A. (1935). A method for investigating fantasies. The Thematic Apperception Test. *Archives of Neurological Psychiatry, 34,* 289–306.

Murray, H. A. (1943). *Thematic Apperception Test.* Cambridge, MA: Harvard University Press.

Plutchik, R. (1962). *The Emotions: Facts, theories and a new model.* New York: Random House.

Plutchik, R. (1980). *Emotion: A psychoevolutionary synthesis.* New York: Harper & Row.

Plutchik, R. (1983). Emotions in early development: A psychoevolutionary approach. In R. Plutchik & H. Kellerman (Eds.), *Emotion: Theory, research and experience* (Vol. 2). New York: Academic Press.

Plutchik, R. (1984). Emotions: A general psychoevolutionary theory. In K. R. Scherer & P. Ekman (Eds.), *Approaches to emotion.* Hillsdale, NJ: Erlbaum.

Plutchik, R., & Kellerman, H. (1974). *Emotions Profile Index.* San Francisco, CA: Western Psychological Services.

Plutchik, R., Kellerman, H., & Conte, H. (1979). A structural theory of ego defenses and emotions. In C. Izard (Ed.), *Emotions in personality and psychopathology.* New York: Plenum.

Rapaport, D., Gill, M. M., & Schafer, R. (1970). *Diagnostic psychological testing.* New York: International Universities Press.

Rorschach, H. (1942). *Psychodiagnostics.* New York: Grune & Stratton.

Rorschach, H., & Oberholzer, E. (1924). The application of the interpretation of form to psycho-analysis. *Journal of Nervous and Mental Diseases, 60,* 225–248, 359–379.

Schilder, P. (1935). *The image and appearance of the human body.* New York: International Universities Press.

Chapter 8

METHODOLOGY IN THE ANTHROPOLOGICAL STUDY OF EMOTION

ROBERT I. LEVY AND JANE C. WELLENKAMP

ABSTRACT

Anthropological studies of emotion in communities whose histories, settings, and sociocultural organization differ greatly from those of the modern world are potential sources of empirical findings and theoretical perspectives that throw a special light on the nature of emotion. Methods for investigating emotion in these studies depend on the special conditions of cross-cultural studies and on the theoretical perspectives of the investigator. This chapter characterizes the anthropological approach to emotion and summarizes the authors' own theoretical orientations and empirical study of emotion in non-Western communities. These summaries provide a background for a discussion of the nature and problems of characteristic anthropological methods that are the basis for the description and interpretation of phenomena related to emotion.

INTRODUCTION

In contrast to the formal methods of experimentally oriented psychology, anthropologists for the most part use relatively informal, flexible techniques of investigation, which permit a search for previously neglected and possibly fruitful aspects of problems, and which respond to the special and often unpredictable conditions of field work. Special techniques are developed as they are needed,

205

motivated by their tentative usefulness and appropriateness in specific settings. Techniques, in such an approach, are flexible, innovative, and always problematic sets of tools for the description and elucidation of the wide range of issues which can be profitably investigated in "anthropological settings." Such settings, which we will characterize below, lend themselves to different kinds of research, many of which are inquiries within the framework of more or less traditional Western sociology, economics, psychology, and so on, carried on for some limited purpose in settings and cultures other than their usual modern Western ones. Such comparative studies differ from what we take to be the anthropological ideal in two ways. First, they are usually less concerned with using local data in a reflexive criticism and modification of their theoretical assumptions. Second, they most often pay insufficient (from an anthropologist's perspective) attention to the effects of context on both phenomena and theory [see Nagel (1961, p. 459f), discussed in Fiske & Shweder (1986, p. 4)].

Anthropological settings in both simple and, in recent years, more complex communities have been the sites for comparative sociology, comparative economics, comparative psychology, and the like [see Edgerton (1974) on the contrast between "comparative psychology" and "psychological anthropology"]. These studies, at their best, attempt to confirm or disconfirm the presence of some theoretically significant phenomenon or relationship carefully designated in advance. Information about human universals, on the one hand, and about culturally variable phenomena, on the other, results from such studies. An important and successful example of this cross-cultural comparative approach is the work of the psychologist Paul Ekman and his associates (Ekman, 1980a, 1980b; Ekman & Oster, 1979) in New Guinea and elsewhere on universals in the facial expression of emotions. Through careful experiments their studies have served to correct widely held relativistic assumptions about the uniqueness of forms of emotional expression in greatly different communities, and, thus, have made problematic the supposedly overwhelming importance of local cultural conventions in emotional expression. Comparative studies in this sense are a legitimate and valuable activity for behavioral scientists. However, there is some consensus in anthropology that there are approaches, problems, and methods which represent the discipline's special insights and responsibilities.

Anthropology, in short, prefers techniques of observation and inquiry which are fluidly responsive to an emerging understanding of local forms. Allied to this preference is a traditional commitment (resembling such fields as ethology in this aspect) to detailed accounts of natural settings and behaviors and to nonintrusive methods of observation in the hope of producing the least possible disturbance of those settings and behaviors. Behavioral observations, with close attention to context, supplemented by interviewing that is open ended and minimally prestructured, are the common first approaches to data collection. At times, however, it inevitably becomes necessary and productive for the investigator to systematically (and cautiously) manipulate the context in which behavior occurs through more structured interviews and other eliciting procedures, but such more intrusive techniques are ideally used only after much background ethnographic work has been completed. Such background work is necessary in order to determine the specific local meanings which enter into the interpretation of and response to various aspects of artificially constructed or manipulated situations, including testing instruments and experimental procedures developed in Western settings [see Price-Williams (1978) on problems in cross-cultural testing for cognitive functions]. These local meanings (including the local significance of details of tests, and of the testing situation itself) have often distorted the results and interpretations of some putatively objective procedures.

The anthropological study of emotion begins with the observation of and inquiries about what the investigator takes to be, in a first approximation, *emotional* behavior and experience, always considered in their social context. The techniques for guiding and facilitating observation and inquiry—which may be characterized as informal, creative, and naturalistic, based on emerging ethnographic understanding, and under methodological surveillance—are more difficult to specify concretely than are formal methods. One is often limited to giving general principles and examples, and saying "this is the type of thing we have in mind." As the choice of techniques is also at the service of questions and theoretical orientations brought to the investigation—questions and orientations which will be in part unfamiliar to the reader from other disciplines—we will combine our discussion of methodology and technique with a discussion of views developed in the course of our own work (Levy, 1973, 1978, 1983, 1984a, 1984b, 1985a, 1985b, in preparation; Wellenkamp, 1984, 1987, 1988; Wellenkamp & Hollan, 1981) as to what is interesting about emotion as it may be studied anthropologically. [For an overview of studies on emotion in anthropology, see Lutz and White (1986).]

A HISTORICAL NOTE

In the last few years, reflecting a renewed interest in emotion within the social and behavioral sciences and philosophy (an interest which represents, in part, a return to problems left neglected by the powerful cognitive orientations and investigations of recent decades), a number of anthropological studies of emotion have been made, for the most part in the radically non-Western communities which have traditionally served as anthropology's main research settings.

In earlier decades, to the limited degree that it was of interest to anthropologists, *emotion* in anthropology had been a vague term put to diverse uses.

If "emotion" is taken to mean "an emotion," a bounded sequence of anger, sadness, fear, and so forth . . . rather than some more abstract or derivative usage, then it has not been of central concern in anthropology until recently. Clyde Kluckhohn, for example, in a forty-seven page review of "Culture and Behavior" (1954), gave only one and one-half rather thin pages to "affect." His emphasis was on the relativistic aspects, noting that although "there may be a sense in which emotions, as biological events, are the same the world over . . . the expression of emotions and the circumstances arousing particular emotions vary culturally." In the second edition of the same handbook the new review of psychologically relevant anthropological studies by George DeVos and Arthur Hippler (1969) dealt with emotion primarily as an element in "expressive affective symbolic behavior," that is, as expressed in such forms as folklore and art in various cultures.

"Emotion" was always taken note of in "culture and personality" studies, but in keeping with the psychoanalytic emphasis of most of those studies it was usually of interest as a clue for the understanding of a psychodynamically conceived "personality organization" [Levy, 1984a, pp. 214–215].

The 194 more recently published studies reviewed by Lutz and White (1986) range across many other topics. These include, among others, emotion terminology in various languages, local cultural conceptions and theories of emotion [including our own "Western folk models of the mind" (D'Andrade, 1987)], the social and cultural regulation of emotion, and the relationship between symbolic action and emotion, topics which have also been of concern to the present authors.

ANTHROPOLOGICAL SETTINGS AND APPROACHES

The anthropological approach in its classic form is in part a function of the kinds of communities anthropologists have studied in their search for communities outside of the major Western tradition, communities which were long isolated and unknown or poorly known to the West, and therefore "exotic." In these small, scattered and often relatively self-sufficient places, the investigator would try to understand the life of the community insofar as possible as a "whole," as a set of systematic and mutually significant relationships. This approach promised to be a powerful strategy not only for describing the multitude of local traditions and social arrangements (which the anthropologist was supposed to describe in detail in his or her ethnographic and humanistic role), but also as an approach to an understanding and eventual explanation of those local arrangements. Questions to be asked about such small communities, when thought of as systems (in one or another sense), might include: what are the power and limits of different settings, ecologies, technologies, scales, traditions, and histories in affecting human minds and social inventions? What are the mechanisms that might produce such effects?

The anthropological sense of the interrelationship of phenomena derives in some part from *a priori* assumptions and in larger part from the realities of small, traditional communities. Understanding of these webs of interrelated phenomena is facilitated by the perspective made possible by the smallness of the community's scale, by the long periods of time the anthropologist spends in the field, and by his or her special and distant position as an outsider. One important implication of the anthropologist's case-centered, systematic, holistic viewpoint is an awareness of the problematic nature of many supposedly universal units of behavioral analysis, such as *emotion,* or *anger,* and the realization that a rigid and unquestioned definition and bounding of phenomena may well impose some arbitrary and Western reification of local phenomena. Such reification may obscure the most significant insights that might be derived from an examination of local processes (Shweder & LeVine, 1984, *passim*). But while the phenomenal and case-oriented, clinical, *idiographic* approach of the anthropologist is sometimes put in an unfavorable contrast to *nomothetic* strategies in searching for more general elements, relations, and laws, many anthropologists, including ourselves, believe that idiographic study provides corrective and suggestive ideas, hunches, and empirical discoveries, toward some more general, less parochial science.

EMOTION IN ANTHROPOLOGICAL SETTINGS: ORIENTING STRATEGIES AND SOME BASIC QUESTIONS

We can now turn toward our main topic and note something of our approach to the anthropological study of emotion and to a set of questions within this approach. Some of what follows will be more narrowly related to our own sometimes idiosyncratic concerns and conceptions; much will apply to the anthropological study of emotions in general. The questions can be ordered into some general *problem fields,* most of which have their own literature and theoretical orientations. The discussion of approaches and questions will serve to introduce the next section's illustrative sample of proposed answers. The questions and answers will, in turn, serve to introduce and frame a discussion of some aspects of technique. We should note that although we have elsewhere dealt descriptively at length with *specific emotions* in some non-Western communities [see, for example, Wellenkamp (1984) on sadness and mourning in Indonesia and Levy (1973, chaps. 9 and 10) on a spectrum of emotions in Tahiti], we are mostly concerned here with the study of emotion in general.

OBSERVATION AND AN ORIENTING SCHEMA FOR CONSIDERING EMOTION AS A SEQUENCE

Observation in an exotic setting starts with an investigator's general capacity for understanding behavior, an understanding developed and educated elsewhere, which is gradually confirmed or modified as a result of a growing experience of the community in which he or she is working. Empathy, intuition, and working analytic schemata serve as essential but problematic instruments in this understanding.

What should one look at if one is interested in *emotion*, or, for our present purposes, how should emotion be thought of so that it will be amenable to an anthropologically interesting analysis? How might we limit and break down the vague overall category of emotion into components which might be useful in a sociocultural approach to emotion?

It seems clear that emotion, like visual perception or any other psychological process, must proceed in a differentiated way through some length of time. We have found it productive [following Ekman, (1980a, 1980b) with appropriate modifications] to begin by conceiving of emotion as a sequence consisting of phases, in which the *feeling* itself is only one (albeit a critical) phase. For our purposes it has been useful to exaggerate linear steplike aspects of the sequence and the separation and distinctions among the steps or phases. Our schematic phases are as follows: (1) The *initial appraisal* of an eliciting situation. This is immediate, and begins out of awareness. (2) The organismic response to that appraised eliciting situation. This is the *feeling phase* of the sequence. Feeling arises in other experiential sequences, e.g., pain and fatigue. The question of how emotion might be distinguished from other sequences entailing feeling must therefore be considered. The feeling phase in an emotion sequence is of central importance in motivating a further response—which has special properties in relation to the local culture, properties which contrast with those of the first, the appraisal, phase. A feeling is also empathically generated in those who are observing someone experiencing an emotion through the *expression* and *communication* of that person's state. It is essential for our purposes to distinguish expression as the indexical signs or symptoms of the state of the individual (for example, flushing), which are under very limited cultural and individual control, from intended communication, which uses locally constructed and conventionalized devices (including controlled or mimicked expression) for purposely informing others about one's condition. Communication is related to what Ekman (1980a, p. 87) calls "display rules." (3) The response by the individual to the feeling. This response entails a *cognitive evaluation* of the situation, which now must take into account the transforming experience of the feeling. The feeling phase motivates this "secondary" movement of understanding—which may be contrasted with the "primary" understanding of the eliciting situation, which had generated the feeling in the first place. Our subsequent discussion will elaborate on this schema, and suggest how these distinctions have seemed useful in analyses of the differential effects of local culture on human experience.

Observations of emotion sequences occurring during the ongoing life of a community during the 1-½ or more years that anthropologists typically spend in residence can often be supplemented by observations of such sequences as they occur within the open-ended interviews we will discuss in a later section. As these interviews are ideally tape recorded, and occasionally video taped, particularly reliable and reaccessible data is obtainable.

In the observation of these sequences it is essential to note aspects of the *contexts* within which they take place, as well as the *role characteristics* (age, gender, positions in the hierarchy of wealth and/or power, etc.) of the people involved.

LOCAL INTERPRETATION AND LOCAL COVERT CONTROLS

Every established community elaborates more or less integrated systems of definition, interpretation, evaluation, and discourse, concerning the self and others. Such systems help to define reality and thus tend to integrate and control behavior and understanding. The investigator must supplement observation of in-context, naturally occurring behavior (including the observation of behavior during interviewing) by asking people to describe what they *think* is (or should be, or should not be) going on. Such queries may be supplemented by the systematic study of vocabulary terms, rules, classifications, evaluations, theories, and so forth, related to specific emotions and to emotion in general, as recognized and defined in the community. Local interpretations of emotion are also related to local theories and interpretations of such problematic things as *self, person* (the morally responsible actor), cause and effect, etc. In addition to the *overt* discursive conscious schemata for emotions, one will also be able to discern analytically *covert* categories by inspection of how things are talked about and responded to. Thus it is possible to argue from an examination of their behavior and conceptions that Tahitians have a covert category of "emotional feeling" in contrast to other kinds of feeling, even though the category is not named or intellectually recognized (Levy, 1984a). We should note that the overt and covert systems for the understanding of emotion of the local culture under investigation and those of the Western observer will only partially correspond.

We are now able to specify other questions. What are the local schemata for understanding and communicating about emotion in general, the various phases of the emotion sequence, the specific emotions? Do such schemata illuminate our own folk and scientific theories of emotion? How do the local theories relate to other aspects of the life and history of the community? What are the relations of these schemata to the actualities of emotion in the community as understood progressively and tentatively by the outside observer? What feedback effects do the schemata have on the various phases of the emotion sequence, and on the responses of others? What, in contrast to these relatively overt cognitive forms, are the community's covert controls of emotion? How do they operate?

We have suggested that the cognitive, classificatory, and discursive forms characteristic of a particular community clearly shape the form of the emotion sequence by controlling or influencing responses to the feeling phase in individuals. It has proved useful to ask whether (and how) forms characteristic of a community also shape the *onset* of the sequence, the initial tendency to respond to a eliciting situation. That is, do different kinds of communities' "task" in the control of emotions once they have been initiated vary because of differences in the "response tendencies" of local people? Can a cultural tradition produce phlegmatic, or irritable, people? How do community life and tradition and learning differentially affect these two aspects of response—the tendency to respond to some class of eliciting situations and the nature of the response once feeling is aroused?

ACQUISITION

Once we have delineated local forms we may ask how they are acquired. For the community as a whole this is a historical process. For individuals in each generation this is, in part, a question of learning. Are different aspects of the phases and forms of emotion differentially affected by culturally patterned learning? We will argue that they are.

DISTRIBUTIONS

What is the significance of variation in aspects of emotion by different roles, situations, and contexts in a community?

THE ADAPTIVE SHAPING OF OUTPUT

Different kinds of emotion sequences may lead to superficially similar types of *behavioral outputs,* outputs which may have great importance to the group. Aggressiveness, courage, timidity, gentleness, suspicion, sensitivity or insensitivity to the responses of others, and concern or lack of concern with shame and guilt are behaviors closely connected with emotion and are of great adaptational significance for one or another kind of community and for the performance of particular social roles within a community. How are such valued outputs shaped in a community so that individuals with quite different experiences and temperaments may act in the proper manner?

CULTURAL TRANSFORMATION AND PROJECTION

In what ways do other cultural forms serve to express, discharge, and disguise emotions which cannot be easily expressed in the course of everyday life?

EXPLANATORY STRATEGIES

Once we have delineated local emotional forms, we can choose to explore various approaches to explanation. The effects of local culture and social structure, local patterns of learning and development, psychodynamic processes influenced by local experience, the community's history, and present adaptations or past ones (the latter often persisting in a dysfunctional form) to one or another environmental feature are overlapping examples of explanatory possibilities.

COMPARATIVE THEORY AND TYPOLOGICAL CONSIDERATIONS

We have put anthropological approaches into some opposition to the uses of anthropological settings for comparative studies in other disciplines. But comparative questions can be asked about phenomena adequately put in context in different kinds of sociocultural systems. For emotion, one may ask whether any aspects of emotional form, expression, local theory, and the like are regularly related to some aspect of community form or setting—ecology, technology, social scale and complexity, etc. Thus it has been suggested that there are some features of anger which may be characteristic of hunter–gatherer groups (Rosaldo, 1984, p. 150), groups which differ in most other respects except in their basic system of livelihood. This is an example of, and suggests the further possibilities of, a *typological* approach, in which some important common feature (or cluster of features) of otherwise dissimilar communities (in this example a hunting and gathering economy) might be regularly associated with some aspect of emotion.

MORAL EMOTIONS

There are certain kinds of emotion sequences which have been the subjects of an independent and very large literature in anthropology and in the psychodynamic tradition that influenced psychological anthropology. These are the emotions thought to be specifically effective in producing self-control as a response to locally constituted moral systems. The specific emotions traditionally thought to be associated with moral controls are shame, embarrassment, guilt, and some aspects of fear [see Levy, 1973 (chap. 10); Piers & Singer, 1971]. Moral emotions are of particular anthropological interest because there are clear differences in the ways they are structured and made use of in different kinds of societies (although it should be noted that the traditional attempt to separate societies into "shame societies" and "guilt societies" has proved conceptually inadequate). There has been recent awareness that still other emotion sequences may be closely related to moral controls (e.g., Levy, 1973, 1985a; Levy &

Rosaldo, 1983). The questions here are which emotions are harnessed in various communities for the internal motivation of moral self-control? How does this work? How are the emotions related to other internalized and external aspects of the moral system?

GLOBAL ISSUES

Based on a study of local forms, can one contribute empirically and methodologically to hypotheses about global questions such as the general biosocial nature of emotion, or the relations of emotion and rationality?

EMOTION IN ANTHROPOLOGICAL SETTINGS: SOME SELECTED PROPOSALS

Answers to (or at least opinions on) many of the foregoing questions and issues have been suggested by ourselves and others. It will be useful to sample some of them here to clarify and expand the questions we have listed and to provide a background for later comments on technique.

We have sketched a model of emotion as a sequence in which *feeling* is only one phase, and have noted some of the issues and questions suggested by such a model. We have made a distinction between a primary understanding, which initiates the emotion sequence in response to an eliciting situation, and a secondary understanding, which is motivated by an awareness of the feeling generated by the primary understanding. The understanding which informs the *appraisal phase,* which turns a perceived situation into an elicitor of some emotion, seems in our cross-cultural studies to be more universally human [Levy, 1973 (chap. 9), 1984a] and probably more related to biological "prewired" modes of understanding than is the secondary understanding. Insofar as the primary response is affected by learning, the learning is of a different type than the learning which affects the phase following the feeling. Some of the learning affecting the primary response is *random* (from the viewpoint of the local cultural order and its conscious educational efforts); some of it is based on *patterns* of experience (Levy, 1976), which are generated by local social and cultural forms whose implications are not generally apparent to local people. This pattern learning affects people's generalized, intuitive reactions to situations. It affects the way that stimuli affect them. The learning which affects the response to the feeling (both in the subject and in the local observers watching and empathically grasping the first signs of the subject's response to some particular context) is much closer to consciousness, to local logic, to verbal discourse, and to the conscious control of self and others, and can be thought of as an important community resource for controlling and integrating behavior. This kind of learning is related to language, values, terminology, systems of classification, and definitions—the local intellectual resources for building a local reality within which "sane" people are expected to operate. The mental precipitates of these two kinds of learning correspond to Leventhal's (1980) distinctions between perceptual memories (or, in his terminology, "schemata") and conceptual memories:

> The schematic and conceptual systems attach different types of cognitive processes to emotion. The schematic is in some sense the more primary and important; it integrates situational perceptions (episodes) with autonomic, subjective, expressive and instrumental responses in a concrete, patterned, image-like memory system. The conceptual system is more sequential and volitional in nature and corresponds more closely to social labelling processes [p. 160].

The feeling phase of the emotion sequence is the first part of the sequence which is unquestionably conscious, and it mobilizes and motivates a new phase of the response which is clearly related to the local culture and to the self. The self can be looked on as, in part, a cultural construction, an internal representation of and response to local systems of definition, control, and integration [for *self* and the related concept of *person* in anthropology, see Carrithers, Collins, & Lukes (1985), Kirkpatrick (1983), Levy & Rosaldo (1983), Marsella, DeVos, & Hsu (1985), and Shweder & LeVine (1984, Pt. II)].

Distinguishing a feeling phase in the emotion sequence suggests the question of the special status of *emotional feelings* among other feelings, and evokes speculations about the critical function of feeling in the emotion sequence itself. *The emotional feeling is a subcategory of feeling which implies a relation, primarily a social relation, between the self and an external world.* "I am angry, therefore (is the implication) someone or something is frustrating me." Nonemotional feelings, in contrast, may be ascribed to a *part* of the body (not, "*I* am sad," but "My tooth is hurting me") or a relation of the self to its *bodily support* ("I feel tired"). Individuals and cultures have the option of interpreting a feeling, which to some observers would seem to be emotional in the above sense, as a nonemotional feeling. This happens when a hypochondriac redefines some emotional feeling as a physical symptom, and when, for example, in rural Tahiti, people systematically, and for good adaptive cultural reasons, interpret a feeling which seems to the outside observer to be, say, sadness (an emotion) as a symptom of spirit-produced illness (a nonemotion). In both these cases the relation of self to another is denied. Another option is to accept a feeling as an emotional feeling in our sense, but mislabel the specific emotion that is felt, by distorting or denying in the later course of the sequence the perceptions and understandings which had initiated the sequence.

The Tahitian example illustrates that the culturally influenced conceptual part of the emotion sequence may be *wrong* from some cross-cultural perspective (Levy, 1985b)—an error shared by all normal members of the community. This misinterpretation at a level of secondary understanding is a distortion of something which had to be properly understood in primary understanding in order for the emotion sequence to be activated at all. As Leventhal (1980) writes in his comments on the distinction between schematic and conceptual systems (above), the conceptual system has to do with "the conclusions we draw about our feelings—our guesses as to what internal events and actions make up emotion as well as the causes and consequences of emotion. Although these beliefs are based on information gleaned from sensory motor and schematic processing, there is no reason to assume that they accurately reflect the mechanisms, responses, eliciting conditions or consequences of emotional processing" (1980, p. 181).

The sources of possible distortion in the different phases of emotion differ. Primary understanding may be distorted through peculiar patterns of experience; secondary understanding, through peculiar patterns of discursive knowledge (Levy, 1985b). The feeling phase may involve its own kind of understanding; it may contain a sort of proposition, "learned" in the course of evolution, about the world or, more narrowly, about relations of self to another in that world. That is, in its *form* the feeling itself may *propose* information (Levy, 1985b) about relationships that may be obscured by consequent cultural and psychological devices. A feeling of rage, for example, is the perception of a state of preparation for an attack on someone. This particular kind of feeling in itself contains the implications that someone has done something to motivate an attack, and thus is a *potential* source of information on one's relation to that person. But what an individual finally makes of this potential understanding may well be systematically distorted and transformed by the peculiarities of internal, discursive, conscious thought, as well as by the perceptions and responses of others, both to the situation and to the subject's behavior.

In the case of *specific emotions,* some cultures (Tahiti being an example) treat some specific emotions with extensive vocabularies and overt rules, while other emotions may be very poorly represented, almost to the point of invisibility within the systems of discursive communication. (This is not to say that such emotions are not represented in other nondiscursive, ambiguous modes of communication—dreams, which are vividly recounted in many places; art; poetry, and other projective forms.) These two extreme cases have been called, respectively, "hypercognition" and "hypocognition" (Levy, 1973). For Tahiti, anger and shame, for example, are "hypercognized," while feelings of loss and guilt are extremely "hypocognized," that is, they are difficult to conceptualize, acknowledge, or talk about, and are, in turn, easily and systematically misinterpreted.

While there may be universal central tendencies for those particular emotion categories, which are named in a particular community as is the case for color categories (Berlin & Kay, 1969; see Levy, 1984a, p. 229), the ways in which emotions are grouped and the boundaries of particular categories may vary culturally. Thus what is a single emotion category or subcategory in one culture may be differentiated into two or more categories or subcategories in another culture. Our categories of *embarrassment* and *shame* are named as one category in Tahiti and also among the Newars, and probably similarly in many non-Western cultures. But Tahitian terminology distinguishes between fear as a present experience ("I am afraid now because the dog is biting me") and anticipatory fear ("I fear that the dog might bite me"; "I am afraid of dogs"). Furthermore, particular experiences or responses may be included in a larger emotion category in some exotic way. The Tahitian language, for example, includes idiosyncratic dislike of foods, of the kind which involves an anticipatory nausea, within one of its named categories for *fear*.

Culturally generated discourse (including that aspect of thought which is internal discourse) about emotion has an interesting and important peculiarity. Local theories of, say, thinking or of perception have minimal effects, if any, on those processes. But the local conception of emotion and, in particular, of specific emotions deeply shapes the emotion sequence and its consequences by augmenting, suppressing, or deflecting the course of the emotion. Response and conception are uniquely interrelated in emotion.

Why do we have feelings and consciousness as essential parts of the emotion sequence? Let us review our model sequence for suggestions for possible approaches to such a fundamental question. The sequence starts from some sort of unconscious or marginally conscious appraisal, which has the peculiar result that it produces a feeling which is conscious. *Feeling* implies awareness *plus* a pressure toward action. The feeling phase in turn *motivates* a thoroughly conscious attempt to understand what is going on. This understanding begins as a problem for the self, a subunit of the mind with particularly important relations to and dependencies on the culturally created forms of the local community, and quickly tends to become a problem for interpretation and action by others.

Psychological anthropology conceives of individuals as embedded in their culture and society, with individual–culture–society as a systemtically interrelated unit for analysis. In this perspective, feeling can be thought of as a *signal* from a system of unconscious orientation, a system which is more generally human, more evolutionarily prewired, more the result of random learning and developmental experiences, to another conscious system where the controlling and integrative devices of local cultures and communities operate. The feeling phase in the emotion sequence in a sense *activates* these culturally formed systems in the individual and in the responses of the others in the community who must deal with that individual. We may speculate that feelings (including nonemotional feelings) may arise as a result of perceptions when some response is required beyond the capability of those nonconscious adjustive systems which automatically and autonomously (from the viewpoint of the self) are able to adjust aspects of an individual's responses to internal and external environments. What becomes necessary now is the kind of complex integrated information which depends on the human (or other) organism's complex experience of and learning about the world in which it finds itself. Feelings arise in such circumstances and motivate the examination of this information. In higher animals, particularly social animals, much of the required information includes knowledge about relationships, which are the special subjects of emotion. Finally, among humans, experience and learning depend in large part on culturally structured information and instruction, which, when mobilized by the feeling with its pressure for action and understanding, are the bases for the individual's conscious question, ''What is going on, and what should I do about it?'' and for whatever answers are arrived at.

OTHER ASPECTS OF CONTROL

We have raised the problem of the shaping of locally valued and sometimes adaptive *emotional outputs,* of importance for the life of different kinds of communities. In some traditional communities one can discern a *hierarchy of redundant controls,* which help ensure the proper outputs of behavior, as is the case for *gentleness* in Tahiti (Levy, 1978). Rosaldo's statements about hunter–gatherers noted above (in our discussion of typological approaches) suggest that some aspects of emotion may vary in accordance with *types* of community. Our work in progress suggests that the way in which emotions are controlled varies in communities of different sizes and degrees of social complexity and of modernity. Moving from simple, to complex traditional, and then to modern communities, there is a progressive shifting of emphasis from control through shared coherent interpretations, that is, through the shared definitions of reality which are possible in small isolated communities, to control through powerful externally provided symbolic forms in large, complex traditional communities (Levy, in preparation), and, finally, to the complex relatively autonomous psychodynamic self-controls of modern society.

CULTURAL TRANSFORMATIONS OF EMOTION

This issue was of central importance in the psychoanalytically influenced work on culture and personality in early research in psychological anthropology (DeVos & Hippler, 1969; LeVine, 1973). Cultural institutions such as healing practices and symbolic productions (e.g., ritual, myth, folk tales, poetry, and drama) are important areas of investigation for their possible functions in expressing or deflecting or defending against emotions which may not be normally expressed in other ordinary, everyday arenas. Such emotions are deflected, as it were, to special peripheral or playful arenas or to *transcendent* ones (that is, to some heightened reality—religion, drama, myth, and legend—beyond the everyday reality of ordinary human actions and experience). In such arenas problematic emotions may be directly expressed, or may be expressed in disguised or ambiguous forms. Among the Egyptian Bedouin, for example, feelings of sadness resulting from loss or neglect are not (because of cultural values stressing independence and the importance of maintaining the public appearance of honor) expressed in ordinary discourse but are expressed in the reciting of and the response to poetry (Abu-Lughod, 1985). The apparent validity of observations that many cultural forms do serve the purpose of channeling, denying, or transforming emotions raises the theoretical question as to why this is necessary, and how it works. While *hydraulic, psychic energy,* and *catharsis* metaphors have become questionable, the phenomenon of emotions that are in some sense not fully expressed or "discharged" being deflected into cultural forms which individuals become passionately attached to or anxiously concerned about requires explanation (see Scheff, 1979). An investigation of emotion that attends to both private and public forms is clearly important for the consideration of such problems.

TECHNIQUE

We have sketched a background of inquiry, orientations, questions, and suggested answers which provide a context for choices of technique. How does one gather the kinds of data which are relevant to such approaches to emotion? In the naturalistic study of the emotions we must be sensitive to the systematic interrelations of very different sorts and levels of data—organismic responses, unconscious processes, ideas, responses of others, traditions, histories, social structures, adaptations, and the like. There are various techniques for approaching each of these areas. The way these analytic levels and areas are to be selected and fitted together for the understanding of a specific cultural or individual case or for some particular problem must be done creatively by investigators with little technical guidance.

It will be convenient for this presentation to divide our discussion into sections. We will consider briefly (and unequally) various areas and modes of study. For some topics we will simply note some relevant references. For others, where the methods and problems are general to the behavioral sciences, we have assumed that citations are not necessary. We have devoted most of our space to discussions of the approaches and problems (e.g., observation and empathy) that are most centrally at issue in the kind of anthropological approach we have presented here. There is one motif that runs through much of what follows: the relation of local forms and interpretations to the observations and interpretations of a foreign investigator, and thus the importance, limits, and peculiarities of that investigator as an instrument. The investigator's observations and ways of thinking about those observations are rooted, when the subject is emotion, in an intuitive and empathic understanding of local forms, an understanding which provides a problematic basis for the subsequent description and analysis of those forms.

Naturalistic Observation

We start by trying to observe what seems to be going on. One begins with one's own naive and problematic (but not necessarily erroneous) understanding, and then turns to the local people's also problematic (and not necessarily correct) understanding of the same event. Our eventual understanding, very possibly transcending *both* viewpoints, is a result of their interaction.

What we attend to has to do with our constantly shifting sense of *significance,* generated in part by the sorts of questions and tentative answers we have presented above, as well as by concerns and interests of a more obscure basis. While identifying the emotional behavior of others is always a matter of interpretation and inference based, ideally, on a number of sources of information (Ekman & Oster, 1979; Plutchik, 1983) and subject to the distortion of idiosyncratic personal needs and orientations, identifying the emotions of persons of a culture very different than one's own presents an additional and special problem. As Solomon (1984) has asked,

> What warrants an anthropologist's attributing emotions of a specific sort to persons in a very different society? A few years ago . . . Marvin Harris expressed shock and professional outrage at the "horrifying confidence" of his colleague Margaret Mead in identifying the emotions of her Samoan subjects. Indeed, where should such confidence come from? Is there any justification for confidence in such matters at all? [p. 245]

As Lutz (1985) notes, "an elaborate and complex body of knowledge is involved in an American's identification and explanation of a case of 'anger' or 'emotionality' " (p. 69), and therefore our attributions and interpretations of the emotions of people in other cultures are based, at least in part, on our culturally derived assumptions about emotions and how they work. "Derived from our own (Western) culture" does not necessarily mean (contrary to the occasional polemics of some cultural relativists) arbitrary or mistaken (Levy, 1984c), but in cross-cultural inference the possibility of *cultural* bias is added to the kind of idiosyncratic intellectual or psychodynamic biases that can produce systematic distortions of understanding even within a culture (Devereux, 1967; Spiro, 1986, p. 275).

One can begin to minimize error and distortion substantially in cross-cultural studies simply through the critical, self-reflective awareness that the problem exists [for more skeptical positions on the ease of overcoming difficulties of observation and, particularly, "representation" in anthropology, see Clifford & Marcus (1986)]. The anthropologist's essential ethnographic responsibility to familiarize himself or herself with and eventually to describe indigenous ways of defining and appraising events and of conceptualizing, expressing, and communicating emotions in itself induces awareness of the possible problems and parochialisms in one's own ways of doing such things. One learns to be careful to avoid unwarranted assumptions about the meaning of various behaviors and to remain self-consciously aware of the grounds on which one attributes a state of emotion or specific emotions to others.

Once sensitive to the special problems of distortion, the anthropologist can begin to educate his or her understanding by making use of such resources as:

1. Verbal accounts, interpretations, and explanations made by the individuals concerned.

2. The investigator's growing understanding of the context. With increasing experience of the life of the community, one learns better to understand when, for example, according to local systems of understanding, someone has been excluded or accepted, insulted or complimented, or defeated or rewarded. One comes to understand also how contexts affect the rules and possibilities of expression.

3. The responses of onlookers to an emotion event in the community. The responses of others, both verbal and nonverbal, to an individual's behavior provide further information on the cultural organization of emotion and the way it is maintained by interactions. Do others in the community validate, ignore, discourage, or reinterpret, the individual's emotional response through their own nonverbal and verbal behavior?

4. Knowledge of the past behavior of an individual. One advantage that an anthropological field worker has over many investigators using other approaches is that he or she can observe the behavior of individuals over time and in a variety of situations. This facilitates the understanding of the effect and power of various situations and contexts in producing and modifying an individual's behavior.

Naturalistic Observation: The Problem of Empathy

A subcategory of intuition of particular importance in the study of emotion is empathy. The *Oxford Universal Dictionary* defines empathy (a term first used only in 1912, from the German *einfühlung*, "in feeling") as "the power of projecting one's personality into, and so fully understanding, the object of contemplation." As such a definition emphasizes, empathy so defined is something other than intellectual and analytic understanding. Empathy, to use a somewhat more contemporary language, begins with an unself-conscious reading of body and vocal signs or symptoms and of contexts, a reading derived from an observer's general competence as a social being (as developed in some particular community) in interpreting such significant behavior, as well as his or her idiosyncratic biases or insights. Such understanding operates in any given encounter with little or no help from reflective and discursive thought, although reflective thought can through time progressively educate and modify, validate, or discount empathy. The validity of the use of such intuitive understanding of feeling across cultures has been warmly contested among more extreme partisans of relativistic and universalistic positions [see discussions by Black (1985), Geertz (1983), Kracke (1981), and Riesman (1977)].

Although many aspects of these expressive behaviors appear from the start to be culturally structured and patterned in some local and exotic fashion, and although these exotic formations necessarily capture attention and interest in foreign places, one seems, in our experience, to be able to read rather easily and directly the general meaning (e.g., doubt, interest, frustration, fear, and anger) of very many expressive and nonverbal communicative signs as illuminated by readings of the contexts in which they are produced. Even ethnographic accounts written by those skeptical about the validity of cross-cultural empathic understanding very often contain statements or inferences based on empathic readings of expressive signs of emotion. For instance, Rosaldo (1980), who was a leading critic of "ethnocentric" readings of emotion, writes in her monograph on Ilongot notions of passion and reason, "Wagat, Tukbaw's wife, *said with her eyes* that all my questions gave her pain . . ." (p. 33, emphasis added).

How might we know if our subjective impressions and readings of another's facial expression, tone of voice, posture, and so forth are accurate, especially when we are dealing with members of another culture? Additional sources of information, such as the context, self-reports, and comments of local observers and commentators, can be used to verify our impressions and readings. But there are occasions when such local reports ("I am tired") *conflict* with one's impressions ("He is depressed") based, in large part, on nonverbal and paralinguistic behaviors (e.g., repeated sighing, facial expression, and posture), causing the investigator to suspect that something is going on other than the individual, or his or her group, maintains.

Nonverbal and paralinguistic behaviors are potentially key sources of information on culturally ignored and poorly articulated feelings. An important issue here is to what degree such behaviors are locally constructed (in the same way that linguistic features such as, say, vocabulary items are), and to what degree they are validly understandable across cultures. The degree to which such behaviors are readable transculturally is open to empirical investigation. Permanent audio and visual records of nonverbal and paralinguistic behaviors can be made and examined and correlated with other indexes of emotional response, and can be presented to judges from other cultures for attempts at interpretation. The results of preliminary studies of this sort [such as Ekman's (1980b) study on facial expression] suggest that many bodily indicators of emotion are widespread and perhaps universal. Levy (1984a) has suggested that in addition to shared species-specific biological factors that make aspects of the expression of emotion generally understandable, there are also *iconic* or *analogic* aspects of expression which can be read with little specific cultural information [for an extreme statement on the uniquely local patterning of expressive paralinguistic features, see Pittenger, Hockett & Danehy (1960, p. 185) and Levy's comment on their assumptions (1984a, p. 231)].

Empathy is problematic, nowhere more so than in its cross-cultural use, but, as is the case with intuition generally, its educated use, that is, its successive subjection to critical self-conscious correction, is necessary as an adjunct to the understanding of emotion as we are considering it here. Not every one is so educable. Some people are not particularly empathic[1] and others for one reason or another are rigid about maintaining and defending their own idiosyncratic or ethnocentric orientations. This is a special problem in the study of emotion that is not an issue in the study of other psychological processes such as perception or cognition. Studying color perception or different words for *snow* does not usually provoke personal reactions and defenses to the same extent as does studying anger, shame, fear, or affection. The study of emotion is in itself an emotionally laden enterprise. Not everyone is capable of using themselves as an instrument in the ways called for in these kinds of participant–observational studies. In order to reduce the possibility of distortion, one must be able to observe oneself and develop some awareness of one's own predispositions, needs, anxieties, blind spots, and limitations. One is then prepared to educate one's empathy in the same ways as one educates one's intuitive understanding.

The Open Interview

Interviewing supplements information obtained through observation. Formal interviewing, which we will consider below, is necessary in the investigation of the systematic cultural forms which serve to integrate and control emotion. Here we will have some comments on open and relatively informal interviews. Such interviews provide two kinds of information about emotion. Individuals being interviewed are used in part as *informants,* providing their own presumably

---

[1]An interesting ethnographic question concerns the differential extent, forms, and uses of empathy by different cultural groups and the extent to which sensitivity to others' emotions is culturally important and fostered. Briggs (1970) reports, for example, that the Utku Eskimo with whom she lived were acutely attuned to subtle changes in each other's emotion states as well as in her own. In Polynesia, empathy, which is one of the central meanings of the familiar term *aloha* (Levy, 1973, 340 ff.), is an important basis for moral actions. In other cultures, including our own, empathy has sometimes been considered as unmanly, a sign of weakness (e.g., a problem with *ego boundaries*), or as being fallacious as a mode of knowing (hence, Behaviorism).

objective reports, views, and interpretations of phenomena related to emotion. At the same time they may serve as *respondents,* objects of systematic study in themselves, in which their discourse—and in particular the *forms* of that discourse and their behavior as they talk—indicates something about the organization of emotion in that particular individual. For such interviews the investigator may devise a check sheet of topics to be used to guide the respondent's discussion in the hope of systematically eliciting accounts, memories, and sometimes episodes (preferably in attenuated form) of emotional behavior (Levy, 1973, App. 1). In open interviews the investigator attempts to let the interview follow the respondent's lead to a large degree, in order to see how the respondent presents his or her statements on the assumption that the organization of these presentations may reveal patterning of both cultural and personal significance. In the course of interviews, personal emotional reactions are probed for by questions such as "How did you feel about that?"; "What did you feel like doing then?"; "What *did* you do?"; "Why?" and the like. Such interviews produce rich material bearing on feelings and understandings about feelings and their transformations throughout various stages of life, on learning, on fantasy, on stress and anxiety, on moral ideas and emotions, on self-concept, and on other such personally centered dimensions of experience. While a question during an interview such as (in Tahiti) "What are the responsibilities of a chief here?" produces, for the most part, cultural information, the probe "What is it like for *you* to be a chief?" will elicit information about personal experience and organization. Many aspects of form can be put to analytic use here—facial expression and body language (capable of being recorded by video tape) as well as paralinguistic features, and a rich field of thematic clumpings, distortions, evasions, hesitations, slips of the tongue, and confusions, all amply illustrated and easily discernible in a close listening to tape recordings of interviews.

These kinds of interviews can only properly be conducted after many months of acquaintance with the people involved and after gaining considerable competence in the local language. They should be conducted at a location affording as much privacy as possible, preferably separate from other residences or structures. Knowledge of the general organization of community life and of conventions and norms governing aspects of the interview situation—for example, what one should and should not talk about with others or with particular sorts of people —needs to be acquired beforehand. (Tactful and careful violation of these norms, however, produces some of the most informative interview materials.) The private setting as well as the open-ended, unstructured nature of the interviews allows the persons being interviewed a measure of freedom in his or her responses. Psychological anthropologists have the advantage over most other kinds of psychological researchers in that they can compare a subject's behavior during interviews (as well as responses to other eliciting instruments) with prolonged observations of the same person's behavior in other settings. The contrasts in discourse and behavior as they vary across settings give important additional clues for understanding the psychological and social structuring of emotion in the community.

One major methodological issue in the study of emotion has to do with the fact that some of the expression of, and most of the communication about, emotion is subject to conscious control. Emotion expression can (within limits) be simulated, suppressed, and manipulated in other ways for various instrumental purposes and in response to various internal and external pressures. Interviews provide an opportunity for individuals to comment upon their behavior, to say such things as, "Yesterday, I wasn't truly angry, I was just acting angrily to discourage the others from asking too much," or "I was very angry at him, but I didn't say anything, because he is known for his knowledge of sorcery and because it would have been shameful to let others see my anger." Such self-reports during the course of interviews are in the direction of private discourse, even of private internal thought. One attempts to create a certain type of interview context, one which is perceived as being safe for the discussion of tensions between the private self and the public world (the main locus of emotion), as these are locally conceived. *Safe* also has the essential implication that the subject has come to trust the interviewer's competence, discretion, and motives. This recognition of a need for trust leads to the question of why an informant should be willing to give the interviewer private information. Our experience, and that of many others who have tried to interview about private experience in other cultures, indicates that the chance to explore, discuss, and formulate relatively private thoughts, feelings, and impulses (a chance which arises much more rarely in many very small traditional communities than in our own) is, when the interviewer has met the proper tests, very frequently willingly made use of and is seemingly satisfying and important to the subject. The usefulness of talking about and reflecting on oneself, particularly in very public communities where role playing is pervasively necessary, seems to be of very widespread, perhaps universal, value.

While informants are very often more willing to disclose some information of a private nature to a tactful and sensitive fieldworker who is from outside the community than to fellow members of their own culture, they may also be more hesitant and unwilling to disclose other information. Sometimes one can elicit sensitive and taboo information (e.g., in Nepal, emotions that young Hindu women feel toward husbands and mothers-in-law in their arranged marriages) by asking informants how *others* feel, thus getting covert reports on the self.

The Projection and Transformation of Emotions into Cultural Forms

The techniques relevant here are the now classical (and sometimes controversial) ones for the investigation of the psychodynamic implications of cultural forms (see DeVos & Hippler, 1969; LeVine, 1973). Major monographic examples of this approach are the corpus of the work of Devereux (summarized in 1978) and Spiro (summarized, to that date, in 1978).

Cultural Schemata

While the miscellaneous collection of historically derived local forms which anthropologists group as *culture* seems to affect (in different ways) the various phases of the sequence of emotion, many of the clearest and most obvious effects are produced by locally constituted schemata which name, interpret, instruct what to do about, and evaluate emotion and specific emotions. These schemata are closely related to language, and thus to discursive communication and to the kind of reflective and discursive thought usually called *cognition*. Such systematic schemata, like all more or less efficient communicative systems, are amenable to study through relatively formal techniques. Such techniques have been extensively developed and discussed in the cognitive anthropology of the last 20 years [for some summary overviews, see Casson (1981), Dougherty (1985), Ember (1977), Spradley (1972), Tyler (1969), and, in a useful overview, Gardner, (1985, chap. 8)].

Some anthropologists approach the study of emotion words and concepts by focusing on certain key terms (e.g., Rosaldo, 1980). Others, using the kinds of formal interviews and eliciting techniques that allow for the systematic exploration of lexicons, taxonomies, evaluations, and the like, have investigated aspects of the formal cognitive structure of emotion, generally using techniques of analysis borrowed from earlier work on conceptual systems (Gerber, 1975, 1985; Lutz, 1982; Ochs, 1986; White, 1985). They have often used such techniques in conjunction with recordings of everyday discourse and behavior, and with interviews designed to elicit general propositions and discourse about emotion. Such formal approaches aim to obtain more explicit and systematic formulations of cultural schemata, schemata which otherwise have to be deduced from their background presence in more informal interviews and observations. Care must be taken, however, to determine the extent to which explicit formulations derived from interviews are culturally shared and natural, that is, really inform everyday interactions rather than being improvised responses to the ethnographer's questions and to the peculiarities of the interview situation. One must be cautious about the temptation for the informant (as well as the investigator) to oversystematize cultural constructs that may in actuality be inconsistent and poorly organized (Howard, 1985).

Some Residual Areas

There are a few remaining areas of inquiry which require some special technical approaches, and which are in themselves the subjects of extensive literatures. These are areas of general concern in anthropology and in the social sciences in general and we will only note them briefly here, referring the reader to the literature for methodological and technical discussions.

1. *Distribution.* Many aspects of emotion understanding and action are differentially distributed in communities, either among *social roles* (men and women; children and adults; people of high, mid, and low status; etc.) or in different *behavioral arenas* of the culture (ordinary life versus festivals; sober life versus occasions when alcohol or drugs are traditionally used; everyday discourse versus poetic expression; etc.). The investigator must be able to discern and take account of significant distributions, and if the scale of the problem requires it, devise sampling and survey techniques which will throw light on important distributions.

2. *Explanatory Options.* We have mentioned some options in strategies of explanation. These all require bringing information about emotion sequences, gathered in such ways as we have discussed, into contact with other kinds of data and theoretical frameworks. Two of them require brief additional comments.

LEARNING AND DEVELOPMENT

The problems of how cultural forms are learned and of the effects of different kinds of early experiences were of central concern in the first decades of psychological anthropology [see, for example, Honigmann (1967, chap. 6–10)]. Traditional psychological learning theory and developmental theory within psychoanalysis, have not (in our opinion) proved adequate to the kind of learning which differentiates the citizens of various kinds of communities. The suggestions made in the past on the learning of forms specific to a culture, particularly aspects of psychological organization, were to a considerable degree speculative, and have been subjected to much criticism. In recent years more sophisticated studies have been made. These characteristically emphasize the learning of cognitive orientations, often by means of studies of verbal interactions between caretakers and children (e.g., Ochs & Schieffelin, 1984), but there have been recent attempts to study the learning of some culturally influenced aspects of emotion [see, for example, the collection of articles on "the socialization of affect" edited by Harkness and Kilbride (1983) and the section on "socialization and the acquisition of emotional competence" in Lutz and White (1986)].

Although *adaptation* has been an important issue in certain branches of anthropology (for example, in ecological anthropology and in evolutionary and primate studies within physical and biological anthropology), the emphasis in the few studies among humans when emotion has been an issue, has been, following Darwin, on species-specific adaptations [see Lutz & White (1986) on ethological and evolutionary approaches]. The adaptive aspect of the culturally specific forms of emotion has been a neglected issue. An important exception is Erikson's (1950) study of the emotional adjustment and adaptation of the Sioux and Yurok Indians of the time.

BASIC QUESTIONS IN THE
MEASUREMENT OF EMOTION

The editors of this volume asked the contributors to consider some basic questions in the measurement of emotion. Some of those questions, those relevant to the peculiarities of anthropological research, have been addressed in this essay.

Emotion does not refer to some given, fixed natural object, but to a process which can be bounded and subdivided in different ways. Measurement and techniques for the study of that process derive from how it is defined and from the special concerns of the investigator and his or her discipline. Many psychologically oriented anthropologists, working in communities which illustrate marked and often unexpected group (as well as individual) variations *and* similarities in the forms of emotion behavior, have come to see emotion as fundamentally a *psychocultural* process. In our argument the *phases* of that process (and the various special emotions) are differentially related to aspects of community organization.

We have suggested that one of the most interesting and often neglected problems of emotion is that it must include (or else it is not an emotion) a feeling phase—which may be thought of as a conscious pressure which evokes an effort at understanding and action. We have speculated that this phase has something essential to do with alerting or mobilizing those particular aspects of an individual's adjustive and adaptive capacities which require understanding of a complex learned-about external environment, an understanding which in humans is profoundly shaped by the social and cultural forms of a community.

Among feelings, *emotional feelings* and *emotion sequences* are special subclasses. While my *tooth* may ache, it is *I* as a unified subject who is angry. And while the nonemotional "I am fatigued" points to the relation of that unified subject to his or her bodily support, what we take to be the properly emotional anger, sadness, lust, guilt, shame, and the like point to a relation of the more or less unified socially constituted subject, the self, to an outer world of persons or personified forces and objects.

Our basic assumption, then, is that emotion, in distinction to other kinds of feeling sequences, has evolved so that it has come to mediate the integration of individuals into social groups. Of great importance in all social animals (as modern ethological primate studies clearly illustrate), in humans emotion has *coevolved* with the capacity for culture, that is, the capacity for creating and understanding patterned symbolic worlds as a common matrix within which members of human groups can live, and which are, in fact, the conditions of their elementary survival. The adequate study of emotion, then, requires a consideration of this integration both in its particular forms and functions in different groups and in its general characteristics throughout the human species.

REFERENCES

Abu-Lughod, L. (1985). Honor and the sentiments of loss in a Bedouin society. *American Ethnologist, 12,* 245–261.

Berlin, B., & Kay, P. (1969). *Basic color terms: Their universality and evolution.* Berkeley, CA: University of California Press.

Black, P. W. (1985). Ghosts, gossip, and suicide: Meaning and action in Tobian folk psychology. In G. M. White & J. Kirkpatrick (Eds.), *Person, self, and experience: Exploring Pacific ethnopsychologies* (pp. 245–300). Berkeley, CA: University of California Press.

Briggs, J. (1970). *Never in anger: Portrait of an Eskimo family.* Cambridge, MA: Harvard University Press.

Carrithers, M., Collins, S., & Lukes, S. (1985). *The category of the person.* Cambridge, England: Cambridge University Press.

Casson, R. W. (Ed.) (1981). *Language, culture, and cognition: Anthropological perspectives.* New York: Macmillan.

Clifford, J., & G. Marcus (Eds.) (1986). *Writing culture. The poetics and politics of ethnography.* Berkeley, CA: University of California Press.

D'Andrade, R. (1987). A folk model of the mind. In N. Quinn & D. Holland (Eds.), *Cultural models in language and thought* (pp. 112–148). Cambridge, England: Cambridge University Press.

Devereux, G. (1967). *From anxiety to method in behavioral sciences.* The Hague, The Netherlands: Mouton.

Devereux, G. (1978). The works of George Devereux. In G. Spindler (Ed.), *The making of psychological anthropology* (pp. 364–406). Berkeley, CA: University of California Press.

DeVos, G., & Hippler, A. (1969). Cultural psychology: Comparative studies of human behavior. In G. Lindzey (Ed.), *The handbook of social psychology* (2nd ed.). Reading, MA: Addison-Wesley.

Dougherty, J. W. (Ed.) (1985). *Directions in cognitive anthropology.* Chicago: University of Illinois Press.

Edgerton R. (1974). Cross-cultural psychology and psychological anthropology: One paradigm or two? *Reviews in Anthropology, 1,* 52–65.

Ekman, P. (1980a). Biological and cultural contributions to body and facial movement in the expression of emotion. In A. O. Rorty (Ed.), *Explaining emotion* (pp. 73–101). Berkeley, CA: University of California Press.

Ekman, P. (1980b). *The face of man. Expressions of universal emotions in a New Guinea village.* New York: Garland STPM Press.

Ekman, P., & Oster, H. (1979). Facial expressions of emotion. *Annual Review of Psychology, 30,* 527–554.

Ember, C. (1977). Cross-cultural cognitive studies. In B. J. Siegel, A. R. Beals, & S. A. Tyler (Eds.), *Annual review of anthropology* (Vol. 6, pp. 35–56). Palo Alto, CA: Annual Reviews.

Erikson, E. H. (1950). *Childhood and society*. New York: Norton.

Fiske, D. W. & Shweder, R. A., (Eds.) (1986). *Metatheory in social science*. Chicago: University of Chicago Press.

Gardner, H. (1985). *The mind's new science: A history of the cognitive revolution*. New York: Basic Books.

Geertz, C. (1983). "From the native's point of view": On the nature of anthropological understanding. *Local knowledge: Further essays in interpretive anthropology* (chap. 3). New York: Basic Books.

Gerber, E. R. (1975). *The cultural patterning of emotions in Samoa*. Ph.D. thesis. San Diego, CA: University of California.

Gerber, E. R. (1985). Rage and obligation: Samoan emotions in conflict. In G. M. White & J. Kirkpatrick (Eds.), *Person, self, and experience: Exploring Pacific ethnopsychologies* (pp. 121–167). Berkeley, CA: University of California Press.

Harkness, S., & Kilbride, P. L. (Eds.) (1983). The socialization of affect. *Ethos* (spec. ed.), *11*.

Honigmann, J. J. (1967). *Personality in culture*. New York: Harper & Row.

Howard, A. (1985). Ethnopsychology and the prospects for a cultural psychology. In G. M. White & J. Kirkpatrick (Eds.), *Person, self, and experience: Exploring Pacific ethnopsychologies* (pp. 401–420). Berkeley, CA: University of California Press.

Kirkpatrick, J. T. (1983). *The Marquesan notion of the person*. Ann Arbor, MI: University of Michigan Research Press.

Kluckhohn, C. (1954). Culture and behavior. In G. Lindzey (Ed.), *Handbook of social psychology*, Reading, MA: Addison-Wesley.

Kracke, W. H. (1981). Kagwahiv mourning; dreams of a bereaved father. *Ethos, 9*, 258–275.

Leventhal, H. (1980). Towards a comprehensive theory of emotion. In L. Berkowitz (Ed.), *Advances in experimental social psychology* (Vol. 13, pp. 139–207). New York: Academic Press.

LeVine, R. A. (1973). *Culture, behavior and personality*. Chicago: Aldine.

Levy, R. I. (1973). *Tahitians: Mind and experience in the Society Islands*. Chicago: University of Chicago Press.

Levy, R. I. (1976). A conjunctive pattern in middle class informal and formal education. In T. Schwartz (Ed.), *Socialization as cultural communication*. Berkeley, CA: University of California Press.

Levy, R. I. (1978). Tahitian gentleness and redundant controls. In A. Montague (Ed.), *Learning non-aggression* (pp. 222–235). New York: Oxford University Press.

Levy, R. I. (1983). Introduction: Self and emotion. *Ethos* (spec. ed.), *11*, 128–134.

Levy, R. I. (1984a). Emotion, knowing, and culture. In R. A. Shweder & R. A. LeVine (Eds.), *Culture theory: Essays on mind, self, and emotion* (pp. 214–237). Cambridge, England: Cambridge University Press.

Levy, R. I. (1984b). The emotions in comparative perspective. In K. Scherer & P. Ekman (Eds.), *Approaches to emotion* (pp. 397–412). Hillsdale, NJ: Erlbaum.

Levy, R. I. (1984c). Mead, Freeman, and Samoa: The problem of seeing things as they are. *Ethos, 12*, 85–92.

Levy, R. I. (1985a). Horror and tragedy: The wings and center of the moral stage. *Ethos, 13*, 175–187.

Levy, R. I. (1985b). Local rationality, ideal rationality and emotion. *Social Science Information, 24*, 325–329.

Levy, R. I. (in preparation). *Mesocosm: The organization of a Hindu Newar city in Nepal*.

Levy, R. I., & Rosaldo, M. Z. (Eds.) (1983). *Self and emotion. Ethos* (spec. ed.), *11*.

Lutz, C. (1982). The domain of emotion words on Ifaluk. *American Ethnologist, 9*, 113–128.

Lutz, C. (1985). Ethnopsychology compared to what? Explaining behavior and consciousness among the Ifaluk. In G. M. White & J. Kirkpatrick (Eds.), *Person, self, and experience: Exploring Pacific ethnopsychologies* (pp. 35–79). Berkeley, CA: University of California Press.

Lutz, C., & White, G. M. (1986). The anthropology of emotions. In B. Siegel (Ed.), *Annual review of anthropology*. Palo Alto, CA: Annual Reviews.

Marsella, A., DeVos, G., & Hsu, F. (1985). *Culture and self. Asian and Western perspectives.* New York: Tavistock.

Nagel, E. (1961). *The structure of science.* New York: Harcourt Brace World.

Ochs, E. (1986). From feeling to grammar: A Samoan case study. In E. Ochs & B. B. Schieffelin (Eds.), *Language socialization across cultures* (pp. 251–272). New York: Cambridge University Press.

Ochs, E., & Schieffelin, B. B. (1984). Language acquisition and socialization. Three developmental stories and their implications. In R. A. Shweder & R. A. LeVine (Eds.), *Culture theory: Essays on mind, self, and emotion* (pp. 276–320). Cambridge, England: Cambridge University Press.

Piers, G., & Singer, M. (1971). *Shame and guilt.* New York: Norton (originally published in 1953).

Pittenger, R., Hockett, C., & Danehy, J. (1960). *The first five minutes.* Ithaca, NY: Martineau.

Plutchik, R. (1983). Emotions in early development: A psychoevolutionary approach. In R. Plutchik & H. Kellerman (Eds.), *Emotion: Theory, research, and experience* (Vol. 2, pp. 221–258). New York: Academic Press.

Price-Williams, D. (1978). Cognition: Anthropological and psychological nexus. In G. D. Spindler (Ed.), *The making of psychological anthropology* (pp. 586–611). Berkeley, CA: University of California Press.

Riesman, P. (1977). *Freedom in Fulani social life: An introspective ethnography.* Chicago: University of Chicago Press.

Rosaldo, M. Z. (1980). *Knowledge and passion: Ilongot notions of self and social life.* Cambridge, England: Cambridge University Press.

Rosaldo, M. Z. (1984). Toward an anthropology of self and feeling. In R. A. Shweder & R. A. LeVine (Eds.), *Culture theory: Essays on mind, self, and emotion* (pp. 137–157). Cambridge, England: Cambridge University Press.

Scheff, T. J. (1979). *Catharsis in healing, ritual, and drama.* Berkeley, CA: University of California Press.

Shweder, R. A., & LeVine, R. A. (Eds.) (1984). *Culture theory: Essays on mind, self, and emotion.* Cambridge, England: Cambridge University Press.

Solomon, R. C. (1984). Getting angry: The Jamesian theory of emotion in anthropology. In R. A. Shweder & R. A. LeVine (Eds.), *Culture theory: Essays on mind, self, and emotion* (pp. 238–254). Cambridge, England: Cambridge University Press.

Spiro, M. E. (1978). Culture and human nature. In G. Spindler (Ed.), *The making of psychological anthropology* (pp. 330–360). Berkeley, CA: University of California Press.

Spiro, M. E. (1986). Cultural relativism and the future of anthropology. *Cultural Anthropology, 3,* 259–286.

Spradley, J. (Ed.) (1972). *Culture and cognition: Rules, maps, and plans.* San Francisco, CA: Chandler.

Tyler, S. (1969). *Cognitive anthropology.* New York: Holt, Rinehart & Winston.

Wellenkamp, J. (1984). *A psychocultural study of loss and death among the Toraja.* Ph.D. thesis. San Diego, CA: University of California.

Wellenkamp, J. C. (1987). The meaning of crying and wailing among the Toraja. Paper presented at the 86th Annual Meeting of the American Anthropological Association. Chicago, IL.

Wellenkamp, J. C. (1988). Notions of grief and catharsis among the Toraja. *American Ethnologist, 15,* 486–500.

Wellenkamp, J. C., & Hollan, D. W. (1981). Self-conceptions, bereavement, and cultural discontinuity. Paper presented at the 25th Annual Meeting of the Kroeber Anthropological Society. Berkeley, CA.

White, G. M. (1985). "Bad ways" and "bad talk": Interpretations of interpersonal conflict in a Melanesian society. In J. W. Dougherty (Ed.), *Directions in cognitive anthropology.* Chicago: University of Illinois Press.

Chapter 9

VOCAL MEASUREMENT OF EMOTION

KLAUS R. SCHERER

ABSTRACT

There is good evidence for phylogenetic continuity of the vocal expression of affective states. In spite of the importance of the vocal–auditory modality as a major channel in social communication, relevant research is scarce due to the difficulties of objectively measuring vocal sounds. This chapter describes recent advances in vocal measurement, including digital signal analysis and discusses the major parameters of vocal affect expression. A theory-based approach to the study of vocal cues of emotion is proposed and specific hypotheses are advanced. Finally, the evidence available from research during the past four decades is reviewed.

THE PHYLOGENETIC HISTORY OF VOCAL
EMOTION EXPRESSION

The use of the voice for emotional expression is such a pervasive phenomenon that it has been frequently commented upon since the beginning of systematic scientific interest in human expressive behavior. Cicero, in his *Orator,* a rhetorics manual, is very explicit on this point: "There are as many movements of the voice as there are movements of the soul, and the soul is strongly affected by the voice" (Cicero, 1975, p. 46). Among many others, Aristotle, Quintillian,

EMOTION
Theory, Research, and Experience
Volume 4

Porta, and Bell have contributed discussions of vocal expression (see Laver, 1975, chap. 1, for a review).

One particularly interesting aspect of human expressive vocalization is its apparent phylogenetic continuity with animal vocalization. Charles Darwin, in his pioneering monograph on emotion expression in man and animals, which has influenced research in this area probably more than any other single publication, considered vocalization one of the primary means of emotion expression. He wrote that "with many kinds of animals, man included, the vocal organs are efficient in the highest degree as a means of expression. . . . when the sensorium is strongly excited, the muscles of the body are generally thrown into violent action; and as a consequence, loud sounds are uttered, however silent the animal may generally be, and although the sounds may be of no use" (Darwin, 1965, p. 83).

In spite of the major role that Darwin attributed to vocal affect expression, he devoted many more pages of his work to bodily and facial expression. Even at the present time a disproportionate emphasis on the visual mode of expression may be due to the fact that body postures and facial expressions are much more readily illustrated by drawings and photographs (which Darwin had collected systematically) and/or described verbally than is the fleeting sound of affect expression, which cannot be illustrated in the print medium nor readily described because of a lack of appropriate verbal labels. The relative neglect of the vocal mode of affect expression is most noticeable in the research tradition on nonverbal communication and affect expression in humans (see Scherer, 1982b). Even in the animal communication literature, where the spectrograph (an electroacoustic device which allows the display of acoustic features of a sound on paper) has been frequently used in studying animal calls, the number of studies dealing with the expression of emotion in animals is relatively small. This may be partially due to the fact that biologists and ethologists have been notoriously reticent to use the terms *affect* and *emotion* to describe animal states and have been somewhat uneasy even with the more general notion of motivational states. It may be instructive to review the three major exceptions, the work by Tembrock, by Morton, and by Jürgens.

Tembrock (1975), who suggests a systems theory approach to animal vocal expression, proposes that the *system state* of the animal affects intensity, frequency, and temporal patterning of vocalization. Based on spectrographic analyses of animal calls, Tembrock suggests the following relationships between system states and phonation characteristics: (1) In the contact range, for calls reflecting states of relaxation and contentment such as comfort and play calls, one tends to find repeated short sounds with relatively low frequencies; (2) low frequencies also characterize dominance calls in agonistic encounters and threat calls (i.e., when critical distances are violated); (3) defense calls, which may be the result of a transition from threat calls, are short, with a high-amplitude onset and a broad frequency spectrum; (4) submission calls, which may be the result of graded transitions from threat or defense calls, are characterized by high frequencies, repeated frequency shifts, and a tendency toward temporal prolongation; (5) attraction calls at a distance are also characterized by high frequencies and temporal prolongation (Tembrock, 1975, pp. 66–68; translated by K.R.S.).

Morton (1977) also attempted to identify relationships between emotional states and acoustic features of vocalization across different species. He proposes a "motivation–structural rule" concept to describe the effects of affective state on acoustic structure: "birds and mammals use harsh, relatively low-frequency sounds when hostile and higher-frequency, more pure tonelike sounds when frightened, appeasing, or approaching in a friendly manner" (Morton, 1977, p. 855). The high-frequency, tonelike structure in fearful or friendly motivational states is explained by the structural similarity to infant vocalizations (attracting adults and soliciting support).

Both Tembrock and Morton argue largely on the basis of published studies of vocalization in various animal species. Generally, the investigators in these studies inferred the motivational or emotional state of the animal from overt behavior and context.

In contrast, Jürgens (1979), studying squirrel monkey (*Saimiri sciureus*) calls, was able to manipulate emotional states by using electrical brain stimulation. The "aversiveness" of the states thus produced was established by the amount of time the animal tolerated stimulation. Forty seven call types were studied using spectrographic analysis. Jürgens proposes the following five groups of calls as related to affect state: (1) purring–growling–spitting (*self-assertiveness*): nonharmonic, clicklike, rhythmic sounds; (2) groaning–cawing–shrieking (*protest*): nonrhythmic, harmonic, or noiselike sounds; (3) chucking–yapping–alarm peep (*worrying, warning*): short, loud sounds with a steep fall of energy from high to low frequencies: (4) chirping–peeping–squealing (*social unease, lack of confidence*): nonrhythmic sounds with high fundamental frequency, little frequency modulation, and at times a short ascending frequency course (to draw attention); (5) twittering–chattering–cackling (*pleasure, confirming social bonds*): rhythmic sounds with different shapes of frequency contours.

Jürgens reports that the aversiveness of a call is positively correlated with its total frequency range as well as with (in high-pitched harmonic calls) a higher fundamental frequency and an irregularity of frequency contours. Given the replication of similar results reported in the literature, Jürgens assumes that the relationship between acoustic structure and functional significance of calls found in his study holds for many primate species, and supports the claims presented by Morton (Jürgens, 1982, p. 61).

As one might expect on the basis of a hypothesis of phylogenetic continuity of vocal affect expression, the patterns described by Tembrock, Morton, and Jürgens remind us strongly of similar features in human vocalization. The parallelity would probably be even stronger, if we were to study more systematically the acoustic features of affect vocalizations or vocal emblems (see Scherer, 1977), i.e., the nonlinguistic affective voice sounds used by humans. Such sounds, which have often been termed interjections, might be considered the direct equivalent of animal affect sounds and it is likely that they, too, are produced by limbic system structures (see Lamendella, 1977; Robinson, 1976). Human speech makes use of voice, of course, which leads to an intricate mingling of cognitive–linguistic and affective–nonlinguistic elements in spoken utterances. As we shall see, one of the major problems in the measurement of vocal affect expression is to tease apart these two components of the speech signal and to extract the emotional aspects of a speech utterance.

MAJOR TRENDS IN RESEARCH

I shall deal with two major traditions of research in this area separately, i.e., with encoding and decoding studies. By encoding studies I mean those research attempts which are aimed at identifying the acoustic (or sometimes phonatory–articulatory) features of vocal utterances accompanying emotional states of a person which have been recorded in the field or induced in the laboratory. In the large majority of studies, these emotional states are not real but are role played or portrayed by actors. In contrast, decoding studies are not concerned with the acoustic features per se, but with the ability of judges to recognize the emotion expressed or portrayed through the ensemble of vocal features used. In some cases, cue isolation or masking techniques (see Scherer, 1982b) are utilized to determine which cues are likely to be primarily used by decoders.

A summary of the findings in the encoding studies based on earlier reviews of the literature (see Scherer, 1979, 1981a, 1981b) shows some of the emerging patterns (see Table 9.1). While there is a rather high degree of replication of these findings, the state of our knowledge remains rather unsatisfactory. This is mainly due to the fact that, as a close inspection of Table 9.1 will show, the findings to date do not provide the means for a clear-cut differentiation of many different discrete emotional states. On the whole, one finds a general distinction between affect states characterized by high excitation and activity (ergotropic states) and more restful, quiet, or passive states (trophotropic states). At most, one could find some evidence for distinguishing the three major dimensions which tend to be found for emotional states, evaluation, activity, and potency (see Scherer, 1981a). The assumption that vocal cues may not be capable of transmitting more discrete emotional information is at odds with the evidence to be reported below, showing that judges seem rather well able to decode a variety of emotional states on the basis of voice alone. One of the major problems in

TABLE 9.1
SUMMARY OF RESULTS ON VOCAL INDICATORS OF EMOTIONAL STATES[a]

| Emotion | Pitch | | | Loudness | Tempo |
	Level	Range	Variability		
Happiness/joy	High	?	Large	Loud	Fast
Confidence	High	?	?	Loud	Fast
Anger	High	Wide	Large	Loud	Fast
Fear	High	Wide	Large	?	Fast
Indifference	Low	Narrow	Small	?	Fast
Contempt	Low	Wide	?	Loud	Slow
Boredom	Low	Narrow	?	Soft	Slow
Grief/sadness	Low	Narrow	Small	Soft	Slow
Evaluation	?	?	?	Loud	?
Activation	High	Wide	?	Loud	Fast
Potency	?	?	?	Loud	?

[a]From Scherer (1981a, p. 206).

encoding research has been that most investigators have focused on very few acoustic variables, generally omitting voice quality, which seems to be one of the most promising vocal features (see Scherer, 1981a, 1986). Furthermore, much of this research suffers from a lack of ecological validity in terms of the emotion displays. In many studies, professional or lay actors have been used to portray vocal emotion displays without too much consideration as to the special problems of this approach (see Ekman, Friesen, & Ellsworth, 1972; Wallbott & Scherer, 1986). Finally, one of the major drawbacks, to which we shall return later, is the essentially atheoretical nature of much of this research, which in general has resembled fishing expeditions more than systematic tests of hypotheses.

Decoding studies will only be dealt with briefly here, since the focus is on vocal measurement. Suffice it to say that a review of these studies (see Table 9.2) shows that the average accuracy across the studies reviewed was about 60% (as compared with an average expected by chance of about 12%). This percentage, based on about 30-odd studies, is rather impressive and slightly higher than the accuracy achieved in studies using facial expression in drawings or photographs (see Ekman et al., 1972). Thus, there can be little doubt that enough differentiated information is available in vocal expression to allow a clear distinction of a fairly large number of discrete emotions. Again, however, one is forced to consider the present state of research rather unsatisfactory due to the nature of the material (in many cases actors are being used for portrayals with little concern for potential problems of this approach) and to a general lack of interest in the

TABLE 9.2

SURVEY OF STUDIES ON EMOTION RECOGNITION FROM SPEECH[a]

Study	Speech sample	Encoders[b]	Decoders	Average % accuracy[c]	Corrected % accuracy[d]
Dusenbury & Knower (1938)	Letters of alphabet	4 m, 4 f students	(a) 135 m, 159 f / (b) 47 m, 17 f students	(a) 83 / (b) 81	(a) 81 / (b) 79
Fairbanks & Pronovost (1933)	Standard passage	6 m amateur actors	64 speech students	79	74
Knower (1941)	Letters of alphabet / (a) voiced forward / (b) whispered forward / (c) voiced reversed / (d) whispered reversed	1 m, 1 f	27 students	(a) 89 / (b) 57 / (c) 43 / (d) 23	(a) 88 / (b) 53 / (c) 37 / (d) 15
Pfaff (1954)	Numerals 1–8	1 m speech instructor	304 students	50	44
Davitz & Davitz (1959)	Letters of alphabet	4 m, 4 f students and faculty members, 1 actress	30 graduate students	37	30
Pollack, Rubenstein, & Horowitz (1960)	Standard sentences / (a) 16 alternatives / (b) 8 alternatives	4	18	(a) 42 / (b) 63	(a) 38 / (b) 58
Soskin & Kauffman (1961)	Excerpts from real life recordings	15 m	22	Significant[e]	—[e]
Lieberman & Michaels (1962)	Standard sentences	3 m	10	85	—[e]
Beldoch (1964)	Standard passage	3 m, 2 f	43 m, 46 f students	54	49
Dimitrovsky (1964)	Standard passage	3 m, 2 f	224 children aged 5–12 years	53	37
Kramer (1964)	Standard passage / (a) American English / (b) filtered version (a) / (c) Japanese	(a–b) 6 m speech students / (c) 3 Japanese students	(a–c) 27 m students	(a) 70 / (b) 61 / (c) 58	(a) 63 / (b) 51 / (c) 48
Levitt (1964)	Standard passage	25 m, 25 f students	8 students	47	36
Levy (1964)	Standard passage	3 m, 2 f	32 m, 42 f students	54	49
Osser (1964)	Single word	1 actress	80	33	26
Turner (1964)	36 nonsense words	6 actors, 6 lay persons	(a) 30 somatically ill patients / (b) 60 schizophrenic patients	(a) 75 / (b) 59	(a) 70 / (b) 52

Study	Stimulus material	Encoders	Decoders	Accuracy A	Accuracy B
Hornstein (1967)	Letters of alphabet	124 f students	124 f students	59	54
Plaikner (1970)	Letters of alphabet	1 German actor	30 m, 19 f Germans	53	49
Wolf, Gorski, & Peters (1972)	Letters of alphabet	25 m students	25 m students (same as encoders)	45	39
Burns & Beier (1973)	(a) Standard sentences (b) Filtered version (a)	(a) 30 students (b) 30 students	(a) 21 students (b) 21 students	(a) 60 (b) 39	(a) 52 (b) 27
Ross, Duffy, Cooker, & Sargeant (1973)	Standard passage (a) full range (b) filtered 75–600 Hz (c) filtered 75–450 Hz (d) filtered 75–300 Hz (e) filtered 75–150 Hz	3 m, 3 f actors	33 students	(a) 70 (b) 57 (c) 55 (d) 49 (e) 26	(a) 66 (b) 52 (c) 49 (d) 43 (e) 17
Schlanger (1973)	Standard sentences (a) normals (b) aphasics	1 m, 1 f		(a) 97 (b)[e]	(a) 96 (b)[e]
Nash (1974)	Standard sentences		(a) 45 m, 52 f hospital staff (b) 43 m, 91 f patients	(a) 45 (b) 32	(a) 40 (b) 25
McCluskey, Albas, Niemi, & Cuevas (1975)	2 improvised, emotion-related sentences, content filtered	(a) 3 f Canadian actresses (b) 3 f Mexican actresses	(a) 10 f Canadian students (b) 10 f Mexican students	(a) 73 (b) 77	(a) 71 (b) 69
Sogon (1975)	Standard sentences	12 Japanese	30 Japanese	57	46
Zuckerman, Lipets, Koivumaki, & Rosenthal (1975)	Standard sentences	27 m, 13 f students	(a) 64 m students (b) 37 f students	(a) 45 (b) 46	(a) 38 (b) 46
Fenster, Blake, & Goldstein (1977)	Standard sentences	30 m adults, 30 m children 10–12 years	(a) 30 m adults (b) 30 boys 10–12 years (c) 30 boys 7–9 years	(a) 30 (b) 28 (c) 23	(a) 16 (b) 14 (c) 8
Brown (1980)	Film description	5 Spanish bilinguals	18 students	34	21
Wallbott & Scherer (1986)	Standard sentences	3 m, 3 f German actors	15 German students	53	37

[a] From Scherer (1981a, pp. 208–210).
[b] m, male; f, female.
[c] Average % accuracy, average percentage of accurate judgments.
[d] Corrected % accuracy, accuracy percentage corrected for chance.
[e] Relevant information not available.

precise nature of the cues that are being used by the judges to decode the vocal expression.

One of the major problems in this area of research is the cleavage between encoding and decoding studies, which tend to represent totally separate traditions. This author has repeatedly argued for the use of more comprehensive research designs, based on the Brunswikian lens models, in which both encoding and decoding strategies are combined to study the role of particular expressive cues in the process of communication and in their influence on emotional meaning (see Scherer, 1978, 1982b). Unfortunately, very few studies of this nature have appeared so far (see Figure 9.1 for an example). On the whole, the general scarcity of research in this area can probably be traced to the serious problems a researcher is faced with when attempting to objectively measure vocal expression. While psychologists working in other areas of expression research have developed a number of techniques for the measurement of facial and bodily expression (see Ekman, 1982; Rosenfeld, 1982), workers in vocal expression research have been dependent on advances in the field of phonetics and acoustical engineering.

VOCAL MEASUREMENT

While simple electroacoustic devices to record some major acoustic features such as energy or the melody curve have existed since the turn of the century, major advances in sound measurement were due to the development of the spectrograph in the 1950s (see Denes & Pinson, 1972; Hollien, 1981, pp. 94–

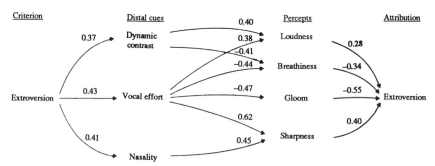

FIGURE 9.1. Example for a Brunswikian lens model demonstrating the accuracy of extroversion inference (from Scherer, 1978). Curvilinear arrows indicate hypothetically assumed causal relationships. Strengths of the relationships are indicated by Pearson *r*s. Other intercorrelations among variables have been omitted to simplify the figure.

96), which made the objective measurement of a number of acoustic parameters in the spectrum (amplitude by frequency display of the components of a sound wave) possible. The development of digital methods of speech analysis and synthesis, particularly in the 1970s and 1980s, together with the development of powerful algorithms for the mathematical description of speech waves, led to a quantum jump in speech research (see Flanagan, 1972; Markel & Gray, 1976). At the present time, we experience an unprecedented rate of technological advances in which these developments provide breakthroughs in areas such as automatic speech and speaker recognition, voice output and input for computers, and the like.

While some psychologists have regularly used this technology for research (particularly in psychoacoustics and some areas of psycholinguistics), researchers in the area of vocal expression have been fairly slow to make use of these methods of measurement. In part, this is probably due to the fairly high expense of the apparatus and/or the unavailability of such apparatus in research areas in which the use of tape recorders and video tape recorders is already counted as a major technological advance. Times are changing, however, and rather sophisticated digital voice analysis methods will be available on standard personal computers in the next few years. Consequently, one could hope for an increased use of objective methods of acoustic assessment in the area of vocal expression research. The following section provides a short survey of the major parameters to be studied.

Of course, the measurement of the acoustic sound wave as it emanates from the mouth and is stored on magnetic tape (or increasingly, directly in digital form) is only one of the levels of analysis possible. Other levels include the physiological level (particularly respiration patterns and excitations of the vocal musculature) and the phonatory–articulatory level of measurement. Since most of these methods require extensive prior training in medicine, physiology, and/or phonetics, these approaches shall not be discussed here (for a more detailed discussion, see Scherer, 1982b).

Figure 9.2 shows a rather simplified diagram of the voice and speech production process with the three major determinants, respiration, phonation, and articulation. For each of these major factors, a number of the most important functional variables which are likely to be affected by emotional arousal and which consequently produce changes of the acoustic sound wave emanating from the mouth (which can then be measured in the acoustic signal) are displayed (for details see Scherer, 1982b).

The major parameters which are determined by these functional variables of the three subsystems of the speech production process are listed in Table 9.3. Figure 9.3 illustrates some of these parameters in terms of their appearance in either the acoustic time signal or in the power spectrum for a segment of the speech wave.

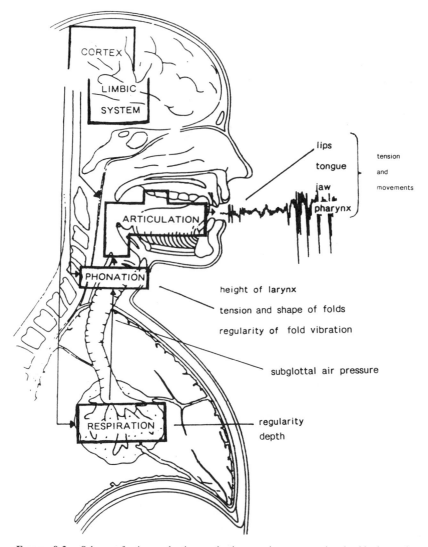

FIGURE 9.2. Schema of voice production mechanisms; major structures involved in the production of vocalization. The labeled boxes identify the system processes that occur at each of the organic units involved in the planning, controlling, and execution of the movements related to the vocalization. The labels attached to these boxes identify some of the most important variables involved in the shaping of the vocal signal.

Almost all of the variables listed in Table 9.3 have been shown in recent research to be heavily implicated in the vocal expression of emotion (e.g., Frick, 1985; Scherer, 1981a, 1985, 1986; Williams & Stevens, 1981), emotional disturbance such as depression (see Darby, 1981; Scherer, 1986), or stress (see

TABLE 9.3
OVERVIEW OF MAJOR ACOUSTIC PARAMETERS[a]

Parameter[b]	Description
F0 perturbation	Slight variations in the duration of glottal cyles
F0 mean	Fundamental frequency (vibration rate of vocal folds as averaged over a speech utterance)
F0 range	Difference between highest and lowest F0 in an utterance
F0 variability	Measure of dispersion (e.g., standard deviation of F0)
F0 contour	Fundamental frequency values plotted over time (intonation)
F1 mean	Frequency of the first (lowest) formant (significant energy concentration in the spectrum) averaged over an utterance
F2 mean	Mean frequency of the second formant
Formant bandwidth	Width of the spectral band containing significant formant energy
Formant precision	Degree to which formant frequencies attain values prescribed by phonological system of a language
Intensity mean	Energy values for a speech sound wave averaged over an utterance
Intensity range	Difference between highest and lowest intensity values in an utterance
Intensity variability	Measure of dispersion of intensity values in an utterance (e.g., standard deviation)
Frequency range	Difference between F0 and highest point in the frequency spectrum where there is still speech energy
High-frequency energy	Relative proportion of energy in the upper frequency region (e.g., > 1 kHz)
Spectral noise	Aperiodic energy components in the spectrum
Speech rate	Number of speech segments per time unit

[a]From Scherer (1986, p. 149). Copyright 1986 by the American Psychological Association. Reprinted by permission.

[b]F0, Fundamental frequency; F1, first formant; F2, second formant.

Scherer, 1981b; Streeter, Macdonald, Apple, Krauss, & Galotti, 1983; Tolkmitt & Scherer, 1986).

Yet another way of studying the importance of these parameters in the vocal communication of affect is the use of resynthesis methods. Digital speech analysis, and in particular the use of linear prediction algorithms (see Markel & Gray, 1976), make it possible to digitize a speech sample, change various parameters (such as energy or fundamental frequency) in a systematic manner, and recreate the voice (using digital-to-analog converters) for presentation to judges. This allows us to vary systematically (in a factorial design, for example) a number of very specific speech parameters using natural speech utterances in order to study their effects on the inference of speaker affect. For example, in our research group we have systematically studied the influence of experimental variations of the fundamental frequency (F0) range, intonation contour, and intensity of judgments of affect. The results show that all of these parameters operate in an essentially continuous fashion on the attribution of various emotions (see Ladd, Silverman, Tolkmitt, Bergmann, & Scherer, 1985).

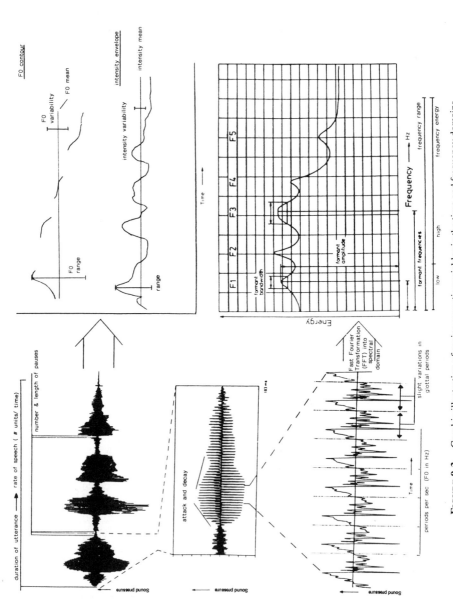

FIGURE 9.3. Graphic illustration of major acoustic variables in the time and frequency domains.

ADVOCATING A THEORETICAL APPROACH TO
VOCAL AFFECT MEASUREMENT

As was mentioned above, one of the major problems in this research area has been the essentially atheoretical approach adopted by most researchers. While this is unavoidable in the early stages of trying to study a phenomenon, it would seem that maturation of a research area requires a move toward more theory-guided approaches. Furthermore, in the area of vocal affect expression, it would seem feasible to make use of admittedly preliminary knowledge concerning the physiological concomitants of emotion and their effects on the voice production process to develop a number of hypotheses concerning the likely vocal effects of particular types of emotional arousal. The present author has attempted to develop a set of theoretical predictions based on a component process model of emotion (see Scherer, 1982a, 1984). In brief, the argument runs as follows (for details, see Scherer, 1985, 1986).

The basic assumption is that a differentiation of the emotional state is produced by the outcomes of a series of "stimulus evaluation checks" (SECs). These checks, including a number of more detailed subchecks, are listed in Table 9.4. They are assumed to always occur in the order given.

TABLE 9.4
SEQUENCE OF STIMULUS EVALUATION CHECKS[a]

---

1. Novelty check. Evaluating whether there is a change in the pattern of external or internal stimulation, particularly whether a novel event occurred or is to be expected.

2. Intrinsic pleasantness check. Evaluating whether a stimulus event is pleasant, inducing approach tendencies, or unpleasant, inducing avoidance tendencies, based on innate feature detectors or on learned associations.

3. Goal/need significance check. Evaluating whether a stimulus event is relevant to important goals or needs of the organism (relevance subcheck), whether the outcome is consistent with or discrepant from the state expected for this point in the goal/plan sequence (expectation subcheck), whether it is conducive or obstructive to reaching the respective goals or satisfying the relevant needs (conduciveness check), and how urgently some kind of behavioral response is required (urgency subcheck).

4. Coping potential check. Evaluating the causation of a stimulus event (causation subcheck) and the coping potential available to the organism, particularly the degree of control over the event or its consequences (control subcheck), the relative power of the organism to change or avoid the outcome through fight or flight (power subcheck), and the potential for adjustment to the final outcome via internal restructuring (adjustment subcheck).

5. Norm/self-compatibility check. Evaluating whether the event, particularly an action, conforms to social norms, cultural conventions, or expectations of significant others (external standards subcheck), and whether it is consistent with internalized norms or standards as part of the self-concept or ideal self (internal standards subcheck).

---

[a]From Scherer (1986, p. 147). Copyright 1986 by the American Psychological Association. Reprinted by permission.

A particular emotional state can be considered as determined by the outcomes of several or all of these checks. A hypothetical prediction table of which types of emotions ought to follow particular patterns of check outcomes is reproduced in Table 9.5.

Component process theory assumes that an emotion (as a psychological construct) consists of changes in the states of five major components or subsystems of an organism: the information-processing subsystem (e.g., subcortical or cognitive appraisal; this is where the checks take place), the physiological changes in the hormonal and autonomic systems (serving as support systems for the organism's actions), an executive system (basically concerned with goal and need priorities and appropriate action tendencies), a motor expression system (with communicative signaling as the major function), and the subjective feeling state (serving as a monitor system for the ongoing processes in the various subsystems). The assumption is that each of the outcomes of the stimulus evaluation checks changes the state of all of these subsystems (a state change which is again modified, obviously, by the outcome of the next check in the sequence). This notion of a continuous change in the various subsystems of the organism, produced by the outcomes of the series of checks, a sequence which is run through continuously, is called a *component* patterning model. This model specifies the relationships between the different components of the emotional state. Table 9.6 shows a hypothetical prediction of the potential effects of various outcomes of the stimulus evaluation checks on some of these major subsystems of the organism.

It might be useful to describe an example for the type of patterning postulated in this model. Let us take the example for a high-power/high-control outcome of the coping potential check. The assumption is that the organismic function of the reaction associated with this check outcome should be the assertion of a goal that is maintained with high priority by the organism. In terms of the social functions, the external expression associated with the reaction should show to conspecifics that the organism is bent on maintaining dominance. In terms of the reaction of the physiological support system, one would expect a balance between ergotropic and trophotropic arousal coupled with increased noradrenalin release and an increase of respiration volume. As far as the somatic muscle system is concerned, one would expect a slight decrease in overall muscle tone [see the detailed justification for this hypothesis in Scherer (1985)] but increased tension in the head and neck regions. In the specific action-system domains, one would expect baring the teeth and tensing the mouth region in terms of facial expression [following the early descriptions given by Darwin (1965)] and a full voice [indicating the dominant and aggressive stands of the individual (see Scherer, 1985)]. In terms of instrumental movement, posture, and locomotion, one would expect agonistic approach behavior. In this manner, functional considerations are used to predict the type of reaction in the various organismic subsystems that

TABLE 9.5

Hypothetical Outcomes of Stimulus Evaluation Checks for Selected Emotional States[a]

Emotional state	Goal/need significance						Coping potential			Norm compatibility	
	Novelty	Pleasantness	Relevance	Expectation	Conduciveness	Urgency	Control	Power	Adjust	External	Internal
Enjoyment/happiness	Low	High	Medium	Consistent	High	Very low	—[b]	—	High	High	High
Elation/joy	High	High	High	Discrepant	High	Low	—	—	Medium	High	High
Displeasure/disgust	Open[c]	Very low	Low	Discrepant	Low	Medium	Open	Open	High	Low	—
Contempt/scorn	Open	Low	Low	Discrepant	Low	Low	Open	High	High	Low	—
Sadness/dejection	Low	Low	High	Discrepant	Obstruct	Low	None	—	Medium	—	—
Grief/desperation	High	Low	High	Discrepant	Obstruct	High	Low	Low	Low	—	—
Anxiety/worry	Low	Open	Medium	Discrepant	Obstruct	Medium	Open	Low	Medium	—	—
Fear/terror	High	Low	High	Discrepant	Obstruct	Very high	Open	Very low	Medium	—	—
Irritation/cold anger	Low	Open	Medium	Discrepant	Obstruct	Medium	High	Medium	High	Low	Low
Rage/hot anger	High	Open	High	Discrepant	Obstruct	High	High	High	High	Low	Low
Boredom/indifference	Very low	Open	Low	Consistent	Obstruct	Low	Medium	Medium	High	—	—
Shame/guilt	Low	Open	High	Discrepant	Obstruct	Medium	High	Open	Medium	Very low	Very low

[a] From Scherer (1986, p. 147). Copyright 1986 by the American Psychological Association. Reprinted by permission.

[b] —, The specific check is not relevant for the respective emotion.

[c] Open, many different outcomes for the respective check are compatible with the emotion in this row.

TABLE 9.6
Component Patterning Theory Predictions of SEC Outcome Effects on Subsystems[a]

SEC outcome	Organismic functions	Social functions	Support system	Action system Muscle tone	Face	Voice	Instrumental	Posture	Locomotion
Novelty									
Novel	Orienting, focusing	Alerting	Orienting response	Local changes	Brows/lids up; open orifices	Interruption; inhalation	Interruption	Straightening, raising head	Interruption
Old	Homeostasis	Reassuring	No change	No change	No change	No change	No change	No change	No change
Intrinsic pleasantness									
Pleasant	Incorporation	Recommending	Sensitization of sensorium	Slight decrease	Expanding orifices; "sweet face"	Wide voice	Centripetal movement	Expanding, opening	Approach
Unpleasant	Expulsion, rejection	Warning, decommending	Defense response, desensitization	Increase	Closing orifices; "sour face"	Narrow voice	Centrifugal movement	Shrinking, closing in	Avoidance, distancing
Goal need significance									
Consistent	Relaxation	Announcing stability	Trophotropic shift	Decrease	Relaxed tone	Relaxed voice	Comfort position	Comfort position	Rest position
Discrepant	Activation	Announcing activity	Ergotropic dominance	Increase	Corrugator	Tense voice	Task dependent	Task dependent	Task dependent
Coping potential									
No control	Readjustment	Indicating withdrawal	Trophotropic dominance	Hypotonus	Lowered eyelids	Lax voice	No activity or slowing	Slump	No movement or slowing
High-power control	Goal assertion	Dominance assertion	Ergo–tropho balance; noradrenaline respiration volume up	Slight decrease; tension in head and neck	Baring teeth; tensing mouth	Full voice	Agonistic movement	Anchoring body: lean forward	Approach
Low-power control	Protection	Indicating submission	Ergotropic dominance; adrenaline; peripheral vasoconstriction; respiration rate up	Hypertonus; tension in locomotor areas	Open mouth	Thin voice	Protective movement	Readiness for locomotion	Fast locomotion or freezing

[a] From Scherer (1985, p. 216).

would seem to be required by the evaluation of an organism's adaptation needs following a specific stimulus evaluation check.

Obviously, this model has a strong psychobiological bent and it would seem that voice production, which is strongly affected by emotion-related physiological changes, is a rather suitable basis for emotion measurement. What are the presumed effects of the stimulus evaluation check outcomes on vocal expression? On the basis of the literature in phonetics and speech physiology, the present author has proposed the list of potential vocal effects shown in Table 9.7. In each case, the effects of the outcome on phonatory and articulatory features as well as the accompanying acoustic consequences are shown.

If one combines the theoretical predictions contained in Tables 9.5 and 9.7, one can produce a set of rather detailed acoustic predictions for differentiated emotional states. This set of hypotheses is shown in Table 9.8. The assumption is that this list of detailed acoustic predictions for different emotional states can serve as a grid for hypothesis-guided research in the area of vocal expression of emotion. While it is certainly highly conjectural and will obviously be in need of continuous modification based on results of further research and increase of knowledge, the schema may at least help to pinpoint parameters and issues which have been neglected by research.

THE EVIDENCE TO DATE

To what extent can the hypothetical predictions presented above be considered supported by research to date? Table 9.9 lists the major encoding studies I have found in the literature. Those predictions that were supported by the results of these studies have been underlined in Table 9.8. On the whole, it would seem that there is a rather impressive degree of support for some of the predictions (see Scherer, 1986). Unfortunately, most of the effects found are related to the basic dimension of tension/relaxation of the vocal apparatus, thus implicating only one of the major variables in voice production (and one that is mainly related to the ergotropic/trophotropic dimension). This is largely due to the fact that those variables which have been fairly easy to measure, such as fundamental frequency, are directly related to this dimension, whereas others, such as voice quality variables, require much more difficult extraction procedures. For example, whereas fundamental frequency can be measured across a whole utterance and does not require segmentation of individual speech units, the extraction of formant frequencies and bandwidth requires the isolation of individual vowels and formant measurement for each vowel. Hopefully, further advances in speech analysis technology will eventually allow us to automatize these procedures further. The same is true for a number of other variables which still require very intensive operator intervention, e.g., the measurement of F0 perturbation.

TABLE 9.7

Component Patterning Theory Predictions of Vocal Changes after Different SEC Outcomes[a]

Evaluation	Outcome	
Novelty check	**Novel** Interruption of phonation Sudden inhalation Silence Ingressive (fricative) sound with a glottal stop (noise-like spectrum)	**Old** No change
Intrinsic pleasantness check	**Pleasant** Faucal and pharyngeal expansion, relaxation of tract walls Vocal tract shortened by mouth, corners retracted upward More low-frequency energy, F1 falling, slightly broader F1 bandwidth, velopharyngeal nasality Resonances raised Wide voice	**Unpleasant** Faucal and pharyngeal constriction, tensing of tract walls Vocal tract shortened by mouth, corners retracted downward More high-frequency energy, F1 rising, F2 and F3 falling, narrow F1 bandwidth, laryngopharyngeal nasality Resonances raised Narrow voice
Goal/need significance check	**Relevant and consistent** Shift toward trophotropic side: overall relaxation of vocal apparatus, increased salivation F0 at lower end of range, low-to-moderate amplitude, balanced resonance with slight decrease in high-frequency energy	**Relevant and discrepant** Ergotropic dominance: overall tensing of vocal apparatus and respiratory system, decreased salivation F0 and amplitude increase, jitter and shimmer, increase in high-frequency energy, narrow F1 bandwidth, pronounced formant frequency differences

Coping potential check

Relaxed voice
  If event conducive to goal: relaxed voice + wide voice
  If event obstructive to goal: relaxed voice + narrow voice

Tense voice
  If event conducive to goal: tense voice + wide voice
  If event obstructive to goal: tense voice + narrow voice

Control

Ergotropic dominance: (see tense voice)

See tense voice

No control

Trophotropic dominance: hypotension of the musculature in the vocal apparatus and respiratory system
Low $F0$ and restricted $F0$ range, low-amplitude, weak pulses, very low high-frequency energy, spectral noise, formant frequencies tending toward neutral setting, broad $F1$ bandwidth
Lax voice

Tense voice

Power

Deep, forceful respiration; chest register phonation
Low $F0$, high-amplitude, strong energy in entire frequency range
Full voice

No power

Rapid, shallow respiration; head register phonation
Raised $F0$, widely spaced harmonics with relatively low energy
Thin voice

Norm/self compatibility check

Standards surpassed

Wide voice + full voice
+ relaxed voice (if expected)
+ tense voice (if unexpected)

Standards violated

Narrow voice + thin voice
+ lax voice (if no control)
+ tense voice (if control)

[a]From Scherer (1985, p. 216).

TABLE 9.8

Changes Predicted for Selected Acoustic Parameters on the Basis of the Voice Type Predictions in Tables 9.5 and 9.7[a]

Voice type	Parameters[b]											
	ENJ/HAP	ELA/JOY	DISP/DISG	CON/SCO	SAD/DEJ	GRI/DES	ANX/WOR	FEAR/TER	IRR/COA	RAGE/HOA	BOR/IND	SHA/GUI
F0												
Perturbation	≤	>			>	>		≥				
Mean	<	≥	>	><	<>	>	>	≥≥	><	> ><	≤	>
Range	≤	≥			≤	>		≥≥	<	≥		
Variability	<	≥			≤	>		≥≥	<	≥		
Contour	=	>			≤	>	>	>	<	=		>
Shift regularity	<	<						<				
F1 mean		<	>	>	>	>	>	>	>		>	>
F2 mean			<	<	<	<	<	<	<		>	<
F1 bandwidth	>	><	<<	<	<>	<>	<	<<	<<	<<	<	<
Formant precision		>	>	>	≤	<	>	>	>	>	<	>
Intensity												
Mean	≤	≥	>	>>	≤	>	>	>	≥	≥≥	<>	
Range	≤	>			<			>	>	>		
Variability	<	>			<			>		>		
Frequency range	>	>	>	>>	><	>>		>>	>	>	>	
High-frequency energy	<	<>	>	>	<	>>	>	≥≥	>>	>>	><	>
Spectral noise	<				≤			≥				
Speech rate	<	≥			≤	>		≥		≥		
Transition time	>	<			>	<		<		<		>

[a] From Scherer (1986, p. 158). Copyright 1986 by the American Psychological Association. Reprinted by permission.

[b] Parameters: ANX/WOR, anxiety/worry; BOR/IND, boredom/indifference; CON/SCO, contempt/scorn; DISP/DISG, displeasure/disgust; ELA/JOY, elation/joy; ENJ/HAP, enjoyment/happiness; FEAR/TER, fear/terror; GRI/DES, grief/desperation; IRR/COA, irritation/cold anger; RAGE/HOA, rage/hot anger; SAD/DEJ, sadness/dejection; SHA/GUI, shame/guilt; F0, fundamental frequency; F1, first formant; F2, second formant; >, increase; <, decrease. Double symbols indicate increased predicted strength of the change. Two symbols pointing in opposite directions refer to cases in which antecedent voice types exert opposing influences.

TABLE 9.9

STUDIES REPORTING DATA ON VOCAL CUES OF EMOTION[a]

Study	Encoding procedure	No. of studies	Analysis methods	Emotions studied[b]
1. Alpert, Kurtzberg, & Friedhoff (1963)	Induction	10	Acoustic	ANX
2. Van Bezooijen (1984)	Simulation	8	Acoustic/rater	CON, DIS, FEAR, INT, JOY, RAGE, SAD, SHA, SUR
3. Bonner (1943)	Induction	52	Acoustic	ANX
4. Bortz (1966)	Simulation	5	Acoustic	BOR, RAGE
5. Coleman & Williams (1979)	Simulation	13	Acoustic	FEAR, JOY, SAD
6. Costanzo, Markel, & Constanzo (1969)	Simulation	33	Rater	ANG, BOR, CON, GRI
7. Davitz (1964)	Simulation	5	Rater	BOR, JOY, RAGE, SAD
8. Duncan, Laver, & Jack (1983)	Natural	1	Acoustic	FEAR
9. Eldred & Price (1958)	Natural	1	Rater	ANG, SAD
10. Fairbanks & Hoaglin (1941)	Simulation	6	Acoustic	BOR, CON, FEAR, RAGE, SAD
11. Fairbanks & Pronovost (1939)	Simulation	6	Acoustic	BOR, CON, FEAR, RAGE, SAD
12. Fonagy (1978)	Simulation	1	Acoustic	FEAR, JOY, RAGE, SAD
13. Green & Cliff (1975)	Simulation	1	Rater	ACT
14. Hargreaves, Starkweather, & Blacker (1965)	Natural	10	Acoustic	SAD
15. Havrdova & Moravek (1979)	Hypnosis	6	Acoustic	JOY, RAGE
16. Hicks (1979)	Induction	?	Acoustic	ANX
17. Höffe (1960)	Simulation	4	Acoustic	ANG, ANX, FEAR, HAP, JOY, RAGE

(continued)

253

TABLE 9.9 (Continued)

	Study	Encoding procedure	No. of studies	Analysis methods	Emotions studied[b]
18.	Huttar (1968)	Natural	1	Acoustic/rater	BOR, HAP, SAD
19.	Kaiser (1962)	Simulation	8	Acoustic	ANG, DIS, HAP, JOY, SAD
20.	Kotlyar & Morosov (1976)	Simulation	11	Acoustic	FEAR, JOY, RAGE, SAD
21.	Kuroda, Fujiwara, Okamura, & Utsuki (1976)	Natural	?	Acoustic	FEAR
22.	Levin & Lord (1975)	Simulation	5	Acoustic	ACT
23.	Markel, Bein, & Phillis (1973)	Induction	50	Rater	ANG, RAGE, SAD
24.	Müller (1960)	Simulation	60	Acoustic	BOR, HAP, JOY, RAGE, SAD
25.	Niwa (1971)	Natural	?	Acoustic	FEAR
26.	Plaikner (1970)	Induction	12	Acoustic	ANX, DIS
27.	Roessler & Lester (1976)	Natural	1	Acoustic	ANG, FEAR, SAD
28.	Roessler & Lester (1979)	Natural	1	Acoustic	FEAR
29.	Scherer (1979a)	Induction	31	Acoustic	DIS
30.	Scherer, Wallbott, Tolkmitt, & Bergmann (1985)	Induction	56	Acoustic	DIS
31.	Sedlacek & Sychra (1963)	Induction	23	Acoustic	JOY, SAD
32.	Simonov & Frolov (1973)	Natural	?	Acoustic	FEAR
33.	Skinner (1935)	Induction	19	Acoustic	JOY, SAD
34.	Sulc (1977)	Natural	15	Acoustic	FEAR
35.	Utsuki & Okamura (1976)	Natural	4	Acoustic	FEAR
36.	Wallbott & Scherer (in press)	Simulation	6	Acoustic	SAD, RAGE
37.	Williams & Stevens (1969)	Natural	4	Acoustic	FEAR, RAGE, SAD
38.	Zuberbier (1957)	Natural	20	Acoustic	SAD
39.	Zwirner (1930)	Natural	2	Acoustic	SAD

[a] From Scherer (1986, p. 160). Copyright 1986 by the American Psychological Association. Reprinted by permission.
[b] Abbreviations: ACT, activation; ANG, cold anger; ANX, anxiety; BOR, boredom; CON, contempt; DIS, disgust; GRI, grief; HAP, happiness; INT, interest; SAD, sadness; SHA, shame; SUR, surprise.

CONCLUSION

The recent technological breakthrough achieved in the area of speech analysis may help to overcome the longstanding neglect of the vocal channel in the study of the expression of emotion. The study of vocal affect expression can help to better understand affect expression, which has long been hindered by the excessive separation of the phenomenon into different channels. In the future, it will be very important to combine studies of vocal and facial affect expression, because there are important interdependencies on the muscular level. Furthermore, apart from its scientific significance, the study of vocal affect expression may have major importance for application in the real world. Quite apart from the obvious relevance for areas such as social skills, attitude change, or persuasion, and for diagnostics in medicine and clinical psychology, engineers working on automatic speech recognition are increasingly cognizant of the fact that computers have trouble understanding emotional speech in human commands. Conversely, in relation to voice synthesis, it is becoming apparent that humans do not like to be talked to by monotone computer voices. In order to equip the robots to speak with affectively appropriate voices and to enable them to understand (and hopefully tolerate) our temper tantrums, we need to learn much more about the human vocal expression of emotion.

REFERENCES

Alpert, M., Kurtzberg, R. L., & Friedhoff, A. J. (1963). Transient voice changes associated with emotional stimuli. *Archives of General Psychiatry, 8,* 362–365.

Beldoch, M. (1964). Sensitivity to expression of emotional meaning in three modes of communication. In J. R. Davitz (Ed.), *The communication of emotional meaning* (pp. 31–42). New York: McGraw-Hill.

Bonner, M. R. (1943). Changes in the speech pattern under emotional tension. *American Journal of Psychology, 56,* 262–273.

Bortz, J. (1966). Physikalisch-akustische Korrelate der vokalen Kommunikation [Physical-acoustical correlates of vocal communication]. *Arbeiten aus dem psychologischen Institut der Universität Hamburg, 9.*

Brown, B. L. (1980). The detection of emotion in vocal qualities. In H. Giles, P. W. Robinson, P. Smith (Eds.) , *Language: Social psychological perspectives* Oxford: Pergamon.

Burns, K. L., & Beier, E. G. (1973). Significance of vocal and visual channels in the decoding of emotional meaning. *Journal of Communication, 23,* 118–130.

Cicero, M. T. (1975). *Orator.* Munich: Heimeran.

Coleman, R. F., & Williams, R. (1979). Identification of emotional states using perceptual and acoustic analyses. In V. Lawrence & B. Weinberg (Eds.), *Transcript of the eighth symposium: Care of the professional voice* (Part I). New York: The Voice Foundation.

Costanzo, F. S., Markel, N. N., & Costanzo, P. R. (1969). Voice quality profile and perceived emotion. *Journal of Counseling Psychology, 16,* 267–270.

Darby, J. (Ed.) (1981). *Speech evaluation in psychiatry.* New York: Grune & Stratton.

Darwin, C. (1965). *The expression of the emotions in man and animals.* Chicago: University of Chicago Press (originally published in 1872 by Murray, London).

Davitz, J. R. (1964). *The communication of emotional meaning.* New York: McGraw-Hill.

Davitz, J. R., & Davitz, L. J. (1959). The communication of feelings by content-free speech. *Journal of Communication, 9,* 6–13.

Denes, P. B., & Pinson, E. N. (1972). *The speech chain: The physics and biology of spoken language* (2nd ed.). Garden City, NY: Doubleday, Anchor (1st ed. published in 1963).

Dimitrovsky, L. (1964). The ability to identify the emotional meaning of vocal expressions at successive levels. In J. R. Davitz (Ed.), *The communication of emotional meaning* (pp. 69–86). New York: McGraw-Hill.

Duncan, G., Laver, J., & Jack, M. A. (1983). A psycho-acoustic interpretation of variations in divers' voice fundamental frequency in a pressured helium-oxygen environment. *Work in Progress, 16,* 9–16.

Dusenbury, D., & Knower, F. H. (1938). Experimental studies of the symbolism of action and voice (III): A study of the specificity of meaning in facial expression. *Quarterly Journal of Speech, 24,* 424–435.

Ekman, P. (1982). Methods of measuring facial action. In K. R. Scherer & P. Ekman (Eds.), *Handbook of methods in nonverbal behavior research* (pp. 45–90). Cambridge, England: Cambridge University Press.

Ekman, P., Friesen, W. V., & Ellsworth, P. (1972). *Emotion in the human face: Guidelines for research and an integration of findings.* New York: Pergamon (2nd ed., P. Ekman (Ed.), published in 1982 by Cambridge University Press, Cambridge, England).

Eldred, S. H., & Price, D. B. (1958). A linguistic evaluation of feeling states in psychotherapy. *Psychiatry, 21,* 115–121.

Fairbanks, G., & Hoaglin, L. W. (1941). An experimental study of the durational characteristics of the voice during the expression of emotion. *Speech Monographs, 8,* 85–90.

Fairbanks, G., & Pronovost, W. (1939). An experimental study of the pitch characteristics of the voice during the expression of emotion. *Speech Monographs, 6,* 87–104.

Fenster, C. A., Blake, L. K., & Goldstein, A. M. (1977). Accuracy of vocal emotional communications among children and adults and the power of negative emotions. *Journal of Communication Disorders, 10,* 301–314.

Flanagan, J. L. (1972). *Speech analysis, synthesis and perception* (2nd ed.). New York: Springer (1st ed. published in 1965).

Fonagy, L. (1978). A new method of investigating the perception of prosodic features. *Language and Speech, 21,* 34–49.

Frick, R. W. (1985). Communicating emotion: The role of prosodic features. *Psychological Bulletin, 97,* 412–429.

Green, R. S., & Cliff, N. (1975). Multidimensional comparisons of structures of vocally and facially expressed emotion. *Perception and Psychophysics, 17,* 429–438.

Hargreaves, W. A., Starkweather, J. A., & Blacker, K. H. (1965). Voice quality in depression. *Journal of Abnormal Psychology, 70,* 218–220.

Havrdova, Z., & Moravek, M. (1979). Changes of the voice expression during suggestively influenced states of experiencing. *Activitas Nervosa Superior, 21,* 33–35.

Hicks, J. W. (1979). An acoustical/temporal analysis of emotional stress in speech. *Dissertation Abstracts International, 41,* 4A.

Höffe, W. L. (1960). Über Beziehungen von Sprachmelodie und Lautsstärke. *Phonetica, 5,* 129–159.

Hollien, H. (1981). Analog instrumentation for acoustic speech analysis. In J. Darby (Ed.), *Speech evaluation in psychiatry* (pp. 79–103). New York: Grune & Stratton.

Hornstein, M. G. (1967). Accuracy of emotional communication and interpersonal compatibility. *Journal of Personality, 35,* 20–28.

Huttar, G. L. (1968). Relations between prosodic variables and emotions in normal American English utterances. *Journal of Speech and Hearing Research, 11,* 481–487.

Jürgens, U. (1979). Vocalization as an emotional indicator. A neuroethological study in the squirrel monkey. *Behaviour, 69,* 88–117.

Jürgens, U. (1982). A neuroethological approach to the classification of vocalization in the squirrel monkey. In C. T. Snowden, C. H. Brown, & M. R. Petersen (Eds.), *Primate communication* (pp. 50–62). Cambridge, England: Cambridge University Press.

Kaiser, L. (1962). Communication of affects by single vowels. *Synthese, 14,* 300–319.

Knower, F. H. (1941). Analysis of some experimental variations of simulated vocal expressions of the emotions. *Journal of Social Psychology, 14,* 369–372.

Kotlyar, G. M., & Morozov, V. P. (1976). Acoustical correlates of the emotional content of vocalized speech. *Sov. Phys. Acoust., 22,* 208–211.

Kramer, E. (1964). Elimination of verbal cues in judgments of emotion from voice. *Journal of Abnormal and Social Psychology, 68,* 390–396.

Kuroda, I., Fujiwara, O., Okamura, N., & Utsuki, N. (1976). Method for determining pilot stress through analysis of voice communication. *Aviation, Space, and Environmental Medicine, 47,* 528–533.

Ladd, D. R., Silverman, K., Tolkmitt, F., Bergmann, G., & Scherer, K. R. (1985). Evidence for the independent function of intonation contour type, voice quality, and F0 range in signalling speaker affect. *Journal of the Acoustical Society of America, 78,* 435–444.

Lamendella, J. T. (1977). The limbic system in human communication. In H. Whitaker & H. A. Whitaker (Eds.), *Studies in neurolinguistics* (pp. 157–222). New York: Academic Press.

Laver, J. (1975). *Individual features in voice quality.* Unpublished doctoral dissertation, University of Edinburgh, Edinburgh, Scotland.

Levin, H., & Lord, W. (1975). Speech pitch frequency as an emotional state indicator. *IEEE Transactions on Systems, Man, and Cybernetics, 5,* 259–273.

Levitt, E. A. (1964). The relationship between abilities to express emotional meanings vocally and facially. In J. R. Davitz (Ed.), *The communication of emotional meaning* (pp. 87–100). New York: McGraw-Hill.

Levy, P. K. (1964). The ability to express and perceive vocal communication of feeling. In J. R. Davitz (Ed.), *The communication of emotional meaning* (pp. 43–55). New York: McGraw-Hill.

Lieberman, P., & Michaels, S. B. (1962). Some aspects of fundamental frequency and envelope amplitudes as related to the emotional content of speech. *Journal of the Acoustical Society of America, 34,* 922–927.

Markel, J. D., & Gray, A. H. T. (1976). *Linear prediction of speech.* New York: Springer.

Markel, N. N., Bein, M. F., & Phillis, J. A. (1973). The relationship between words and tone-of-voice. *Language and Speech, 16,* 15–21.

McCluskey, K. W., Albas, D. C., & Niemi, R. R., et al. (1975). Cross-cultural differences in the perception of the emotional content of speech: A study of the development of sensitivity in Canadian and Mexican children. *Developmental Psychology, 11,* 551–555.

Morton, E. F. (1977). On the occurrence and significance of motivation-structural rules in some bird and mammal sounds. *American Naturalist, 111,* 855–869.

Müller, A. L. (1960). *Experimentelle Untersuchungen zur stimmlichen Darstellung von Gefühlen.* Unpublished doctoral dissertation, Universität Göttingen, Göttingen, West Germany.

Nash, H. (1974). Perception of vocal expression of emotion by hospital staff and patients. *Genetic Psychology Monographs, 89,* 25–87.

Niwa, S. (1971). Changes of voice characteristics in urgent situations (2). *Reports of the Aeromedical Laboratory, Japan Air Self-Defense Force, 11,* 246–251.

Osser, H. A. (1964). A distinctive feature analysis of the vocal communication of emotion. *Dissertation Abstracts, 25,* 3708.

Pfaff, P. L. (1954). An experimental study of the communication of feeling without contextual material. *Speech Monographs, 21,* 155–156.

Plaikner, D. (1970). *Die Veränderungen der menschlichen Stimme unter dem Einfluß psychischer Belastung.* Unpublished doctoral dissertation, Universität Innsbruck, Innsbruck, Austria.

Pollack, I., Rubenstein, H., & Horowitz, A. (1960). Communication of verbal modes of expression. *Language and Speech, 3,* 121–130.

Robinson, B. W. (1976). Limbic influences on human speech. *Annals of the New York Academy of Sciences, 280,* 761–776.

Roessler, R., & Lester, J. W. (1976). Voice predicts affect during psychotherapy. *Journal of Nervous and Mental Disease, 163,* 166–176.

Roessler, R., & Lester, J. W. (1979). Vocal patterns in anxiety. In W. E. Fann, A. D. Pokorny, I. Koracau, & R. L. Williams (Eds.), *Phenomenology and treatment of anxiety.* New York: Spectrum.

Rosenfeld, H. M. (1982). Measurement of body motion and orientation. In K. R. Scherer & P. Ekman (Eds.), *Handbook of methods in nonverbal behavior research* (pp. 199–286). Cambridge, England: Cambridge University Press.

Ross, M., Duffy, R. J., & Cooker, H. S. et al. (1973). Contribution of the lower audible frequencies to the recognition of emotions. *American Annals of the Deaf, 118,* 37–42.

Scherer, K. R. (1977). Affektlaute und vokale Embleme. In R. Posner & H. P. Reinecke (Eds.), *Zeichenprozesse—Semiotische Forschung in den Einzelwissenschaften* (pp. 199–214). Wiesbaden, FRG: Athenaion.

Scherer, K. R. (1978). Personality inference from voice quality: The loud voice of extraversion. *European Journal of Social Psychology, 8,* 467–487.

Scherer, K. R. (1979). Nonlinguistic indicators of emotion and psychopathology. In C. E. Izard (Ed.), *Emotions in personality and psychopathology* (pp. 495–529). New York: Plenum.

Scherer, K. R. (1979a). Nonlinguistic vocal indicators of emotion and psychopathology. In C. E. Izard (Ed.), *Emotions in personality and psychopathology* (pp. 493–529). New York: Plenum Press.

Scherer, K. R. (1981a). Speech and emotional states. In J. Darby (Ed.), *Speech evaluation in psychiatry* (pp. 189–220). New York: Grune & Stratton.

Scherer, K. R. (1981b). Vocal indicators of stress. In J. Darby (Ed.), *Speech evaluation in psychiatry* (pp. 171–187). New York: Grune & Stratton.

Scherer, K. R. (1982a). Emotion as a process: Function, origin and regulation. *Social Science Information, 21,* 555–570.

Scherer, K. R. (1982b). Methods of research on vocal communication: Paradigms and parameters. In K. R. Scherer & P. Ekman (Eds.), *Handbook of methods in nonverbal behavior research* (pp. 136–189). Cambridge, England: Cambridge University Press.

Scherer, K. R. (1984). On the nature and function of emotion: A component process approach. In K. R. Scherer & P. Ekman (Eds.), *Approaches to emotion* (pp. 293–317). Hillsdale, NJ: Erlbaum.

Scherer, K. R. (1985). Vocal affect signaling: A comparative approach. In J. Rosenblatt, C. Beer, M. C. Busnel, & P. J. B. Slater (Eds.), *Advances in the study of behavior* (Vol. 15, pp. 198–244). Orlando, FL: Academic Press.

Scherer, K. R. (1986). Vocal affect expression: A review and a model for future research. *Psychological Bulletin, 99,* 143–165.

Scherer, K. R. (1987). *Vocal assessment of affective disorders.* In J. D. Maser (Ed.), *Depression and expressive behavior* (pp. 57–82). Hillsdale, NJ: Erlbaum.

Scherer, K. R., Wallbott, H. G., Tolkmitt, F. J., & Bergmann, G. (1985). *Die Stressreaktion: Physiologie und Verhalten.* Göttingen, West Germany: Hogrefe.

Schlanger, B. B. (1973). Identification by normal and aphasic subjects of semantically meaningful and meaningless emotional toned sentences. *Acta Symbolica, 4*, 30–38.

Sedlacek, K., & Sychra, A. (1963). Die Melodie als Faktor des emotionellen Ausdrucks. *Folia Phoniatrica, 15*, 89–98.

Simonov, P. V., & Frolov, M. V. (1973). Utilization of human voice for estimation of man's emotional stress and state attention. *Aerospace Medicine, 44*, 256–258.

Skinner, B. R. (1935). A calibrated recording and analysis of the pitch, force and quality of vocal tones expressing happiness and sadness. *Speech Monographs, 2*, 81–137.

Sogon, S. (1975). A study of the personality factor which affects the judgment of vocally expressed emotions. *Japanese Journal of Psychology, 46*, 247–254.

Soskin, W. F., & Kauffman, P. E. (1961). Judgment of emotions in word-free voice samples. *Journal of Communication, 11*, 73–81.

Streeter, L. A., Macdonald, N. H., Apple, W., Krauss, R. M., & Galotti, K. M. (1983). Acoustic and perceptual indicators of emotional stress. *Journals of the Acoustical Society of America, 73*, 1354–1360.

Sulc, J. (1977). To the problem of emotional changes in the human voice. *Activitas Nervosa Superior, 19*, 215–216.

Tembrock, G.(1975). Die Erforschung des tierlichen Stimmausdrucks (Bioakustik). In F. Trojan (Ed.), *Biophonetik*. Mannheim, FRG: Bibliographisches Institut.

Tolkmitt, F., & Scherer, K. R. (1986). Effects of experimentally induced stress on vocal parameters. *Journal of Experimental Psychology, Human Perception and Performance, 12*, 302–313.

Turner, J. le B. (1964). Schizophrenics as judges of vocal expressions of emotional meaning. In J. R. Davitz (Ed.), *The communication of emotional meaning* (pp. 129–142). New York: McGraw-Hill.

Utsuki, N., & Okamura, N. (1976). Relationship between emotional state and fundamental frequency of speech. *Reports of the Aeromedical Laboratory, Japan Air Self-Defense Force, 16*, 179–188.

Van Bezooijen, R. (1984). *The characteristics and recognizability of vocal expressions of emotion*. Dordrecht, The Netherlands: Foris.

Wallbott, H. G., & Scherer, K. R. (1986). Cues and channels in emotion recognition. *Journal of Personality and Social Psychology, 51*, 690–699.

Williams, C. E., & Stevens, K. N. (1969). On determining the emotional state of pilots during flight: An exploratory study. *Aerospace Medicine, 40*, 1369–1372.

Williams, C. E., & Stevens, K. N. (1981). Vocal correlates of emotional states. In J. Darby (Ed.), *The evaluation of speech in psychiatry*. New York: Grune & Stratton.

Wolf, G., Gorski, R., & Peters, S. (1972). Acquaintance and accuracy of vocal communication of emotions. *Journal of Communication, 22*, 300–305.

Zuberbier, E. (1957). Zur Schreib- und Sprechmotorik der Depressiven. *Zeitschrift für Psychotherapie und Medizinische Psychologie, 7*, 239–249.

Zuckerman, M., Lipets, M. S., & Koivumaki, J. H., et al. (1975). Encoding and decoding nonverbal cues of emotion. *Journal of Personality and Social Psychology, 32*, 1068–1076.

Zwirner, E. (1930). Beitrag zur Sprache des Depressiven. *Phonometrie III, Spezielle Anwendungen I* (pp. 171–187). Basel: Karger.

Chapter 10

MEASURING ANIMAL AGGRESSION

DAVID BENTON

ABSTRACT

The various experimental conditions used to generate aggressive behavior and the basic offensive and defensive strategies of rodents are described. The choice of the stimulus animal and the type of measure recorded are discussed. It is concluded that aggressive behavior is most easily generated if the conditions are chosen to mimic, as closely as possible, those facing the feral animal. The adjective aggressive is used to describe a wide range of behavior that reflects various underlying biological mechanisms. It is suggested that we should record a range of measures and not generalize too readily from one situation to another. The concept of dominance as an explanation of rodent social structure is evaluated; it is concluded that winning a social encounter does not simply predict a priority of access to scarce resources. Finally, ethical factors and the advantages and disadvantages of concentrating research effort on rodents are considered.

INTRODUCTION

Considerable effort is being made to study the endocrinological, neurochemical, neuroanatomical, pharmacological, and genetic aspects of aggressive behavior. A very striking observation is that in the vast majority of these types of studies, enormous care and trouble are taken with both the theoretical back-

261

EMOTION
Theory, Research, and Experience
Volume 4

ground of the biology and the technical aspects of any physiological manipulation. In contrast, the measurement and conception of the behavior very frequently seem extremely crude. It is easy to gain the distinct impression that workers whose basic training has been in biology have turned to the study of physiological influence on behavior expecting simple behavioral assays. Frequently there has been a failure to understand the complexity, the conception, and the dynamic nature of behavior: animals have been used as if they are rigid instruments with unvarying characters. It seems likely that a great deal of experimental effort is to a large extent wasted for the lack of concepts and behavioral measures of appropriate sophistication. Because the vast majority of aggression research has used rats or mice, this review will primarily reflect this emphasis.

SOME BASIC BEHAVIOR IN RODENTS

OFFENSE IN THE RAT

Rats are social animals that will readily attack a stranger in a stereotyped way. The dominant, or alpha, male in the group will sniff the perianal region of the intruder. Almost invariably piloerection occurs in the alpha animal but not in the stranger, making the alpha male appear larger. Shortly after piloerection the alpha animal bites and chases the intruder, who will stop running and turn to face the attacker. It rears up on its hind legs, using its forelimbs to push off the alpha animal in the so-called boxing posture. The alpha rat starts a *lateral display,* also called the *offensive sideways posture* or *broadsiding* (Figure 10.1A). The back is arched, the legs nearest the opponent are fully extended, and the head and posterior are curved toward the opponent. In this posture the alpha rat moves sideways toward the intruder, crowding and even pushing it off balance. The alpha rat may make a quick lunge around the body to attempt a bite at the back. In response to such a lunge the defender usually pivots on its rear feet so as to keep its ventral surface toward the attacker and protect its back. After a number of lateral attacks, and especially if the defendant has been bitten, it slowly rolls backward from the boxing position to lie on its back (Figure 10.1B). The attacker positions itself on top of the supine rat, digging at its sides with the forepaws. If the alpha animal can turn the other over to expose the dorsal regions then it will bite. The defensive animal will move in the direction of the attacker's head so to keep the ventral surface uppermost. Although this behavior varies, it is possible to distinguish a characteristic sequence starting with a bite by the alpha animal, followed by flight by the defendant, chase, boxing, lateral attack, lying on the back, and standing on top.

Blanchard and Blanchard (1981) have analyzed the targets in a large number of intruder-resident encounters. They report that between 85 and 90% of bites are

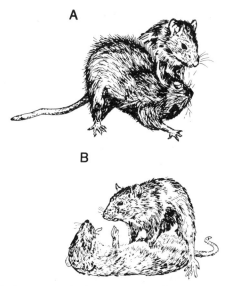

FIGURE 10.1. Offensive postures in the rat. (A) The alpha rat displays a sideways offensive posture; the submissive animal is boxing. (B) The full aggressive and full submissive postures.

on the intruders' backs. If only the ventral surface is available, the biting of the alpha animals is to a very large extent inhibited. It is tempting to suggest that such a consistent behavior must satisfy some adaptive function. An obvious suggestion is that such an attack will drive off a young animal, causing it to colonize another area, and that this animal is likely to share genes with the attacking animal.

Thus boxing and lateral attack can be seen as a unit. The defending animal is attempting to keep its back away from the attacker by offering the ventral surface in the boxing posture. When the need arises, lying on the back is an alternative way of achieving the same end. The lateral attack is the optimal strategy for the alpha rat that is trying to get around the opponent to bite its back.

DEFENSE IN THE RAT

Although the most common bite is directed by the alpha animal toward the back, another type of bite can be distinguished. The rat being attacked may on occasion bite defensively, although the strategy differs. This latter type of bite is made by the intruder and never the alpha animal, and is associated with a number of defensive behaviors directed toward different parts of the anatomy. The bite of an attacker is a crucial event in retaliatory biting. If while being bitten the attacked rat can reach the head of the alpha, then it may bite in return. Nearly all such retaliation occurs within a few seconds of the alpha bite, although this is relatively rare since usually the attacker's head is inaccessible. Increasingly the targets to which bites are directed are being used by researchers to distinguish offensive from defensive aggression.

AGGRESSION IN THE MOUSE

In the mouse, attack and defense can also be differentiated. A resident mouse will initially sniff an intruder and after a period of time will often display the characteristic upright offensive posture: the ears are flattened, the eyes are slitted, and piloerection occurs (Figure 10.2). The subordinate animal displays an upright defensive posture, the ears are upright, the eyes are open, and the snout is raised, a position often associated with vocalization. The strategy is similar to that of the rat; the attacking mouse attempts to get around the opponent and direct attacks to the rump and back. The defending animal pivots on its rear feet to keep the ventral surface toward the opponent and so protect the rear. The mouse shows no tendency to lie on the back or to display the characteristic on-top behavior of the rat. A lateral attack or sideways offensive posture and circling are other strategies against the upright boxing defender in this species. Although there is a very strong preference for the back as a bite target in the mouse, Blanchard and Blanchard (1981) noted that there is less inhibition than in the rat

FIGURE 10.2.   Offense and defense in the mouse. The upright offensive posture (animal on the right) is met by the upright defensive posture.

Offensive attack

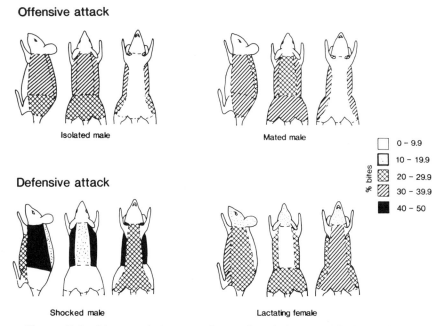

Defensive attack

FIGURE 10.3. Bite targets in four aggression paradigms in the mouse. The data are from Brain (1981).

to bite the stomach and thorax, perhaps because the mouse tends only to nip while the rat produces more severe wounds.

Figure 10.3, using data taken from Brain (1981), illustrates the bite targets in the mouse. Both isolated males and males living with females very clearly avoid attacks to the ventral surface. In contrast, males subjected to electric shock, or lactating females facing a male, do not display the same inhibition. The first two examples presumably reflect offensive attacks whereas the final two reflect defensive motivated behavior.

THE CONCEPT OF AGGRESSION

In any species we can use the adjective *aggressive* to describe a wide range of behavior. Eibl-Eibesfeldt (1979) classified as aggressive "all behaviour patterns that lead to the spacing out of conspecifics by means of the repelling principle or to the domination of one individual over other": thus, for example, the singing of birds to maintain a territory would be included. One danger of such wide definitions is that they may foster the assumption that all items so labeled reflect a common underlying mechanism. A major problem in aggression research is the assumption that one behavioral measure will predict behavior in another situation for no other reason than that our language classifies both situations as aggressive. Unfortunately common parlance is in itself no proof of the correctness of this assumption and in fact it has been emphasized, with increasing frequency, that aggression is not a unitary phenomenon.

An early and very influential classification of different types of aggression was produced by Moyer (1968). He listed seven situations where aggression may occur:

1. *Predatory aggression*—an animal kills and eats a member of a prey species.
2. *Intermale aggression*—fighting between two male conspecifics who have not as yet established a dominant/subordinate relationship.
3. *Fear-induced aggression*—conflict that is preceded by attempts to escape and is provoked by some threat-inducing stimulus.
4. *Territorial aggression*—threat or fighting that occurs on the boundary of some defended area.
5. *Irritable aggression*—the important factors were said to be an attackable object or organism and a predisposing influence such as fatigue or pain.
6. *Maternal aggression*—conflict associated with the defense of the nest, eggs, or young.
7. *Instrumental aggression*—any of the above may change the environment such that the animal is reinforced; in this way it may learn to be aggressive in another context.

Clearly the important factors in Moyer's classification are the provoking stimuli and the situations in which the events take place. The production of such a list immediately forces one to question whether the items included have anything in common apart from the use of the ill-defined term *aggression*. There have been numerous objections to this schema, often associated with complaints about the criteria used and the obvious overlap between some categories. Subsequently an increasing amount of work has examined neuroanatomical, hormonal, neurochemical, and behavioral aspects of these various paradigms, and taking account of this information other schemes have been proposed. Blanchard and Blanchard (1981) made a basic distinction between offensive and defensive aggression that differs in terms of their underlying biology and behavioral strategies. Brain (1981) distinguished five types of aggression:

1. *Self-defensive behavior*—this results from threat and is accompanied by fear; it is preceded by an attempt to escape and usually does not involve a strategy that limits any damage to the opponent (attacking the vulnerable ventral surface).

2. *Parental defense*—involving an attack on an intruding animals to defend the young or nest site.
3. *Reproduction termination*—for example, pup killing in rodents.
4. *Predatory attack*.
5. *Social conflict*—including intermale, territorial, and fighting associated with obtaining a mate.

The vague nature of the term *aggression* and the wide range of the phenomena included in studies in this area have led some to reject the term: in its place Scott (1966) defines agonistic behavior as "a system of related behavior patterns having the common function of adaption to situations of conflict between members of the same species." A message implicit in the present chapter is that research will benefit from the realization that there are a number of behavior patterns that we associate with the phenomena that we label as aggressive, and that it should not be assumed that even closely related behavior patterns reflect common underlying biological mechanisms. In places, the term *aggression* will be used as a convenient shorthand, although it should be always remembered that it is at best a generic term that includes many disparate phenomena.

MODELS OF AGGRESSION INITIATION

ISOLATION

Individual housing is probably the most common means of encouraging rodents to fight: although frequently used, this method continues to raise a number of questions. There is little doubt that isolation predisposes the majority of [but not all (Krsiak, 1975)] mice to fight. However, there are markedly different ways of interpreting this observation; some see the effect of isolation as pathological, while others view them as similar to defending a territory. Although frequently a part of an experimental design, the value of isolation in studies using rats is much more difficult to defend.

The Individual Housing of Rats

In her review of the experimental methods used in this area of research, Huntingford (1980) found that 17 out of 18 rat studies she examined had used isolation in their experimental procedures. This frequent use of isolation may well reflect the difficulty in obtaining spontaneous aggression in laboratory rats; the assumption seems to have been made frequently that, by analogy with the mouse, isolation would encourage aggression, an assumption not in fact supported by the data.

The results of social isolation on gregariousness are unequivocal; both male and female isolates spend more time than grouped rats in contact with another rat of the same gender (Latane, Cappell, & Joy, 1970; Latane, Schneider, Waring, & Zweigenhaft, 1971; Latane, Nesbitt, Eckman, & Rodin, 1972). In general the nature of the resulting behavioral interactions has been poorly reported, although the animals are described as "benign and playful" (Sloane & Latane, 1974). Certainly this type of study, which measures the distance between two animals in a familiar arena, presents no support for the use of isolation as a means of inducing aggression.

Although it is often assumed that isolation induces aggression in the rat, there is remarkably little evidence to support this position. When two isolated or group-housed rats are introduced for a short trial of between 4 and 20 minutes, little or no overt fighting occurs (Ahmed & Harvey, 1968; Bernstein & Moyer, 1970; Korn & Moyer, 1968), unless the animals have been isolated for 3 to 6 months (Sigg, Day, & Colombo, 1966). Blanchard and Blanchard (1981) reported that a period of isolation can slightly enhance the tendency to attack a strange male introduced into an isolate's home cage, although it was important that it was the home cage, and should perhaps be regarded as a variant of the colony model. It was, however, hardly a robust phenomenon, since less than 10% of Long–Evans and only 2.6% of Wistar rats showed a lateral attack to a stranger after 30 days of individual caging. They found that isolation had an even smaller influence in a neutral arena.

The Individual Housing of Mice

There is no doubt that the individual housing of mice is associated with a striking increase in aggression (Brain & Benton, 1983), an effect that is greater when it occurs in young animals and increases with the length of housing until a plateau is reached (Goldsmith, Brain, & Benton, 1976). This change in behavior is not disputed although it has been interpreted in markedly different ways.

Valzelli (1973) talked of an isolation syndrome in terms of three major aspects. First, he saw isolation as producing somatic changes that include an increase in muscle tonus, hypertension, and facilitation of gastric ulceration. Critically, Valzelli points to evidence that isolated mice, given the opportunity to fight, have heavier adrenal glands and higher plasma corticosterone levels. Behavioral changes make up the second part of the postulated syndrome; these include increased aggression, impaired exploration, decreased sexual activity, and learning deficits. The final aspects of the syndrome are changes in brain neurochemistry, including the transmitters acetylcholine, serotonin, norepinephrine, and dopamine. Together these characteristics were said to reflect a pathological state resulting from changes in the limbic system that paralleled psychoneurosis.

In contrast, Brain and Benton (1977) argued that isolation was not a source of stress for the male mouse. They pointed out that the majority of studies that have been quoted as evidence of "isolation stress" employed female rodents or alternatively looked at adrenal activity only after stressing the animal. As the individual housing of female mice is associated with the stimulation of estrogen production, and because these steroids cause adrenocortical hypertrophy, such findings may not reflect changes related to stress. It may alternatively be argued that isolation per se is no more stressful than group housing. For example, Benton, Goldsmith, Gamel-el-Din, Brain, and Hucklebridge (1978) examined mice that had not been subjected to behavioral testing: they reported no difference in plasma corticosterone titer, and a higher adrenal weight in grouped rather than in isolated mice. The effects of increasing time durations of individual housing on "basal" and "stressed" corticosterone values were reported by Goldsmith et al. (1976). Samples for the former were taken following rapid decapitation and in the latter case following the stress of ether anesthesia. For periods of isolation up to 40 weeks no differences in basal corticosterone levels were found and isolates were similar to group-housed animals. Under the stress condition isolated mice had lower levels in the early phase of differential housing, although after 8 weeks the picture reversed.

A hypothesis, strikingly different from Valzelli's, has been proposed; rather than seeing isolated mice as displaying pathological characteristics, it has been suggested that their behavior and physiology have aspects in common with dominant animals. Valzelli (1969) distinguished "normal and aggressive mice," a strange dichotomy as it implies that aggressive behavior is abnormal and indeed pathological. Lorenz (1966) discussed the many benefits that result from aggressive behavior; in many species it helps in obtaining a mate, food, and a territory in which the young can be safely kept, all factors associated with increased biological fitness.

Relevant data come from studies that have contrasted the behavior of isolated, dominant, and subordinate mice. Both isolated and dominant mice are significantly more aggressive than subordinates (Benton & Brain, 1979; Parmigiani, Mainardi, & Pasquali, 1981); in fact, Mainardi, Mainardi, Parmigiani, and Pasquali (1977) found that dominant mice were more aggressive than isolates. Unless one wishes to take the position that dominants are pathological in the extent to which they display aggression, then it can only be concluded that isolated mice are not abnormal in this respect. Valzelli makes great play of the range of other isolation-associated changes, including decreased exploration, increased emotionality, and impaired sexual functioning. When Benton and Brain (1979) examined various measures of emotionality the picture of isolated mice was similar to that presented by Valzelli, but was identical to that demonstrated by dominant, but not subordinate, mice. Again the similarity of the dominant and isolated mice makes it difficult to describe the behavior as pathological. On an anthropomorphic basis, Valzelli assumes that a more cautious or emotional response to novelty is pathological; in the hard world of the feral mouse this may well not be the case. The effect of isolation on sexual behavior is equivocal, and there are reports that it is disruptive (Lagerspetz, 1969), without influence (King, 1956), or actually has a facilitating influence (de Catanzaro & Gorzalka, 1979).

A recent observation is that isolation in the female mouse leads to a high level of submissive behavior in the presence of a strange male, an observation that has been used to examine drug effects (Benton, 1985).

THE COLONY MODEL

An increasingly used technique in aggression research involves the introduction of a strange animal into an established group. Wilson (1975) noted that an intruder entering an established group stimulated aggression in a wide range of social animals. The behavior of rats under this condition was described above (see Offense in the Rat). Luciano and Lore (1975) found that isolation-reared intruders received serious wounds from a colony of group-reared rats but not from a colony made up of previously isolation-reared rats. However, the greatest time spent fighting in the first hour of a 21-hour test occurred between a colony of isolation-reared residents and isolated intruders. Lore and Flannelly (1977) also reported that isolation-reared intruders seemed to learn from their experience such that they no longer elicited aggression on a second test in a different colony. Brain, Benton, Howell, and Jones (1980) found that female intruders into a colony of mixed sex tended to be attacked by the female residents, whereas male intruders were attacked by males.

PARENTAL AGGRESSION

Gestation is associated, in the mouse, with an increased likelihood of attacking a male intruder (Noirot, Goyens, & Buhot, 1975), something rarely observed in virgin females. Svare (1977), however, claimed that it is only characteristic of certain strains of mice. Cohabitation with a pregnant cagemate increases the likelihood of nonpregnant females attacking male intruders (Buhot-Averseng & Goyens, 1981). It seems that pregnant mice produce odors that have pheromonal influences. Brain, Benton, and Bolton (1978) found that male mice living with a pregnant female fought more than did isolated animals.

The lactating female mouse is particularly aggressive, directing attacks to the ventral surface and head (Figure 10.3), offering maximal discouragement to intruding males that may cannibalize the young (Al-Maliki, Brain, Childs, & Benton, 1980). Lactating female mice will even attack intruding rats. The behavior varies with the stage of lactation, being optimal some days after parturition. Although attack is not dependent on the presence of a litter, the removal of the pups eventually reduces aggressiveness (Al-Maliki et al., 1980). Svare (1977) reviewed the evidence that demonstrated that the suckling of the nipples appears to be necessary for the maintenance of maternal aggression.

Mice resident in a group will also direct attack toward a lactating female (Haug, Spetz, Ouss-Schlegel, Benton, & Brain, 1986). Although this is strain dependent (Haug & Mandel, 1978), it is an interesting phenomenon in that the influence of gonadal hormones is quite different as compared to many other paradigms. Thus, only when they are castrated will male residents vigorously attack lactating intruders; it is more common for female residents to initiate an attack, although this is inhibited by administering testosterone.

Infanticide is displayed by both rats and mice, although it is not necessarily a common response. Gandelman (1983) commented that less than 5% of his laboratory mice killed young. This type of behavior has been commonly included in classifications of the different types of aggression. It is interesting that Gandelman (1983) argues that androgens play a role in the expression of pup killing.

SHOCK-INDUCED AGGRESSION

Many workers have used noxious stimuli, particularly electric shock to the feet or tail, to generate agonistic behavior. Until very recently the most common means of inducing aggression in rats has been to place them in a small chamber and to encourage them to fight by administering repeated electric shocks; the assumption is made that painful stimuli are involved in spontaneous encounters (Ulrich, 1966). In both mice and rats an upright posture (boxing) is assumed, with both animals facing each other; biting occurs only infrequently (Figure 10.4). Most well-conducted studies have found that isolated rats showed less shock-induced aggression than was shown by grouped rats (Hutzell & Knutson, 1972; Knutson & Kane, 1980; McGivern, Lobaugh, & Collier, 1981).

Blanchard and Blanchard (1981) compared the same rats regarding colony-related and shock-induced fighting. In a colony, the alpha animals displayed offensive patterns such as lateral attacks that were directed to the back and rump. When shocked, the same animals changed to a pattern of defense, assumed an upright posture, and directed their attacks toward the snout. These workers believe that boxing is a reflex attempt to push the other animal away, rather than an attempt to strike it.

Pain-induced aggression involves the delivery of a tail shock to a rat that is confined in a tube (Azrin, Rubin, & Hutchinson, 1968). Although the usual measure is the biting of a wooden dowel following shock, this is unnecessary, because spontaneous biting occurs with confinement. It may be that biting and

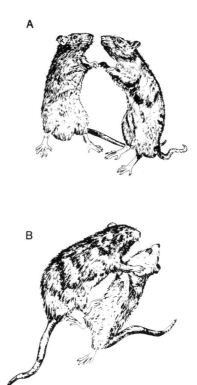

FIGURE 10.4.   Defensively motivated behavior in the rat. (A) The boxing position. (B) A jump attack.

chewing in this situation represents the rats attempts to chew their way out of confinement.

PREDATORY ATTACK

This involves the study of attacks that one species directs to a member of another species. Examples of this type include mouse killing (muricide) or frog killing (ranicide) by the rat and attacks on locusts by mice. Many workers have reservations about including such behavior as examples of aggression, rather than being reflections of the need to eat. Often there is a lack of obvious fear or competitiveness, and gonadal hormones do not seem to be involved in locust killing (Brain & Al-Maliki, 1979).

O'Boyle (1974) argued that muricide is essentially predation because it is related to eating and is behaviorally distinct. A rat kills a mouse in a stereotyped way; it chases it and holds it by the forepaws and then bites the nape of the neck, a sequence of behavior quite unlike that in other aggressive encounters. The relationship to eating is unclear, as some rats will never kill, even if they are in need of food (Karli, 1956), something not to be expected in a predatory animal. In contrast, the incidence of locust killing was significantly increased by food deprivation (Brain & Al-Maliki, 1979). Blanchard and Blanchard (1977) concluded that mouse killing may represent not predatory aggression but something very similar to conspecific attack. van Hemel (1975) similarly argued that muricide has features in common with agonistic behavior that are not shared with eating, for example, the controlling areas of the brain.

Thus the situations used to examine predatory aggression have been interpreted in very different ways. It may be that the resulting measures reflect several mechanisms; possibly aspects more traditionally described as aggression may be stimulated if the prey fights back and is capable of damaging the attacker. This possibility may arise when a rat confronts a mouse. In other situations, for example, when a mouse eats a locust, it may be that the motivation is primarily hunger, as a small and defenseless opponent is unlikely to stimulate aggression.

BRAIN STIMULATION-INDUCED ATTACK

Implanting a stimulating electrode into a specific area of the rat hypothalamus produces highly reproducible aggressive attacks (Kruk, Meellis, van der Poel, & Mos, 1981). The basic attack is a strong bite directed toward the head and upper back. More fierce forms may arise, such as attack jumps (Figure 10.4); less aggressive forms, such as skin pulling, may also be observed. Such an approach offers a stability of behavior that allows the effects of drugs and hormones to be conveniently quantified. A striking aspect of hypothalamic aggression is the lack of concern for the consequences of fighting; rolling on the back does not inhibit attacks, the lateral attack posture is never seen, and the rat seems unaware of the significance of the behavior in which it is involved. The jump attack seems to reflect a lack of caution and would be used, for example, to escape when cornered by a predator.

AN EVALUATION OF THE
MODELS OF AGGRESSION

Much of the variation in the success of the methods that have been used to encourage agonistic behavior may be explained by examining the ecological appropriateness of the test. If testing situations are chosen to reflect the natural social organization and life experiences of the species in question, it is possible to readily demonstrate the behavior required. In contrast, when such factors are ignored, then the behavior is difficult to obtain and impossible to interpret.

Mackintosh (1973) pointed out that the natural social organization of the feral rat consisted of multimale groups, whereas male mice defend territories against other males (Crowcroft & Rowe, 1963; Mackintosh, 1970). This observation may explain why many paradigms are able (or not able, as the case may be) to induce aggressive behavior. The close parallels between the behavior (Benton & Brain, 1979) and physiology (Benton et al., 1978) of individually housed and dominant mice suggest a possible genesis of isolation-induced aggression in this species. Individually housed mice may be viewed as dominants without a subordinate, or territory holders without an intruder.

Because of their feral social organization, the isolation of rats seems ecologically inappropriate. It is not surprising that in the rat isolation does not reliably induce aggression, although it is troubling that it is so commonly employed in experimental designs. The ready way in which grouped rats attack intruders may reflect the use of appropriate social organizations. Wilson (1975) concluded on the basis of observations of a wide variety of animal species in their natural habitats that the appearance of a stranger was the "strongest evoker" of attack in virtually all species of socially organized animals. This approach has also been used to demonstrate attack in laboratory studies of birds, fish, hamsters, gerbils, and monkeys. A major advantage is that the social organization reflects what naturally occurs and the absence of long periods of isolation removes the criticism that social deprivation and gross physiological changes may have resulted.

Adverse comments have been repeatedly made about shock-induced fighting. Repeated administration of electric shock seems unnatural, and the circumstances in which the feral animal would suffer this type of repeated pain are not clear. The significance of the rat's boxing position is uncertain. Chance (1968) has commented on the facile assumptions made about this posture in the rat; correlations between shock-induced boxing and other behaviors suggest that it has offensive as well as defensive components (Chance, 1968). It has been proposed that the behavior of shocked animals closely resembles defensive–submissive rather than offensive–dominant patterns. Blanchard and Blanchard (1981) concluded that pain-elicited attack is a rare form of attack in intraspecific encounters. They say that, as it is now used, shock-induced fighting does not provide a good measure of defensive attack. Kicking and striking are not, according to the Blanchards, measures of defensive attack, and since these behaviors are much more commonly observed than are defensive bites, the traditional adding of bites, kicks, and strikes swamps the single but uncommon genuine measure. They similarly comment that biting a dowel following shock is unrelated to defensive attack. It seems likely that historically the frequent use of shock-induced aggression has reflected the lack of alternative methods capable of reliably inducing fighting. As more convenient methods have become available that are more natural and easily interpretable, and also involve much less distress for the animals, the justifications for the use of this paradigm have declined.

In contrast, the ease with which aggression develops in parturient female rodents again illustrates the advantage of using ecologically relevant situations. When a researcher taps the natural predispositions of an animal, then aggression is easily generated. Goyens and Noirot (1977) speculated that the attacking of males by pregnant females may serve to protect them from postpartum mating by unfamiliar males. The pup-killing model is more difficult to understand. A case can be made for it being a means of recycling resources when breeding conditions are not optimal, or alternatively it may be a means of population control (Gandelman, 1983). A third explanation in that it reflects the breakdown of maternal behavior under stressful conditions.

One may conclude that the use of grossly unnatural resting conditions must prejudice the validity and generality of any results. Clearly any laboratory differs markedly from the natural habitat of the species prior to domestication; however, some laboratory procedures seem more unnatural than others. The data seem to readily support the impression that attempts to mimic the social organization and life events of the feral animal will make the observation of the desired behavior more probable. In addition, it becomes possible to understand it in an evolutionary context.

THE STIMULUS ANIMAL

By its very nature it takes two to fight. Having experimentally manipulated one animal there is always the risk that any difference in aggression reflects the partner and not the experimental animal. The solutions to this problem are varied. One approach is to dispense with the second animal and use an inanimate object in its place. Thus the response of an animal to being poked with a pencil (Brayley & Albert, 1977) or the biting of a block of wood or a telegraph key (Wagner, Beuving, & Hutchinson, 1979) may be recorded. These stimuli have in common that they bear little resemblance to a live conspecific. If you view agonistic encounters as progressing through a sequence during which the animals investigate each other, threaten, fight, and finally establish a dominant/subordinate relationship, these types of inanimate objects can be expected to produce at the best a limited picture of an animal's aggressive response. At the very least there is an obligation on the part of those using these techniques to demonstrate that they reflect physiological mechanisms similar to the more usual methods of measuring aggression. In the case of the biting of telegraph keys there is evidence that it has little in common with more traditional methods (Brain, 1981).

The second group of solutions to the problem of an appropriate stimulus is the use of so-called standard opponents. The aim is to produce an opponent whose behavior is uniform. One approach is to physically restrict the opponent, for example, by sticking the tail to the floor or restricting movement by the use of elastic bands. These approaches seem unnecessarily cruel and are open to the valid criticism that they obviously lead to unnatural interactions. Alternative approaches have been to render animals either permanently or temporally anosmic, procedures that produce nonaggressive animals. A similar goal can be achieved by using castrated or group-housed animals.

The aim of such approaches is usually to obtain an opponent that does not initiate aggressive encounters, thus any differences in observed fighting is assumed to reflect the experimental manipulation of the test animal. In practice, things are not as simple as this rationale implies. Brain, Benton, Childs, and Parmigiani (1981) compared three types of nonaggressive opponents, anosmic, juvenile, and repeatedly defeated mice. Anosmic mice were more likely to display submissive postures and flee than were the other two categories. The animals previously subjected to defeat spent more time defending themselves than did the other categories. It is clear that an aggressive encounter is a dynamic interaction between two mice; the nature of the interaction depends in subtle ways on the nature of the supposedly standard opponent. It is essential that the history of all animals is recorded and that the measures reflect the nuances of the interaction.

THE MEASUREMENT OF AGGRESSION

Having chosen the situation so that aggressive behavior is likely to result, the next problem is to decide what to record. The strategies vary and are discussed in the following subsections.

A SINGLE MEASURE

The most common approach is to use a single measure. The following measures are among the most common:

1. The latency to start fighting.
2. The total time spent fighting.
3. A single rating of aggression on (say) a 1–5 scale.
4. The percentage of animals that fight.
5. The number of bouts of fighting.

COMPOSITE SCORES

A second approach is to rate or count a number of activities and then add these to produce a composite score. Brayley and Albert (1977) rated the reaction of a rat on a scale of 0–3 in six situations, such as being picked up or tapped with a pencil, and then added these together.

AUTOMATED TECHNIQUES

A submissive mouse will squeak when bitten or threatened and a relatively simple electronic device can be used to filter out the relevant frequencies. These vocalizations correlate well with traditional measures such as the latency, duration, and frequency of biting attack (Brain, Benton, Cole, & Prowse, 1980). When such a device is used in combination with a microcomputer the possibility of long-term monitoring arises, allowing the asking of questions precluded by traditional observational methods (Benton, 1984). Benton, Brain, Jones, Colebrook, and Grimm (1983) examined the drug Fluprazine, which has been suggested to allow the establishment of a dominant/subordinate relationship without overt fighting. They reported a powerful antiaggressive influence, but when the drug action decreased after several hours, fighting resulted.

ETHOLOGICAL APPROACHES

A recent trend has been to use the techniques of the ethologist (Benton et al., 1983; Miczek, Kruk, & Olivier, 1984). This involves the detailed and precise observation of the behavior of animals under as nearly natural conditions as possible, at the level of individual movement patterns. Table 10.1 lists one way in which a dyadic encounter between two male mice may be analyzed (Benton et al., 1983); in this detail a 10-minute sequence may produce as many as 300 or 400 behavioral elements. Unfortunately, different workers may use similar lists that differ in minor respects, either in the labels they apply to a posture or in the postures they record. Naturally the situation in which the animals are examined will to some extent determine the behavioral elements that are observed. The table in no way attempts to present a definitive list that will comprehensively describe the full range of possible behavior in every situation.

The recording of this detail brings with it problems of synthesis and analysis. The solutions are mathematical and will be only briefly mentioned. Cluster analysis techniques are simply numerical methods of grouping objects; they search for natural groupings in the data. There are two basic strategies, and the methods may be agglomerative or divisive; the former method, by serial fusions, groups the entities into larger clusters; the latter method starts at the other end with all the observations and separates them into successively smaller clusters. Depending on the techniques used the resulting clusters may or may not contain overlapping items.

TABLE 10.1

POSTURES OBSERVED IN A DYADIC ENCOUNTER OF MALE MICE

Posture	Comments
Offensive	
Aggressive groom	Vigorous grooming of immobilized opponent
Biting attack	Bites standard opponent
Chase	Pursues standard opponent
Circle	Cyles of approaching and leaving with no intervening activity, e.g., rear
Fight	Intense biting and kicking of opponent
Lunge	An "intention movement" for biting standard opponent
Sideways offensive	Attention to opponent, eyes slitted, and ears flattened; orientation toward opponent with at least one forepaw on the substrate
Tail rattle	Tail vibrated against substrate
Upright offensive	Upright or vertical position, ears flattened, eyes slitted; head horizontal and extended toward opponent
Defensive	
Crouch	All paws on substrate, body hunched; generally immobile with slight scanning movements of the head
Flee	Runs from standard opponent
Freeze	Immobile in any position except crouch
Kick	Fends off other mouse with hindpaws or forepaws
Sideways defensive	Lateral orientation to opponent, head up, eyes open and ears extended; at least one forepaw on the substrate
Upright defensive	Forepaws off the ground, head up, eyes open, and ears extended; sometimes regarded as a submissive response
Flag/evade	Avoids standard opponent
Social	
Approach	Moves towards standard opponent
Attempted mount	Palpation of opponents sides with forepaws, pelvic thrusting
Attend	Directs head toward standard opponent
Body sniff	Sniffs standard opponent's body
Crawl under	Tunnels under standard opponent
Follow	Moves after standard opponent
Groom	Grooms standard opponent
Genital sniff	Sniffs perianal region of standard opponent
Head groom	Grooms head of standard opponent
Head sniff	Sniffs head of standard opponent
Leave	Ambulates away from standard opponent
Nose to nose	
Stretched attention	Orientating to opponent at a distance—an extreme version of attend
Walk round	Locomotion around opponent at close quarters
Nonsocial	
Abbreviated dig	Forepaws kick sawdust backward
Back rear	One or both forepaws on opponent's back without nose or whisker contact

TABLE 10.1 (*Continued*)

Posture	Comments
Dig	Substrate displaced backward; forepaws and hindpaws used in alternation
Explore	Ambulation around cage with sniffing
Jump	
Push dig	Forepaws push sawdust forward
Scan	Scanning movements of head while standing; attention not on opponent
Scratch	Scratches self, often with hind paw, cf. a dog
Self-groom	Autogrooming

One of many approaches can be illustrated by an example (Jones & Brain, 1985):

1. A video tape of an interaction between two male mice is described as a temporal sequence of 300 to 400 behavioral elements based on Table 10.1.

2. A transition matrix is compiled, each behavioral element is considered in turn as a "first act," and the types and frequencies of the elements found to immediately follow it are calculated.

3. All permutations of rows in the transition matrix are then compared using the Chi-square statistic, the test being used not as a test of significance, but rather as a measure of the similarity of the distribution of elements. The behavioral elements that tend to be followed by the same elements, at similar frequencies, yield the smallest Chi-square values and are considered to be the most closely associated.

4. The resulting Chi square values were then subjected to a hierarchical cluster analysis using the method of Ward (1963). At any stage the loss of information that results from grouping elements into clusters can be measured in terms of the total sum of the squared distances of every element from the center of the cluster to which it belongs [also known as the error sum of squares (ESS)]. Thus at every step the union of every possible pair of clusters is considered and the two whose fusion results in the smallest increase in the sum of squared distances are combined.

5. The results are plotted as dendrograms, a visual means of displaying the association between elements (Figure 10.5). The compactness of clusters may be inferred from increments in the ESS and separation from other clusters.

A highly simplified example is given in Figure 10.5, illustrating the pattern of results from the study of the antiaggressive drug Fluprazine (Benton *et al.*, 1983). For clarity, instead of 30 or 40 elements, only 6 are reported. In the control condition, groups of elements occur that represent nonsocial, social, and

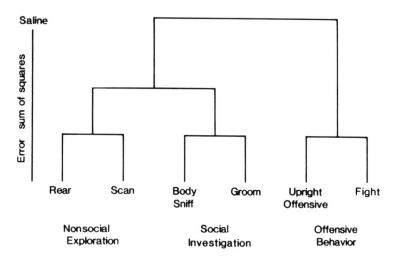

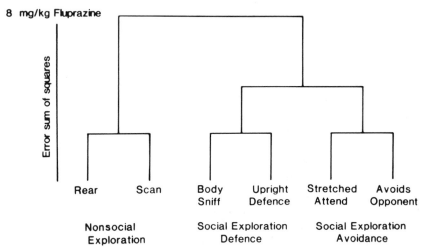

FIGURE 10.5. A dendragram as a means of displaying ethologically derived data. The data based on Benton, Brain, Jones, Colebrook, and Grimm (1983) compares control animals with those treated with an antiaggressive drug. For illustrative purposes, only 6, instead of 30 to 40, postures are described in a simplified manner.

offensive behaviors. In the drug-treated animals, the behavioral elements are differently arranged. The offensive elements are missing and social investigation is associated with defense and avoidance of the partner.

The time-consuming nature of the ethological recording and analysis of behavior means that it is unlikely to be routinely used in many laboratories; rather it

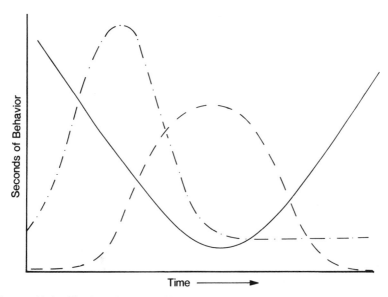

FIGURE 10.6. The dynamic nature of behavior. In an idealized way, the changes in various categories of behavior, which occur when two mice meet, are described. Note that in a period as short as 10 minutes, the incidence of various behaviors changes rapidly. —, Nonsocial behavior; -··, social investigation; ---, offensive behavior.

will be kept in reserve for occasions when such a fine-grain analysis is profitable. Many will feel that it is more cost effective to use less sophisticated methods allowing more questions to be tackled. A solution with much to recommend it is that our understanding of rodents be used to record broad categories of behavior instead of specific postures. Thus with the use of readily available multichannel recorders the time spent in nonsocial, social, offensive, and defensive behaviors can be recorded in real time. Such an approach involves no more time than more traditional approaches that, for example, report one measure, such as the total time spent fighting. Figure 10.6 shows, in an idealized manner, the types of data that result when two mice interact for the first time. Figure 10.6 also illustrates the dynamic nature of behavioral interactions; typically there is a period of nonsocial investigation, followed by social investigation. Fighting occurs, leading to the establishment of dominance, after which offensive behavior rapidly declines. The study of changes in the frequency of different types of behaviors over time also has much to recommend it; if one is planning to examine animals for 10 minutes, it is easy to examine five 2-minute blocks. An encounter in which fighting takes place immediately is a very different situation than one where the same amount of fighting occurs in the middle or the end of the period of observation. The more experienced and confident animal will fight quickly. If anxious or in a novel situation, the animal will postpone aggression.

A COMPARISON OF THE METHODS
OF MEASUREMENT

Aggression is a broad category of behavior rather than a single behavior pattern, giving rise to the problem as to which aspects should be measured and recorded. By far the majority of studies that have used rodents report only one index of aggression; Huntingford (1980) found that this was true in 71% of the papers she examined. The demonstration of high correlations between the commonly used indexes of aggression, such as the total time spent attacking, latency of attack, and ratings of threat, supports this position (Brain, Benton, Cole, & Prowse, 1980). The tendency for certain activities to occur closely together in time and to appear in similar circumstances is the best justification for the use of a single measure.

Most investigators classify aggression in terms of its causal basis, as they are interested in underlying mechanisms; it is hoped that the various behavior patterns grouped together as aggression share internal and external stimuli and a common neural substrate. Almost always this is an assumption that remains largely untested and in fact is only rarely explicitly discussed. To a large extent the classification of aggression in terms of common causal bases reflects implicit assumptions rather than experimentally demonstrated facts.

When the biological bases of a range of measures of agonistic behavior have been examined, the evidence suggests that different causal mechanisms are involved. Adams (1979) analyzed the studies that have stimulated and lesioned areas of the brain prior to the observation of aggression. He found it necessary to hypothesize three motivational systems: offense, defense, and submission, each reflecting different brain pathways. This provides parallels to the suggestion that offensive and defensive behavioral strategies differ in the rat (Blanchard & Blanchard, 1981), and to the fact that the hormonal bases of dominant and submissive behaviors have been found to be distinct (Leshner, 1981). Unlike dominance, subordination is not androgen dependent, although pituitary–adrenocortical activities influence this latter class of behavior. Thus there is considerable evidence that the range of behaviors that we observe during an aggressive encounter reflects several underlying mechanisms. In addition, the novelty or fear-inducing characteristics of the situation in which the fighting occurs may lead to other behavior, such as nonsocial exploration or signs of anxiety.

The implications for measurement are widespread. Those studies that examine only one measure seem to be wasting data. They are being misleading if they imply they are looking at aggression per se, when in fact they are looking at only one aspect of a behavioral sequence that reflects many mechanisms. There are good reasons to believe that the physiological measures that they examine may not influence all aspects of the sequence in a similar way. Those who use a composite score have even more problems. If you record one simple measure then you are able to talk about this at the end of the experiment. If you add two, three, or more activities then you risk mixing characteristics that reflect different biological factors. The resulting score may be nonsense; the use of composite scores can only be justified by extensive research into the basis of the behavior.

DOMINANCE AND SUBORDINATION

When examining aggressive encounters, the concept of dominance is frequently invoked; it has been seen as governing social interactions and the ability to compete for resources such as food, space, and a mate. Although the concept had been extensively debated (Bernstein, 1981), there has been surprisingly little attention paid to assessing its value in the area of rodent behavior.

It is possible to distinguish two major approaches to the definition of dominance (Benton, 1982); in the first, the defining characteristic is the nature of the social interaction. In this tradition a hierarchy of chickens is described as a *peck order*. Klopfer (1974) says "Dominance is inferred whenever one individual is able to chastise another with impunity." A major problem in rodent studies, for those wishing to distinguish dominance, is that overt aggression is rarely observed in established groups as social order is maintained by odors, threats, and submissive postures.

This difficulty in observing overt fighting has led to a second way of defining aggression: van Kreveld (1970) suggested that "dominance is a priority of access to an approach situation or to leaving an avoidance situation that one individual has over another." An advantage of this second approach is that dominance can be measured by removing a resource and observing which animal has priority when it is replaced. The assumption has been made that these two types of definition reflect a common mechanism, although this is rarely tested, and when it has been examined the data tend not to support the assumption.

Syme (1974) reviewed those studies that in the rat have compared competition for various resources. Syme observed that when more than one competitive test was compared there was a tendency to find a low correlation between them. Benton, Dalrymple-Alford, and Brain (1980) carried out one of the few studies of dominance in the laboratory mouse. They reported no relationship between gaining priority of access to water, to a receptive female, or to space. Syme (1974) sensibly commented that if each group is required to have a large number of dominance orders then the concept is useless. A similar rationale suggests that if dominance is a fundamental determinant of rodent behavior then indexes of overt aggression should relate to competitive measures. Syme in this context concluded "That there is not necessarily a high correlation between aggressive and competitive orders.'' Benton et al. (1980) found that mice that won aggressive encounters had greater access to sexually receptive females, but not to water when thirsty, and did not have a priority when space was limited. It is difficult to avoid the conclusion that the various measures of dominance do not reflect a single underlying mechanism and that competitive tests do not tap the social organization of the animals' studied.

Given the widespread connotations associated with the concept of dominance, it would perhaps be better if workers stopped using the term. There seems good reason to believe that animals that win or lose an aggressive encounter will differ in many important respects, although these are not often predictable by describing one as dominant. Rather than relying on an abstract concept we would be better to take an empirical, observational approach. Distinguishing winners and losers seems of great heuristic value. The losers of aggressive encounters are more active but habituate to novelty more rapidly (Benton and Brain, 1979), and they are less aggressive in subsequent encounters and are less likely to investigate a receptive female (Benton et al., 1980).

THE SPECIES USED IN AGGRESSION RESEARCH

In 1950 Beach pointed out that comparative psychology was suffering from an overreliance on the study of domesticated strains of *Rattus norvegicus*. Throughout this century more and more experiments have been carried out on fewer and fewer species. When Huntingford (1980) carried out a similar although more limited exercise, looking at research on the biological aspects of aggression, she found a similar phenomenon. Looking at three relevant journals over a 2-year period, she found that only 10% of papers used nonmammalian vertebrates. In contrast, almost 80% of the studies had used rodents, almost exclusively rats and mice.

The popularity of rodents reflects several associated advantages: they are universally available, cheap to maintain, easy to rear, hardy, and well adapted to laboratory life. The young psychologist in particular is unlikely to be familiar with many other species and will often turn to rodents with little thought; the question is whether this is desirable.

The concentration of research effort on a few species undoubtedly brings advantages. When the same behavior is examined in terms of associated neuroanatomy, neurophysiology, neurochemistry, endocrinology, and genetics then it is possible to compare, check, and integrate the findings. The expectation is that the ways in which various physiological mechanisms interact will become apparent. It is difficult to underestimate the potential advantage of such a concentration of research. If we wish to understand the relationship between what takes place in single cells and the behavior of the entire organism, then we need a complete picture from the most micro to macro level of analysis. Aggression offers such an opportunity where characteristic behavior can be related to particular neural circuits, hormones, and neurochemistry, as well as to past experience.

At the same time an overwhelming concentration on rats and mice can cause problems; there is much to be gained from a comparative approach. Are domesticated mice and rats representative of other species? In fact, are they typical of feral mice and rats? Have we gained a distorted or even absurd picture of mammalian behavior by concentrating on these species and mistaking the particular for the general? The inescapable fact is that until we study other species to a greater extent it is impossible to answer these questions.

When interpreting rodent behavior in the laboratory a common approach is to analyze it in terms of the evolutionary background of the rat's feral ancestors. Some workers have, however, questioned the extent to which domesticated rats are typical of the feral strains from which they were derived (Lockard, 1968). With domestication at the Wistar Institute, *R. norvegicus* became heavier, and while the weight of the brain and adrenal glands decreased, the pituitary and thyroid increased. Naturally a primary objective of domestication was to change the behavior to suit laboratory life. Relevant in this context are the following remarks: "They [domesticated *R. norvegicus*] had lost much of their viciousness and their fear of man; females rarely killed the young returned to the nest after being handled . . . Rats of the later generations had not, however, overcome their aversion to the presence of strange individuals, and such intruders were killed as promptly as in the earlier generations" King and Donaldson (1929).

In a similar vein Tolman (1959) commented that, following domestication; "Fighting is incomplete, immature, and rather harmless in character, resembling play. Placed together in a chamber and shocked, norvegicus pairs fight savagely while many albino varieties do not."

Blanchard and Blanchard (1981) found wild rats to be much more defensive than their laboratory cousins. Laboratory rats show almost no defensiveness to human approach, whereas wild rats run away and, if cornered, turn, rear up, squeal, and display the teeth and leap toward the head. In 70% percent of cases, Karli (1956) reported that *R. norvegicus* killed mice, although this was true for only 12% of albino strains. Particularly in rats it may be that this lack of aggressivness has led to the use of testing situations that lack ecological validity, for example, the use of electric shocks. An alternative explanation is that the lack of an ecologically appropriate test situation has resulted in difficulty in producing aggressive behavior in the rat. Laboratory rats living in a group will readily fight with a strange intruder; it appears that, because feral rats live in social groups, the intruder paradigm is ecologically valid. In contrast, the ready way in which isolation induces aggressive behavior in the mouse also reflects the importance of ecologically valid testing situations. Since the feral male mouse readily defends a territory and drives off others to remain solitary, the individual housing of a male mouse can be viewed as appropriate.

ETHICAL CONSIDERATIONS

The work of any scientist occurs within boundaries prescribed by the society in which it takes place. These boundaries may be stated in legal terms or less formally in widely held attitudes and values. Increasingly the use of animals for scientific purposes is a matter of concern in many countries, and any scientist, when planning to use animals, is well advised to consider the ethical implications. By its nature, research involving aggressive encounters is likely to attract the attention of those concerned with animal welfare. Several of the methods historically used can reasonably be thought to involve suffering, although our more recent understanding of animal behavior allows the concerned scientist to turn to other approaches that seem to involve only minor discomfort.

The decision as to whether a particular experiment is justified involves the weighing of the balance between the likely value of the information gained and the suffering caused, if any, to the animals involved. It should not be assumed that every possible experiment will produce useful scientific information (Huntingford, 1984). Even the most productive line of research will eventually reach a stage when the additional information gained is so insignificant as to be viewed as trivial or repetitive. Such work is to be deplored as a waste of limited research funding and is unlikely to benefit the individual's career. Turning to the other side of the equation, the possible suffering of animals, it is easy for the ill-informed to imagine that when animals fight this inevitably leads to a lingering, bloody death.

In fact, those who are familiar with animal behavior know that in many species intraspecific aggression has been ritualized in such a manner that often threat takes the place of overt fighting. When fighting does occur it is often ritualized and directed toward nonvulnerable areas of the body; its duration is limited by mechanisms that aid the rapid establishment of a dominant/subordinate relationship. Any competent researcher should be able to use our understanding of the behavior of particular species to design methodologies that minimize both the duration of encounters and any distress caused to the animals. If the species examined or the experimental conditions employed are known to result in either intense or prolonged fighting, then workers may consider a measure such as latency to attack that correlates highly with the total time spent fighting (Brain, Benton, Cole, & Prowse, 1980). Workers may wish to consider if more information may be gained by using a situation or strain of animals known to produce only limited amounts of fighting. Apart from the humanitarian issues there is arguably a scientific advantage. With mice, for example, it is easy to arrange within a 10-minute period a sequence of several behaviors. A period of initial investigation of the surroundings will be followed by social investigation of the opponent. A period of fighting leads to the rapid establishment of dominance that occurs several minutes before the end of the period of observation (Figure 10.6). It is possible to observe a range of behavior by ensuring that the period of fighting is brief. As well as commenting on aggression, a great deal of other information can be gained. For example, Krsiak et al. (1984) noted that most anxiolytic drugs stimulate sociability. The increased behavioral detail will allow the distinguishing of general from specific influences, for example, whether a change is merely indicative of general sedation. Thus some thought about the experimental situation can give more information while using fewer animals that are caused less distress.

CONCLUSIONS

The value of future research on biological aspects of aggression will be greatly increased if more care is taken in choosing the paradigm, the particular conditions of the test, and the measures of behavior. In general, aggression is easier to observe if the test taps the natural behavior of the animal. Thus, for example, the introduction of an intruder into the territory of a naturally solitary animal, or a group of established social animals, will reliably and rapidly produce characteristic offensive postures. In contrast, the use of unnatural acts, such as repeatedly shocking rats, has led to results that are difficult to interpret and are a continuing cause of controversy.

It is unreasonable to assume that a single measure will adequately reflect the multiple factors that will inevitably influence the behavior of an animal in a particular situation. As one example the degree of familiarity with a situation is a critical variable that may lead to exploration, nervousness, or even fear: at a later stage, following habituation, these responses will diminish. It is obvious that the importance of variables such as these will change throughout a single test, and from day to day, in the light of experience. The recording of a number of behavioral measures will allow indications of behavioral tendencies, other than aggression, to be obtained. Such an approach need not add greatly to the effort associated with the recording of behavior, and will greatly facilitate the interpretation of the findings.

Finally, it should be recognized that aggression is not a unitary phenomenon and that measures obtained in different situations, and in fact several measures obtained from the same situation, may not reflect common biological substrates. It follows that findings should be generalized only with great caution.

REFERENCES

Adams, D. B. (1979). Brain mechanisms for offense, defense and submission. *The Behavioral and Brain Sciences, 2*, 201–241.

Ahmed, S. S., & Harvey, J. A. (1968). Long term effects of septal lesions and social experience in shock-elicited fighting in rats. *Journal of Comparative and Physiological Psychology, 66*, 596–602.

Al-Maliki, S., Brain, P. F., Childs, G., & Benton, D. (1980). Factors influencing maternal attack on conspecific intruders by lactating female TO strain mice. *Aggressive Behavior, 6*, 103–117.

Azrin, N. H., Rubin, H. B., & Hutchinson, R. R. (1968). Biting attack by rats in response to aversive shock. *Journal of the Experimental Analysis of Behavior, 11*, 633–639.

Beach, F. A. (1950). The snark was a boojum. *American Psychologist, 5*, 115–124.

Benton, D. (1982). Is the concept of dominance useful in understanding rodent behaviour? *Aggressive Behavior, 8*, 104–107.

Benton, D. (1984). The long-term effects of naloxone, dibutyryl cyclic CMP and chlorpromazine on aggression in mice monitored by an automated device. *Aggressive Behavior, 10*, 79–89.

Benton, D. (1985). Mu and kappa opiate receptor involvement in agonistic behaviour in mice. *Pharmacology, Biochemistry and Behavior, 23*, 871–876.

Benton, D., & Brain, P. F. (1979). Behavioural comparisons of isolated, dominant and subordinate mice. *Behavioural Processes, 4*, 211–219.

Benton, D., Brain, P. F., Jones, S., Colebrook, E., & Grimm, V. (1983). Behavioural examinations of the anti-aggressive drug fluprazine. *Behavioral and Brain Research, 10*, 325–338.

Benton, D., Dalrymple-Alford, J. C., & Brain, P. F. (1980). Comparisons of measures of dominance in the laboratory mouse. *Animal Behaviour, 28*, 1247–1279.

Benton, D., Goldsmith, J. F., Gamel-el-Din, L., Brain, P. F., & Hucklebridge, F. H. (1978). Adrenal activity in isolated mice and mice of different social status. *Physiology and Behavior, 20*, 459–464.

Bernstein, H., & Moyer, K. E. (1970). Aggressive behavior in the rat: Effects of isolation and olfactory bulb lesions. *Brain Research, 20*, 75–84.

Bernstein, I. S. (1981). Dominance: The baby an the bathwater. *The Behavioral and Brain Sciences, 4*, 419–457.

Blanchard, R. J., & Blanchard, D. C. (1977). Aggressive behavior in rats. *Behavioral Biology, 21*, 197–224.

Blanchard, R. J., & Blanchard, D. C. (1981). The organization and modeling of animal aggression. In P. F. Brain & D. Benton (Eds.), *The biology of aggression* (pp. 529–561). Alphen aan den Rijn, The Netherlands: Sijthoff & Noordhoof.

Brain, P. F. (1981). Differentiating types of attack and defense in rodents. In P. F. Brain & D. Benton (Eds.), *Multidisciplinary approaches to aggression research* (pp. 53–78). Amsterdam: Elsevier/North-Holland.

Brain, P. F., & Al-Maliki, S. (1979). A comparison of effects of simple experimental manipulations on fighting generated by breeding activity and predatory in TO strain mice. *Behaviour, 69*, 183–200.

Brain, P. F., & Benton, D. (1977). What does individual housing mean to a research worker? *IRCS Journal of Medical Science, 5*, 459–463.

Brain, P. F., & Benton, D. (1983). Conditions of housing, hormones and aggressive behavior. In B. B. Svare (Ed.), *Hormones and aggressive behavior* (pp. 351–372). New York: Plenum.

Brain, P. F., Benton, D., & Bolton, J. C. (1978). Comparison of agonistic behavior in individually-housed male mice with those cohabiting with females. *Aggressive Behavior, 4*, 201–206.

Brain, P. F., Benton, D., Childs, G., & Parmigiani, S. (1981). The effect of the type of opponent in tests of murine aggression. *Behavioural Processes, 6*, 319–327.

Brain, P. F., Benton, D., Cole, C., & Prowse, B. (1980). A device for recording submissive vocalizations of laboratory mice. *Physiology and Behavior, 24,* 1003–1006.

Brain, P. F., Benton, D., Howell, P. A., & Jones, S. E. (1980). Resident rats aggression towards intruders. *Animal Learning and Behavior, 8,* 331–335.

Brayley, K. N., & Albert, D. J. (1977). Suppression of VMH-lesion-induced reactivity and aggressiveness in the rat by stimulation of lateral septum but not medial septum or cingulate cortex. *Journal of Comparative and Physiological Psychology, 91,* 290–299.

Buhot-Averseng, M.-C., & Goyens, J. (1981). Effects of cohabitation with another female on aggressive behaviour in pregnant mice. *Aggressive Behavior, 7,* 111–121.

Chance, M. R. A. (1968). Ethology and psychopharmacology. In C. R. B. Joyce (Ed.), *Psychopharmacology dimensions and perspectives* (pp. 283–318). London: Tavistock.

Crowcroft, P., & Rowe, F. P. (1963). Social organization and territorial behaviour in the wild house mouse (*Mus musculus* L.). *Proceedings of the Zoological Society of London, 140,* 517–532.

de Catanzaro, D., & Gorzalka, B. B. (1979). Isolation-induced facilitation of male sexual behavior in mice. *Journal of Comparative and Physiological Psychology, 93,* 211–222.

Eibl-Eibesfeldt, I. (1979). *The biology of peace and war.* New York: Viking.

Gandelman, R. (1983). Hormones and infanticide. In B. B. Svare (Ed.), *Hormones and aggressive behavior* (pp. 105–118). New York: Plenum.

Goldsmith, J. F., Brain, P. F., & Benton, D. (1976). Effect of age at differential housing and the duration of individual housing on intermale fighting and adrenocortical activity in TO strain mice. *Aggressive Behavior, 2,* 307–323.

Goyens, J., & Noirot, E. (1977). Intruders of differing reproductive status alter aggression differentially in early and late pregnant mice. *Aggressive Behavior, 3,* 262–267.

Haug, M., & Mandel, P. (1978). Strain differences in aggressive behaviour of female mice against lactating and non-lactating individuals. *Neuroscience Letters, 7,* 235–238.

Haug, M., Spetz, J. F., Ouss-Schlegel, Benton, D., & Brain, P. F. (1986). Effects of gender, gonadectomy and social status on attack directed towards female intruders by resident mice. *Physiology and Behavior, 37,* 533–537.

Huntingford, F. A. (1980). A review of the methods used to describe and measure aggressive behaviour in physiological studies. *Aggressive Behavior, 6,* 205–215.

Huntingford, F. A. (1984). Some ethical issues raised by studies of predation and aggression. *Animal Behaviour, 32,* 210–215.

Hutzell, R. R., & Knutson, J. F. (1972). A comparison of shock-elicited fighting and shock-elicited biting in rats. *Physiology and Behavior, 8,* 477–480.

Jones, S. E., & Brain, P. F. (1985). An illustration of simple sequence analysis with reference to the agonistic behavior of four strains of laboratory mouse. *Behavioural Processes, 11,* 365–388.

Karli, P. (1956). The Norway rat's killing response to the white mouse: An experimental analysis. *Behaviour, 10,* 81–103.

King, H. D., & Donaldson, H. H. (1929). Life processes and size of the body and organs of the gray Norway rat during ten generations in captivity. *American Anatomical Memoirs, 14,* 1–106.

King, J. A. (1956). Sexual behavior of C57BL/10 mice and its relation to early social experience. *Journal of Genetic Psychology, 88,* 223–229.

Klopfer, P. H. (1974). *An introduction to animal behavior: Ethology's first century.* Englewood Cliffs, NJ: Prentice-Hall.

Knutson, J. F., & Kane, N. (1980). The effects of social isolation on two shock-induced aggressive responses in rats. *Animal Learning and Behavior, 8,* 167–170.

Korn, J. H., & Moyer, K. E. (1968). Behavioral effects of isolation in the rat: The role of sex and time of isolation. *Journal of Genetic Psychology, 113,* 263–273.

Krsiak, M. (1975). Timid singly-housed mice: Their value in prediction of psychotic activity of drugs. *British Journal of Pharmacology, 55,* 141–150.

Krsiak, M., Sulcova, A., Donat, P., Tomasikova, Z., Dlohozkova, N., Kosar, E., & Masek, K.

(1984). Can social and agonistic interactions be used to detect anxiolytic activity of drugs? In K. A. Miczek, M. R. Kruk, & B. Olivier (Eds.), *Ethopharmacological aggression research* (pp. 93–114). New York: Liss.

Kruk, M. R., Meelis, W., van der Poel, A. M., & Mos, J. (1981). Electrical stimulation as a tool to trace physiological properties of the hypothalamic network in aggression. In P. F. Brain & D. Benton (Eds.), *The biology of aggression* (pp. 383–395). Alphen aan den Rijn, The Netherlands: Sijthoof & Noordhoff.

Lagerspetz, K. M. J. (1969). Aggression and aggressiveness in laboratory mice. In S. Garattini & E. G. Sigg (Eds.), *Aggressive behaviour* (pp. 77–85). Amsterdam: Excerpta Medica.

Latane, B., Cappell, H., & Joy, V. (1970). Social deprivation, housing density and gregariousness in rats. *Journal of Comparative and Physiological Psychology, 70,* 221–227.

Latane, B., Nesbitt, P., Eckman, J., & Rodin, J. (1972). Long and short term social deprivation and sociability in rats. *Journal of Comparative and Physiological Psychology, 81,* 69–75.

Latane, B., Schneider, C., Waring, P., & Zweigenhaft, R. (1971). The specificity of social attraction to rats. *Psychonomic Science, 23,* 28–29.

Leshner, A. I. (1981). The role of hormones in the control of submissiveness. In P. F. Brain & D. Benton (Eds.), *Multidisciplinary approaches to aggression research* (pp. 309–322). Amsterdam: Elsevier/North-Holland.

Lockard, R. B. (1968). The albino rat: A defensible choice or a bad habit? *American Psychologist, 23,* 734–742.

Lore, R., & Flannelly, K. (1977). Rat societies. *Scientific American, 236,* 106–116.

Lorenz, K. (1966). *On aggression.* London: Methuen.

Luciano, D., & Lore, R. (1975). Aggression and social experience in domesticated rats. *Journal of Comparative and Physiological Psychology, 88,* 917–923.

Mackintosh, J. H. (1970). Territory formation by laboratory mice. *Animal Behaviour, 18,* 177–183.

Mackintosh, J. H. (1973). Factors affecting the recognition of territory boundaries by mice. *Animal Behaviour, 21,* 464–470.

Mainardi, D., Mainardi, M., Parmigiani, S., & Pasquali, A. (1977). Relationship between aggressiveness due to isolation and social status in the house mouse. *Accademia Nazionale dei Lincei, 63,* 120–125.

McGivern, R. F., Lobaugh, N. J., & Collier, A. C. (1981). Effect of naloxone and housing conditions on shock elicited reflexive fighting: Influence of immediate prior stress. *Physiological Psychology, 9,* 251–256.

Miczek, K. A., Kruk, M. R., & Olivier, B. (Eds.) (1984). *Ethopharmacological aggression research.* New York: Liss.

Moyer, K. E. (1968). Kinds of aggression and their physiological basis. *Communications in Behavioral Biology, 2,* 65–87.

Noirot, E., Goyens, J., & Buhot, M. (1975). Aggressive behavior of pregnant mice towards males. *Hormones and Behavior, 6,* 9–17.

O'Boyle, M. (1974). Rats and mice together: The predatory nature of the rat's mouse-killing response. *Psychological Bulletin, 81,* 261–269.

Parmigiani, S., Mainardi, D., & Pasquali, A. (1981). A comparison of aggressiveness in dominant subordinate and isolated house mice. In P. F. Brain & D. Benton (Eds.), *The biology of aggression* (pp. 563–570). Alphen aan den Rijn, The Netherlands: Sijthoof & Noordhoff.

Scott, J. P. (1966). Agonistic behavior in mice and rats: A review. *American Zoologist, 6,* 683–701.

Sigg, E. B., Day, C., & Colombo, C. (1966). Endocrine factors in isolation-induced aggressiveness in rodents. *Endocrinology (Baltimore), 78,* 679–684.

Sloane, L., & Latane, B. (1974). Social deprivation and stimulus satiation in the albino rat. *Journal of Comparative and Physiological Psychology, 87,* 1148–1158.

Svare, B. B. (1977). Maternal aggression in mice: Influence of the young. *Biobehavioral Reviews, 1,* 151–164.

Syme, G. J. (1974). Competitive orders as measures of social dominance. *Animal Behaviour, 22,* 931–940.

Tolman, E. C. (1959). *Behavior and psychological man.* Berkeley: University of California Press.

Ulrich, R. E. (1966). Pain as a cause of aggression. *American Zoologist, 6,* 643–662.

Valzelli, L. (1969). The exploratory behaviour in normal and aggressive mice. *Psychopharmacologia, 15,* 232–235.

Valzelli, L. (1973). The isolation syndrome in mice. *Psychopharmacology, 31,* 305–320.

van Hemel, P. E. (1975). Rats and mice together: The aggressive nature of mouse killing by rats. *Psychological Bulletin, 82,* 456–459.

van Kreveld, D. A. (1970). Selective review of dominance–subordination relations in animals. *Genetics and Psychology Monographs, 81,* 143–173.

Wagner, G. C., Beuving, L. J., & Hutchinson, R. (1979). Androgen dependency of aggressive target-biting and paired fighting in male mice. *Physiology and Behavior, 22,* 43–46.

Ward, J. H. (1963). Hierarchical grouping to optimize an objective function. *Journal of the American Statistical Association, 58,* 236–244.

Wilson, E. O. (1975). *Sociobiology: The new synthesis.* Cambridge, MA: Harvard University Press.

AUTHOR INDEX

293

SUBJECT INDEX

297

CONTENTS OF PREVIOUS VOLUMES

312

VOLUME 2: EMOTIONS IN EARLY DEVELOPMENT

VOLUME 3: BIOLOGICAL FOUNDATIONS OF EMOTION

Part I General Models of Brain Functioning

Part II Ethological and Evolutionary Considerations